Counsel for Kings:
Wisdom and Politics in Tenth-Century Iran

VOLUME I

Edinburgh Studies in Classical Arabic Literature
Series Editors: Wen-chin Ouyang and Julia Bray

This series departs from conventional writing on Classical Arabic Literature. It integrates into its terms of enquiry both cultural and literary theory and the historical contexts and conceptual categories that shaped individual writers or works of literature. Its approach provides a forum for path-breaking research which has yet to exert an impact on the scholarship. The purpose of the series is to open up new vistas on an intellectual and imaginative tradition that has repeatedly contributed to world cultures and has the continued capacity to stimulate new thinking.

Books in the series include:

The Reader in al-Jāḥiẓ
Thomas Hefter

Recognition in the Arabic Narrative Tradition: Deliverance and Delusion
Philip F. Kennedy

Counsel for Kings: Wisdom and Politics in Tenth-Century Iran
Volume I: *The* Naṣīḥat al-mulūk *of Pseudo-Māwardī: Contexts and Themes*
L. Marlow

Counsel for Kings: Wisdom and Politics in Tenth-Century Iran
Volume II: *The* Naṣīḥat al-mulūk *of Pseudo-Māwardī: Texts, Sources and Authorities*
L. Marlow

Al- Jāḥiẓ: In Praise of Books
James E. Montgomery

Al- Jāḥiẓ: In Censure of Books
James E. Montgomery

Hikayat Abi al-Qasim*: A Literary Banquet*
Emily Selove

The Literary Qur'an
Shawkat M. Toorawa

www.edinburghuniversitypress.com

Counsel for Kings: Wisdom and Politics in Tenth-Century Iran

Volume I

The *Naṣīḥat al-mulūk* of Pseudo-Māwardī: Contexts and Themes

L. Marlow

EDINBURGH
University Press

to

SAM and DJL

Edinburgh University Press is one of the leading university presses in the UK. We publish academic books and journals in our selected subject areas across the humanities and social sciences, combining cutting-edge scholarship with high editorial and production values to produce academic works of lasting importance. For more information visit our website: www.edinburghuniversitypress.com

Edinburgh University Press Ltd
The Tun – Holyrood Road
12 (2f) Jackson's Entry
Edinburgh EH8 8PJ

Typeset in 11/15 Adobe Garamond by
Servis Filmsetting Ltd, Stockport, Cheshire,
and printed and bound in Great Britain by
CPI Group (UK) Ltd, Croydon CR0 4YY

A CIP record for this book is available from the British Library

ISBN 978 0 7486 9690 1 (hardback)
ISBN 978 0 7486 9691 8 (webready PDF)
ISBN 978 1 4744 0650 5 (epub)
Volumes I and II available as a two-volume set: ISBN 978 0 7486 9756 4

Contents

Illustrations

Preface

This book is the result of several years' study of the Pseudo-Māwardian text known as *Naṣīḥat al-mulūk*, 'Counsel for Kings'. When I began my research for this project, I intended to produce an annotated translation of Pseudo-Māwardī's book, a tenth-century Arabic mirror for princes. Work on the translation necessarily involved close attention to the text's *Sitz im Leben*, and the project developed into a broader study of the text's relationship to the milieu in which it was composed. On account of its early date, its distinctive intellectual-cultural setting and its presentation of a multifaceted mentality, *Naṣīḥat al-mulūk* is a mirror of very considerable interest. This book, in which large sections of translation still appear (especially in the second volume), constitutes an attempt to evoke this mentality and to situate *Naṣīḥat al-mulūk* in its historical and literary contexts.

I am deeply grateful to Nicola Ramsey, Commissioning Editor, and to Edinburgh University Press for accepting the book for publication. I owe a particularly deep debt of gratitude to Julia Bray, Laudian Professor of Arabic at Oxford University, and Wen-chin Ouyang, Professor of Arabic and Comparative Literature at the School of Oriental and African Studies, co-editors of the Edinburgh University Press series Studies in Classical Arabic Literature. I am profoundly grateful to them for their willingness to accept a two-volume work into the series, their meticulous reading of the manuscript, their exceptional generosity with their time and knowledge, and their numerous and invaluable suggestions for improvement. Their critical advice has saved me from many errors; I am responsible, of course, for all remaining mistakes and infelicities.

I have incurred many debts in the course of my years of study of Pseudo-Māwardī's *Naṣīḥat al-mulūk*. My first and primary debt is to Patricia

Crone, who with unerring discernment recognised the interest and importance of the text, and was kind enough to bring it to my attention. It is a pleasure and a privilege to thank the School of Historical Studies at the Institute for Advanced Study in Princeton for the opportunity to spend a term there as Willis F. Doney Member in 2012. I am grateful to the faculty, members and staff of the Institute, and I should particularly like to acknowledge the assistance of Kirstie Venanzi, who obtained a digital copy of the manuscript of *Naṣīḥat al-mulūk* on my behalf. I should similarly like to thank my colleagues at Cambridge University, among them James Montgomery, Christine van Ruymbeke and Basim Musallam, for their hospitality during the Michaelmas Term of 2012, which I spent at the university as an Academic Visitor. It is a pleasure to acknowledge my gratitude to Wellesley College for the approval of a sabbatical leave, and I should like to mention in particular the staff in the college's Interlibrary Loan Department; without their patient work on my behalf I would not have been able to pursue my research. I remain very grateful to W. Luke Treadwell, who offered instructive comments on an early draft of parts of the present book. For his swift reading of and invaluable comments on drafts of four chapters, as well as his generous sharing of work not yet published, I am deeply grateful to Jürgen Paul. Similarly, I should like to thank Elvira Wakelnig for her kindness in sharing proofs prior to publication. For stimulating and helpful conversations, assistance and advice of various kinds I am indebted to Hassan Ansari, Dianne Baroz, Houchang Chehabi, Barbara Geller, Hugh Kennedy, Beatrice Manz, Charles Melville, Firuza Melville, Carolyn Morley, Roy Mottahedeh, Bilal Orfali, Maria Eva Subtelny and Deborah Tor. As a glance at this book will reveal, I am indebted to the scholarship of many of these individuals as well as to numerous other specialists. I should also like to express my thanks to the two anonymous readers who provided comments to Edinburgh University Press.

For expert assistance in preparing the two maps, I am grateful to Scott Walker of the Lamont Library, Harvard University, and for his careful preparation of the genealogical chart (Figure 2), to Richard Bourque, Wellesley College. I am also grateful to Edinburgh University Press for permission to produce and publish, as Figure 1, a modified version of the dynastic table from Clifford Edmund Bosworth, *The New Islamic Dynasties: A Chronological and Genealogical Manual* (New York: Columbia University Press, 1996), p. 170.

Finally, I offer my thanks, and my love, to my family, whose patience and encouragement during the years that it has taken to complete this project have consistently supported me.

Notes on Transliteration and Dates

I have adopted a slightly modified version of the *IJMES* system for the transliteration of Arabic and Persian words and names. In my transliterations of Persian words and names, I have substituted *ż* for Arabic *ḍ*, and *v* for *w*. Arabic and Persian personal names appear in full transliteration. Persian names are rendered according to their Persian forms (Shāpūr, Anūshīrvān) except in cases of direct transliteration from Arabic (Sābūr, Anūshīrwān). I have used modern Turkish spelling for Turkish words.

Place names used in English appear in anglicised forms (Mosul, Mecca, Homs). The names of less well-known locations appear in transliteration, but without diacritics (Andarab, Panjhir, Chaghaniyan). Dynastic names used in English appear in their anglicised forms (Abbasid, Ottoman); less familiar dynastic names appear in anglicised transliteration, but without diacritics (Tahirid, Samanid). Common terms are either translated or transliterated without italicisation (ḥadīth, sharīʿa, ʿulamāʾ), except where they appear in quotations. 'Amir' appears without diacritics and is capitalised only when it denotes a particular individual. I have adopted the commonly used anglicised forms Sunni, Shiʿite, Ismaʿili and Muʿtazilite rather than the fully transliterated forms Sunnī, Shīʿī, Ismāʿīlī and Muʿtazilī.

In the translations, I have attempted to provide the non-linguist with reliable independent access to the primary sources. Accordingly, I have translated titles of books and key terms at first mention, and repeated the main terms, in Arabic or Persian, in parentheses in subsequent passages. The main terms appear in the Glossary. In order to convey the repetitions and emphases of the original, I have quite often employed a single translation for key terms. The adoption of a consistent rendering for central Arabic and Persian terms is intended not to imply fixed limits of meaning, but to assist the reader in appreciating the resonance that the term carries as it reappears in multiple contexts.

In the translated passages, I have used parentheses to indicate words or phrases that do not appear in the original text but are intended to clarify my interpretation, and square brackets to supply identifying or explanatory information. In citing Qurʾānic passages, I have consulted several translations, especially Muhammed Marmaduke Pickthall, *The Glorious Koran: A Bi-Lingual Edition with English Translation, Introduction and Notes* (London: George Allen& Unwin, 1976) and Ahmed Ali, *Al-Qurʾān: A Contemporary Translation* (Princeton, NJ: Princeton University Press, 1993). Unless otherwise indicated, however, all translations are the author's.

Numerical dates are rendered according to the Hijrī and Gregorian calendars; the Hijrī date precedes the Gregorian date. In the case of dates that precede the Islamic era, and dates for which the Hijrī calendar is not characteristically used, Gregorian dates appear alone. For reasons of brevity, references to centuries appear only according to the Gregorian calendar (e.g., eleventh century, not fifth/eleventh century). The names of months and festivals are transliterated without diacritics (Safar, Ramadan, Nawruz, Mihragan).

Glossary

adab (pl. *ādāb*)	literary culture; appropriate and pleasing behaviour; in the plural, maxims, notable sayings, instructive examples
^{c}ahd (pl. *^{c}uhūd*)	a contract or covenant; a 'testament' or 'charge', a literary composition in which a senior figure, frequently a father, offers advice or exhortation for the benefit of his son(s) or successors (see also *waṣiyya*)
ahl al-sunna wa-l-jamā^{c}a	a grouping that defined itself by its emphasis on the importance of normative practice (*sunna*), especially that of the Prophet, and distinguished itself from the Shi^{c}a; precursor of the later Sunni community; see also *sunna*, *jamā^{c}a*
^{c}ajam	collective term for speakers of a language other than Arabic (contrasted with *^{c}arab*, speakers of Arabic); very often, speakers of Persian; *^{c}ajamī* (pl. *^{c}ajā$^{\circ}$im*), individual member(s) of this group
^{c}āmma	collective term for the common people; *^{c}āmm* (pl. *^{c}awāmm*), commoner(s)
^{c}aṣabiyya	partisan loyalty, communal solidarity; see also *ta^{c}aṣṣub*
aṣlaḥ	better, more righteous, more conducive to well-being; *al-aṣlaḥ*, the best or most righteous; the theological doctrine that God must act in the manner that is optimal for His creatures

athar (pl. *āthār*)	a trace, track or lasting effect; a reported utterance or action; a 'tradition', that is, a saying or action of the Prophet or one of his Companions, passed down by an authenticated chain of transmitters (see also *ḥadīth*)
aʿwān	'assistants', aides; a category of individuals closely identified with the ruler, often present at the court and involved in the discharge of the ruler's affairs
bidʿa	innovation
budd (pl. *bidada*)	a buddha; *al-Budd*, Siddartha Gautama the Buddha
dāʿī	an individual who summons people to faith, a missionary; agent of a *daʿwa* (q.v.)
daʿwa	summons to faith or call to allegiance and support; see *dāʿī*
dihqān (pl. *dahāqīn*)	in the late Sasanian period, a member of the landed gentry, often involved in military, administrative and fiscal activities; in tenth-century eastern Iran, a landed military commander; in later usage, an agriculturalist
diyāna	religion, religious practice
ghazw	raiding or military campaigning
ghishsh	deceit, deception
ghulām (pl. *ghilmān*)	an attendant or servant; a military slave; member of a military retinue or bodyguard, sometimes of servile status, bound by personal ties
ḥadīth (pl. *aḥādīth*)	a transmitted report of the words or actions of the Prophet; the corpus of these authenticated accounts
ḥakīm (pl. *ḥukamāʾ*)	a wise person or sage, philosopher, physician; especially in eastern Iran, an honorific title for a respected scholar or religious figure
ḥākim (pl. *ḥukkām*)	judge; holder of authority
ḥaqq (pl. *ḥuqūq*)	a rightful claim

hawā	desire; caprice; erroneous religious belief; *ahl al-ahwāʾ*, people who hold erroneous beliefs, i.e., heretics, free-thinkers
ḥikma (pl. *ḥikam*)	wisdom; philosophy; a wise saying
ilḥād	heresy, atheism; see *mulḥid*
jamāʿa	community, collectivity; the whole community of believers
kalām	speech; rational or dialectical theology
khādim (pl. *khadam*)	a servant; a eunuch; an individual employed in the ruler's service, pledged to an overlord (*makhdūm*)
khāṣṣa	collective term for the 'special' or 'distinguished' people, privileged social groups; an élite; *khāṣṣ*, pl. *khawāṣṣ*, an individual in close proximity to the ruler
khidma	service; a type of relationship contracted between an individual, whether slave-born or free-born, and his superior
khuluq (pl. *akhlāq*)	a characteristic, (moral) disposition
madhhab (pl. *madhāhib*)	a path, grouping of people bound by a common interest or affiliation; a legal school
mamlūk (pl. *mamālīk*)	'a thing possessed', a slave, especially a military slave
maʿrifa	knowledge, including intuitive or experiential as opposed to rational knowledge
maṣlaḥa	well-being, welfare; the common or public good; see also *ṣalāḥ*
mawʿiẓa	exhortation, admonition
milla	religious community; see also *umma*
mulḥid	heretic, atheist
muruwwa	manly virtue
mutakallim	rational theologian; religious specialist
mutanabbiʾ	pseudo-prophet
mutaṭawwiʿa, *muṭṭawwiʿa*	groups of volunteers involved in military activities, especially at the frontier

naqīb (pl. *nuqabā*ʾ)	leader, especially of a distinct social group, such as the descendants of the Prophet
naṣīḥa	advice, counsel
nāsik (pl. *nussāk*)	ascetic(s)
naẓar	rational speculation, rational enquiry
niʿma (pl. *niʿam*)	favour, bounty
raʾīs	leader of an urban constituency or neighbourhood
raʾy	opinion, rational judgement
ṣalāḥ	goodness, righteousness; well-being, welfare; see also *maṣlaḥa*
sawād	mass, generality (of the population)
shukr	gratitude
siyāsa	governance; training, discipline; especially in Persian usage, also punishment
sunna (pl. *sunan*)	a normative practice, especially of the Prophet; the body of literature that records the Prophet's authenticated sayings and actions; see also *ḥadīth*
taʿaṣṣub	factional or communal attachment
tafḍīl	preference
taqrīb	bringing (a person) close, showing favour
taqwā	consciousness of God, fear of God, godliness
umma (pl. *umam*)	community
wafāʾ	loyalty, trustworthiness, fulfilment of one's word
waqf (pl. *awqāf*)	in Islamic law, a charitable trust or endowment
waṣiyya (pl. *waṣāyā*)	a 'testament' (see also *ʿahd*)
zāhid (pl. *zuhhād*)	renunciant(s)
zuhd	austerity, renunciation, asceticism; *al-zuhd fī l-dunyā*, renunciation of the world

Introduction

ᶜAlī Ibn Razīn, an author in early twelfth-century Mosul, narrates the story of a man, a commoner, who wished to buy a book solely because he had heard that it was popular with 'a king of our time'. So desperate was the man to purchase a copy that he went to the extremity of selling items of his clothing to raise the necessary funds. The man acquired the book, which, Ibn Razīn adds, was useless to him. But the efforts to which he had gone to obtain it left him famished and exposed during two nights of extreme cold, and as a result of these privations he contracted a long illness. Ibn Razīn relates this account in order to impress upon his intended reader, a king, the importance of keeping his reading matter secret.[1] It was essential to good governance that the king's affairs should remain hidden from his subjects, and this necessity for secrecy extended to the contents of the king's library.[2]

The present study concerns a tenth-century Arabic book that is both for and about kings. Its author, who expresses firm opinions regarding their appropriate and inappropriate reading matter and much else besides, doubted that its intended recipient would welcome it. Indeed, whether this book, an unusually pointed 'mirror for princes' or work of advice for a ruler, ever reached the king's ear is unknown. Several other details are likewise unknown or uncertain, since the author of the book suppressed both his own name and that of his imagined reader. At some point in its transmission, however, this mirror for princes acquired an illustrious attribution, which doubtless accounted in significant measure for its survival.

The mirror for princes in question is the *Naṣīḥat al-mulūk* ('Counsel for Kings') attributed to the renowned scholar, jurist and polymath Abū l-Ḥasan ᶜAlī b. Muḥammad b. Ḥabīb al-Māwardī (364–450/974–1058). Available in three editions,[3] *Naṣīḥat al-mulūk* has also been translated into Turkish.[4]

An important stimulus to this substantial investment of scholarly attention in the text surely lies in its association with al-Māwardī. While several scholars have, over the years, accepted this attribution,[5] Fuʾād ʿAbd al-Munʿim Aḥmad questioned al-Māwardī's authorship of the mirror as early as 1977,[6] and refuted it in definitive fashion in the introduction to his critical edition of 1988 as well as, at greater length, in a separate monograph.[7] Since the appearance of Aḥmad's publications, several scholars have followed his rejection of al-Māwardī's authorship of *Naṣīḥat al-mulūk*, a conclusion also assumed in the present study.[8]

The Manuscript and its History

At present, only one manuscript copy of the *Naṣīḥat al-mulūk* of Pseudo-Māwardī, as I shall refer to the unidentified author, is known to have survived.[9] Preserved in the Bibliothèque nationale de France (BnF), this copy forms part of a collection, a *majmūʿa*, in which it has been bound together with a copy of the *Muʿīd al-niʿam wa-mubīd al-niqam* ('The Returner of Favours and Averter of Punishments') of Tāj al-Dīn al-Subkī (728–71/1327–70) and part of the *Sulūk al-mālik fī tadbīr al-mamālik* ('The Conduct of the Ruler in the Administration of the Kingdoms') of Ibn Abī l-Rabīʿ. As its copyist informs us, the manuscript was completed in Egypt in the year 1007/1598–9, that is, during the period in which that country formed a province of the Ottoman Empire. The combination of these three works, all of which treat aspects of ethical conduct, in a single collection evokes the cultural and intellectual location of *Naṣīḥat al-mulūk* in the context of an early modern Egyptian readership of Arabic edificatory prose. I shall return to the subject of the book's reception by this readership after a review of its history, its physical appearance and the documentary evidence of its annotations.

The manuscript formed part of the 219 Arabic manuscripts held in the personal library of Cardinal Mazarin (1602–61), who, in a pattern established by his predecessor Cardinal Richelieu (1585–1642), sent the ambassador to Constantinople, at that time Jean de La Haye, to the Levant and elsewhere to search for and acquire manuscripts in their original languages. It was during the reign of Louis XIV (r. 1643–1715) and especially through the efforts of Jean-Baptiste Colbert (1619–83), Controller General of Finances, that a large expansion of the royal collections took place, both through acquisitions of personal libraries and through expeditions to locate and purchase manuscripts in the Ottoman territories. In 1668, the Bibliothèque du roi, predecessor of the BnF, acquired a large part of Mazarin's library, amounting to 343 Oriental manuscripts and including 164 Arabic manuscripts, among them *Naṣīḥat al-mulūk*.[10] A year earlier, in 1667, the Bibliothèque du roi had acquired part of the library of the orientalist Gilbert Gaulmyn; that acquisition included 247 Arabic manuscripts, 214 Turkish and Persian manuscripts, and 240 Hebrew manuscripts, as well as printed books in Hebrew, and Syriac, Coptic and Armenian manuscripts.[11] Thus, *Naṣīḥat al-mulūk* was among the earliest Arabic texts to arrive in France and to enter the royal collection, where it formed part of the *ancien fonds*. The manuscript appeared in the library's first catalogue, written in Latin and dated 1739.[12]

It would seem that the earliest surviving documentation of *Naṣīḥat al-mulūk*'s ascription to al-Māwardī lies in the manuscript itself. Many Arabic manuscripts contain an abundance of written materials in addition to the copied text(s); copious notations, frequently added by different individuals at different dates, appear in the folios that precede the opening of texts, in the colophons that follow them, and in the margins of the copied texts themselves. These notes differ in kind and in purpose. Some notations document a manuscript's commissioning and ownership; some consist of certificates of audition (*samāʿāt*) or licences for transmission (*ijāzāt*); some record the reactions of readers, who might supply glosses for unfamiliar terms, add comments related to the subject matter and inscribe verses of poetry in the margins.[13] The BnF's copy of *Naṣīḥat al-mulūk* contains several annotations that provide important documentary information. In two locations, a librarian, or possibly the individual who commissioned the copy, has labelled it with the 'title' *Naṣīḥat al-mulūk*, 'Counsel for Kings', and identified it as the work of al-Māwardī. The same person, in all likelihood, supplied the brief biography of al-Māwardī that appears at the end of the manuscript. The individual responsible for these supplementary sections employed a larger script and a more ornate calligraphic style than that used for the copying of the text. Many manuscripts, like *Naṣīḥat al-mulūk*, include 'titles' attached in a conspicuous manner in the pages that precede the text or in the colophons that appear at the end. Sometimes these added designations reproduce the title announced by the text's author, typically with the phrase *wa-sammaytuhu*

. . . ('I have called [this book] . . .'). Very commonly, however, they take the form of shortened, simplified or paraphrased versions of the author's title, or, if as in the present case the text provides no indication of the author's title, they ascribe a title that identifies the genre or subject matter of the text. These short titles facilitated the essential functions of classification and retrieval of books stored in libraries and collections. The use of a contrasting colour of ink or an ornamental script allowed for the quick location of the book, categorised according to its genre and content, and also added to the owner's satisfaction and pleasure in possessing and perusing it.[14]

In the BnF's copy of *Naṣīḥat al-mulūk*, the first of the two instances in which the attribution to al-Māwardī appears takes the form of a disk-shaped *shamsa*, a decorative inscription that precedes the text of the work.[15] The inscription reads:

> The book *Naṣīḥat al-mulūk*, composition of the learned *shaykh* and *imām*, the most perceptive scholar and illustrious judge (*al-qāḍī al-ajall*), Supreme Judge (*aqḍā l-quḍāt*) Abū l-Ḥasan ᶜAlī b. Muḥammad b. Ḥabīb known as al-Māwardī [364–450/974–1058], may God support him by His mercy and make him dwell in the amplitude of His Paradise, through Muḥammad and his family. Amen.[16]

On the facing folio, an individual involved in the production of the manuscript has traced a rectangular box, in which a calligrapher, probably the same individual who wrote the text of the *shamsa*, has inscribed the *basmala*,[17] followed by the notice, 'Table of contents for the book *Naṣīḥat al-mulūk* of the learned al-Māwardī. He assembled it in ten chapters, praise be to God'.[18] Beneath this heading, the calligrapher has recorded the topics of the ten chapters in two columns. Marginal annotations to this table of contents indicate that the titles of the chapters were verified with reference to either the text itself or perhaps the copy (or copies) from which it was made.

The text that follows, written in a considerably smaller script, covers some 100 folios. The copyist had at his disposal at least one exemplar, his use of which for purposes of collation and correction is evident from his several marginal notations of *ṣaḥḥa* ('it [this wording] is correct') and *balagha* ('it [a collation] has been completed').[19] When he had reached the end of the work, the copyist wrote:

> The book *Naṣīḥat al-mulūk* is finished, praise be to the only God and prayers and peace upon him after whom there are no further prophets. The finishing of the copying of this blessed copy corresponds to Sunday, 4 Safar 1007 [= 5 September 1598]. It is finished.[20]

Beneath this inscription, in a further notation contained within an inverted triangular frame, the copyist has 'signed' his work:

> Acknowledging his sin and shortcoming, the poor and wretched servant Ismāᶜīl b. Sulaymān b. Ismāᶜīl al-Bījūrī, servant of the sandals of the Khalwatiyya Masters (*khādim niᶜāl al-sāda al-khalwatiyya*), may God pardon them all, appended (it) by his failing hand.[21]

This signature supplies some suggestive pieces of information regarding the context for the manuscript's production. It indicates that the copyist was affiliated with the Khalwatiyya Sufi organisation. From eastern Anatolia, the Khalwatiyya (Turkish Halvetiye) order began to establish itself in Egypt in the late Mamluk period. Like the Bektaşiyye, the Khalwatiyya remained largely limited to Turkish circles in Cairo for a long time. The order thrived among the Ottoman soldiery stationed in the province and was popular with the Ottoman governors, but did not flourish among the indigenous population for approximately another two centuries.[22] In the eighteenth century, the organisation would become virtually universal among Egypt's higher ᶜulamāᵓ, and it would remain strong in the nineteenth and twentieth centuries.[23] In the period in which the copyist produced the manuscript of *Naṣīḥat al-mulūk*, the individuals affiliated with the Khalwatiyya in Cairo remained predominantly Ottoman and Turkish in background.

After the copyist's signature, which marks the end of his text, an individual, departing from the small and unadorned script of the copied text and adopting a more visually assertive calligraphic style, has added:

> The biography of the author of this book
>
> He is the learned imam and Supreme Judge (*aqḍā al-quḍāt*) Abū l-Ḥasan ᶜAlī b. Muḥammad b. Ḥabīb al-Māwardī al-Baṣrī al-Shāfiᶜī, author of the book *al-Ḥāwī* ('The Comprehensive') on jurisprudence (*fiqh*) in approximately twenty volumes. He has no parallel in the [Shāfiᶜī] legal school (*madhhab*). He wrote [another] book on jurisprudence that he called

> *al-Iqnā*ᶜ ('The Provision'); it contains profitable and unusual materials found nowhere else. He also composed a book that he called *Adab al-dīn wa-l-dunyā* ('Good Conduct in Matters Religious and Mundane'),[24] and a commentary (*tafsīr*) of the Glorious Qurʾān; he called (this commentary) *al-Nukat* [*wa-l-*ᶜ*uyūn*] ('Points' ['and Principles']). He was a leader in jurisprudence, the principles [of jurisprudence] (*uṣūl*) and scriptural exegesis (*tafsīr*), and he was discerning in Arabic. He undertook the judgeship in several lands, and then settled in Baghdad. He lived, may Almighty God have mercy on him, for 86 years. He studied jurisprudence with (*tafaqqaha* ᶜ*alā*) Abū l-Qāsim [ᶜAbd al-Wāḥid b. al-Ḥusayn] al-Ṣaymarī [d. after 387 /996–7][25] in Basra and with Shaykh Abū Ḥāmid [Aḥmad b. Muḥammad al-Isfarāʾinī, 344–406/955–1016][26] in Baghdad. He related ḥadīth from (*ḥaddatha* ᶜ*an*) al-Ḥasan [b. ᶜAlī b. Muḥammad] al-Jīlī,[27] who was the companion (*ṣāḥib*) of Abū Khalīfa [al-Faḍl b. al-Ḥubāb] al-Jumaḥī,[28] and his group, and others. Abū l-ᶜIzz [Aḥmad b. ᶜUbaydallāh] b. Kādish related from him (*rawā* ᶜ*anhu*).[29] He died, may God have mercy upon him, in the year 450 [1058] of the *hijra* (emigration) of the Prophet. Among that which is recounted of him is that when he wished to cite a verse of poetry from an ode (*qaṣīda*) that he had memorised, he committed the entire *qaṣīda* to memory. May God Almighty have mercy on him and be pleased with him.[30]

At the bottom of this last folio, the individual who ordered the copy, and who perhaps added the preceding and concluding materials in the larger script, has 'signed' his commission:

> The wretched servant of Almighty God, calligrapher and secretary (*rāqim al-ḥurūf kātib*) ᶜUlwān b. ᶜAbd al-Nabī b. ᶜUlwān al-Qaramānī al-Ḥanafī, one of the clerks of the noble ordinances (*min katabat al-aḥkām al-sharīfa*) of the high courts (*al-abwāb al-*ᶜ*āliyya*) and recorder of documents (*tezkereci*) at the administrative council (*dīwān*) of Cairo (Miṣr al-maḥrūsa), may God pardon him and his parents and all Muslim men and all Muslim women, asked for this book to be written for himself so that he might benefit from it and learn from its contents. Amen.[31]

The manuscript, then, was copied in Ottoman Egypt for the use of an Ottoman secretary assigned to the provincial judicial administration in

Cairo.[32] The same individual commissioned the other major work copied in the manuscript, the *Muᶜīd al-niᶜam* of al-Subkī,[33] a work that similarly and explicitly combines the perspectives of religion and the mundane world, *dīn* and *dunyā*.[34] From his *nisba* (the element in a personal name that indicates geographical roots or association, genealogical descent or professional or legal affiliation), al-Qaramānī (Karamanlı), it would appear that the manuscript's commissioner was of Turkish heritage; it is possible that he was a recent immigrant.[35] The region of Karaman, it might be added, played a prominent role in the rise of the Khalwati (Halveti) Sufi organisation in its Anatolian phase, and al-Qaramānī was perhaps, like the copyist, affiliated with the Khalwatiyya.[36]

The Book's Commissioning and Reception

Given his professional involvement in the Egyptian branch of the Ottoman administration and his training in calligraphy, al-Qaramānī was necessarily fully proficient in Arabic. He also identifies himself as an affiliate of the Ḥanafī legal school (*madhhab*, pl. *madhāhib*). It is quite likely that he was among the numerous Ḥanafī officials whom the Ottomans, as part of their promotion of the Ḥanafī school of law, posted to provincial capitals. In these provincial locations Ḥanafīs sometimes constituted a minority in relation to the adherents of other legal schools, who continued in their existing affiliations. In Egypt, the Mamluks (648–923/1250–1517), whose rule preceded that of the Ottomans, had continued the policy of their predecessors, the Ayyubids (564–650/1169–1252 in Egypt), in treating the four legal schools equally, and had constructed educational institutions (*madāris*, sing. *madrasa*) for all of them. Under Ottoman authority, notwithstanding the Ottomans' official sponsorship of Ḥanafī law, Cairo's leading mosque and *madrasa* al-Azhar continued to accommodate all four of the Sunni legal schools. In Cairo, as well as in Lower Egypt, it was the Shāfiᶜī *madhhab* that predominated. This predominance is perhaps related to the combination of *Naṣīḥat al-mulūk*, conspicuously attributed to the great Shāfiᶜī jurist al-Māwardī, with the work of al-Subkī, another eminent Shāfiᶜī authority and author of *Ṭabaqāt al-shāfiᶜiyya* ('Generations of the Shāfiᶜīs'), in the *majmūᶜa* in which it was bound. Given the status of the Shāfiᶜī legal school in Cairo and his professional responsibilities, al-Qaramānī perhaps found it advantageous to acquire a familiarity with Shāfiᶜī scholarship and with the broader, non-juristic literature produced by celebrated Shāfiᶜī writers. It is perhaps also significant that rivalries within the Khalwatiyya in sixteenth-century Cairo appear to reflect tensions between Turkish immigrants and the indigenous Egyptian ᶜulamāᵓ, and suggest a certain antagonism between adherents of the Shāfiᶜī and Ḥanafī schools.[37] Critical to the Khalwatiyya's eventual spread in Egypt was its appeal to adherents of different Sunni legal schools. Whereas it had originated in an almost entirely Ḥanafī milieu, by the mid-eighteenth century its Egyptian members included large numbers of Shāfiᶜīs and Mālikīs as well.

Al-Qaramānī's commissioning (*istiktāb*) of *Muᶜīd al-niᶜam* is documented in precisely the same language as his request for *Naṣīḥat al-mulūk*.[38] In both instances, he describes his professional identity in terms of multiple occupations.[39] His standing in the administrative hierarchy fell among the middling ranks,[40] and his commissioning and owning of *Naṣīḥat al-mulūk* attest to the expansion of book possession and reading beyond the élites to the urban middle classes in Ottoman Cairo. Nelly Hanna has demonstrated that in the seventeenth and eighteenth centuries, books came within the economic reach of numerous members of the Cairene middle class, and that these individuals were able to build modest personal libraries; indeed, Hanna invokes the *fonds arabe* in the Bibliothèque nationale as an example of the increase in Arabic book production in the seventeenth and eighteenth centuries.[41] The commissioning of *Naṣīḥat al-mulūk* and *Muᶜīd al-niᶜam* might suggest that the trend had begun as early as the later sixteenth century.

In its physical appearance, the manuscript emphasises the text's association with al-Māwardī, which evidently contributed significantly to its importance to its commissioner-owner. The manuscript record for Ottoman Egypt suggests a considerable interest in the advisory works of al-Māwardī.[42] The Ottoman Egyptian readership, indeed, sought to acquire edificatory works in several genres. Compilations of proverbs were among the books produced in abundance for the seventeenth-century Cairene middle classes,[43] and diverse advisory writings, whether addressed to the ruling élites on the exercise of power or to city-dwellers wishing to live their lives in a thoughtful and ethical manner, appear to have enjoyed considerable popularity in both Cairo and Istanbul.[44] The Ottoman élites appreciated works of counsel (*naṣīḥa*), and Arabic and Persian mirrors addressed to kings and kings-in-waiting contributed significantly to the development of the Turkish 'book of counsel' (*nasihatname*).[45] The celebrated eleventh-century Persian mirrors, the *Qābūsnāmeh* ('Book of Qābūs') or *Andarznāmeh* ('Book of Counsel') (475/1082–3) of the Ziyarid ruler ᶜUnṣur al-Maᶜālī Kaykāʾūs b. Iskandar (r. 441–80/1049–87), the *Siyar al-mulūk* ('Conduct of Kings'), also known as the *Siyāsatnāmeh* ('Book of Governance'), of the vizier Niẓām al-Mulk (410–85/1019–92), and the *Naṣīḥat al-mulūk* ('Counsel for Kings') attributed to Abū Ḥāmid al-Ghazālī (450–505/1058–1111), were all available in Ottoman Turkish translations.[46] Ottoman literature of the sixteenth and seventeenth centuries reflects a growing preoccupation, especially among the élites involved in governance, with the theme of 'the corruption of the time' (*fasād al-zamān*), manifested in perceived social and political shortcomings, and their remedies.[47] As subsequent chapters will demonstrate, *Naṣīḥat al-mulūk* anticipates this Ottoman interest in its thorough attention to the causes of, and solutions to, religious, moral and political problems. The problems of defining and realising just and legitimate rule, of imagining and perfecting a type of sovereignty for the good of the entire society, were matters of interest and concern not only for rulers and their assistants, but also for many members of the population. It is possible that al-Qaramānī, as an administrative employee, particularly appreciated books that, like *Naṣīḥat al-mulūk*, treated the cultivation of the inner life in combination with involvement in the exercise of power. Pseudo-Māwardī's *Naṣīḥat al-mulūk* and al-Subkī's *Muᶜīd al-niᶜam* address an audience fully engaged in the politics and economics of the mundane world, from which they nevertheless encourage a certain detachment.[48] The Khalwatis' accommodation of the present world as well as the world of the hereafter facilitated the entry of middle-ranking individuals, such as the calligrapher and secretary, into their community.[49] It is quite likely that these factors contributed to readers' receptions of Pseudo-Māwardī's book.

The Author and his Milieu

The first owner of the manuscript, as the preceding discussion indicates, believed it to represent the work of al-Māwardī. It is possible and perhaps likely that the identification of the work as al-Māwardī's was present in the exemplar(s) available to the copyist. In the absence at this juncture of further known manuscripts, assessment of the attribution's history depends on circumstantial evidence, including the various listings and descriptions of al-Māwardī's writings provided by his pre-modern biographers, and on the comparison of *Naṣīḥat al-mulūk* with writings for which al-Māwardī's authorship is undisputed. The remainder of this Introduction addresses the bibliographic record, and summarises the principal scholarly arguments for and against the mirror's attribution to al-Māwardī.

None of the period's most authoritative bio-bibliographers – among them Yāqūt (d. 626/1229), Ibn Khallikān (608–81/1211–82), Ibn Kathīr (*c.* 700–74/1300–73), al-Dhahabī (673–748 or 753/1274–1348 or 1352), al-Ṣafadī (696–764/1297–1363) and al-Subkī (d. *c.* 769/1368) – refers to a *Naṣīḥat al-mulūk* among the works of al-Māwardī.[50] In the single known manuscript, namely, that preserved in the BnF, the designation *Naṣīḥat al-mulūk* appears, as has been described, *hors de texte*. The absence of the 'title' from the biographers' lists need not negate al-Māwardī's authorship, however. Titles of books were rarely fixed; on the contrary, they underwent frequent reformulation and, as has been mentioned, writings appeared under different titles in different libraries or collections.[51] In the case of al-Māwardī's works, the leading pre-modern bio-bibliographers listed varying numbers of compositions under somewhat mutable titles, and they did not pretend to supply exhaustive inventories. Al-Khaṭīb al-Baghdādī (392–463/1002–71), a student of al-Māwardī, stated simply that his teacher wrote 'many books on the principles and branches of jurisprudence, and other subjects'.[52] In his *Ṭabaqāt al-fuqahā'* ('Generations of the Jurists'), the eleventh-century scholar al-Fīrūzābādī stated of al-Māwardī that he composed 'many works in jurisprudence, scriptural exegesis, the principles of jurisprudence and literary culture' (*lahu muṣannafāt kathīra fī l-fiqh wa-l-tafsīr wa-uṣūl al-fiqh wa-l-adab*).[53] In the fourteenth century, al-Subkī described al-Māwardī as the 'author of *al-Ḥāwī* and *al-Iqnā'* on jurisprudence, *Adab al-dīn wa-l-dunyā*, *al-Tafsīr*, *Dalā'il al-nubuwwa* ("The Proofs of Prophecy"), *al-Aḥkām al-sulṭāniyya* ("The Governmental Ordinances"), *Qānūn al-wizāra wa-siyāsat al-mulk* (or *Qānūn al-wizāra* and *Siyāsat al-mulk*) ("The Principle of the Vizierate["] and ["]Governance of Sovereignty"), and other works (*wa-ghayr dhālika*)'.[54] Al-Subkī's entry, specific in its details yet explicitly open-ended, illustrates the varying designations under which some of al-Māwardī's writings circulated. Lists of al-Māwardī's writings commonly begin with the subject of jurisprudence, for which he was principally known. Ibn Kathīr, for example, described al-Māwardī as 'author of *al-Ḥāwī*' (*muʾallif al-Ḥāwī*), a work that the biographer declared to be unequalled in its contribution to the subject; Ibn Kathīr then added, 'And he wrote the "Commentary", the "Governmental Ordinances", "Proper Conduct in Matters Religious and Mundane", and other useful compositions' (*wa-ghayr dhālika min al-muṣannafāt al-nāfiʿa*).[55] These entries demonstrate the contrast between the general formulations of the earliest records and the specific information supplied in the later reports, in which the details vary to some degree from one account to another.

Al-Māwardī's established writings on the subjects of authority and statecraft, many of them mentioned in the accounts of his biographers, include *al-Aḥkām al-sulṭāniyya wa-l-wilāyāt al-dīniyya* ('Governmental Ordinances and Religious Appointments'); *Qawānīn al-wizāra (wa-siyāsat al-mulk)* ('Principles of the Vizierate [and the Governance of Sovereignty]');[56] *Tashīl al-naẓar wa-taʿjīl al-ẓafar* ('The Facilitation of Reflection and the Hastening of Victory'), the two parts of which address, respectively, the moral characteristics (*akhlāq*) that the ruler should cultivate and the governance that he should pursue; and, more loosely, *Adab al-dunyā wa-l-dīn*.[57] Al-Māwardī's writings on these subjects reflected and were related both to his scholarly training and his professional experience. As the leading Shāfiʿī jurist of the period, well versed in all four Sunni legal schools, al-Māwardī had held judgeships in various (unspecified) locations, and taught for several years in Basra and Baghdad.[58] Controversially, in 429/1037–8, Caliph al-Qāʾim (r. 422–67/1031–75) bestowed on al-Māwardī the title of Supreme Judge, *aqḍā l-quḍāt*.[59] In further indications of al-Māwardī's close relations with the most powerful figures of his age, the Abbasid caliphs secured his ambassadorial and advisory services on several occasions, and the Buyids (320–454/932–1062; in Iraq, 334–447/945–1055), rulers of Iraq and western Iran during al-Māwardī's lifetime, likewise dispatched him with their communications and held him in high esteem (according to the biographer Yāqūt, 'he possessed a [high] station among the Buyid kings' (*kāna dhā manzila min mulūk banī Buwayh*)).[60]

In his important study, *Politics and Revelation: Mawardi and After*, the research for which was conducted well before the appearance of published editions of *Naṣīḥat al-mulūk*, Hanna Mikhail considered the question of its authorship and decided in favour of al-Māwardī.[61] Among his arguments, Mikhail noted that in *Adab al-dunyā wa-l-dīn*, al-Māwardī accounted for his relatively brief treatment of governance with the explanation that he had (already) 'devoted a separate book to the subject of governance (*siyāsa*)'.[62] Mikhail proposed that this reference applied to the work known as *Naṣīḥat al-mulūk*.[63] Two additional works devoted to governance, *Durar al-sulūk fī siyāsat al-mulūk* ('Pearls of Conduct in the Governance of Kings') and *al-Tuḥfa al-mulūkiyya fī l-ādāb al-siyāsiyya* ('The Royal Gift in Good Governmental Practices'), survive, like *Naṣīḥat al-mulūk*, in single manuscripts attributed to al-Māwardī. Fuʾād ʿAbd al-Munʿim Aḥmad, who prepared editions of both these works, has accepted al-Māwardī's authorship of *Durar al-sulūk*, which was commissioned by and dedicated to the Buyid ruler of Iraq, Bahāʾ al-Dawla (r. 379–403/989–1012), and was probably composed in approximately 393/1002–3.[64] Aḥmad has further proposed that al-Māwardī's reference in *Adab al-dunyā wa-l-dīn* to his previously composed 'book on the subject of governance' applies not to *Naṣīḥat al-mulūk*, but to *Durar al-sulūk*.[65] The second book, *al-Tuḥfa al-mulūkiyya*, has ostensibly survived in a manuscript that bears the early date of 543/1148–9. Aḥmad has rejected the ascription of this text to al-Māwardī, and also demonstrated that the manuscript is dated far earlier than it can actually have been copied.[66]

The earliest external reference to a *Naṣīḥat al-mulūk* in connection with al-Māwardī appears in a somewhat confusing entry in the bibliographic encyclopaedia of the Ottoman polymath Ḥājjī Khalīfa (d. 1067/1657). Ḥājjī Khalīfa's entry is at odds with the evidence of the text preserved in the Bibliothèque nationale, and appears to conflate this text with the *Naṣīḥat al-mulūk* of al-Ghazālī. The relevant passage, which suffers from at least one lacuna, reads as follows:

> *Naṣīḥat al-mulūk*: This is *al-Tibr al-masbūk* ('Fashioned Gold') in Persian, by the Imām Abū Ḥāmid Muḥammad b. Muḥammad al-Ghazālī, and its translation, *Natījat al-sulūk* ('The Outcome of Conduct'), translated by Ṣafī al-Dīn Abū l-Ḥasan al-Irbilī, who died in . . . [and was] the paternal uncle

> of Ibn al-Mustawfī. [He translated it] into Arabic without changing anything in the structure of the book according to its arrangement and form. A further [work of this title] is that of Māwardī in *Muᶜīd al-niᶜam*. Someone translated it from Persian into Arabic, and called it *al-Durr al-masbūk fī naql Naṣīḥat al-mulūk* ('The Fashioned Pearl on the Translation of *Counsel for Kings*'). It begins: Praise be to God for His bounties and His favours, etc. Someone translated it into Turkish.[67]

It will be apparent that this passage hardly constitutes a straightforward reference to the *Naṣīḥat al-mulūk* in question.[68] First, Ḥājjī Khalīfa states that the work was translated from Persian into Arabic. Although, as the following chapters will demonstrate, there is substantial evidence to suggest that the text was initially composed in a Persian-speaking environment, the text is silent regarding any derivation from a Persian precursor. It might be added that none of al-Māwardī's biographers report that he composed any of his writings in Persian, or even that he was proficient in that language. Secondly, Ḥājjī Khalīfa states that in its Arabic form, the text was called *al-Durr al-masbūk fī naql Naṣīḥat al-mulūk*. Neither this title nor any other name appears in the manuscript. Thirdly, as Aḥmad has conclusively indicated, the opening words cited by Ḥājjī Khalīfa correspond not with the beginning of the *Naṣīḥat al-mulūk* attributed to al-Māwardī, but with the beginning of *al-Tibr al-masbūk*, the Arabic version of the *Naṣīḥat al-mulūk* of al-Ghazālī.[69] The evidence strongly suggests that Ḥājjī Khalīfa conflated the *Naṣīḥat al-mulūk* of al-Ghazālī, which was indeed translated from Persian into Arabic, with the Arabic work to which al-Qaramānī, perhaps following an established supposition, attached the same 'title', and which Ḥājjī Khalīfa appears to have encountered, apparently in the same copy, as an accompaniment to *Muᶜīd al-niᶜam* with which it was bound. In short, the limited corroboration of al-Māwardī's authorship of *Naṣīḥat al-mulūk* available in the pre-modern and early modern literature is at best problematic.

Aḥmad's principal arguments against al-Māwardī's authorship of *Naṣīḥat al-mulūk* arose, however, from internal evidence. While he explored several areas of contrast between this mirror and the works of al-Māwardī, the foundation of Aḥmad's rejection of al-Māwardī's authorship lies in his comparative analysis of the legal ordinances (*al-aḥkām al-fiqhiyya*) recorded in the known works of al-Māwardī and in *Naṣīḥat al-mulūk*:[70] by this means he documented numerous indications that the author of *Naṣīḥat al-mulūk* tended towards Ḥanafī rather than Shāfiʿī positions in matters of law.[71] In his edition of *Naṣīḥat al-mulūk*, Aḥmad advanced the tentative proposal that it might represent the work of the philosopher and polymath Abū Zayd Aḥmad b. Sahl al-Balkhī (d. 322/934).[72] A participant in the intellectual lineage of the philosopher Abū Yūsuf Yaʿqūb al-Kindī (*c.* 183–256/800–70), Abū Zayd al-Balkhī spent most of his later life in eastern Khurasan, where he became the primary direct exponent of the 'Kindian tradition', the continuing development and dissemination of al-Kindī's philosophical approach and teachings.[73] Although Aḥmad did not pursue the hypothesis of Abū Zayd al-Balkhī's authorship in his later study, it remains a perceptive suggestion, and evokes the early tenth-century eastern Iranian environment in which *Naṣīḥat al-mulūk* certainly arose.

More recently, Ḥasan Anṣārī has addressed the theological importance of *Naṣīḥat al-mulūk*, and has demonstrated in definitive manner its strongly Muʿtazilite background.[74] The Muʿtazila, a religious movement that originated in Iraq in the eighth century and developed extensively in the ninth and tenth centuries, came to comprise a diverse grouping of rationalist theologians (*mutakallimūn*, sing. *mutakallim*). By the early tenth century, the various perspectives and doctrines taught by the Muʿtazila had settled into two principal groupings classified as 'Basran' and 'Baghdadi'.[75] Although the Muʿtazilite movement lost its social-political prominence in later centuries, it left lasting traces in many branches of intellectual activity; indeed, in some respects al-Māwardī's writings suggest similarities with Muʿtazilite perspectives.[76] Anṣārī, rejecting the possibility of Abū Zayd al-Balkhī's authorship, has posited instead the authorship of a student of the Muʿtazilite theologian Abū l-Qāsim ʿAbdallāh al-Kaʿbī al-Balkhī (d. 319/931), the principal theologian of the Baghdadi school of Muʿtazilite theology in early tenth-century Khurasan. Specifically, Anṣārī has proposed that the author of *Naṣīḥat al-mulūk* was al-Kaʿbī's student Abū l-Ḥasan ʿAlī b. Muḥammad al-Ḥashshāʾī al-Balkhī. Noting that al-Ḥashshāʾī's name and patronymic (*kunya*) are identical to those of al-Māwardī, Anṣārī postulates that in the manuscript from which the extant copy was made the copyist either encountered a lacuna in place of the *nisba* 'al-Ḥashshāʾī' or found it illegible, and accordingly replaced it with 'al-Māwardī', and in this way occasioned the misattribution of the work.[77] Although this proposal is not subject to positive verification at the present time, it is at once appealing and plausible.

Most important for the present study are *Naṣīḥat al-mulūk*'s connections, implied in the prior studies of both Aḥmad and Anṣārī, with an early tenth-century Balkhi origin. In this book, I seek to demonstrate, and shall thereafter assume, an early tenth-century Balkhi context for the mirror's composition by an unknown author to whom, for purposes of the current discussion, I refer as 'Pseudo-Māwardī'. In further development of the lines of enquiry initiated by Aḥmad and Anṣārī, the following chapters find extensive evidence of Pseudo-Māwardī's affinity with both the Kindian tradition, developed in the eastern regions by Abū Zayd al-Balkhī and his students,[78] and Muᶜtazilite intellectual techniques and doctrines, especially those associated with the Baghdadi Muᶜtazila and developed in Khurasan by Abū l-Qāsim al-Kaᶜbī. The two Balkhīs, Abū Zayd and Abū l-Qāsim al-Kaᶜbī, studied logic together in their youth, worked alongside one another in the employ of the governor of Khurasan, Aḥmad b. Sahl, and appear to have remained friends throughout their lives.[79] Both men engaged, if to differing degrees, with philosophy (*falsafa*) and rational theology (*kalām*); the philosophical perspective of al-Kindī, inherited and developed by Abū Zayd al-Balkhī, displays affinities with the rational theology that would come to be associated with the Muᶜtazila, and Abū l-Qāsim al-Kaᶜbī, like other Muᶜtazilite theologians, incorporated aspects of *falsafa* into his writings.[80]

Furthermore, Abū Zayd al-Balkhī and Abū l-Qāsim al-Kaᶜbī were fluent in and contributed to the Arabic literary culture of *adab*, a fundamental component of the intellectual-cultural context for *Naṣīḥat al-mulūk*. In fact, Ibn al-Nadīm (*c*. 320–80/932–90) of Baghdad, the leading tenth-century bibliographer and specialist in the culture of book-writing, classified Abū Zayd, notwithstanding his learning in the ancient and modern sciences, among the secretaries (*kuttāb*) because of his greater affinity with them than with the philosophers (*falāsifa*).[81] Some years later, Abū Ḥayyān al-Tawḥīdī (*c*. 315–411/927–1023), who himself combined literary virtuosity with an extensive knowledge of philosophy, reported Abū Zayd's reputation as 'the Jāḥiẓ of Khurasan', that is, the counterpart in the east to the leading Iraqi literary figure of the previous century.[82] As for al-Kaᶜbī, Yāqūt (d. 626/1229), the previously mentioned specialist in the biographies and compositions of Arabic writers not only includes an entry for him in his expansive dictionary of littérateurs, but also describes him as *al-mutakallim al-mufassir al-adīb*, 'theologian, exegete and littérateur', and records some of his poetry.[83] In short, the two friends of Balkh, Abū Zayd and Abū l-Qāsim al-Kaᶜbī, participated in a mentality that was grounded in scripture, rationalist, steeped in Arabic poetry and linguistics, sharpened through disputation, and unapologetically indebted to the wisdom of peoples of the past. This mentality thrived in Balkh in the first half of the tenth century, and, I shall argue, produced *Naṣīḥat al-mulūk*.

The term *adab* (pl. *ādāb*) encompasses many meanings. Several of these interconnected meanings carry ethical connotations.[84] In many instances the term denotes a custom, a mode of comportment, manners or etiquette; in the plural, *ādāb*, it denotes rules of ethical behaviour and laudable habits, as well as maxims or aphorisms.[85] *Adab* also refers to the voluminous literature that offers its audiences pleasure and entertainment, exemplary illustrations of pleasing and meritorious behaviour, and the knowledge necessary for the cultivation of ethical qualities. Among the numerous figures who contributed to the formation of *adab* in the early Islamic period were several secretaries in caliphal employ.[86] These men of letters, some of whom will appear in the following pages, produced an Arabic prose literature that encompassed a variety of genres. In some cases they also adapted, directly or indirectly, Middle Persian, Greek, Syriac and Sanskrit texts into Arabic, and these texts contributed significantly to the shaping of Arabic literary culture. As it developed, the literary culture associated with *adab* embraced a vast range of topics and deployed a correspondingly ample repertoire of cultural materials. Usefully likened to the concept of *paideia*,[87] *adab* is closely related to *taʾaddub*, the process of acquiring the knowledge necessary for the cultivation of the humane virtues, and to *taʾdīb*, the process of instruction designed to illustrate and instil magnanimity of disposition and encourage correspondingly meritorious conduct.

Naṣīḥat al-mulūk, a substantial work of Arabic prose, participates in several literary genres. It takes the form of an extended discursive treatise in which several perspectives, disciplines and cultural materials combine. It is, as its author Pseudo-Māwardī announces, a work of advice (*naṣīḥa*); more specifically, it undertakes the duty of offering counsel and instruction to the ruler. *Naṣīḥat al-mulūk* is also a work of 'wisdom', or *ḥikma*, in the capacious sense that this term had developed from the ninth century onwards. The term evoked the knowledge attained through the experience of multiple peoples and communities transmitted from the past; particularly in the eastern regions of the Islamic world, it also connoted rational philosophy, also designated *falsafa*, and the knowledge accessible to reason in conformity with religious or revealed truth. In addition, *Naṣīḥat al-mulūk* participates incidentally in the discourses of rational theology (*kalām*), jurisprudence (*fiqh*) and lexicography (*lugha*). In formal and conceptual terms, *Naṣīḥat al-mulūk* bears the imprint of the Qurʾān, which supplies many of Pseudo-Māwardī's categories and portions of his vocabulary, and from which he quotes explicitly more than from any other source. Deeply rooted in the Qurʾānic text and its interpretation, *Naṣīḥat al-mulūk* is also richly informed by the diverse literary and conceptual heritages available to its tenth-century author. In all these regards, *Naṣīḥat al-mulūk* provides an example of the manifold and interconnected senses of the term *adab*: it involves its audience in an expansive and varied body of literary and cultural knowledge; it promotes appropriate and pleasing conduct; and it instructs by means of logical argument and carefully selected illustrative texts.

The Present Study

This book seeks to demonstrate the multiple discourses in which *Naṣīḥat al-mulūk* participated and to explore the complex meanings that it may have purveyed to its early tenth-century audience. Mirrors for princes are, in Judith Ferster's phrase, 'camouflaged' texts:[88] their authors negotiated the uncertain ground between critical advice and awed subservience, and characteristically packaged their counsels in the form of clichés and maxims, and stories set long ago in far-away locales.[89] Modern readers are sometimes deterred by their apparently tedious repetition of well-worn quotations and anecdotes. Historians have often found mirrors lacking in readily usable historical information, and literary scholars have rarely found them conspicuously elegant examples of literary prose.[90] It is perhaps for these reasons that scholars have tended to approach mirrors for princes, above all, as expressions of 'political thought';[91] this perspective has, indeed, greatly enhanced scholars' appreciation of the range and subtlety of that category.[92]

The present study reads *Naṣīḥat al-mulūk* as a product of, and a response to, a specific historical milieu and moment. By situating the mirror in its historical and literary contexts, I have attempted to demonstrate Pseudo-Māwardī's skills and infer his purposes in his deployment of familiar, seemingly timeless, materials in ways that respond to the particularities of his circumstances. To achieve their purposes, the authors of mirrors availed themselves of the intellectual, rhetorical and imaginative resources of literary culture. Despite the superficially distancing effect that their techniques sometimes create, mirrors, as a number of studies have shown, reflect the specific character of the times and places in which they were produced.[93]

From time to time, including in its title, this book refers to 'Iran'. Since this term does not appear in Pseudo-Māwardī's Arabic text, its use in the present study requires some explanation. Fluent in the late antique cultural heritage of his region,[94] Pseudo-Māwardī was probably familiar with the Sasanians' uses of the term 'Iran' (Middle Persian *Ērān*), which appears in the titles of the dynasty's founding monarch, Ardashīr I (r. *c.* 224-40 or 242), and his successors. Far more commonly used in the Arabic sources of Pseudo-Māwardī's period, however, are the terms *fārs* and *furs*, applied to a region and persons related to it respectively. The phrases *Īrān-zamīn* (the land of Iran), *shahr-i Īrān* and *Īrān-shahr* (the city or land of Iran), which expressed territorial ideas of 'Iran', appear more frequently in New Persian, which became established as a literary language during Pseudo-Māwardī's lifetime. Moreover, writers of Khurasanian background in particular brought territorial and residential conceptions to their interpretations of Qur᾽ānic categories,[95] and Pseudo-Māwardī is likely to have understood the term 'Iran' in a territorial and residential sense.[96]

Like many authors, Pseudo-Māwardī employs the Arabic terms *ᶜarab* and *ᶜajam*. This pair of terms distinguished between native speakers of Arabic and non-Arabic-speaking populations. For Pseudo-Māwardī, *ᶜajam* connoted above all speakers of Persian (and perhaps other Iranian languages), and in most instances his *mulūk al-ᶜajam*, 'kings of the *ᶜajam*', designated the Sasanian monarchs.[97] He possessed a powerful sense of the past's lasting meaning; if he imagined an 'Iranian' communal past, it is likely that territorial and linguistic factors predominated in his understanding. In most situations, as Sarah Savant has stressed, contemporaries attached greater significance to regional affiliations than to the relatively abstract idea of 'Iran';[98] local identities also proved strong and enduring.[99] For Pseudo-Māwardī and many of his contemporaries, 'Iran' is likely to have represented a loosely defined territorial space that encompassed several regional locations and possessed a highly diverse population, and it is in this sense that I employ the term 'Iran' in the present work.

In two volumes, this book approaches *Naṣīḥat al-mulūk* as a product and reflection of the Samanid realm in the first half of the tenth century. The first volume addresses aspects of the work's context, and interweaves the evidence of the text with the attestations of a variety of contemporary and near-contemporary sources. Part I, consisting of two chapters, introduces the early tenth-century Samanid context and situates *Naṣīḥat al-mulūk* within it. Chapter 1 addresses the mirror's historiographical contents and argues, on the basis of this material, for *Naṣīḥat al-mulūk*'s composition in the first half of the tenth century and during the reign of the Samanid Amir Naṣr b. Aḥmad (r. 301–31/914–43). Chapter 2 treats the possible locations in which Pseudo-Māwardī might have lived and argues for his composition of *Naṣīḥat al-mulūk* in an eastern Iranian location, probably Balkh. Part II, in two chapters, explores Pseudo-Māwardī's presentation of the character of Samanid governance and its relationship with the diverse populations that lived in the Samanid domains. Chapter 3 examines Pseudo-Māwardī's representation of kingship, the titles and vocabulary that he applies to rulers and figures invested with differing levels of power and authority. Pseudo-Māwardī's portrayal of governance, the chapter argues, presupposes the absolute quality of royal power; yet he warns repeatedly of the ease with which the ruler may lose or compromise his sovereignty. Chapter 4 explores his treatment of social categories, and the implied links of mutual dependence and reciprocal obligation by which the individuals who composed these categories were bound, directly or indirectly, to the king and other persons at high levels of power. In a reflection of the indirect character of Samanid governance, Pseudo-Māwardī urges the king to attend properly to the indispensable nurturing of his relationships with the categories of his subjects. Part III, in four chapters, explores the religious landscape of the tenth-century Samanid domains.

A recurrent theme is Pseudo-Māwardī's conception of a multi-confessional community, and of a plurality of religiously specific communities; the king, he insisted, was responsible for the welfare of the entire population, and had, in addition, specific responsibilities with regard to the Muslim religious community. Chapter 5 treats the region's diverse religious character and the various discourses that reflected and responded to it. In this context, Chapter 6 explores the practices of the Samanid amirs. Chapter 7 presents Pseudo-Māwardī's exposition of the ills that befall kingdoms and their remedies; it details the interconnections that he perceives between religion and kingship. In conclusion, Chapter 8 addresses Pseudo-Māwardī's religious sensibility and intellectual-theological disposition.

Volume II concentrates on *Naṣīḥat al-mulūk*'s design and rhetorical method. Part I, consisting of two chapters, addresses the structure and presentation of the mirror and Pseudo-Māwardī's methods of argument and persuasion. Chapter 1 presents an analysis of *Naṣīḥat al-mulūk*'s preface and first chapter, in which the theme of counsel (*naṣīḥa*) governs the literary techniques by which Pseudo-Māwardī seeks to establish a relationship with his audience. Chapter 2 explores the numerous and highly diverse textual authorities, written or otherwise, available to Pseudo-Māwardī and invoked in *Naṣīḥat al-mulūk*. It addresses Pseudo-Māwardī's use of what Julia Bray has termed a 'strategy of eclecticism',[100] by which he brings an abundance of examples of ancient wisdom to bear on recent developments, and thereby infuses new elements of meaning into the living expressions of his region's ancient cultural heritage. Part II, in three chapters, offers detailed expositions of the three chapters, devoted to the three branches of Aristotelian practical philosophy, ethics, economics and politics, that form the heart of the book. Chapter 3 studies Pseudo-Māwardī's longest chapter, 'On the governance and discipline of the self'; Chapter 4 addresses his chapter 'On the governance of the élites'; Chapter 5 presents his chapter 'On the governance of the common people'. These chapters attempt to convey the integration in the conceptual framing and literary articulation of Pseudo-Māwardī's mirror of the sacred sources, a rationalist theological–philosophical discourse, wisdom literatures of diverse provenances and the Arabic narrative and poetic repertoires. The Conclusion considers Pseudo-Māwardī's literary act in terms of the circumstances to which he responded and the genre in which he wrote.

As a product of the first half of the tenth century, *Naṣīḥat al-mulūk* constitutes one of the earliest extant book-length examples of Arabic advice literature. It marks a significant stage in the conceptual expansion of the genre, which had as its proximate antecedents the treatise devoted to a particular subject, such as *Kitāb al-Kharāj*, the treatise on taxation submitted by the jurist Abū Yūsuf (d. 182/798) to Caliph Hārūn al-Rashīd (r. 170–93/786–809), and the 'testament' or moral exhortation (*waṣiyya* or *ᶜahd*), such as that of the first ruler of the Tahirid dynasty in Nishapur, Ṭāhir b. al-Ḥusayn (r. 205–7/821–2), who composed it for his son ᶜAbdallāh on the occasion of the latter's appointment to the governorship of Diyar Rabiᶜa in 206/821. Far larger in scope than these earlier compositions, Pseudo-Māwardī's work in some respects bears comparison with the *Akhlāq al-mulūk* of the ninth-century Iraqi author al-Taghlibī; like this work, commonly known as *Kitāb al-Tāj*, *Naṣīḥat al-mulūk* integrates the experience and wisdom of the Sasanian heritage into an Arabic text that addressed a highly cosmopolitan audience. *Naṣīḥat al-mulūk* also anticipates the book-length *Ādāb al-mulūk* ('Customs of Kings') of the celebrated poet and philologist Abū Manṣūr ᶜAbd al-Malik al-Thaᶜālibī (350–429/961–1038), who spent almost all his life in the eastern regions, and who wrote his work of advice between 403/1012 and 407/1017 for the Khwārazmshāh Abū l-ᶜAbbās Maᵓmūn II (r. 399–407/1009–17), and the previously mentioned eleventh-century Persian *Qābūsnāmeh* (475 /1082–3) of Kaykāᵓūs, who composed his encyclopaedic book, addressed to his son Gīlānshāh, in forty-four thematic chapters. *Naṣīḥat al-mulūk* is roughly contemporary with the anonymous mid-tenth-century Arabic work known as *Siyāsat al-mulūk* ('The Governance of Kings'), apparently the work of a secretary who wrote during the Buyid period; this book, however, is half the length of Pseudo-Māwardī's *Naṣīḥat al-mulūk* and considerably more circumscribed in its scope.[101] Accordingly *Naṣīḥat al-mulūk* is of interest not only for its historical testimony – it amplifies the scant body of available sources produced during the earlier decades of the Samanid period - but also for its substantial literary and cultural significance.

PART I

SITUATING THE TEXT

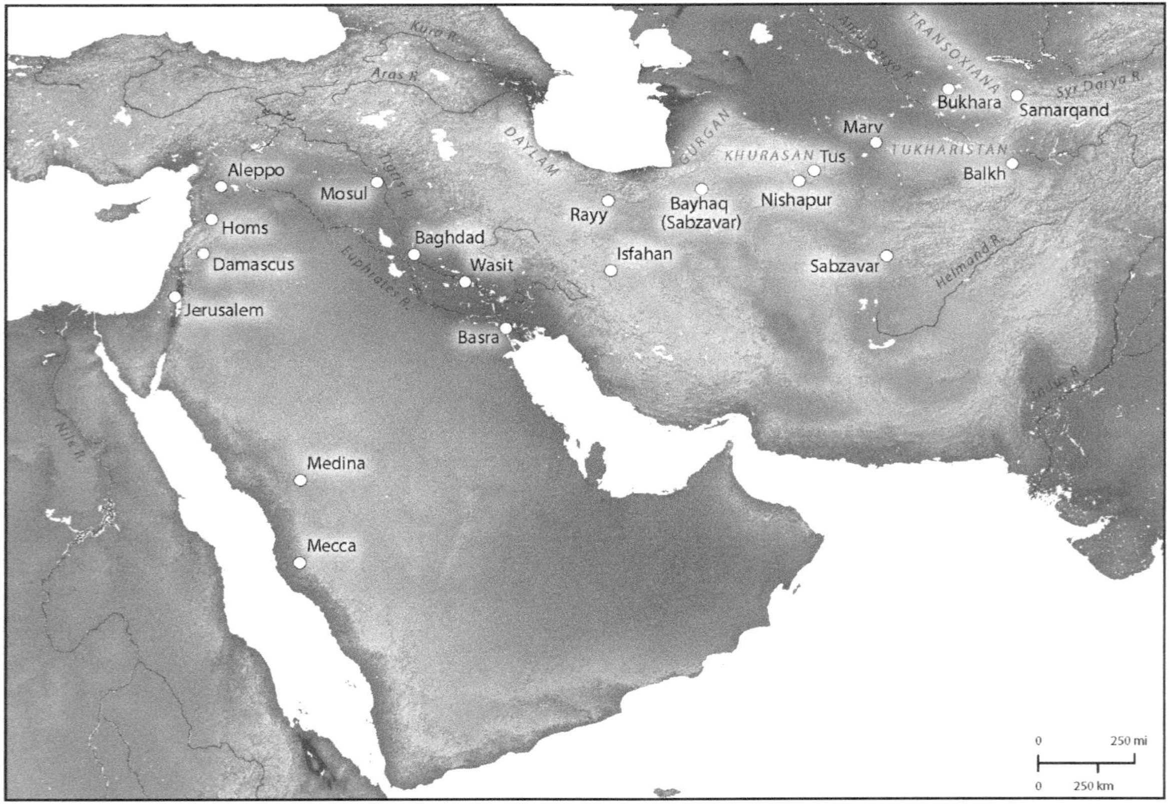

Map 1 The Nile-to-Oxus Region in the Tenth Century

I

An Early Samanid View of History: The Dating of *Naṣīḥat al-mulūk*

In around 204/819, the Abbasid Caliph al-Maʾmūn (r. 198–218/813–33), through his governor in Khurasan, Ghassān b. ʿAbbād (202–5/817–20), appointed four Samanid brothers, sons of Asad b. Sāmānkhudā, to the governorships of the four principal towns of Transoxiana, Bukhara, Samarqand, Shash and Farghana, and inaugurated the era of Samanid dynastic rule (204–395/819–1005). The Samanids had successfully assisted al-Maʾmūn in the caliphate's efforts to suppress the revolt of Rāfiʿ b. al-Layth, who in 190/806 had initiated in Samarqand a rebellion that spread across Transoxiana and attracted the involvement of surrounding peoples and regions.[1] After Ghassān's dismissal in 205/821 and the appointment in the same year of al-Maʾmūn's commander Ṭāhir b. al-Ḥusayn (159–207/776–822) as Amir of Khurasan, the Samanids retained their posts and their strength in Transoxiana grew steadily during the ensuing period of the Tahirids' governance in Khurasan.[2]

Information regarding the earlier history of the Samanid family is sparse but suggestive. Of particular interest is the Samanids' claim, widely accepted among their contemporaries and later commentators, to an ancestral lineage from the general Bahrām-i Chūbīn.[3] A scion of the Arsacid (Parthian) family of Mihrān, one of the great families of late antique Iran, Bahrām, probably born in Rayy, led a major rebellion in 590–1 against the Sasanian monarchs Hurmuzd IV (r. 579–90) and Khusraw II (r. 590–628). His challenge to the legitimacy of Sasanian rule found strong support in the formerly Parthian domains of the northern and eastern regions of the Iranian cultural world, where Sasanian power had always been tenuous.[4] It was in these regions that, some three centuries later, the Samanids rose to power; their long-standing rivals the Buyids (320–454/932–1062) held the heartlands of the former Sasanian Empire in western Iran and Iraq. The Samanids' association with

Bahrām-i Chūbīn strengthened their ancestral claims to the eastern regions,[5] where, according to the pre-eminent geographers of the middle decades of the tenth century, al-Iṣṭakhrī and Ibn Ḥawqal, Bahrām-i Chūbīn's 'reputation among the Persians for strength and courage has remained current' (*sāra dhikruhu fī l-ᶜajam bi-l-baʾs wa-l-najda*).[6] The geographers' language attests to the continuing force in this region of the Samanids' claimed lineage, and implies that their association with Bahrām contributed effectively to the establishment of their legitimacy.[7] Several reports situate the Samanids' heritage specifically in the lands adjacent to the River Oxus, and identify their ancestors with Balkh, in the vicinity of which their forebears had perhaps owned land.[8] Through his analysis of a figured medallion produced in Bukhara in 358/969, Luke Treadwell has recently strengthened the case for a Bactrian and possibly Hephthalite background to the Samanids.[9]

It is the premise of this book that the *Naṣīḥat al-mulūk* of Pseudo-Māwardī reflects perspectives formed in the earlier tenth-century portion of the Samanids' rule. This period exhibits substantial continuity with preceding historical patterns established under the Tahirids (205–59/821–73) and Saffarids (247–393/861–1003), as well as the emergence of new factors that would contribute to lasting transformations in the later Samanid and subsequent periods. The present chapter situates *Naṣīḥat al-mulūk* in the context of the Samanid domains in the first half of the tenth century. It consists of three parts. The first section surveys the development of the Samanid polity until approximately the middle of the tenth century, and concentrates on contests for the position of 'senior amir' within the dynastic family. The second section examines Pseudo-Māwardī's chronological presentation of the history of virtuous leadership. This part of *Naṣīḥat al-mulūk* provides strong evidence for its composition in the first half of the tenth century, and also, incidentally, reveals both the Muᶜtazilite doctrines that shaped the book's conceptual underpinnings and Pseudo-Māwardī's employment of the rich resources of *adab*. The third section addresses some of the recurrent themes in Pseudo-Māwardī's portrayal of virtuous leadership, and studies the brief passages with which he concludes his historiographical survey. The chapter finishes with a discussion of *Naṣīḥat al-mulūk*'s implications for Samanid relations with the caliphate, and a consideration of the principal piece of internal evidence that might suggest a later date for *Naṣīḥat al-mulūk*'s composition.

The Samanid Polity in the Late Ninth and Early Tenth Centuries

Al-Maʾmūn's simultaneous appointment of four members in one generation of the Samanid family to different localities in Transoxiana conformed to and extended the model of familial governance practised by the Tahirids and Saffarids. While one member of the family attained leading status, resided in the capital and often (but not invariably) enjoyed the prior or eventual recognition of caliphal investiture, the system permitted more than one branch to establish strong bases of local support and to contest the position of 'senior amir', which did not necessarily continue in a single line of succession.[10] In the Samanid case, the early period saw an alternation between fraternal and filial patterns of succession, and it was not until the mid-tenth century, when Nūḥ I b. Naṣr (r. 331–43/943–54) followed his father Naṣr II b. Aḥmad (r. 301–31/914–43) as senior amir and became the third lineal descendant of Ismāʿīl b. Aḥmad (r. 279–95/892–907) to hold the position, that the assumption of hereditary succession from father to son seemed privileged. Among the four brothers in the first generation, the senior leadership lay initially with the eldest, Nūḥ b. Asad, in Samarqand. At Nūḥ's death, his brother Aḥmad (I) b. Asad, governor of Farghana from 204/819, succeeded him, and when Aḥmad died in 250/864, his son Naṣr (I) b. Aḥmad (r. 250–79/864–92) assumed the position of senior amir.[11] Ismāʿīl b. Aḥmad succeeded his brother Naṣr at the latter's death, and the Samanid leadership continued, albeit amid repeated challenges, in Ismāʿīl's line.

During Naṣr I's amirate, the Tahirids and Saffarids competed for control of Khurasan in a contest that resulted, in 259/873, in the Saffarids' eviction of the Tahirids from Nishapur. These conditions permitted Naṣr, from his base in Samarqand, gradually to extend his authority across the whole of Transoxiana, and in 260 or 261/874 or 875, Caliph al-Muʿtamid (r. 256–79/870–92) confirmed him in the governorship of the entire province, 'to the extremity of the lands of the *mashriq*', that is, of the eastern regions.[12] In the same year, Naṣr appointed his younger brother Ismāʿīl b. Aḥmad to the governorship of Bukhara, where the names of Naṣr and Ismāʿīl replaced that of the Saffarid Yaʿqūb b. al-Layth (r. 247–65/861–79) in the *khuṭba*, the oration delivered in the mosques in conjunction with the Friday noontime prayer, which, by custom, included a prayer for the well-being of the current ruler, identified by name, and accordingly proclaimed the political allegiance of the community.[13]

Within the Samanid family, Naṣr's leadership elicited the rivalry of Ismāᶜīl, who in 272/886 initiated a protracted military conflict against his brother, from which, following three years of strife, the younger brother emerged victorious. At the conclusion of hostilities, the brothers reached an agreement whereby Ismāᶜīl would remain in his governorship of Bukhara and succeed Naṣr on the latter's death, which occurred at Samarqand in 279 /892.[14] A third brother, Isḥāq b. Aḥmad, had in 275/888 given his support to Ismāᶜīl in the conflict between his brothers. Isḥāq had held a number of governorships, including Farghana, and eventually assumed the governorship of Samarqand, probably at Naṣr's death. By the time of Ismāᶜīl's death in 295/907, Isḥāq's position in the Samanid polity was firmly established: his authority in the pre-eminent city of Samarqand was secure, and he enjoyed the prestigious status of brother and supporter of Ismāᶜīl, and senior member of the Samanid dynastic family (the later historian Ibn al-Athīr (555–630 /1160–1233) refers to him as such, calling him *shaykh al-Sāmāniyya*).[15]

Having assumed the rank of senior amir, Ismāᶜīl (r. 279–95/892–907) continued the expansion of the Samanid territories in energetic fashion. He conquered and deposed the Afshins of Ushrusana and, on both sides of the River Oxus, asserted Samanid suzerainty over other local rulers, including the Abu Dawudids, or Banijurids, of Tukharistan and Khuttal and the Muhtajids (Āl-i Muḥtāj) of Chaghaniyan.[16] He also extended the Samanid dominion over the ancient kingdom of Khwarazm. To the west, he extended his authority over the Zaydi imams of the Caspian region.[17] He further strengthened his position by achieving a decisive victory over the Saffarid Amir ᶜAmr b. al-Layth (r. 265–87/879–900), who had assumed leadership of the Saffarids after the death in 265/879 of his brother Yaᶜqūb. In 285/898, Caliph al-Muᶜtaḍid (r. 279–89/892–902) appointed ᶜAmr to the governorship of Transoxiana, which the caliph's predecessor al-Muᶜtamid (r. 256–79/870–92), as noted above, had granted to Naṣr I. In 287/900, Ismāᶜīl confronted and defeated ᶜAmr at Balkh, took him prisoner and sent him to Baghdad, where he was executed soon after the death of al-Muᶜtaḍid in 289/902.[18] Following the Samanid victory, al-Muᶜtaḍid awarded the governorship of Khurasan and Transoxiana to Ismāᶜīl, who thereby assumed authority over the former Tahirid dominions in eastern Iran and joined them to the Samanids' territories in Transoxiana.[19] Accordingly, in a formal enactment of the already decreasing political and military significance of the River Oxus,[20] the Samanid polity combined into a single structure the regions to the west and south of the river with the lands to the east and north. As the anonymous author of the geographical work *Ḥudūd al-ᶜālam* ('The Boundaries of the World'), completed in 372/982, perhaps in Chaghaniyan on the eastern side of the upper Oxus, put it, 'The king of Khorāsān (pādshāy-i Kh.) in the days of old was distinct from the king of Transoxiana but now they are one'.[21]

Rather than re-settling the centre of the polity in Khurasan, with its established status and importance in Islamic political, economic, intellectual and cultural life and its rapidly increasing urban populations, Ismāᶜīl opted to transform Bukhara, the seat of his personal power, into the capital of the Samanid dynastic or 'monarchical' 'state'.[22] Although a significant consideration in Ismāᶜīl's decision was, reportedly, Bukhara's relative proximity to Khurasan, the choice ensured that the Samanid polity would retain its foundation in Transoxiana.[23] As Luke Treadwell has aptly observed, it was more than eighty years after Nūḥ b. Asad had arrived in Samarqand that Samanid armies occupied Khurasan, and the dynasty never established a court in Nishapur, the former centre of the Tahirids' polity; instead, the Samanid amirs delegated authority over Khurasan to their governors.[24] Bukhara's location in Transoxiana conditioned the Samanid amirate in numerous respects. It promoted the formation of a 'Turko-Persian Islamicate culture',[25] and, as Michael Bonner has pointed out, like other societies at the frontier, it lent the polity a distinctive character in that it not only 'emerge[d] and gr[e]w on the physical periphery', but it also engaged 'constantly [in] discovering and testing the inner limits and meanings of Islamic society'.[26]

Three features of the Samanid polity, each related to its physical–geographical location, demand brief attention. The first feature concerns the frequent military activities, during the earlier Samanid period, at the frontier between the cultivated lands and the steppe. Their location in Transoxiana placed the Samanids in immediate propinquity to the peoples of the Turkic regions. Like their Tahirid predecessors, the Samanids fortified their cities with walls and ramparts, and constructed networks of defensive fortresses and military outposts, or *ribāṭāt* (sing. *ribāṭ*), along the frontier.[27] In the later decades of the ninth century, the brothers Naṣr I, Ismāᶜīl and Isḥāq continued the military campaigns of the previous generation of Samanid amirs and extended the settlement of Transoxiana.[28] Following his accession to the senior amirate, Ismāᶜīl, in 280/893, launched an expedition into the steppe, where he defeated the Qarluq (Karluk) Turks and captured Talas (= Ṭarāz), site in the previous century of a decisive Arab-Muslim victory in 133/751 over a Chinese army.[29] In part it was Turkish offensives that provoked the Samanids' initially punitive responses.[30] When Ismāᶜīl returned from his victory at Talas, he brought with him large numbers of captives, including the wife of the kāghān, as well as numerous animals.[31] Although the Samanids' purposes in the ninth century were also expansionist in nature, this element receded during the tenth century, when, as Peter Golden and C. E. Bosworth have indicated, economic interests appear to have provided the principal motivation for the continuing military campaigns. Due to their liminal location, the Samanids, in a perpetuation and expansion of the practices of their Tahirid and Saffarid predecessors, played the principal role in the trade in Turkic slaves, some of whom they retained for their own use, and some of whom they dispatched further west.[32] Though ostensibly military in nature, the proliferating *ribāṭāt*, constructed at the frontier between steppe and cultivated land and sometimes in the steppe itself, served a variety of functions, possibly including, as Jürgen Paul has proposed, the provision of facilities related to the capture and trading in slaves.[33]

Secondly, the situation of the Samanid polity rendered it a centre of extensive and lucrative commercial activity. Located at the intersection of several, often ancient, trade routes, the amirate created a political and economic framework within which numerous, diverse peoples, including Slavs, Turks, Indians, Tibetans and Chinese, as well as Muslims from western Asia and North Africa, encountered one another. The linking of these regions and their inhabitants facilitated extensive mobility, large-scale commercial undertakings and significant prosperity. The vast distances across which quantities of Samanid coins have been found, from the Volga to Scandinavia and western and southern Europe, attest to the scale of engagement on the part of the Samanid polity in long-distance trade and the high regard in which widely separated contemporaries held its silver currency.[34] As the geographers invariably remarked, the Samanid territories contained abundant deposits of silver; G. C. Miles identified as many as forty-seven mints from Farghana to Tabaristan known to have issued coins in the name of the Samanids, and for purposes of long-distance trade the dinar of Nishapur maintained its preferred status into the Seljuk period.[35]

Thirdly, the Samanids' close identification with the frontier involved them in important diplomatic activities and enabled them to acquire not only products, but also knowledge from neighbouring and more distant regions. It was within the Samanid domains, although not, apparently, at the Samanid court, that the polymath Abū Zayd al-Balkhī (d. 322/934) produced his highly regarded maps and, followed by al-Iṣṭakhrī, a significant body of geographical writing. (According to al-Muqaddasī, al-Balkhī, citing his fear of crossing the River Oxus, declined the summons to Bukhara of *ṣāḥib Khurāsān*, presumably Naṣr II b. Aḥmad, so that the latter could avail himself of his expertise (*li-yasta*ᶜ*īna bihi*).)[36] Al-Muqaddasī, who composed his geographical compendium in the later tenth century and towards the end of the Samanid period, reports having located geographical works in 'the library of the ruler of Khurasan' (*fī khizānat amīr Khurāsān*) and in a private library in Nishapur.[37] It was similarly in Bukhara that Naṣr II's vizier al-Jayhānī received the envoy Ibn Faḍlān, whom in 309/921 Caliph al-Muqtadir (r. 295–320/908–32) had sent to the king of the Bulghars of the Volga.[38] Al-Jayhānī, in concert with other figures in the courtly élite, promoted the collection of intelligence related to other peoples, especially those who inhabited the regions that surrounded the Samanid polity. The vizier is associated with the production of a geographical work, usually designated by the numerous near-contemporaries who consulted it as the *Kitāb al-Masālik wa-l-mamālik* ('Book of Routes and Kingdoms') of al-Jayhānī; this work, which evidently circulated under the name of 'al-Jayhānī', is quite likely to have been, as Charles Pellat surmised, the result of a collective familial project.[39] Political and military considerations, in part, stimulated the gathering of such knowledge: in the introduction to his own geographical work, al-Muqaddasī recalled the shortcomings of the efforts of his predecessors, and mentioned specifically Abū ᶜAbdallāh al-Jayhānī, 'vizier to the Amir of Khurasan' (*wazīr amīr Khurāsān*), whose motivation in gathering strangers and eliciting from them information about various lands, their revenues and the condition of the roads that led to them al-Muqaddasī described as 'the conquest of the lands' (*futūḥ al-buldān*) and the acquisition of knowledge regarding their revenues.[40] The interests of al-Jayhānī and other members of the Samanid élites in gathering and transmitting knowledge related to neighbouring populations was, however, not limited to military and other instrumental purposes; by al-Muqaddasī's report, al-Jayhānī studied *falsafa*, astrology and astronomy, frequently classified as 'ancient' or 'foreign' sciences, and the geographical work associated with the Jayhānī family appears to have addressed a broad spectrum of interests, particularly with regard to the regions to the east and south. The historian Gardīzī, who composed his Persian *Zayn al-akhbār* ('The Adornment of [Historical] Accounts') in the mid-eleventh century at the court of the Ghaznavid ᶜAbd al-Rashīd (r. *c.* 440–3/1049–52), identified Abū ᶜAbdallāh Jayhānī's *Kitāb-i Tavārīkh* ('Book of Histories') as his source for certain Indian materials.[41] In general terms, the promotion of such investigations in the Samanid domains addressed several interests, among them the furthering of commercial activities, the acquisition of medical and other forms of practical and scientific knowledge, and the provision of a potential means to facilitate the integration of the diverse peoples living in their dominions.

When at the death of Ismāᶜīl in 295/907, the senior amirate passed to his son Aḥmad II, Isḥāq b. Aḥmad, governor of Samarqand and brother of Naṣr I and Ismāᶜīl, prepared to challenge Aḥmad's accession.[42] The contest, as Treadwell has indicated, replicated the alignments of the earlier conflict between Naṣr and Ismāᶜīl in that it demonstrated the active competition between the urban centres of Samarqand and Bukhara,[43] perhaps anticipated in Samarqand's loss of political stature to its rival and also manifested in the frequency with which the urban population participated in revolts and factional conflicts.[44] Aḥmad prevailed against his uncle's incipient challenge, and eventually restored Isḥāq to his governorship of Samarqand.[45] In 301 /913–14, however, Aḥmad was assassinated at the hands of a small number of his *ghilmān* (sing. *ghulām*), military slaves, in this instance apparently the amir's bodyguards. Although the motives for the act remain obscure, it seems that among the various groupings of *mamālīk* (sing. *mamlūk*, a slave, in this context employed principally in a military capacity) certain powerful constituencies had withheld their support from Aḥmad.[46]

Upon Aḥmad's death his young son Naṣr (II), almost universally said to have been eight years old, and whom eight years later the envoy Ibn Faḍlān still considered a beardless youth, was elevated to the amirate.[47] This time in a major contest for power, Isḥāq and his supporters, whose strength lay in Samarqand and the surrounding territories, waged a second attempt to wrest the senior amirate from Ismāᶜīl's line. According to the pre-eminent historian al-Ṭabarī (224–310/839–923), Aḥmad's *ghilmān*, his administrative and secretarial staff (*kuttāb*) and a significant number of his senior commanders (*jamāᶜa min quwwādihi*) transferred their allegiance to Naṣr, who also received the support of the notables of Bukhara.[48] The fullest account, however, is that of the later historian Jamāl al-Dīn ᶜAlī Ibn Ẓāfir (d. 613/1216), who indicates the importance of the support of the *mamlūk*s, often designated 'Turks' (*al-atrāk*), for Isḥāq. Treadwell has suggested that it was perhaps the senior *mamlūk*s, who had been affiliated with Ismāᶜīl, who rallied to support Isḥāq, whereas the younger *mamlūk*s supported Naṣr. Against them, the deceased Amir's deputy (*nāʾib*) in Bukhara mobilised large numbers of the city's voluntary forces, the *mutaṭawwiᶜa* or *muṭṭawwiᶜa*, sometimes enlisted in the service of the faith, and *ᶜayyārūn*, members of armed chivalric bands.[49] Al-Ṭabarī mentions more than one encounter, one of which took place at the gates of Bukhara, where the forces mobilised in support of Naṣr defeated the supporters of Isḥāq. Captured in 301/913–14, Isḥāq appears to have remained in Bukhara until his death, possibly in prison.[50] Despite the failure of his two efforts to seize the amirate, Isḥāq enjoyed the firm support of Samarqand, and evidently disposed of considerable power. The gravity of his challenge is suggested by the fact that coins were minted in his name in Samarqand and in Nishapur in the year 301/913–14,[51] and near-contemporary and later writers frequently remark on the striking disparity in strength between Isḥāq and Naṣr.[52] Furthermore, several of Isḥāq's sons continued his resistance to Naṣr's leadership in the years after their father's death.[53]

Pseudo-Māwardī's History of Exemplary Rulers

For the purposes of establishing its date and historical context, the most critical passage in *Naṣīḥat al-mulūk* occurs in Pseudo-Māwardī's review of the history of virtuous governance. This discussion falls in the book's third chapter, devoted to the 'Clarification of the factors that cause disorder (*ikhtilāl*) and corruption (*fasād*) to appear in kingdoms and in the conditions of kings'. Towards the end of this chapter, Pseudo-Māwardī provides a chronologically arranged presentation of exemplary rulers. He selects rulers, including recent Samanid amirs, and emphasises particular qualities and deeds imputed to them in order to demonstrate that virtuous rulers have always succeeded in combining their exercise of power with 'obedience to God and justice towards His creation and His creatures' (*ṭāᶜat Allāh wa-l-ᶜadl fī khalīqatihi wa-bariyyatihi*).[54] The invocation of these figures accentuated the compelling, persuasive power of the ruler's personal ancestry as well as more distant antecedents. The remainder of this chapter situates Pseudo-Māwardī's presentation, by way of translation and paraphrase, in its tenth-century Samanid context.

Pseudo-Māwardī introduces his theme in this manner:

> There is nothing that we shall put down in this book of ours for which, when we have wished to cite as a witness for it the saying of a king, a caliph or an amir – and we shall adduce many of their sayings – we could not find such a saying, recorded and written down, transmitted and preserved. We have also been able to find examples of kings who inclined in their conduct towards the purport of the saying, professed it, privileged it and acted in accordance with it. However much we might doubt in a thing, there is no doubt that God has had prophets, messengers and friends (*anbiyāᵓ wa-mursalūn wa-awliyāᵓ*) who have ruled the world, led troops and armies, and subjugated the lands with their forces. Neither the loftiness of their station, nor the greatness of their sovereignty, nor the abundance of their armies, nor the toughness of their troops, nor the multitude of their populations (*sawād jumūᶜihim*) have prevented them from choosing obedience to God, and justice towards His creation and His creatures (*īthār ṭāᶜat Allāh wa-l-ᶜadl fī khalīqatihi wa-bariyyatihi*). They lived as kings and they died as kings, and yet the reports of their deeds have endured, and the tongue of honest sincerity (*lisān al-ṣidq*) [continues to speak favourably] concerning them, so that it is as if they were alive although they are dead, and present although they are absent (*ka-annahum . . . shuhūd wa-in ghābū*).[55]

In this passage, Pseudo-Māwardī acknowledges the worldliness inherent in the status of kings, but elevates their standing by associating the best of them with prophets and the friends of God. Like prophets, the worthiest kings have succeeded in winning lasting renown through their obedience to God and their justice towards their subjects. By observing this pair of ethical commitments, the virtuous kings accepted their subordination to the divine law, a condition in which they resembled their subjects, and their position of responsibility over the population. To convey the population in its entirety, Pseudo-Māwardī employs the term *sawād*, a common usage particularly in the eastern Iranian regions, where it appears, as a later chapter will indicate, in the title of the theological treatise *al-Sawād al-aᶜẓam*, 'The Great Multitude'.[56] After these prefatory remarks, the author begins his chronologically sequenced presentation of exemplary rulers with Qurʾānic figures:

> There was Sulaymān b. Dāʾūd [= Solomon], the tidings of whom God has narrated to us. He has informed us that He softened steel for him,[57] humbled the strong for him, subjugated the jinn and humanity for him, as well as the beasts, domestic and wild, all the species among the animals. At his command the winds blew as a gentle breeze wherever he so indicated. And before him was his father Dāʾūd [= David], peace be upon them both, whom God made a vicegerent on earth and a steward over humankind (*jaᶜalahu Allāhu khalīfatan fī l-arḍ wa-amīnan ᶜalā l-khalq*).
>
> Among them also were the prophet Yūsuf [= Joseph], God's prayers and peace be upon him, and Dhū l-Qarnayn ['The Two-Horned'], whom God commended. Then there were Mūsā b. ᶜImrān [= Moses] and Yūshaᶜ b. Nūn [= Joshua] and their kinsfolk.[58]

This section draws on the Qurʾānic presentations of several prophets, among whom the prophet-kings Solomon and David receive particular attention. Closely associated with these emblems of blessed world governance is Dhū l-Qarnayn, often explicitly identified with Alexander the Great.[59] The societies of late antique western Asia cultivated a vast range of stories and sayings associated with the figure of Alexander; Pseudo-Māwardī cites Iskandar, usually in connection with Aristotle, in numerous instances. In the present passage, he follows the name Dhū l-Qarnayn with the formula 'whom God commended' (*alladhī athnā Allāhu ᶜalayhi*), a mark of the figure's elevated but not quite prophetic status. In all likelihood, Pseudo-Māwardī shared the prevalent contemporary view that four ancient kings had held sovereignty over the whole world; two, Solomon and Dhū l-Qarnayn, had been Muslims (that is, monotheists), and two, Nimrod and Nebuchadnezzar, had been unbelievers.[60]

Pseudo-Māwardī continues with the example of the Prophet Muḥammad:

> Then there was the Seal of the Prophets and the Lord of the Messengers, our Prophet, God's prayers and peace be upon him, whom God made sovereign over many of His lands during his lifetime. He led armies, formed cavalries, accomplished conquests and administered affairs, and none of that prevented him from obedience to God and carrying out His command, from eschewing that which He prohibited, or from practising austerity in this life and anticipating the next (*al-zuhd fī l-dunyā wa-l-raghba fī l-ākhira*).[61]

In a pattern common to the conceptual frameworks of universal histories, such as the *Taʾrīkh al-rusul wa-l-mulūk* ('History of Prophets and Kings') of al-Ṭabarī, Pseudo-Māwardī's historical survey comprises prophets, caliphs and kings. After a brief mention of the Rightly Guided Caliphs and the Prophet's Companions, 'who conquered the lands and triumphed over the people of resistance (*ahl al-ʿinād*)',[62] he turns to the Umayyad Caliph ʿUmar b. ʿAbd al-ʿAzīz (r. 99–101/717–20), of whom he observes:

> [He belonged to] the Banū Marwān, who wrought chaos in the earth, altered the established practices (*gharrarū al-sunan*) and manifested innovations (*aẓharū al-bidaʿ*). There had previously been none other among them like him. He ordered the distribution of the revenues amassed in the treasuries (*bayʿ al-khazāʾin*), he redressed grievances, and he put an end to the cursing of the family of the Prophet.[63] He desired knowledge, spread excellence, and showed favour to the people of knowledge and austerity (*ahl al-ʿilm wa-l-zuhd*). The corruption of the people of his time and of his relatives and peers did not prevent him from his righteousness, his religious commitment and his quest for truth (*min ṣalāḥihi wa-tadayyunihi wa-taḥarriyyihi l-ḥaqq*).[64]

Despite his critical attitude towards the Marwānid caliphs, to whom he refers elsewhere as 'kings', Pseudo-Māwardī's treatment of 'kingship' (*mulk*) and his uses of the term 'king' (*malik*) are often positive, and he cites several Umayyad caliphs, notably Muᶜāwiya, in positive contexts. In assigning an exceptional standing to ᶜUmar b. ᶜAbd al-ᶜAzīz, whose capacity to choose virtue over corruption he affirms, he follows an established pattern in Abbasid historiography.[65] His positive treatment of a second Umayyad, Yazīd (III) b. al-Walīd (r. 126/744), however, indicates his specifically Muᶜtazilite perspective.[66] Yazīd, who instigated the assassination of the Umayyad al-Walīd II (r. 125–6/743–4) and assumed the caliphal office in his place, appears to have adopted the religious–political perspectives of the Qadariyya. Associated with the doctrine of human free will and the denial of God's creation of evil, the term Qadariyya connoted a loose grouping of individuals, including the religious–moral exemplar al-Ḥasan al-Baṣrī (21–110/642–728). In their political and theological inclinations, the Qadariyya anticipated the larger religious movement of the Muᶜtazila, with whose emergence they are often linked through al-Ḥasan al-Baṣrī's students and associates, Wāṣil b. ᶜAṭāʾ (d. 131/748–9) and ᶜAmr b. ᶜUbayd (80–144 /699–761).[67] Like the Muᶜtazilite theologian al-Kaᶜbī (d. 319/931), the historian and polymath al-Masᶜūdī (d. 345/956) would link Yazīd's beliefs and his revolt (*khurūj*) against al-Walīd, when the latter fell into corruption (*fisq*) and injustice (*jawr*), to the Muᶜtazila (*kāna . . . maᶜa shāʾiᶜa min al-muᶜtazila*).[68] Pseudo-Māwardī not only ascribes virtue to Yazīd, whose reign, inaugurated by the overthrow of his cousin and predecessor, lasted less than a year, but also reproduces the entire text of the contractual speech that he made upon his accession:

> Yazīd b. al-Walīd was similar [to ᶜUmar b. ᶜAbd al-ᶜAzīz], for he manifested religion and was zealous in it (*aẓhara l-dīn wa-taᶜaṣṣaba lahu*), and he spread justice. He killed his paternal cousin [al-Walīd] on account of his oppression (*ẓulm*), injustice (*jawr*), heresy (*ilḥād*) and unbelief (*kufr*).[69]
>
> Then he rose to deliver an oration to the people. He praised and extolled God, and prayed for His Prophet, on whom be peace. Then he said, 'By God, I have not rebelled [against al-Walīd] in insolence or pride, nor in avidity for the world or craving for sovereignty. Nor do I flatter my (lower) self; [on the contrary] I despise it. Rather I rebelled out of anger on behalf of God and His religion, in a summons to (*dāᶜiyan ilā*) the Book of God and the practice (*sunna*) of His Prophet, since the signposts

of guidance had been demolished, the light of the people of godliness had been extinguished, and the obstinate person (*ᶜanīd*), who regarded every forbidden thing (*ḥurma*) as licit and embarked on every form of innovation (*bidᶜa*), had appeared. By God, he (al-Walīd) did not believe in the Day of Judgement. Although he was my paternal cousin in acquired merit (*ḥasab*) and my equal in lineage (*nasab*), when I saw [his shortcomings], I asked God for guidance as to what was best in my affair and petitioned Him not to burden me with [the demands of] my (lower) self; I sought the assistance of those pledged to obey me among the people of my province, until God delivered His bondsmen from him (al-Walīd) and purified the lands of him by His might and power, not by my might and strength.

'O people, I pledge to you that I shall not place a single stone upon a stone, nor construct a single water channel, nor accumulate wealth, nor on any account give it to a wife and children, nor transfer wealth from one land to another until I have stemmed the poverty of that land and restored the prosperity of its people in accordance with their satisfaction; rather, if a surplus remains, I shall transfer it to the land that is next to it among those that are most in need of it. It is my responsibility not to require your service at the frontiers for excessive periods of time, lest I try you and your families. I shall not lock my door against you so that the strong among you are free to consume the weak, and I shall not impose on the people liable to the poll-tax among you such hardship that I cause them to abandon their lands and deprive their progeny. But you are entitled to your stipends (*aᶜṭiyāt*) each year and your allowances (*arzāq*) each month, so that the livelihood of the Muslims shall be abundant and the most distant of them (as prosperous) as the most proximate. If I fulfil this charge to you (*fa-in anā wafaytu lakum bi-hādhā*),[70] then you are bound to hear and obey, and to supply aid and mutual support. If I do not fulfil this charge to you, then you have the right to depose me; except that you should call me to repent, and if I repent, then you should accept it from me. If you consider or know someone renowned for excellence and righteousness, someone who will give to you of his own accord in the way that you would wish to receive, and you wish to pledge allegiance to him, then I shall be the first to pledge allegiance to him and to enter into obedience to him. O people, there is no obedience due from the creature in disobedience to the Creator (*innahu lā ṭāʿata li-makhlūq fī maʿṣiyat al-khāliq*). I speak these words of mine, and I beg God's pardon for myself and for you.'[71]

Yazīd's oration, recorded in several historiographical works but unexpected in a mirror for princes, reflects the perspectives of the Qadariyya, who had opposed Umayyad rule for some decades and some of whom appear to have participated in Yazīd's seizure of the caliphate in 126/744. Yazīd's rhetoric indicates his adoption of a Qadarī conception of the caliphate in which the caliph, like his subjects, was subordinate to the divine law and whose right to his subjects' obedience was conditional on his observance of the law. By asserting these Qadarī principles, Yazīd claimed religious legitimation for his overthrow of al-Walīd.[72] Pseudo-Māwardī's incorporation in full of Yazīd's pledge into his otherwise abbreviated account of exemplary history indicates the importance that he attached to its contents. The speech attempts to justify rebellion against a ruler perceived to have lapsed into *ẓulm* and *jawr*, oppression and injustice, through his breach of his subjects' rights and his neglect of their well-being, and into *ilḥād* and *kufr*, heresy and unbelief, through his engagement in illicit behaviour. As later chapters will demonstrate, the themes of rulers' duties towards their subjects, the conditional nature of their legitimacy, and the corollary limitations to the subjects' duty of obedience recur throughout *Naṣīḥat al-mulūk*.[73]

Turning to the Abbasids, Pseudo-Māwardī notes that few of them, or 'few of the virtuous among them', lacked praiseworthy qualities, the adoption and imitation of which would have been meritorious. He selects certain caliphs for particular mention. He begins with Abū l-ʿAbbās (al-Saffāḥ, r. 132–6/749–54), the first of the Abbasid caliphs, who 'displayed austerity and was abundant in excellence and knowledge' ([*kāna*] *ẓāhir al-zuhd kathīr al-faḍl wa-l-ʿilm*), and his brother Abū Jaʿfar al-Manṣūr (r. 136–58/754–75), also abundant in knowledge and strong in his religious conviction (*kathīr al-ʿilm shadīd al-iʿtiqād fī l-dīn*). In an implicit suggestion of a model from which contemporary rulers might benefit, Pseudo-Māwardī pays considerable attention to al-Manṣūr's association with the previously mentioned theologian ʿAmr b. ʿUbayd, who was reputed for his personal austerity as well as his inclination to rational engagement in theological matters. Before his accession to the caliphate, Abū Jaʿfar (al-Manṣūr) 'acquired knowledge and religion from him [ʿAmr]' (*akhadha ʿanhu al-ʿilm wa-l-dīn*), and he was 'the most eager of people to benefit from him' during his caliphate as well. 'His son' (al-Mahdī, r. 158–69/775–85), according to Pseudo-Māwardī, followed the same path as his father (*kāna . . . ʿalā madhhabihi*).[74]

Hārūn al-Rashīd (r. 170-93/786-809), Pseudo-Māwardī writes, displayed religiosity and attachment to Islam and religion (*kāna . . . mutadayyinan shadīd al-taʿaṣṣub lil-Islām wa-lil-diyāna*) and astuteness in his governance; he protected the pillars of the religious community and promoted religion ([*kāna*] *. . . ẓāhir l-shahāma jaladan fī-l-siyāsa wa-l-ḥimāya dhābban ʿan arkān al-milla munkamishan fī l-daʿwa*). He led campaigns and went on pilgrimage both on foot and mounted; indeed, there were few years in which he engaged in neither a campaign (*ghazwa*) nor the pilgrimage, a point commemorated by 'his panaegyrist'. Pseudo-Māwardī adds that Hārūn cultivated jurists, brought scholars close, was solicitous of religious affairs, and was praised for his godliness (*taqwā*) and fear of God (*khashya*). Again, Pseudo-Māwardī cites the verses of Abū Nuwās (d. between 198/813 and 200/815), this time identified, and concludes with the line: 'An imam who fears God, to the point that / It is as if he expected to see Him by the morrow.'[75]

Pseudo-Māwardī reserves his most effusive admiration for al-Maʾmūn (r. 198–218/813–33), who had forged close ties with the eastern regions of the Abbasid domains during the years of his governorship in Khurasan (193–8/809–13), and had also, as described at the beginning of this chapter, inaugurated the Samanid dynastic family in their Transoxianan strongholds. His praise of al-Maʾmūn, to whom he proceeds without mention of his brother and rival al-Amīn (r. 193–8/809–13), is also likely to reflect Pseudo-Māwardī's Ḥanafī and Muʿtazilite leanings, since this caliph shared with many Ḥanafīs and Muʿtazilites certain attitudes and convictions, including a critical stance towards the reports of the Prophet's normative practice or *sunna*. Al-Maʾmūn also held and promoted the doctrine of *khalq al-Qurʾān*, namely, that God had created the Qurʾān in time rather than its being co-eternal with Him. Often associated with the Muʿtazila, this doctrine perhaps had its roots in Ḥanafī jurisprudence, in which al-Maʾmūn was well versed.[76] Shortly before his death, al-Maʾmūn instituted the 'inquisition', or *miḥna*, in order to enforce adherence to this doctrine among judges, notary-witnesses, scholars of ḥadīth and jurists.[77] Although *Naṣīḥat al-mulūk* provides evidence of several Muᶜtazilite doctrines, this particular doctrine is not mentioned; Pseudo-Māwardī perhaps alludes to the *mihna* in a later passage, however. Of al-Maᵓmūn, Pseudo-Māwardī writes:

> If this community (*umma*) were, with his example, to compete against all other nations (*sāᵓir al-umam*) over their kings, then this one would prove to be the best, and this community would be found to prevail against the other nations by virtue of his superiority in excellence (*faḍl*), knowledge (*ᶜilm*), intellect (*ᶜaql*), literary training (*adab*), resolve (*ḥazm*), purpose (*arab*), judgement (*raᵓy*), understanding (*fahm*), astuteness (*shahāma*) and determination (*ᶜazm*); in his investigation of matters of governance, his disputation in matters of religious knowledge and his independent reasoning (*ijtihād*) in the selection of religious paths (*ikhtiyār al-madhāhib*); in his love of religious knowledge and those who practise it, his zeal (*taᶜaṣṣub*) for the [doctrine of the] divine unity (*tawḥīd*), his fulfilment of due claims with regard to the remaining matters of sovereignty (*tawfīran ᶜalā sāᵓir abwāb al-mulk ḥaqqahā*), and giving them their due measure. Celebrated and widely circulating books contain many substantiated reports and transmitted accounts concerning him.[78]

In this laudatory portrayal of al-Maᵓmūn, Pseudo-Māwardī emphasises the caliph's engagement with rational approaches (evoked by the terms *ᶜaql, raᵓy, naẓar, ijtihād*) to religious knowledge, together with his accomplishments in the field of literary culture (*adab*). Pseudo-Māwardī's presentation of al-Maᵓmūn resembles that of the grammarian, lexicographer, mathematician and traditionist Abū Ḥanīfa al-Dīnawarī (Persian Dīnavarī, d. between 281 and 290/894 and 903):

> He was astute (*shahm*), far in aspiration, and self-denying. He was the star among the offspring of al-ᶜAbbās in knowledge (*ᶜilm*) and philosophical wisdom (*ḥikma*); he acquired a good measure of every science and contributed a portion to it. It was he who obtained the 'Book of Euclid' from the Byzantines and ordered its translation and explication. During his caliphate he held assemblies (*majālis*) for the debate of the various religions (*adyān*) and theological doctrines (*maqālāt*). His teacher in these matters

was [the Muᶜtazilite] Abū l-Hudhayl Muḥammad b. al-Hudhayl al-ᶜAllāf (d. *c.* 227/841).[79]

Pseudo-Māwardī and al-Dīnawarī convey al-Maᵓmūn's engagement with the entire range of the sciences, 'ancient' or 'foreign' and religious, or, in Pseudo-Māwardī's phrasing, *ᶜaql* (reason, rationality), *ᶜilm* (religious knowledge), and *adab* (literary culture). Both authors also draw attention to the caliph's personal involvement in religious affairs, and refer to his convening of inter-confessional and inter-sectarian debates.[80] The holding of staged debates began during the Umayyad period,[81] and several of the earlier Abbasid caliphs, followed by the local rulers who rose to power from the beginning of the ninth century onwards, adopted the practice as well.[82] Pseudo-Māwardī praises al-Maᵓmūn's investigation of and exercise of *ijtihād* with regard to the competing religious paths, including his interrogation and evaluation of diverse religious arguments.[83] His reference to 'choice' (*ikhtiyār*) resonates with the theological–philosophical doctrine that asserted human freedom of choice in the realm of action,[84] encountered previously in connection with Yazīd III and the Qadariyya; Pseudo-Māwardī's reference to the caliph's reported 'zeal for the doctrine of the divine unity' similarly suggests an affinity with the Muᶜtazila, the 'people who adhered to the doctrines of divine justice and the divine unity' (*ahl al-ᶜadl wa-l-tawḥīd*). A near-contemporary writer in the eastern regions, al-Maqdisī (fl. 355/966), probably a Muᶜtazilite and certainly inclined towards rational speculation into religious matters, wrote of al-Maᵓmūn that he ordered 'the examination of judges and transmitters of Prophetic traditions' (*amara bi-imtiḥān al-quḍāt wa-l-muḥaddithīn*).[85] Unlike al-Maqdisī, Pseudo-Māwardī omits overt reference to the *miḥna* in connection with al-Maᵓmūn; but he employed the figure of the caliph to promote the principle of the ruler's rational speculation into religious matters.

Next Pseudo-Māwardī turns to Caliph al-Muᶜtaṣim (r. 218–27/833–42), the abundance of whose campaigns and battles he describes as the subject of numerous celebrated reports. This caliph was, Pseudo-Māwardī writes, observant in religion, steadfast, fearless, astute, a defender of religion and a protector of the honour of the Muslims (*kāna mutadayyinan jaladan bāsilan shahman dhābban ᶜan al-dīn ḥāmiyan ᶜan ᶜawrat al-muslimīn*).[86] The string of epithets resembles the list of qualities ascribed to Hārūn al-Rashīd. As in the case of Hārūn, the final element in the list introduces a particular demonstration of al-Muᶜtaṣim's virtue. Pseudo-Māwardī proceeds to narrate the famous incident in which, 'it is said' (*qālū*), the caliph heard mention of a Muslim woman taken prisoner by the Byzantines in the course of battle. The woman called on the caliph's name: 'O Muᶜtaṣim!' The caliph had responded immediately, '*Labbayki labbayki*', a phrase evocative of the cry of pilgrims called to Mecca and suggesting a response to a divine summons. He set out immediately, rallied his élites (*khāṣṣa*) and retinue (*ḥāshiya*), and had his army (*jaysh*) and pledged forces (*khadam*) join him one by one.[87] He did not rest until he had reached Byzantine territory, found and liberated the woman, and inflicted severe damage upon the Byzantines.[88] The narrative refers to al-Muᶜtaṣim's triumphant campaign against the Byzantines in 223/838, when he seized ᶜAmmūriyya (Amorium) in a punitive response to a Byzantine raid on the frontier town of Zibatra in the course of which several Muslims had been taken prisoner. In connection with his account, and in an indication of his command of the repertoire of Arabic poetry, Pseudo-Māwardī quotes the celebrated verses of Abū Tammām (188–231/804–46), whose *qaṣīda* commemorated the siege of Amorium attributed to al-Muᶜtaṣim's response to 'the Zibatran woman's cry'.[89]

The last of the Abbasid caliphs selected for mention in *Naṣīḥat al-mulūk* is al-Wāthiq (r. 227–32/842–7):

> Al-Wāthiq was remembered for his strong inclination towards religion and his passion for religious knowledge and those who practised it (*kāna l-Wāthiq madhkūran bi-shiddat raghbatihi fī l-dīn wa-wulūᶜihi bi-l-ᶜilm wa-ahlihi*); his promotion of them, his convening of assemblies with them and his seeking to profit from their learning (*[bi-] taᶜẓīmihim wa-mujālasatihim wa-l-istikthār minhum*); his speculation into the divine unity (*tawḥīd*) and divine justice (*ᶜadl*), and his examination of opponents and disputations with them, and his urging them to accept the truth (*[bi-] imtiḥānihi al-mukhālifīn wa-munāẓarātihim wa-ḥamlihim ᶜalā qubūl al-ḥaqq*).[90]

Pseudo-Māwardī's positive references to religious disputation, and to the doctrines of *tawḥīd* and *ᶜadl*, the divine unicity and divine justice, provide further indications of his Muᶜtazilite disposition. In a probable allusion to al-Wāthiq's aggressive prosecution of the *miḥna* at the beginning of his reign,

Pseudo-Māwardī also mentions the caliph's engagement in *imtiḥān*, the examination of theological opponents.[91] His praise of al-Maᵓmūn and al-Wāthiq is consistent with his Muᶜtazilite disposition and his vigorous promotion elsewhere in his book of the role of dialectical theologians, *mutakallimūn*, in 'protecting' the borders of the religious community.[92]

His representation of al-Wāthiq marks the conclusion of Pseudo-Māwardī's discussion of caliphs. He adds the summary remark, 'and other caliphs of the Banū ᶜAbbās', and proceeds to direct his attention to 'the amirs among the rulers of Khurasan':

> Then there were the amirs among the rulers of Khurasan (*al-umarāᵓ min wulāt Khurāsān*), including the Tahirids (205–59/821–73). They have left remarkable traces, and they exercised sound governmental principles (*siyāsāt sadīda*), such as the strengthening of religion and the guardianship of sovereignty (*iᶜzāz al-dīn wa-ḥiyāṭat al-mulk*); the encouragement of learning (*ᶜilm*) and literary culture (*adab*); the honouring of their practitioners and the adornment of their assemblies with them; the pursuit of the most excellent among them in the provinces (*buldān*) and their conveyance from distant regions; their solicitude in the writing and correcting of books (*[min] ᶜināyatihim bi-kitbat al-kutub wa-taṣḥīḥihā*); association with the people trained in the literary arts (*ahl al-ādāb*) and moral excellence (*faḍl*); care in promoting the right (*iṣṭināᶜ al-maᶜrūf*) and spreading the good (*baththal-khayr*), investigating the affairs of the subjects, and protection of the territory (*ḥawza*) – until, when the last of them faltered in these matters, it was a reason for the disappearance of their kingdom, the termination of their turn in power and the passing of their era (*ḥattā idhā fatara fī hādhihi l-asbāb ākhiruhum kāna dhālika sababan li-nuzūl mamlakatihim wa-nqiḍāᵓ dawlatihim wa-taṣarrum muddatihim*).[93]

At this point in his historical survey, then, Pseudo-Māwardī turns from Iraq to Khurasan and from caliphs to *umarāᵓ*. In keeping with tenth-century usage, he refers to the Tahirids and Samanids as *wulāt Khurāsān*, rulers of Khurasan; the lost but much cited history of the mid-tenth-century Abū ᶜAlī Ḥusayn b. Aḥmad al-Sallāmī, which appears to have covered the period up to approximately the middle of the century, was entitled *Taᵓrīkh wulāt Khurāsān* ('History of the Rulers of Khurasan').[94] Pseudo-Māwardī praises the Tahirids, as he had lauded Caliph al-Maʾmūn, for their accomplishments in *ᶜilm*, religious learning, and *adab*, literary culture, which encompassed several genres of edificatory poetry and prose; and for their generous patronage of specialists in both of these meritorious fields of intellectual and cultural activity.

Turning to Khurasan, Pseudo-Māwardī's historical narrative acquires a distinct regional quality. Among the activities distinguished by Pseudo-Māwardī in his praise of the Tahirids is their copying and 'correction' (*taṣḥīḥ*) of books. The Tahirids were celebrated for their patronage of Arabic cultural activities, and several members of the family were accomplished writers and poets.[95] Furthermore, as Pseudo-Māwardī's account indicates, the Tahirids enjoyed high regard in this milieu: the father of al-Kaᶜbī, the Muᶜtazilite theologian whose doctrines are discernible in *Naṣīḥat al-mulūk*, had served in the Tahirid administration, and al-Kaᶜbī composed a *Kitāb Maḥāsin Āl Ṭāhir* ('Book of the Fine Qualities of the Tahirids'), a *Kitāb Mafākhir Khurāsān* ('Book of the Praiseworthy Features of Khurasan') and a *Taʾrīkh Naysābūr* ('History of Nishapur'), said to have been destroyed by fire.[96] Pseudo-Māwardī also quotes ᶜAbdallāh b. Ṭāhir (r. 213–30/828–45) on two occasions.[97] The reference to the Tahirids' copying and correction resonates with reports of the reclamation of the cultural legacies of late antiquity, especially by means of the translation and adaptation into Arabic of materials that subsequently contributed to the shaping of Arabic literary culture. Ibn al-Nadīm, the erudite tenth-century bibliographer and bookseller of Baghdad, describes the 'transmission' or 'correction' (of a previously translated version) of the 'Letters of Aristotle to Alexander' performed by Sālim Abū l-ᶜAlāʾ, the accomplished secretary (*kātib*) under Caliph Hishām (r. 105–25/724–43).[98] Several reports record the philosopher al-Kindī's 'correction' of texts; since al-Kindī appears not to have been proficient in Greek but sponsored the translations undertaken by members of his circle, he presumably corrected these texts in their Arabic versions.[99] The scientist and polymath al-Bīrūnī (362–after 442/973–after 1050) states that the poet Abū ᶜAlī Muḥammad b. Aḥmad al-Balkhī claimed in his *shāhnāmeh* ('book of kings' [of Iran], a literary genre) that he had 'corrected his reports' (*ṣaḥḥaḥa akhbārahu*) against the *Kitāb Siyar al-mulūk* ('Chronicle of Kings'), then compared his text with the version of the Zoroastrian Bahrām al-Haravī al-Majūsī.[100] The same process is mentioned in the 'Bāysunghurī Preface' (829/1425–6) appended, albeit many centuries later, to the recension of Firdawsī's *Shāhnāmeh* initiated by the Timurid prince Ghiyāth al-Dīn Bāysunghur (799–837/1397–1433).[101] This preface describes the ancient Persian kings, 'especially the Sasanians, and among them especially the Just King Anūshīrvān', as avid collectors of the reports of their predecessors, and engaged in 'correcting the accounts of their lives and the stories about them' (*taṣḥīḥ-i aḥvāl-o ḥikāyāt-i īshān*).[102] Whether it was to these processes of cultural reclamation that Pseudo-Māwardī referred in his reference to the Tahirids' copying and correcting of books is uncertain. Such a supposition need not, however, be at odds with the Tahirids' evident attachment to Arabic culture, and despite the assertions in some later sources that they evinced no interest in or were actively hostile to Persian culture, C. E. Bosworth drew attention nearly fifty years ago to evidence of a more expansive attitude.[103]

Also evocative of a tenth-century Perso-Islamic cultural milieu is the author's account of the Tahirids' eventual loss of their kingdom (*mamlaka*), their dynastic term (*dawla*) and their period (*mudda*) of sovereignty. He depicts an order in which dynasties rise, maintain their turn in power (*dawla*) as long as they uphold their responsibilities to religion and their subjects, and lose their sovereignty when they fail in these responsibilities.[104] The causative role of moral decay in precipitating the fall of dynasties constitutes a *topos* in, not uniquely but especially, Persianate literary culture, where it is frequently invoked, as in this instance, with reference to Muḥammad b. Ṭāhir (r. 248–59/862–73), the last Tahirid ruler.[105] The historian Gardīzī, who wrote under the Ghaznavid dynasty that rose to power under and eventually supplanted the Samanids, described Muḥammad b. Ṭāhir as 'heedless and lacking in regard for consequences' (*ghāfil va-bī-ᶜāqibat*), preoccupied with drinking, amusement and gaiety; his negligence, according to Gardīzī, provoked revolts, the loss of Tabaristan and Gurgan, and eventually his eviction from Khurasan through the agency of the Saffarid Yaᶜqūb b. Layth.[106] The anonymous *Tārīkh-i Sīstān* ('History of Sistan')[107] includes a narrative in which Yaᶜqūb chances upon a poem inscribed on the wall of a ruined house; in the poem, the fall of the Barmakids, a powerful family of administrators originally from Balkh, abruptly dismissed from office in 187/803 under Hārūn al-Rashīd, prefigures the fall of the Tahirids, and Yaᶜqūb identifies himself as the foretold agent of their demise.[108] The theme receives particular emphasis in *Naṣīḥat al-mulūk*, and Pseudo-Māwardī's invocation of the Tahirids provides his early tenth-century audience with an immediate and recent reminder of the contingency of royal power. After the Ghaznavids, formerly in the Samanids' service, rose to power, the secretary and historian Abū l-Fażl Bayhaqī (385–470/995–1077) composed in 451/1059 a thirty-volume Persian *Tārīkh* ('History'),[109] in which he treated the theme of the contingency and transience of worldly power to justify the new dynasty's claim to legitimate rule in the absence of an illustrious genealogy.[110]

In the final section of his chronological treatment of exemplary rule, Pseudo-Māwardī passes from the Tahirids, without mention of the Saffarids, to the Samanids:[111]

> The conditions of the recent kings of Sāmān (*aḥwāl mulūk Sāmān al-muḥdathīn*) were similar.[112] Naṣr b. Aḥmad [= Naṣr I b. Aḥmad, r. 250–79 /864–92] was a religiously observant and austere amir (*kāna . . . min ᶜubbād al-umarāʾ wa-zuhhādihim*), in comparison with those before and after him (*bi-l-iḍāfa ilā man kāna qablahu wa-baᶜdahu*).
>
> The Late Amir (al-Amīr al-Māḍī)[113] Abū Ibrāhīm [= Ismāᶜīl I b. Aḥmad, r. 279–95/892–907] engaged in frequent military campaigns (*kāna . . . kathīr al-ghazw*), displayed humility ([*kāna*] *ḥasan al-tawāḍuᶜ*) and lofty aspiration, supported the external aspect of the law ([*kāna*] *nāṣiran li-ẓāhir al-sharīᶜa*), was merciful towards the subjects, intense in his devotion to fear of God and in manifesting the precepts of the religious community ([*kāna*] *shadīd al-raghba fī l-khashya wa-iẓhār farāʾiḍ al-milla*). He pursued justice (*ᶜadl*) and manifested the truth (*yuẓhiru l-ḥaqq*), even though he belonged among the worldly-minded people (*wa-in kāna min abnāʾ al-dunyā*).
>
> Isḥāq b. Aḥmad [= Isḥāq b. Aḥmad I] is remembered for his learning (*ᶜilm*) and literary culture (*adab*) and his love of its practitioners (*al-maḥabba li-ahlihi*), his numerous assemblies with them, and his attentive companionship with them (*al-istiʾnās bihim*).
>
> The Martyr (al-Shahīd) [= Aḥmad II b. Ismāᶜīl, r. 295–301/907–14] is described by the attribute of justice for his implementation of the ordinances (*al-ᶜadl fī l-aḥkām*), his equal treatment (*al-taswiya*) of the near

> and the far and the noble and the humble with regard to (the ordinances), his investigation of the affairs of the subjects and his mercy towards them (*al-naẓar fī umūr al-raᶜiyya wa-l-raḥma bihā*). He sought to alleviate their burdens and showed kindness towards them ([*kāna*] . . . *yataḥarrā al-takhfīf ᶜanhā wa-l-rifq bihā*).[114]

This passage is of critical importance in establishing the date for the composition of *Naṣīḥat al-mulūk*.[115] Pseudo-Māwardī's reference to two amirs, al-Amīr al-Māḍī and (al-Amīr) al-Shahīd, by their posthumous titles (*laqab*s), indicates that he wrote after their deaths. Since al-Shahīd was killed in 301 /914, the passage establishes the work's composition after that date. At the earliest, it must have been written during the reign of Aḥmad's successor Naṣr II b. Aḥmad (r. 301–31/914–43), who is conspicuously absent from the author's list of exemplary rulers.[116] Pseudo-Māwardī's reference to 'the recent kings of the house of Sāmān' could suggest that the Samanid dynastic era had recently come to an end; but the absence of all the later Samanid rulers from his exemplary inventory renders this interpretation much less likely than the alternative possibility, namely, that he referred to a recent generation or sequence of Samanid amirs.

More suggestive evidence for the dating of *Naṣīḥat al-mulūk*'s composition appears in Pseudo-Māwardī's inclusion of Isḥāq b. Aḥmad I among the exemplary Samanid amirs. Isḥāq, as mentioned previously, was the brother of Naṣr I and Ismāᶜīl. Although he never attained the leading rank, Isḥāq bore the same title, 'amir', as his brothers.[117] Pseudo-Māwardī's inclusion of an amir of more local significance in a list that otherwise consists only of prophets, caliphs and senior amirs suggests a date at which the generation represented by the three sons of Aḥmad remained immediately meaningful among the inhabitants of the Samanid polity. Also noteworthy is Pseudo-Māwardī's reference to Ismāᶜīl b. Aḥmad by his *kunya*, Abū Ibrāhīm. It was customary to refer to the amirs by their *kunya*s during their lifetimes and by their posthumous *laqab*s after their deaths.[118] Pseudo-Māwardī adopts both modes of address in referring to Ismāᶜīl, a detail that strengthens the likelihood that he lived during and remembered Ismāᶜīl's reign. A dating during the reign of Naṣr II would account for the inclusion of Isḥāq, whose claims to the amirate would become increasingly distant as the Samanid dynasty continued, after the accession of Naṣr's son Nūḥ, in Ismāᶜīl's line, and for the reference to Ismāᶜīl as Abū Ibrāhīm, who had not yet passed beyond living memory. Such a dating would also coincide with the sporadic revolts raised by Isḥāq's sons, whose challenges to Naṣr II's authority attested to the continuing relevance of their father to considerations of legitimacy in the Samanid domains. In sum, it seems likely that Pseudo-Māwardī was a younger contemporary and admirer of the generation of Naṣr I, Ismāᶜīl and Isḥāq and that he assimilated Aḥmad to this group.

Pseudo-Māwardī's portrayal of Ismāᶜīl coincides with other contemporary and near-contemporary accounts. The historian Narshakhī, who composed a *Taᵓrīkh Bukhārā* ('History of Bukhara'), in Arabic and presented it to the Amir Nūḥ b. Naṣr (r. 331–43/943–54) in 332/943–4,[119] describes Ismāᶜīl as an intelligent, just and compassionate man (*mardī ᶜāqil-i ᶜādil-i mushaf-fiq*), possessed of sound judgement and skill (*ṣāḥib-i rāy va-tadbīr*), and obedient to the caliphs.[120] Like Pseudo-Māwardī, Narshakhī states that Ismāᶜīl 'manifested the traces of justice and fine conduct' (*āthār-i ᶜadl va-sīrat-i khūb ẓāhir kard*). He punished anyone who had committed an injustice; none of the Samanids was 'greater in governance than he was, although he was austere in the exercise of his sovereignty' (*hīch kas az Āl-i Sāmān bā-siyāsat-tar az vey nabūd bā ān-keh zāhid būd dar kār-i mulk*).[121] Several of the early amirs held sessions for the redress of grievances (*maẓālim*) in person. According to a frequently cited report, Ismāᶜīl endured extreme personal hardship, including long exposure to conditions of rain and snow, in order to maintain his subjects' access to his person; such stories of devotion to the cause of justice for the least of his subjects contributed significantly to the shaping of the amir's royal persona.[122] His son Aḥmad, Narshakhī remarks, resembled him in conduct, practised justice and dispensed perfect equity to the subjects (*ᶜadl mīkard va-inṣāf-i raᶜiyyat bi-tamāmī dād*), and the subjects lived in ease and comfort.[123] Other sources report that Isḥāq also presided over sessions of *maẓālim*, a point that passes unmentioned in Narshakhī's account, which is markedly favourable to Ismāᶜīl and his lineal descendants.[124]

Elsewhere, Ismāᶜīl and his forces are reported to have enjoyed a reputation for their zeal in performing prayer and reading the Qurᵓān. In his confrontation with ᶜAmr b. al-Layth Ismāᶜīl, described in *Tārīkh-i Sīstān* as *mardī ghāzī* ('a man dedicated to military campaigns [for the faith]'), is said to have induced some of ᶜAmr's commanders to defect to his side by claiming, 'We are *ghāzīs*; we do not possess wealth. This man [ᶜAmr] continues to seek this world (*hamī dunyā ṭalab kunad*), whereas [our concern is with] the next. What does he want from us?'[125] Narshakhī similarly described the Amir as 'austere' (*zāhid*) in his governance, and Pseudo-Māwardī evokes Ismāᶜīl's cultivation of a world-renouncing demeanour (he was 'intense in his fear of God'). The quality of austerity (*zuhd*), as Chapter 6 will indicate, formed a component of a distinctive culture associated with the Central Asian frontier. Like Ismāᶜīl, several of his brothers also participated in military activities at and beyond the border with the steppe.[126] In later decades, the amirs' involvement in the direction and sponsorship of the activities conducted at and from the *ribāṭ*s appears to have diminished, and it was increasingly local leaders who furnished the *ribāṭ*s' requirements and volunteers (*mutaṭawwiᶜa*) who undertook the campaigns.[127] Pseudo-Māwardī's mention of *ghazw* is compatible with the hypothesis that he lived within memory of the generation of the sons of Aḥmad b. Asad, whose personal involvement in warfare contributed to the construction of their legitimacy.

In the light of the continuing tensions between the cities of Bukhara and Samarqand, it is quite likely that *Naṣīḥat al-mulūk* reflects a perspective other than that of the capital. Pseudo-Māwardī's high regard for Isḥāq is in contrast to the hostile and belittling treatment of the amir meted out in sources composed from a point of view closer to the centre of the polity. The vizier Abū l-Faḍl Balᶜamī (d. 329/940),[128] who embodied the perspective of the central administration, transmitted a report that delegitimised Isḥāq in his contest for leadership by impugning his conduct towards the religious scholars – a matter, incidentally, for which Pseudo-Māwardī explicitly praises him. According to Balᶜamī, Ismāᶜīl and his brother Isḥāq had been in Samarqand, where they received a visit from the eminent Shāfiᶜī jurist and ḥadīth scholar (*muḥaddith*) Muḥammad b. Naṣr al-Marwazī (202–94 /817–906), who, after extensive travels, had settled in Samarqand.[129] Ismāᶜīl greeted the scholar with warmth and courtesy, but Isḥāq refrained from extending a welcome to him. That night, Ismāᶜīl saw the Prophet in a dream. The Prophet predicted that the dominion of Ismāᶜīl and his progeny would grow strong, whereas that of Isḥāq and his sons would fail on account of the latter's slighting of Muḥammad b. Naṣr.[130] The eleventh-century scholar, historian and littérateur al-Khaṭīb al-Baghdādī (392–463/1002–71) reports, similarly transmitted on Bal^c^amī's authority, a slightly fuller version of the narrative. In this account, Ismā^c^īl was in Samarqand, sitting for the redress of grievances (*maẓālim*), with his brother Isḥāq by his side when the scholar entered. Ismā^c^īl, in a first-person narrative, relates that he rose in respect for the scholar's learning (*qumtu lahu ijlālan li-^c^ilmihi*). When the scholar had left, Isḥāq berated his brother Ismā^c^īl for rising in honour of one of his subjects. He remarked, 'You are the ruler of Khurasan, yet when one of your subjects enters your presence, you rise before him! That's the way to lose power' (*anta wālī Khurāsān yadkhulu ^c^alayka rajul min ra^c^iyyatika fa-taqūmu ilayhi wa-bi-hādhā dhahāb al-siyāsa*). In Ismā^c^īl's subsequent dream, the Prophet turns to him and declares that his sovereignty and that of his descendants will grow firm on account of his display of respect (*ijlāl*) for Muḥammad b. Naṣr, and then turns to Isḥāq and pronounces that his sovereignty and that of his children will dissipate because of his belittlement (*istikhfāf*) of him.[131] The tendentious purposes of Bal^c^amī's account emerge clearly from al-Khaṭīb al-Baghdādī's report that in actuality Ismā^c^īl and Isḥāq provided equal, and generous, support to Muḥammad b. Naṣr, and that the people of Samarqand donated a similar amount for the scholar's benefit.[132]

In another example of the discrediting of Isḥāq's claims, Narshakhī, who presented his *Tārīkh-i Bukhārā* to Ismā^c^īl's great-grandson, describes Ismā^c^īl as 'the first of the holders of authority [*salāṭīn*] of the Samanids', and 'a truly deserving and meritorious king' (*bi-ḥaqīqat pādshāh-i sazāvār bā-istiḥqāq būdeh*), and presents Isḥāq, in explicit contrast to his brother Ismā^c^īl, in a consistently negative light.[133] For example, according to Narshakhī, at the conclusion of the conflict between Naṣr and Ismā^c^īl, Isḥāq refused to dismount before the former. When Ismā^c^īl, who displayed exemplary deference, chastised Isḥāq for his temerity, the latter became abject, kissed the ground before Naṣr and offered as an excuse the explanation that his horse was too wild for him to be able to dismount quickly.[134] Similarly, Gardīzī, who glossed over certain contentions among the Samanids, depicts Isḥāq as the plotter of rebellions, against Aḥmad II b. Ismā^c^īl in 296/908, and, aided by his son Ilyās, against Naṣr II.[135] Pseudo-Māwardī represents a contrasting, possibly in part regional, point of view, in which not only Ismā^c^īl but also other Samanid amirs of his generation represent the models of sovereignty from which, by implication, Ismāᶜīl's grandson Naṣr had deviated.

Models of Sovereignty in *Naṣīḥat al-mulūk*

Pseudo-Māwardī's depiction of prophets, caliphs and kings accentuates their combination of the just exercise of power with reasoned engagement in the religious sphere. The qualities that recur in his descriptions include religious observance (his exemplars are *mutadayyin*), learning (*ᶜilm*), literary culture (*adab*), excellence or humanistic knowledge (*faḍl*) and austerity (*zuhd*). Among the most prevalent lexical items in his presentation are words related to the root *ẓ-h-r*, especially the terms *ẓāhir*, external, and *iẓhār*, outward demonstration. With regard to religious matters, Pseudo-Māwardī's *iẓhār*, as Chapter 7 will indicate, expressed his endorsement of the exterior dimension of the religious law, as opposed to the interior (*bāṭin*) dimension promoted by some of his contemporaries. In his description of Ismāᶜīl b. Aḥmad, Pseudo-Māwardī employs terms derived from the root *ẓ–h-r* three times (*kāna . . . nāṣiran li-ẓāhir al-sharīᶜa . . . shadīd al-raghba fī . . . iẓhār farāʾiḍ al-milla . . . wa-yuẓhiru l-ḥaqq*).[136] The last phrase, which appears on precious metal coinage from the time of al-Maʾmūn to the Mongols,[137] evokes the Qurʾānic passage, 'It is He who has sent His Prophet with guidance and the religion of truth, in order that He should cause it to prevail over all religion' (*huwa alladhī arsala rasūlahu bi-l-hudā wa-dīni l-ḥaqqi li-yuẓhirahu ᶜalā l-dīn kullihi* (Q. 9: 33, 48: 28, 61: 9)). Also striking is Pseudo-Māwardī's repeated appreciation of rulers devoted to *tawḥīd*, the doctrine of the divine unity, and to rational speculation (*naẓar*) into religious matters, including the staging of religious debates. Later in the century, the unidentified author(s) of *Tārīkh-i Sīstān* praised the Saffarid Khalaf b. Aḥmad (r. 352–93/963–1003), governor of Sistan, for, among other virtuous practices, his convening of sessions dedicated to religious learning, disputation and the hearing of ḥadīths.[138]

Pseudo-Māwardī's treatment of the Samanid amirs in his third chapter concludes his linear presentation of virtuous rulers. It is indicative of the cultural location of author and audience that he follows this chronologically ordered account with the general observation that these commendable practices were also the customs of the best of the Sasanian kings in earlier times (*wa-ka-dhālika kāna ḥāl afāḍil al-mulūk min Āl Sāsān min qablu*).[139] In a sign of his perception of continuity and consistency with the past, Pseudo-Māwardī, who shared with his near-contemporary al-Masᶜūdī a strong sense of the enduring usefulness of the wisdom attained by and passed down from earlier communities, cites reports related to the most celebrated of the Sasanian kings, Ardashīr (= Ardashīr I, r. *c.* 224–40 or 242), Anūshīrvān (= Khusraw I, 'The Immortal Souled', r. 531–79) and Shāpūr (= Shāpūr I, r. 239 or 240–70 or 273), and Aristotle's apocryphal correspondence with his royal pupil Alexander the Great.[140] To support this observation, he cites a set of materials rendered into Arabic from Middle Persian texts, themselves likely to have passed through multiple redactions and, in some cases, languages before acquiring the sixth-century form in which the translators of the early centuries of the Islamic era found them.[141] First, he cites two quotations from *ᶜAhd Ardashīr*, the 'Testament of Ardashīr', 'that he (Ardashīr) made as a model for the exercise of sovereignty' (*jaᶜalahu dastūran lil-mulk*). Next, he states that he has read in 'the Testament(s) of Anūshīrvān and Shāpūr' about the honouring and defence of religion, exertion in protecting and preserving it, 'and we have related several of their reports and narrative accounts'. Pseudo-Māwardī's references to the experiences of earlier peoples finish with four quotations that he has read in Aristotle's 'Epistle to Alexander' (*Risāla ilā l-Iskandar*).[142] He concludes with the statement that there are many similar reports of kings distinguished by virtues and their avoidance of vices, but that the amount that he has mentioned will suffice as a sign of what he intends to convey.[143]

In his quotations from the 'Testament of Ardashīr' and Aristotle's *Risāla ilā l-Iskandar*, Pseudo-Māwardī selects passages that recapitulate the theme, ubiquitous in Sasanian-derived writings, of the interdependence of religion and sovereignty. He begins with the frequently cited passage from the 'Testament of Ardashīr':

> Know that religion and sovereignty are twin brothers, neither one of which endures without its partner. For religion is the foundation of sovereignty, and sovereignty in its turn becomes the guardian of religion. Sovereignty depends on its foundation, and religion depends on its guardian. For whatever lacks a guardian vanishes, and whatever has no foundation crumbles.[144]

Pseudo-Māwardī adduces this passage at the conclusion of his chronological treatment of prophets, caliphs and kings. This section forms the last part of his third chapter, devoted to the causes of corruption in kingdoms and in the conditions of kings. Earlier in his book, as Chapter 7 of the present volume will demonstrate, Pseudo-Māwardī had already detailed the dangers of heterodoxy, and urged his royal audience to assume a critical posture in matters of religion. His descriptions of model rulers reflect these themes, which he emphasises further through the quotations with which he concludes his chapter.

Pseudo-Māwardī continues his concluding remarks with a second quotation from *ᶜAhd Ardashīr*:

> Know that two leaders – a secret leader in religion and an overt leader in sovereignty – can never be united in a single kingdom, without the leader in religion extracting whatever lies in the hands of the leader in sovereignty. For religion is a foundation and sovereignty is its pillar, and the possessor of the foundation takes precedence with regard to the entire edifice over the possessor of the structure (*ᶜumrān*).[145]

Pseudo-Māwardī introduced the theme of the danger posed to the king and the kingdom by rival religious figures earlier in his book. His citation supports his urging of the ruler to take an active role in guiding the religious affairs of the kingdom.[146] In adducing these two passages from *ᶜAhd Ardashīr*, Pseudo-Māwardī has reproduced a large portion of the opening pages of this text in its surviving Arabic version.[147]

The cluster of quotations ascribed to Aristotle, all common to the text known as *al-Siyāsa al-ᶜāmmiyya* ('General Governance'), echo the theme articulated in the passages from the 'Testament of Ardashīr':

> Any king who makes his sovereignty a servant to his religion is worthy of kingship. Any king who makes his religion a servant to his sovereignty, then for him sovereignty is a calamity.[148]

> Whoever cleaves to normative practice (*sunna*), his blood is forbidden to you, and likewise visiting humiliation upon him.[149]

> Defend your religion (and) you will improve your final end.[150]

> Make this world a protection (*wiqāya*) for your next life; do not make the next life a protection for your life in this world.[151]

Pseudo-Māwardī's use of sources associated with perennial wisdom, whether in the voices of Sasanian monarchs, Greek philosophers or Indian kings, receives attention in Chapter 2 of Volume II. In the present context, these materials, deftly deployed to engage a diverse audience of Pseudo-Māwardī's contemporaries, demonstrate the importance to author and audience of the wisdom of the past. Rather than rupture, Pseudo-Māwardī perceives continuity, and, in keeping with a dominant strand in the political culture of his time, his frame of reference is hybrid and multifaceted. It is consistent with the catholicity of cultural interests exemplified by Caliph al-Maʾmūn, for whom he expresses particular admiration; this caliph was conversant with the ideas and texts of the Middle Persian repertoire, and took an exceptional interest in the transmission into Arabic of scientific knowledge.[152]

Pseudo-Māwardī's abandonment of his narrative of caliphal history after al-Wāthiq in favour of a focus on the rulers of Khurasan strongly suggests an eastern location for the composition of his text. It finds a parallel in his seventh chapter, 'On the governance of the common people' (*fī siyāsat al-ʿāmma*). In a brief, selective and chronologically arranged section devoted to the ruler's responsibility to dispatch observers and spies amongst the subjects, the author again begins with the Rāshidūn, the 'Rightly Guided Caliphs', proceeds through selected Umayyads (described, incidentally, as 'kings', usually a positive term in *Naṣīḥat al-mulūk*), mentions certain Abbasid caliphs (so designated), and then turns his attention to Khurasan and the Tahirids:

> As for his (the Prophet's) Rightly Guided Caliphs, it is related regarding ʿUmar, may God be pleased with him, that he exercised a remarkable command and firm governmental practice in this regard; to the extent that they used to say of him that he knew that which occurred in the provinces of his terrain as well as he knew that which issued directly from him, so that each of his officials suspected that the persons closest to him might raise a complaint against him.[153]
>
> Among the kings (*mulūk*), Muʿāwiya (b. Abī Sufyān, r. 41–60/661–80) was similar, and this was one of his distinguishing achievements. [The caliph's

> governor in Iraq] Ziyād b. Abīhi (d. 53/673) followed in his tracks in this respect. It is said of him (Ziyād) that a man entered his presence with a petition and addressed him regarding it. Assuming that Ziyād did not know the petitioner, the latter disclosed the identity of his father and his people (*qawm*) to him. Ziyād smiled and said, 'Are you introducing yourself to me? I know you, your father, your mother, your grandfather and your grandmother, and I know this garment that you are wearing: it belongs to So-and-so son of So-and-so'. The man was astonished and so alarmed that he trembled with fear.[154] Among the Umayyads, ᶜAbd al-Malik b. Marwān (r. 65–86/685–705) was similar in this regard.
>
> Among the Abbasid caliphs, Abū Jaᶜfar al-Manṣūr, al-Rashīd and al-Maʾmūn were similar. For each of these caliphs, in this matter there are many transmitted accounts (*āthār*) and reports (*akhbār*), the mention of which would lengthen this chapter greatly. It is even related of many of them that they went out in disguise and walked about in the markets, and that they went out in the dead of night and listened to the voices of their servants (*khadam*) in their palaces and households.
>
> In Khurasan ᶜAbdallāh b. Ṭāhir used to go out frequently into the street, and ask those passers-by whom he met about his conduct and the conduct of his officials among them.[155]

In this passage, Pseudo-Māwardī presents his materials in the same sequenced fashion, and with the same turn from the caliphate to the east, that he had employed in his chronological portrayal of the virtuous ruler-prophets, caliphs and kings. His accounts of ᶜUmar, Muᶜāwiya and Ziyād coincide with a section that appears in *Akhlāq al-mulūk*, commonly known as *Kitāb al-Tāj* ('Book of the Crown') of al-Taghlibī (or al-Thaᶜlabī), a ninth-century composition that addressed a variety of topics appropriate to kings and the life of the court.[156] Despite a considerable number of such coincidences, Pseudo-Māwardī does not acknowledge *Akhlāq al-mulūk*, and I shall argue in Volume II that Pseudo-Māwardī and al-Taghlibī are likely to have drawn upon a common source.[157] Unlike al-Taghlibī, who wrote in Iraq, Pseudo-Māwardī, in an indication of the strength of regional identities, added to the previously mentioned cases of royal intelligence gathering the example of ᶜAbdallāh b. Ṭāhir.

Relations with the Caliphs

Pseudo-Māwardī's diversion from the Abbasid caliphs to the Tahirids and Samanids is consistent with the Samanids' relations with the caliphs in the first half of the tenth century. Narshakhī avers that Ismāᶜīl b. Aḥmad consistently displayed obedience to the caliphs, and regarded it as obligatory to follow them.[158] Yet, for all Narshakhī's affirmation of the propriety of Ismāᶜīl's relations with the Abbasids, the amir's interactions with Caliph al-Muᶜtaḍid suggest a combination of the appearance of deference with a high degree of functional autonomy. Samanid coins carried the names of the caliphs together with those of the amirs, and the amirs supplied the caliphs with 'gifts' and slaves, but not, it seems, with regular submissions of tax or tribute; relations were, in Michael Bonner's phrase, 'correct but cool'.[159] The amirs welcomed caliphal investiture, but they also cultivated several other sources of legitimation, such as lineage, the defence of the frontier, the conduct of *ghazw*, economic prosperity, patronage of various kinds of cultural production and respectful relations with the ᶜulamāᵓ in their cities. Tellingly, Pseudo-Māwardī cites the examples of individual caliphs, but displays no interest in the office of the caliphate. His treatment is consistent with a milieu in which rulers interacted in an irregular fashion with particular caliphs, but in which the office of the caliphate was insignificant in matters of local governance, and caliphal investiture only one source of legitimation among many.

In the later Samanid period, the amirs became increasingly involved in conflicts with members of the Buyid dynastic family, their principal rivals to the west. This intensifying rivalry had repercussions for the Samanids' relations with the Abbasids as well as with regional holders of power. The Buyids prevailed upon Caliph al-Muṭīᶜ (r. 334–63/946–74), for example, to recognise one of the Samanids' vassals, Abū ᶜAlī Aḥmad al-Ṣaghānī (Persian Chaghānī) (d. 344/955) of the Āl-i Muḥtāj of Chaghaniyan,[160] as Amir of Khurasan. Having led repeated campaigns on the Samanids' behalf against the Buyids, Abū ᶜAlī, who governed Khurasan in the years 327–31/939–43 and was reappointed to his post in about 340–2/951–3, had latterly entered into negotiations with them.[161] After the Buyids took Baghdad in 333/945, their scope for such interventions increased.[162] It was largely in response to the Buyids' involvement in the installation and deposition of caliphs that the Samanids likewise began to grant, and sometimes withhold, recognition of authority to the caliphs; for example, they offered shelter to the pretender Muḥammad b. al-Mustakfī and refused to recognise al-Qādir (r. 381–422 /991–1031).[163] In the changing conditions of the second half of the tenth century, during which period the establishment of the Fatimid caliphate not only in North Africa, but also from 358/969 in Egypt posed an overt challenge to Abbasid authority, the later Samanid amirs periodically asserted and manifested their independence from the Abbasid caliphs. The Samanid-sponsored 'translations' (in fact, re-writings in Persian) of the 'History' and *Tafsīr* ('Commentary' [on the Qurʾān]) of al-Ṭabarī suggest a changing attitude, and occasionally display a quite critical posture towards the Abbasids.[164]

Several historians have observed that the Samanids emulated the Abbasids, especially in the arrangement of their administration.[165] This debt notwithstanding, the Samanid polity and the diverse communities accommodated within it operated in an autonomous context. The polity developed more in response to local conditions than in emulation of the Abbasid imperial model, and participated in the construction of a confident, distinctive identity to which the religion of Islam, the Iranian past and its lasting cultural expressions, the wisdom of the diverse communities in its midst and neighbouring regions, and the Arabic and Persian languages all contributed. Its geographical location, its position at the centre of numerous converging trade routes, its vast and diverse terrain, its extensive and varied resources, and its economic prosperity enabled the Samanid amirate to function with little reference to an Abbasid 'centre'. Perhaps to a greater degree than its counterparts in the far western region of al-Andalus, the Samanid polity developed distinctive social–cultural patterns that display little evidence of a perception of relativism to a distant focal point. *Naṣīḥat al-mulūk*, in keeping with this perspective, appears not as the product of a peripheral environment, but rather as an example of 'regionalism'.[166] Its disregard of caliphs after al-Wāthiq and its seemingly complete neglect of the office of the caliphate suggest less an attitude of competition or hostility than a sense of their lack of immediate relevance. This perspective is consistent with the evidence of relations between the Samanids and the Abbasids for the first half of the tenth century.

On the basis of the arguments adduced in this chapter, the present study assumes that *Naṣīḥat al-mulūk* is a product of the Samanid domains, and that it was first composed during the reign of Naṣr II b. Aḥmad (r. 301–31 /914–43), perhaps in the third decade of the tenth century. Later chapters will argue that it is in the context of Naṣr's reign that much of the concern explicit and implicit in Pseudo-Māwardī's writing seems most plausibly situated. If the book was indeed written at this time, it is among the earliest known Arabic mirrors of such length and complexity to have survived, and, as the present volume aims to demonstrate, a valuable source for Samanid history and culture in its own right.

The Inclusion of Later Materials

Certain parts of *Naṣīḥat al-mulūk* suggest a dating later than the early tenth century. For example, the term *sulṭān*, which in the early tenth century sometimes designated 'power' or 'authority' in an abstract sense and sometimes a holder or holders of power, occasionally appears in a form that suggests its later usage to refer to a specific individual.[167] Hanna Mikhail identified another indication that might undermine the case for an early tenth-century dating of *Naṣīḥat al-mulūk*. Pseudo-Māwardī, in an example of his extensive use of the resources of *adab*, cites numerous verses of Arabic poetry, for which in some cases he identifies the poet, and which in other cases appear without attribution. Among the verses that Pseudo-Māwardī introduces with the simple phrase *wa-qāla ākhar* ('another [poet] said') and for which he supplies no additional identifying information are the following lines:

> If the leader (*ṣadr*) of the *majālis* is not a *sayyid*
> Then there is no good in those whom the *majālis* appoint as leaders (*man ṣaddarathu al-majālisu*)
> How many a speaker (says): 'Why do I see you walking?'
> And I say to him, 'It's a surprise that you are riding!'[168]

The pre-eminent littérateur of the eastern regions Abū Manṣūr al-Thaᶜālibī (350–429/961–1038) records these verses in his discussion of the grammarian and *adīb* Ibn Khālawayh. Ibn Khālawayh was born in Hamadan, arrived in Baghdad in 314/926, settled in Aleppo at the court of the Hamdanids (293–394/906–1004; in Aleppo, from 333/944) and died in 370 or 371/980. He apparently attained a high reputation during his lifetime and attracted many students in *ᶜilm* and *adab*.[169] Mikhail identified the quoted stanza as the latest datable citation in *Naṣīḥat al-mulūk* and, in Mikhail's interpretation, its inclusion constituted evidence of the work's composition during the lifetime of al-Māwardī.[170]

In the light of the text's other indications, it is necessary to consider alternative explanations for the inclusion of the verse. The accuracy of al-Thaᶜālibī's attribution, for example, is not entirely beyond doubt. A number of scholars have observed that his compendium of poets *Yatīmat al-dahr wa-maḥāsin ahl al-ᶜaṣr* ('The Matchless Pearl of the Age and the Fine Qualities of the People of the Time') is a work of uneven character; since al-Thaᶜālibī spent his entire life in the east and never travelled to distant Syria, the Syrian section is the least reliable part of the collection.[171] Furthermore, al-Thaᶜālibī's attribution of this particular verse to Ibn Khālawayh perhaps evinces a certain reserve. Al-Thaᶜālibī opens his section devoted to Ibn Khālawayh with the statement, 'Of his poetry only this has survived . . .', and cites a lengthy extract with commentary. He then adds, 'And he said' (*wa-qāla*), an apparent afterthought for which he specifies neither a written nor an oral source, and it is at this point that he reproduces the verse that also appears in *Naṣīḥat al-mulūk*.[172] In short, al-Thaᶜālibī's inclusion of the verse under Ibn Khālawayh's name need not constitute definitive proof of its origination. More importantly, even if it is assumed that Ibn Khālawayh composed the verses in question, their appearance in *Naṣīḥat al-mulūk* is not incompatible with the proposed early to mid-tenth-century dating for the text. Perhaps the most likely explanation is that a later writer, through whose hands the text passed, added this couplet to *Naṣīḥat al-mulūk*.

In sum, the balance of the evidence overwhelmingly suggests an early to mid-tenth-century dating for the text's initial composition. It is possible that the verse by Ibn Khālawayh, and perhaps other additions and modifications, entered the text at the point of a later, possibly eleventh-century reworking.

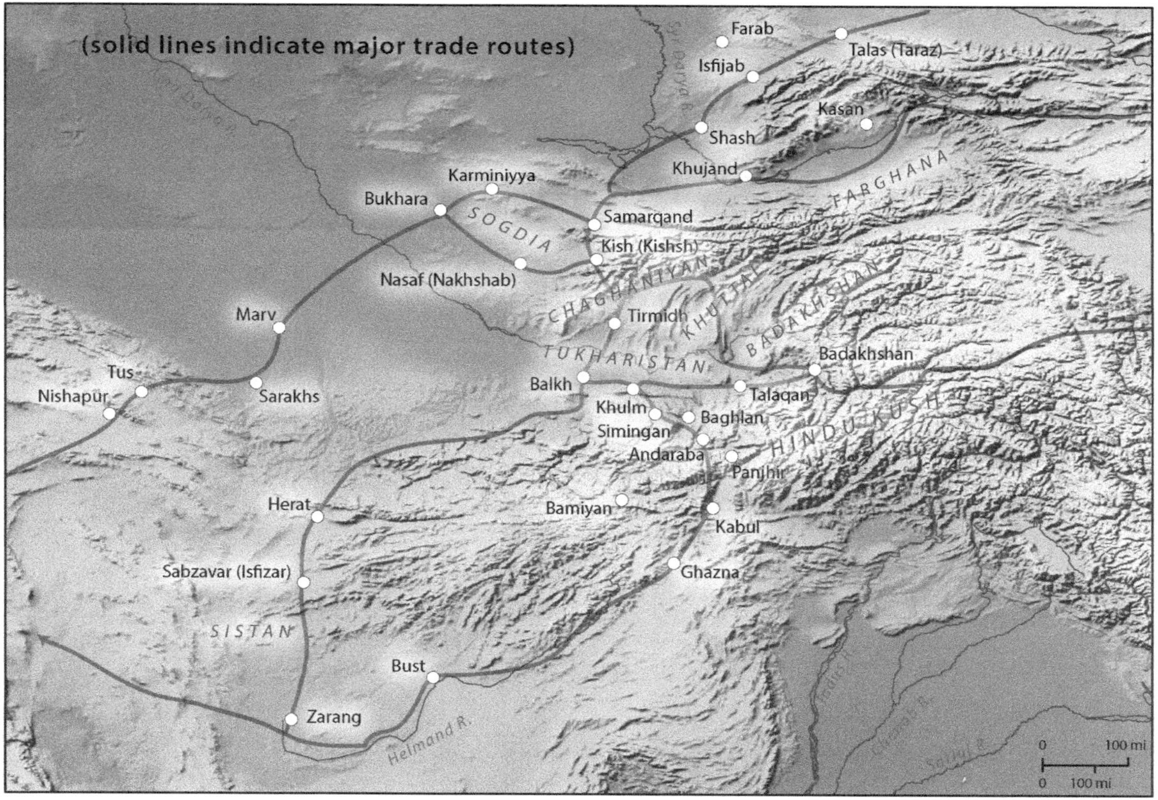

Map 2 The Oxus Regions in the Ninth and Tenth Centuries

2

A Liminal Setting: The Location of *Naṣīḥat al-mulūk*

Chapter 1 sought to establish a Samanid context and an early to mid-tenth-century date for *Naṣīḥat al-mulūk*'s first composition. This chapter addresses its possible location within the Samanid domains. After brief preliminary comments regarding the major regions subsumed within the Samanid polity, Transoxiana, Khurasan and Tukharistan, the chapter examines the cultural and linguistic evidence of the text, offers an analysis of the locations named in the text, and presents arguments for its provenance from, first and probably, Balkh, and, secondly and possibly, Samarqand.

As indicated in Chapter 1, the Samanid amirate had its beginnings in Transoxiana or, in the terminology of the Arabic sources of the early centuries, Mā warāʾ al-nahr.[1] The designation connoted the Muslim regions beyond the River Oxus, and its usage evolved, as Étienne de la Vaissière has observed, in such a way that it came to correspond largely with the region known to Xuanzang (d. 664), the Chinese Buddhist monk who travelled overland to Buddhist sites in India and along the Silk Road between 629 and 645 and visited the region's monasteries and holy sites in 630, as Sogdia.[2] The major Transoxianan cities to which members of the family had first been appointed by al-Maʾmūn as governors, especially Bukhara, Samarqand and to a lesser extent Farghana, remained the principal bases of the Samanids' power. Ismāʿīl's decision to locate his court and capital in Bukhara ensured the continuing centrality of that region in the Samanid polity and its orientation towards the frontier, a strategic location that brought with it the responsibility for defending and maintaining the borders as well as the economic advantages of a site of convergence for a network of routes involved in an active overland trade.

Bukhara and Samarqand developed distinctive urban characters and their rulers and inhabitants, as observed in Chapter 1, not infrequently vied with one another for power and status. Both cities emerged in the Samanid era as centres for intellectual activity and religious scholarship. At an unknown date, Bukhara, its name possibly derived from the term applied to a Buddhist monastery, *vihāra*,[3] acquired the epithet 'the noble' (*sharīf*) due to its sustained prominence in the Islamic sciences.[4] An early example of Bukhara's stature in religious scholarship is provided by Muḥammad b. Ismāᶜīl al-Bukhārī (194–256/810–70), celebrated for the pre-eminent Sunni collection of ḥadīth that bears his name; al-Bukhārī lived and taught in Bukhara, although he died near Samarqand.[5] The city became renowned for its abundance of books and well-appointed libraries. Ibn Sīnā (d. 428/1037), whose scholarly career began in Bukhara, was famously impressed by the superlative quality of the city's libraries, and especially the holdings of the library of Nūḥ II b. Manṣūr (r. 365–87/976–97).[6] As the political–administrative–military centre of the Samanid polity, a thriving commercial centre and an intellectual centre,[7] Bukhara might seem the most probable site for the composition of a Samanid mirror for princes. Yet the text of *Naṣīḥat al-mulūk* offers little information to support the conjecture of a Bukharan provenance.

A more likely location, especially in the light of Pseudo-Māwardī's positive representation of its governor Isḥāq b. Aḥmad, is Samarqand, which retained much of its regional eminence even after Ismāᶜīl's adoption of Bukhara as the Samanid capital. Al-Muqaddasī remarked explicitly that despite Bukhara's status as the political capital and location of the administrative offices, *dār al-mamlaka wa-mawḍiᶜ al-dawāwīn*, it did not constitute the region's centre, its *miṣr*; indeed, the Samanids themselves had moved there from Samarqand.[8] Samarqand, 'the capital of Sogdia' (*qaṣabat al-Sughd*),[9] enjoyed a position at the intersection of trade routes from India and Afghanistan via Balkh and Tirmidh, and from western Iran via Marv. From Samarqand, these routes led northwards and eastwards into the Turkish steppes and along the Silk Road to eastern Turkistan and China. The city also flourished because of the great fertility of the surrounding district; the highly irrigated basin of the River Zarafshan supported a dense agricultural population. Largely on account of its location, size and its established status in the conduct of long-distance overland trade, Samarqand remained the primary commercial centre of Transoxiana. It was, according to al-Iṣṭakhrī, 'the entrepôt of Transoxiana and the meeting place of merchants' (*hiya furḍat mā warāʾ al-nahr wa-majmaᶜ al-tujjār*).[10] In its fostering of religious scholarship, Samarqand emerged at an early date as a leading regional centre. The city produced an exceptionally large number of religious scholars, as the *Kitāb al-Qand fī maᶜrifat ᶜulamāʾ Samarqand* ('Book of Candy on Knowledge of the Scholars of Samarqand'), with its 1,232 entries in the (published) Arabic version of Abū Ḥafṣ ᶜUmar b. Muḥammad al-Nasafī (d. 537/1142–3), renders evident.[11] Although the author of *Naṣīḥat al-mulūk* does not refer to Samarqand any more than he refers to Bukhara, several characteristics of the text are compatible with a Samarqandi environment.

Pseudo-Māwardī, as Chapter 1 showed, refers more than once to 'the rulers of Khurasan', and his understanding of the political–geographical designation of Khurasan is likely to have included the region in which he lived and wrote. It was in this compound sense that the anonymous author of *Ḥudūd al-ᶜālam* wrote of Khurasan, 'The *mīr* of Khorāsān resides at Bukhārā'.[12] As a territorial category, the name of Khurasan still subsumed a vast terrain, the boundaries of which were variously, and often imprecisely, defined, and which encompassed a correspondingly diverse set of physical and human geographies.[13] Noting the contrasts combined in the designated region, Richard Bulliet and Parvaneh Pourshariati have distinguished between 'Inner Khurasan' and 'Outer Khurasan'.[14] In Inner Khurasan, the population of Nishapur, the region's major city, grew considerably in the course of the Samanid period: Bulliet has calculated that the city's population, approximately 5,000 in the mid-seventh century, reached roughly 150,000 in the year 1000. He has further concluded that the most rapid growth occurred in the ninth and tenth centuries, during which period the demographic increase in the Muslim community reflects extensive conversion to Islam, possibly associated with movement from rural to urban locations.[15] The population became increasingly heterogeneous, especially as Khurasan's contiguity with Transoxiana and the Turkic sphere of Inner Asia created unprecedented opportunities for travel, trade and migration.

Of particular importance in the present context is the region of Tukharistan, the term applied to the ancient district of Bactria, which possessed as its centre the ancient city of Balkh. Like that of other regions, the spatial definition of Tukharistan fluctuated, but in a general sense the designation applied to the highlands dependent on Balkh on both sides of the River Oxus.[16] Chaghaniyan, which bordered on the Oxus, possessed extensive political and cultural links with the city of Balkh.[17] Although the Abbasids initially dispatched commanders to govern Tukharistan and from the early ninth century assigned the region to the governance of the Tahirids, the Tahirids' seat of power in Nishapur lay some 500 miles to the west, and it was local dynastic families, most notably the Abu Dawudids (Daʾudids) or Banijurids, who controlled the region, including its highly productive silver mines. The Amir Abū Dāʾūd Muḥammad b. Aḥmad ruled in Balkh from 260/874, and remained in office as late as 285–6/898–9, when, according to Narshakhī, ʿAmr b. Layth summoned him, Aḥmad b. Farīghūn[18] and Ismāʿīl b. Aḥmad to obedience. It was near Balkh, as described in Chapter 1, that Ismāʿīl defeated and captured ʿAmr in 287/900.[19] If the dating of *Naṣīḥat al-mulūk* to the reign of Naṣr II is correct, these last events are likely to have occurred during the lifetime of Pseudo-Māwardī.

The disparate pieces of information regarding the Banijurids,[20] like other dynastic families of the region, present a sparse and not entirely consistent record, but it appears that, despite his earlier support for the defeated ʿAmr, Abū Dāʾūd Muḥammad b. Aḥmad retained his position at Balkh.[21] The management of Balkh, like that of most other major cities within the Samanid domains, seems to have proceeded with a large degree of independence from the Samanid senior amirs, who periodically required the cooperation of the city's leading families and eminent individuals (individuals who resisted Samanid power also took up positions there). In what appears to have been a common pattern, Abū Dāʾūd controlled not only Balkh, but also Andarab and Panjhir in Badakhshan. Andarab, where the Abū Dāʾūdids minted coins over several decades of the later ninth and the beginning of the tenth centuries, lay on one of the two main routes across the Hindu Kush to Kabul and India.[22] If, as the present chapter proposes, Pseudo-Māwardī lived in Tukharistan in this period, he lived in circumstances particularly conducive to mobility and access to the south and east.[23]

The region's location ensured its continuing contact with an exceptionally broad set of geographical–cultural areas. It had a long history of contact with China: when in 116/734 al-Ḥārith b. Surayj (d. 128/746), who at that time controlled Balkh, rebelled against caliphal suzerainty, he enlisted the support of the local princes of Tukharistan, who continued to send embassies to the Imperial Chinese court with requests of help against the Arab armies even after the Arab-Muslim victory at Talas.[24] Tukharistan also had long-standing relations with Turkic peoples,[25] who seem, moreover, to have constituted a distinct grouping within the population; the geographical work *Ḥudūd al-ᶜālam* mentions the presence of Khallukh (= Kharlukh, Karluk) Turks in the region's steppe lands.[26] The Hephthalites, long-standing adversaries of the later Sasanian monarchs and encountered by the first Arab armies in their turn, appear in a late eighth-century set of documents written in Bactrian,[27] and as late as the latter half of the tenth century the secretary Abū ᶜAbdallāh Muḥammad b. Aḥmad al-Khwārazmī still knew of and described the 'group(s) (*jīl* or *jiyal*) of people who possessed power (*shawka*) and possessed the lands of Tukharistan', the Hephthalites (Ar. Hayāṭila).[28] A set of Arabic documents, produced like the Bactrian group in the area between Balkh and Bamiyan in the late eighth century, attests to the continuing use of both languages during this period, and reflects the heterogeneity of the local population.[29] The Arabic documents reflect numerous cultural groups, and record Arabic, Iranian and Turkish personal names; some of these names appear in the Bactrian documents as well. Collectively, the Bactrian and Arabic documents indicate the prevalence of diverse forms of Mazdaism and a variety of local religious cultures. A subset of the Bactrian texts, some bearing drawings of figures, attests to the presence of Buddhism.[30] The linguistic, ethnic and religious diversity indicated in these late eighth-century documents decreased and mutated over the course of the following centuries,[31] but left a lasting imprint in many aspects of Tukharistan's culture.

By the late ninth and tenth centuries, Balkh had grown prosperous. The historian and geographer al-Yaᶜqūbī (d. after 292/905), who served in Khurasan under the Tahirids until their fall in 259/873 and completed his *Kitāb al-Buldān* ('Book of Countries') in 278/891, stressed the city's size and status, and a century later al-Muqaddasī compared it with Damascus and even Bukhara.[32] As the *Fażāʾil-i Balkh* ('The Virtues of Balkh') of Shaykh al-Islām Vāᶜiẓ, composed in Arabic between 584/1188–9 and 610/1214 and rendered into Persian in 676/1278,[33] and the biographical collection *al-Ansāb* ('Genealogies') of ᶜAbd al-Karīm al-Samᶜānī (506–62/1113–66), who hailed from Marv, attest, Balkh too produced numerous scholars, as well as several individuals renowned for their practice of austerity (*zuhd*).[34] Al-Iṣṭakhrī observed that the most excellent of the people of Khurasan were the people of Balkh and Marv in jurisprudence, religion, rational speculation and dialectical theology (*anjabu ahl Khurāsān ahl Balkh wa-Marw fī l-fiqh wa-l-dīn wa-l-naẓar wa-l-kalām*).[35] As the present chapter seeks to demonstrate, Balkh, which, unlike Bukhara, Samarqand or Nishapur, is mentioned in *Naṣīḥat al-mulūk*, emerges as the most likely setting for the work's initial composition.

Cultural and Linguistic Indications

Pseudo-Māwardī's presentation of history, especially his informed portrayals of the Tahirids and the Samanids, indicates his links with, and probably residence in, the eastern regions or *mashriq*. Other aspects of *Naṣīḥat al-mulūk* confirm this impression. That the author lived in a non-Arabic-speaking environment is implicit in his recommendation that princes should learn the Qurʾān 'with Arabic' (*maʿa al-lugha al-ʿarabiyya*), that is, in conjunction with their instruction in the Arabic language.[36] By the tenth century, Persian had emerged as the spoken lingua franca of the eastern regions, and was gradually replacing the indigenous Iranian languages and dialects; in the course of the century, differences between Persian-speakers and Turkish-speakers probably became more pronounced. Pseudo-Māwardī reveals no familiarity with Turkish words, but he sometimes employs Persian vocabulary in his Arabic text. In a telling passage, he refers to *afsānaqāt*, 'stories' – a usage in which he attaches the Arabic feminine sound plural to the Persian singular noun *afsān* or *afsāneh*.[37] The use of this form, in a context in which the author refers to collections of stories such as *Hazār afsān* ('The Thousand Stories'), denoted by its Persian name, and the Persian- or Indic-associated 'Book of Sindbād', suggests that it was particularly a profusion of Persian stories that he had in mind when he discouraged their pursuit:

> It is necessary that the prince commit to memory, by way of historical narratives (*akhbār*), the biographical accounts of the Prophet (*akhbār al-maghāzī wa-l-siyar*)[38] and the transmitted reports concerning the caliphs (*āthār al-khulafāʾ*) – rather than the reports of lovers (*āthār al-ʿushshāq*), or books of stories (*kutub al-afsānaqāt*) such as the *Book of Sindbad* (*Kitāb Sindbād*), the *Thousand Stories* (*Hazār afsān*) and the like.[39]

In another case, Pseudo-Māwardī adopts the Persian word *bāghbān*, in the phrase 'like the clever gardener (*ka-l-bāghbān al-ḥādhiq*) who is eager for the prosperity of his orchard'.[40] These occurrences in *Naṣīḥat al-mulūk* suggest a largely Persian-speaking milieu. While several locations would fulfil this condition, Bukhara, unlike Samarqand, was unlikely to be among them. By contemporary accounts, in the early tenth century Sogdian, if in a modified form, remained the principal spoken language of the Samanid capital, and Dari, derived from the language spoken at the Sasanian court, took the place of a secondary language.[41] In an intriguing comment on Bukhara's attachment to Sogdian culture, Étienne de la Vaissière speculates that Narshakhī, who in 332/943 composed his (lost) *Taʾrīkh Bukhārā*, 'so little Islamic in its spirit', may have been prompted by a sense that knowledge of the city's Sogdian past would be lost without deliberate efforts to preserve its memory.[42] In contrast to Bukhara's continuing attachment to Sogdian culture and the Sogdian language, Balkh, by the tenth century, appears to have had a largely Persian-speaking population. In the later tenth century, Ibn al-Nadīm (d. *c.* 380/990), who wrote in Baghdad, associated Balkh with the prevalence of the language of Dari, the use of which as a lingua franca had been growing over the course of centuries.[43] Al-Muqaddasī, writing in the same period, suggests the expressive, indeed literary, qualities associated with the language of Balkh when he reports that one of the local rulers (*mulūk Khurāsān*) had ordered his vizier to gather men from the five principal provincial areas (*kuwar*) of Khurasan, namely, Sijistan, Nishapur, Marv, Balkh and Herat. Once they had assembled, the vizier commented on the qualities of each man's speech, and pronounced that of the Balkhi to be fit for use in official correspondence (*risāla*).[44] Shaykh al-Islām Vāʿiẓ, by his sobriquet an esteemed religious teacher and a preacher, employed numerous earlier materials in his early thirteenth-century 'history' of the city (Arabic *Faḍāʾil Balkh*, accessible in a later thirteenth-century Persian translation, *Fażāʾil-i Balkh*), and reported, on the basis of traditional lore ('it is recorded in the transmitted reports', *dar āthār āmadeh ast*) that the language of the angels surrounding the throne of God is Dari Persian (*fārsī-yi darī*), and more specifically that the revered authority of the early period al-Ḥasan al-Baṣrī (21–110/642–728) had declared the language of the denizens of Paradise to be Persian (*pārsī*). He added that Naḍr b. Shumayl (122–203/739–818), judge of Marv, had remarked that 'Dari Persian is the language of the people of Balkh' (*pārsī-yi darī zabān-i ahl-i Balkh ast*).[45]

The centrality of the wisdom of the past to Pseudo-Māwardī's mentality is evident in virtually every section of his mirror. In particular he demonstrates, in D. G. Tor's words, 'the use of and reference to the pre-Islamic Iranian past as a living cultural heritage and model for emulation in the author's own time'.[46] Many of the more extensive and detailed items in the author's Iranian repertoire, such as his several citations from the 'Testament of Ardashīr' and the 'Testament of Shāpūr', are associated with the specifically Sasanian past and its expression in Middle Persian literature.[47] Pseudo-Māwardī's acquaintance with a large repertoire of materials transmitted from earlier Middle Persian texts is evident not only in attributed quotations, but also in his occasional retention, in Arabised form, of items of Middle Persian vocabulary. In one instance, he employs the term *āʾīn* (from *ēwēn*) as a synonym for 'modes of conduct' (*siyar*).[48] His several generic references to, for example, 'the Persian kings' (*mulūk al-ᶜajam*) and 'the conduct [ways] of the Persians' (*siyar al-ᶜajam*), for which he provides no specific indication of a source, suggest that these materials, sometimes replete with Middle Persian lexical items, circulated in a fluid body of oral and written versions in his environment. In one case, Pseudo-Māwardī refers to an unspecified, possibly oral source (introduced by the phrase *wa-balaghanā*, 'it has come to our knowledge'), and relates that, in times of crisis, the Persian kings (*mulūk al-aᶜājim*) used to summon three persons, the chief priest (*mōbadān mōbad*), the leading minister (*dabīrbad*) and the 'minister of war' (*wazīr al-ḥarb*);they ate only bread, onions, vinegar, salt and the simple Persian food *bazm-āvard*. The report also appears in the mid-ninth-century *Akhlāq al-mulūk*, likewise without any indication of a source.[49]

It is invariably the more recent, 'historical' Iranian past to which Pseudo-Māwardī refers. Notwithstanding the industrious production of written *shāhnāmeh*s within the Samanid domains during his lifetime, Pseudo-Māwardī never invokes the legendary Pishdadi and Kayani kings or, with one possible exception, the heroes or *pahlavān*s of the Sistani cycle.[50] In a single passage, he mentions a certain Rustam, of whom he reports, 'They have said: The inscription on Rustam's signet ring (read), "Jest is a defect, lying a source of ruin, injustice a calamity".' This Rustam, introduced as if the information were in oral circulation, is perhaps the *pahlavān*, son of Zāl or Dastān, from whom the Tahirids claimed descent, or perhaps the celebrated general Rustam (b. Farrukhhurmuz) of the late Sasanian era, whom he mentions elsewhere (as the following paragraph will show).[51]

Pseudo-Māwardī's perception of the continuing usefulness of the Iranian historical past also emerges in his treatment of military matters. In his ninth chapter, for example, he refers to the *siyar al-ᶜajam*, possibly, but not necessarily, a text (*wa-li-dhālika mā ḥukiya fī siyar al-ᶜajam*, 'similar is that which is related concerning the ways of the Persians' or 'in "The Ways of the Persians"'); on this authority Pseudo-Māwardī paraphrases the Persians' reported calculations for the number of troops necessary for campaigns in different regions.[52] When he turns his attention to confrontations between the Qurʾānic categories of *muʾmin*, 'believer', and *mushrik*, 'associator' (of other phenomena with God), or, loosely, 'polytheist', he cites the examples of the 'Battle of Bakr b. Wāʾil'[53] and the Battle of al-Qadisiyya (between 14/635 and 16/637), both remembered as Arab victories over Persian (*ᶜajamī*) armies. He provides detailed accounts, including statistics (in both cases, the victors triumphed over disproportionately larger forces), and he identifies by name the leaders of the defeated *ᶜajamī* troops.[54] In treating the defeat of the Sasanian forces under the command of Rustam, 'who was that day their king (*malik*) and their leader (*zaᶜīm*)', at al-Qadisiyya, he observes that Rustam's *ᶜajamī* army possessed great courage (they were *ūlū l-baʾs al-shadīd*), 'as God mentioned in the Qurʾān according to the commentaries (*tafāsīr*)'.[55] By contrast, the Byzantine border appears remote in *Naṣīḥat al-mulūk*. Pseudo-Māwardī mentions only as a general assertion that relatively small numbers of believers had triumphed more than once over larger Byzantine armies, and resorts by way of illustration not to specific encounters, but to Qurʾānic texts.[56]

The religious content of *Naṣīḥat al-mulūk* forms the subject of Part III of this volume. It may be observed here that the book reflects a multiconfessional environment and a culturally pluralistic one; it also reflects an environment in which several observers associated religious movements with struggles for power, in a process for which Pseudo-Māwardī provides an analysis. These characteristics are similarly consistent with the hypothesis of an early tenth-century eastern Iranian milieu.

Geographical Indications

To situate the text's genesis more precisely within the Samanid domains of the *mashriq*, it is instructive to examine Pseudo-Māwardī's limited references to geographical locations. *Naṣīḥat al-mulūk* includes references to three cities: Mecca (twice), Homs (twice) and Balkh (once). Mecca provides the setting for a narrative in which the Umayyad Caliph ᶜAbd al-Malik (r. 65–86 /685–705) addresses a Muslim gathering and elicits vociferous remonstrance from a disaffected tribesman, who objects to the discrepancy between the caliph's exhortation of others and his personal behaviour.[57] Such encounters illustrate a *topos* prevalent in early Arabic prose; several caliphs, including the Umayyad ᶜAbd al-Malik and notably the Abbasid al-Manṣūr, feature in anecdotes of this kind, examples of admonition (*mawᶜiẓa*) deployed to cautionary effect. The two mentions of the ancient Syrian town of Homs appear in communications to the urban population. In the first case, the Companion of the Prophet Abū l-Dardāᵓ, who died in Damascus in 32/652 and acquired a reputation for austerity (*zuhd*), religious knowledge (*ᶜilm*) and wisdom (*ḥikma*), addressed an exhortation to 'the people of Homs'; in the second instance, Ibrāhīm b. al-ᶜAbbās writes a letter on behalf of the caliph to 'the people of Homs'.[58]

Mecca, especially on the occasion of the pilgrimage, provided the setting for several homiletic caliphal orations; the references to Homs, incorporated into the caliphal lands at an early date, reflect a similarly exhortative literary strain. Neither location implies a particular geographical location for the composition of *Naṣīḥat al-mulūk*; the anecdotes indicate instead Pseudo-Māwardī's familiarity with early Arabic literary culture and his adept deployment of its resources for edificatory and instructive purposes.

Pseudo-Māwardī's second reference to Mecca is quite different in character. It appears in his last chapter, which is dedicated to controversial matters of particular relevance to kings. In a discussion of the moral and legal status of music, Pseudo-Māwardī reports the prevailing disagreement with regard to the legality of listening to the music of flutes, mandolins and stringed instruments (*al-samāᶜ min al-mazāmir wa-l-ṭanābīr wa-l-maᶜāzif*). Many persons, he reports, consider the activity forbidden, and the generality of the people of religion, scruple and excellence avoid it (*taḥarraja ᶜanhu ᶜāmmat ahl al-dīn* *wa-l-wara*ᶜ *wa-l-faḍl*). These individuals regard it as 'diversion and play' (*lahw wa-la*ᶜ*b*) and as a deviation from the way of God (*ṣadd* ᶜ*an sabīl Allāh*), all of which have been prohibited in the Qurʾān (6: 70, 23: 115).[59] But some people, Pseudo-Māwardī continues, regard it as permitted as long as it does not involve the singing of distasteful lyrics that incite fornication (*al-zinā*), obscenity (*fāḥisha*), unbelief (*kufr*) or mockery (*hijāʾ*). The members of this group adduce as their authority the Prophet's endorsement, on the occasion of weddings and nuptial processions, of the custom of using the tambourine (*duff*), accompanied by the soft vocalising of truthful words (*kalām ṣidq*). This practice, Pseudo-Māwardī asserts, had remained widespread in the Hijaz and in Mecca 'until our own time'.[60] This notation, apparently based on personal observation, indicates that Pseudo-Māwardī was acquainted with the Hijaz and had almost certainly visited Mecca, probably as a pilgrim. That Pseudo-Māwardī had performed the pilgrimage is entirely likely, and consequently this second mention of Mecca, though it occurs in a very different context from the first, similarly reveals little concerning his place of residence.

Much more suggestive than these references to Mecca and Homs is Pseudo-Māwardī's single reference to Balkh. In this case, the passage in question takes the form of a reference to a historical event. The episode involves an encounter between the Umayyad armies and the forces of the Abbasid call to allegiance (*da*ᶜ*wa*). Pseudo-Māwardī alludes to an encounter at a bridge in or near Balkh (*Qanṭarat al-S.r.ḥān bi-Balkh*) between supporters of the Abbasid *da*ᶜ*wa* and 'the Arabs of the Umayyad armies'.[61] The latter are numbered at the stereotypical 40,000 cavalry,[62] while 'Abū Dāʾūd' (almost certainly Abū Dāʾūd Khālid b. Ibrāhīm al-Dhuhlī (d. 140/757), one of Abū Muslim's generals in eastern Khurasan) commanded only a small number of men. (Abū Muslim (d. 137/755), probably born in Marv, was the central figure in the building of the Abbasid *da*ᶜ*wa* in Khurasan.[63]) Pseudo-Māwardī's account of the event suggests detailed local knowledge:

> We have heard (*balaghanā*) that when Abū [Dāʾūd] Khālid al-Aᶜwar [= Abū Dāʾūd Khālid b. Ibrāhīm][64] encountered the Arabs of the Umayyad armies (*al-*ᶜ*arab min juyūsh banī Umayya*) at Qanṭarat al-S.r.ḥān [= the Bridge of Sarjanān?] at Balkh, the force that met him amounted to 40,000 horsemen drawn from the officers (*quwwād*), the courageous (*anjād*), the

> chiefs (*wujūh*), the notables (*aᶜyān*), the brave (*abṭāl*) and the cavalrymen (*fursān*) of the Arabs,[65] while Abū Dāʾūd commanded only a small number of men. When the two sides met, a crier among them (the Umayyad forces) exclaimed, 'We are a victorious army' (*naḥnu jamīᶜun muntaṣir*, Q. 54: 44). Abū Dāʾūd heard that, and responded with the words by which God answered the people who had made that call: 'The army will be defeated and they will turn their backs in flight' (*sa-yuhzamu l-jamᶜu wa-yuwallūna l-dubur*, Q. 54: 45) – and so it was.[66]

The copyist of the manuscript, unfamiliar with the name of the location at which this episode took place, provides only an undotted consonantal outline: al-S.r.ḥān.[67] The vicinity of Balkh suggests more than one possible reading of this place name. Two sites experienced extensive military activity during Qutayba b. Muslim's campaigns into Transoxiana, especially against Nīzak Ṭarkhān, in 91/709–10.[68] It is possible to read the word as a reference to the Surkhāb, an alternative name for the River Vakhsh.[69] Castles stood at each relay along the Surkhab, and in this year Qutayba b. Muslim pursued Nīzak in the gorges of the Surkhab River, between Baghlan and Bamiyan.[70] Another possible reading is Siminjān, one of the towns that belonged to Balkh. From Balkh to Khulm the distance was two stages, and from Khulm to Siminjān a further two stages.[71] Siminjan lay close to Ruʾb or Rūb on the upper course of the Khulm River, and probably corresponded to the modern location of Haybak.[72] Nīzak was defeated and killed in this area in 91/709–10.

The most likely reading for al-S.r.ḥān, however, is Sarjanān. It was at the River Sarjanan, in 130/747–8, that Abū Dāʾūd Khālid b. Ibrāhīm, one of Abū Muslim's leading generals in the region, led a force that killed large numbers of anti-Abbasid rebels from Balkh, Tirmidh and nearby locations.[73] By this date, Abū Muslim controlled much of Khurasan, including the cities of Marv, Marv-al-Rud and Herat; but before he could move against Naṣr b. Sayyār (d. 131/748), the Umayyad governor whose forces were drawn up to the west in Nishapur, he needed control of Balkh in order to secure his position to the east. Accordingly, Abū Muslim dispatched Abū Dāʾūd Khālid b. Ibrāhīm, who took the city and overthrew Ziyād b. ᶜAbd al-Raḥmān, Naṣr b. Sayyār's governor of the city. Abū Muslim installed Yaḥyā b. Nuᶜaym as his governor in Balkh, and directed Abū Dāʾūd to return to Marv. But

Yaḥyā b. Nuᶜaym, apparently long ambivalent towards Abū Muslim and the *daᶜwa*, quickly entered into negotiations with Ziyād b. ᶜAbd al-Raḥmān, and established a large force composed of, according to al-Ṭabarī, the Muḍar, the Yaman, the Rabīᶜa 'and the Persians who were with them' (*wa-man maᶜahum min al-aᶜājim*) in order to fight against the black-clad forces of the Abbasid *daᶜwa* (*al-musawwida*).[74] Consequently, Abū Muslim sent Abū Dāᵓūd back to Balkh, where he defeated the allied forces in a brief engagement at the River Sarjanān and recaptured the city.[75] It is highly likely that it was this encounter to which Pseudo-Māwardī referred. *Fażāᵓil-i Balkh* implies widespread opposition among the people of Balkh to the Abbasid *daᶜwa* and Abū Dāᵓūd Khālid b. Ibrāhīm's army. The book further indicates that religious leaders led the popular opposition; after the Abbasid victory, these men went into hiding until Khālid b. Ibrāhīm granted them a safe conduct, whereupon some of them still refused to return.[76]

In *Naṣīḥat al-mulūk*, the episode appears not as part of a historical narrative, but as an illustration of the auguring power of scriptural and poetic texts. The presaging force of adeptly deployed Qurᵓānic verses in battle constitutes a *topos* in early Arabic literature. In this case, it seems likely that the *topos* shaped local memories of an encounter that took place perhaps some two centuries before the author wrote his book. This aspect of the account suggests that Pseudo-Māwardī drew on local knowledge, a proposal that finds further support in *Fażāᵓil-i Balkh*, where the account of the aftermath of these events mentions the copious use of Qurᵓānic quotations, although not this particular example, in communications among the parties. It must be conceded that, at variance with the reports contained in *Fażāᵓil-i Balkh*, Pseudo-Māwardī's account represents a pro-Abbasid perspective. Pseudo-Māwardī's pro-Abbasid point of view is consistent with his Muᶜtazilism, which perhaps overlaid his interpretation of a local memory. More generally, it is significant that among countless examples of the deployment of sacred and poetic texts in moments of confrontation and crisis, Pseudo-Māwardī cited an example situated in Balkh.

The highly cosmopolitan qualities of *Naṣīḥat al-mulūk*, and particularly its allusions to the Buddha and other Indic-related cultural materials, provide additional support for the hypothesis that Pseudo-Māwardī was a Balkhi. The following section addresses the conditions and character of Balkh in the first half of the tenth century and seeks to establish its suitability as a location for the production of *Naṣīḥat al-mulūk*.

A Balkhi Provenance

Balkh enjoyed the status of a regional capital.[77] Although the limited accessibility of the physical evidence and the complexities involved in interpreting the literary sources (composed by indigenous writers and by visitors) complicate efforts to reconstruct the social and physical environments of Balkh,[78] it seems certain that the city's location at the intersection of many major trading routes left a deep and distinctive impress. Many of the routes across Eurasia remained active in the Samanid period, and the evidence of centuries of cross-cultural contact, as well as the city's multi-ethnic and multi-religious character, survived in the names of its gates, such as Bāb al-Hinduwān ('Gate of the Indians') and Bāb al-Yahūd ('Gate of the Jews').[79] Writing in the late ninth century, al-Yaᶜqūbī mentions merchants' travels in the course of his extensive discussion of Balkh, in which he specifies the city's position in relation to several locations across the Oxus, including Bamiyan, the mountains of which contained the sources of several rivers, including one that flowed to Balkh, the regions of Tibet and the lands of the Turks.[80] Of particular significance in the present context, Balkh provided opportunities for close contact with north-western India, with access via the River Oxus, also known as the River of Balkh (Nahr Balkh or Balkhāb) to Kabul, and thence over the Hindu Kush.[81] The author of *Ḥudūd al-ᶜālam* describes the city as 'the resort of merchants' and 'the emporium (*bār-kadha*) of Hindūstān';[82] and several writers identified the towns of Kabul[83] and Ghazna,[84] with which Balkh was linked, with an extensive trade in commodities from India.[85] Travellers between India and China also passed through Balkh, from which some routes led eastward to the Himalayas and ultimately to Tibet.

Several of Pseudo-Māwardī's contemporaries associated Balkh with the borders of the accessible and familiar lands of the Islamic cultural sphere. Ibn al-Faqīh, the ninth-century author whose *Kitāb al-Buldān* ('Book of Countries'), composed in about 290/903, survives in an abridgement,[86] ascribed Balkh to a peripheral location when he defined the fourth *iqlīm*, the middle clime and the best in disposition (*mizāj*), as stretching from Ifriqiya to Balkh to 'the east of the earth' (*min Ifrīqiyā ilā Balkh ilā mashriq al-arḍ*).[87] Other accounts similarly associate Balkh with a liminal location. According to the anonymous author of the Persian *Mujmal al-tavārīkh va-l-qiṣaṣ* ('Compendium of Histories and Tales', 520/1126), the boundaries of the land of Iran (*zamīn-i Īrān*) ran from the River of Balkh to Azerbaijan and Armenia, or from the Oxus to the Euphrates.[88] Balkh's proximity to the River Oxus (Jayḥūn), intensified its associations with extremity;[89] the river remained a natural and perhaps an imaginative barrier, even if it had ceased to constitute a political or military one.

If the city of Balkh, at the limits of the accessible world, implied for later ninth- and tenth-century observers distance in space, it also evoked distance in time: it was steeped in antiquity. Balkh, the geographers reported, was among the cities constructed by Alexander.[90] Many accounts in Arabic and Persian suggest that by, and in the course of, the tenth century, the city's associations with Alexander had become overlaid and somewhat eclipsed by a plethora of associations with the Iranian past (to which, as the *Shāhnāmeh* of Firdawsī indicates, Alexander had been significantly assimilated). Examples of these connections include historical figures, such as the Sasanian monarch Qubād b. Fīrūz (= Kavād I, r. 488–96, 499–531), who reportedly selected Balkh as one of the 'purest' (*anzah*) sites among his dominions.[91] Several cases of Iranian associations occur in *Mujmal al-tavārīkh va-l-qiṣaṣ*, where it is the legendary Pishdadi king Ṭahmūrath who, having subdued the demons, oversaw the construction of Balkh; he undertook the building of cities, notably Balkh, alongside other foundational activities, such as the initiation of reading and writing, the instruction of the demons and the learning of hunting.[92] According to the same author, Balkh was the site of several conflicts and struggles involving the hero or *pahlavān*, Rustam.[93] It was the site of fire-temples even before the appearance of Zoroaster in the reign of Gushtāsb, who embraced the religion and died in the vicinity of Balkh,[94] and after Zoroaster made his way from Azerbaijan to Balkh, the city became the centre of his teaching. The (legendary) Kayanid queen Humāy reportedly made her capital at Balkh, and the Kayanid king Kayqubād died there.[95]

Although, as the previously cited reports indicate, Balkh was strongly associated among medieval authors in Arabic and Persian with Zoroastrianism, among its most remarkable features was the Nawbahār, a major site for Buddhist pilgrims. Before the Arab-Muslim conquest, Tukharistan had formed the westernmost part of the vast terrains in which Buddhism was practised, and through Buddhism its population shared in social, artistic and intellectual traditions common to the regions to its south and east.[96] The city's Buddhist heritage renders Balkh a particularly likely location for the production of *Naṣīḥat al-mulūk*.

In earlier centuries, Buddhists had lived in several Iranian locations, including Marv.[97] The number of Buddhists in most of these places, however, appears to have diminished very considerably before the Arab-Muslim conquests.[98] Xuanzang's account of his journey through the region in the early seventh century suggests a fairly widespread diminution of Buddhist monasteries: at Tirmidh, he reported the presence of about ten monasteries (*sanghārāma*) with about 1,000 monks; in Chaghaniyan, he found only five *sanghārāma*s, with 'a few monks'; Khulm possessed about ten convents and 500 monks.[99] (Xuanzang observed a similar decrease in the Buddhist presence in some other regions through which he passed.) An exception to the trend of diminishing communities occurred in Tukharistan, and particularly Balkh and its environs: at Balkh (Po-ho), called the 'Little Rājagriha' because of the numerous Buddhist sites in the vicinity, Xuanzang estimated 100 monasteries and 3,000 monks. He commented particularly on the Nawbahār (*Navasanghārāma*), which contained a richly ornamented image of the Buddha as well as relics of the Buddha. He observed many additional monasteries and stupas containing relics in the surrounding areas, where the population practised the Hinayana ('Lesser Vehicle') (Theravada) form of Buddhism.[100] A century later, another Buddhist monk, Huichao, who was born in about 700 in Korea and in his youth travelled to China to study Buddhism, embarked on a pilgrimage. Having travelled through north-western India and Central Asia, Huichao reached Kucha at the end of 727, returned to his home in about 729, and died soon after 780. When Huichao visited Fu-ti-ya, Balkh, in about 726, shortly after an Arab-Muslim garrison had settled in Balkh in 107/725, he described it as the residential city of the king of Tukharistan, and reported that since Arab troops had occupied the city, the ruler had fled to Badakhshan. A full century after Xuanzang's arrival, however, Huichao observed that the population – the king, the great people and the ordinary people – practised Hinayana Buddhism and venerated the *triratna*, the three jewels or refuges,[101] and that the city possessed abundant monasteries and monks.[102]

Furthermore, several writers, including al-Yaᶜqūbī, al-Iṣṭakhrī and the author of *Ḥudūd al-ᶜālam*, commented on Balkh's relative proximity and connection to Bamiyan.[103] Balkh and Bamiyan lay on the ancient route that connected south-eastern Iran with India, in a region where the figure of Maitreya, the Buddha whose manifestation lies in the future, seems to have provided the focal point of a flourishing form of Buddhism.[104] At Bamiyan (Fan-yen-na), Xuanzang observed ten convents and about 1,000 priests; he also described the colossal statues in the mountain to the north-east, and local Buddhist relics.[105] A growing body of literary and material evidence suggests that Buddhism continued to flourish in the area that embraced Balkh and Bamiyan for a considerable period of time, possibly centuries, after the advent of Muslim rule. When he arrived in the region in about 726, Huichao reported that, at the time of his visit, the king of Bamiyan possessed numerous and powerful troops and, unlike most of the local rulers who had come under the suzerainty of 'the Arabs', was subservient to no other ruler; as in Balkh, he found that the king, nobles and ordinary people were devoted to the *triratna*, and that the town possessed abundant monasteries and monks; in Bamiyan, the population practised Mahayana (the 'Greater Vehicle') and Hinayana forms of Buddhism.[106] Deborah Klimburg-Salter has proposed that at Balkh and probably Bamiyan, the indigenous population, predominantly Buddhist, co-existed with the new Muslim settlers and converts, initially a small number, for some 200 years after the initial invasions, and that this co-existence was reflected in settlement patterns, with Buddhist and early Muslim cities in close proximity to one another.[107] Kevin van Bladel has found that in Tukharistan, Buddhism and indigenous religious cultures co-existed with Arab-Muslim rule for a period of decades, and has noted, in addition to the living presence of Buddhism evident in the fragmentary texts and material remains, the continuous traditions of learning both in Sanskrit and probably also in Bactrian, during the eighth century.[108] Al-Yaᶜqūbī reports that the indigenous ruler, known as the *shēr* of Bamiyan, converted to Islam under the Abbasid Caliph al-Manṣūr (r. 136–58/754–75),[109] but in nearby Kabul, despite the fact that the city was under the rule of the governor of Khurasan, the population followed various religions, and it is likely that the majority remained Buddhist in the tenth and eleventh centuries.[110] Of Kabul, al-Iṣṭakhrī reported, 'In (Kabul) there are (some) Muslims, and their suburb (*rabaḍ*) includes Indian infidels' (*kuffār min al-hind*);[111] Ibn Ḥawqal noted the presence in the *rabaḍ* of *kuffār* (infidels) and *yahūd* (Jews);[112] the author of *Ḥudūd al-ᶜālam* described Kabul's inhabitants as 'Muslims and Indians', and stated that 'there are idol-temples in it';[113] and al-Muqaddasī noted Kabul's mixed Indian and Muslim population, as well as its function as a gathering place for merchants.[114] Geoffrey Khan concludes that most local rulers in the region did not embrace Islam in the early Abbasid period, and that the indigenous beliefs of eastern Afghanistan remained dominant, in some areas until the Ghaznavid campaigns of the eleventh century.[115] Contacts between Muslims and Buddhists also occurred: the celebrated renunciant Shaqīq b. Ibrāhīm al-Zāhid al-Balkhī (d. 194/810), member of a wealthy family in Balkh, reportedly travelled to Turkistan for trading purposes with the Kharlukhiyya (probably the Karluks), who 'worshipped idols' (*wa-hum yaᶜbudūna al-aṣnām*), and met an elderly man (*shaykh kabīr*), the 'servant of the idols' (*khādim aṣnāmihim*), who became the occasion for Shaqīq's renunciation (*zuhd*) (or repentance, Persian *tawbeh*).[116] Moreover, even as the number of local converts to Islam grew, the converts' familiarity with and attachment to their cultural and religious heritage are likely to have endured. Al-Yaᶜqūbī describes the telling example of intermarriage between the families of Bamiyan's local ruler and the Muslim at whose hands he converted to Islam, Muzāḥim b. Bisṭām; in a pattern reminiscent of the Barmakids, the family of *shērs*, now Muslims but retaining their ancestral title, attained prominent positions in Baghdad and elsewhere under the early Abbasids.[117]

Such familiarity and attachment found continuous reinforcement in the massive imprint of Buddhist devotion in the landscape.[118] From Marv to Balkh, from Bukhara to Bamiyan and Kabul, Muslims, whether local residents or visitors, found themselves in the midst of Buddhist monuments. Not surprisingly, the material evidence of the two great sanctuaries of Iranian Buddhism, Balkh and Bamiyan, features prominently in the Arabic and Persian geographical accounts of the region.[119] At least in Bamiyan, the Buddhist sites that such writers witnessed were not necessarily abandoned, ruinous or ill-maintained. Klimburg-Salter has concluded that the carving of the colossal Buddhas stood at the beginning of a period of intense artistic activity, in the course of which the most active period of expansion through the secondary valleys of the Hindu Kush occurred between the eighth and the tenth centuries; furthermore, she has found that most of the architectural units in the Bamiyan Valley, as well as all the centres in the secondary valleys, were decorated in the course of the late seventh and early eighth centuries.[120] The author of *Ḥudūd al-ᶜālam* wrote, 'In it there are two stone idols (*but*) of which the one is called Red Idol (*surkh-but*) and the other White Idol (*khing-but*)'.[121] Although his indication of their location is imprecise, Ibn al-Nadīm's reference to two colossal religious images (*ṣanamāni*) incised out of mountains on both sides of a deep valley, visible from a great distance and a site of a pilgrimage among Indians, almost certainly refers to the two Buddhas of Bamiyan.[122] In about 616/1219, the literary biographer and polymath Yāqūt travelled in the region, and described Bamiyan, its paintings and its 'two colossal sculptures carved in the mountain from its base to its peak' (*ṣanamāni ᶜaẓīmāni nuqirā fī l-jabal min asfalihi ilā aᶜlāh*).[123]

The hypothesis that Pseudo-Māwardī was a resident of Tukharistan finds support in his discussion of the means by which kings and sages have sought to perpetuate their memory – a meritorious activity, the value of which he impressed upon his royal audience. Of their several techniques for effecting such enduring reputation, Pseudo-Māwardī begins with a reference to leaving a lasting visual imprint on the landscape:

> The intelligent among the kings of the worlds and the virtuous among the believers have never ceased to strive for this quality of remembrance and to exert themselves in the attainment of it. They have sought to purchase it through their bodies, possessions, souls and properties and they have seen that an enduring memory constitutes perpetuation for the one remembered, to the point that many kings and sages have adopted various strategies for the purpose. Some among them have sought lasting memory by the construction of strong and remarkable buildings, and fine images, cut into the mountains and rocks and painted in buildings and residences (or palaces) (*ibtināʾ al-abniya al-ᶜajība al-wathīqa wa-l-taṣāwīr al-anīfa al-manqūra fī l-jibāl wa-l-ṣukhūr wa-l-manqūsha fī l-abniya wa-l-dūr*), that endure over the course of the ages.[124.]

In this passage, it seems likely that Pseudo-Māwardī evoked the visual environment in which he wrote. Although it is possible that he had in mind the

Achaemenid and Sasanian sites of western Iran, it is more probable, given his interests in Khurasan, that he was responding to the Buddhist (and possibly other) imagery that surrounded him in such structures as the Nawbahār and the rock reliefs and sculptures of Bamiyan. This interpretation finds support in *Ḥudūd al-ᶜālam*, whose author described Balkh as 'a large and flourishing town, formerly the residence of the Sasanian kings . . . In it are found buildings of the Sasanian kings with paintings (*naqsha*) and wonderful works (*kārkird*), (which) have fallen into ruins. (That place) is called Nau-bihār.' The reference to royal buildings adorned with paintings and *kārkird*, perhaps sculptures, is reminiscent of the passage in *Naṣīḥat al-mulūk*. Slightly later the author of *Ḥudūd al-ᶜālam* describes nearby Simingan as 'a town lying in the mountains. There are in it mountains of white stone similar to marble (*rukhām*) in which dwellings have been cut (*kanda-ast*), as well as halls (*majlis*), pavilions (*kūshk*), idol-temples, and horse-stables, with all the implements (*ālāt*) appertaining to pavilions. On it [the rock] various figures are painted in the fashion of the Indians (*az kirdār-i H[ind]*).'[125] To a greater extent than any other religion in the region, Buddhism had marked the landscape with sculptures hewn into the rock, paintings, and the surviving monasteries and stupas, the grandeur and durability of which evidently impressed the authors of *Naṣīḥat al-mulūk* and *Ḥudūd al-ᶜālam*.

The Buddhist sites that most attracted the attention of Muslim observers were the Nawbahār at Balkh, sometimes thought, as *Ḥudūd al-ᶜālam* indicates and is perhaps implied in the passage in *Naṣīḥat al-mulūk*, to have functioned as a Sasanian palace, and the Buddhist sculptures and paintings at Bamiyan.[126] For the travellers and geographical writers of the ninth and tenth centuries, closely associated with the religious life of the Nawbahār were its custodians, the Barmakids, who later entered the service of Hārūn al-Rashīd and rose to the highest levels of power in the caliphate before their sudden and complete elimination.[127] Al-Yaᶜqūbī, who locates the structure of the Nawbahār within the *rabaḍ* (suburb) of Balkh, glosses it as 'the stations (or habitations) of the Barmakids' (*manāzil al-barāmika*).[128] Although their understandings of the Nawbahār's specifically Buddhist functions and significance not surprisingly exhibit interference from the more familiar lore surrounding ancient Arabian and Zoroastrian religious cultures, the writers who discussed the Nawbahār continued to associate it with the office of the *barmak* and with the Barmakid family.[129] The assimilation of Buddhism to Zoroastrianism is endemic: when Narshakhī refers to the *but-khāneh* at Bukhara, on the site of which the commander Qutayba b. Muslim (49–96 /669–715) in 94–5/712–13 erected the city's first mosque and incorporated into it *spolia* from its predecessor, it is impossible to judge from his account whether the pre-existing structure was Buddhist or Zoroastrian.[130] According to al-Masᶜūdī (d. 345/956), who travelled overland to India via Balkh in about 305/917, the legendary Iranian king Manūchihr had ordered the Nawbahār's construction in the name of the moon; its priests were appointed to exalt the kings, and *barmak* was the name, or title, of their overseer (*kāna al-muwakkil bi-sadānatihi yudᶜā al-barmak*).[131] According to Ibn al-Faqīh, who wrote at the beginning of the tenth century, the Barmakids had been a noble family in Balkh since before the Arsacids (*mulūk al-ṭawāʾif*). Their religion, in Ibn al-Faqīh's terminology, was the 'worship of idols' (*ᶜibādat al-awthān*), and it was they who had built the Nawbahār, which they modelled on the accounts that had reached them of Mecca, the Kaᶜba and the religion of Quraysh and the Arabs. In fact, Ibn al-Faqīh claims, the name Barmakī, adopted by all of them who held authority there, derived from *Bāb Makka*, which connoted 'the ruler of Mecca' (*wālī Makka*).[132] Ibn al-Faqīh drew analogies between the sanctuary of the Nawbahār and the Kaᶜba, but he also recorded details specific to the Buddhist site. The *ᶜajam*, he wrote, venerated the Nawbahār and visited it as pilgrims. They made offerings to the image in it, dressed it in silk, and attached banners (*aᶜlām*) to the shrine or dome (*qubba*), which they called *al-Ashbat*, Ibn al-Faqīh's rendering, in the judgement of many scholars, of the term *stupa*.[133] He reports further that the kings of China and the Kabulshah, king of Kabul, followed this religion, and that when they came on pilgrimage, they prostrated themselves before the chief idol.[134]

Al-Masᶜūdī's and Ibn al-Faqīh's presentations of Buddhist phenomena reflect interference from their understandings of religions that they held to be comparable.[135] Many authors who discussed the Sumaniyya, the term by which Buddhists were commonly known, linked them with the Sabians, and, as Patricia Crone has argued, regarded both groups as practitioners of an ancient paganism.[136] In many cases, they linked both groups with the figure of 'Būdhāṣaf' (also spelled 'Būdhāsaf' or 'Būdāsaf'), a name derived from the term *bodhisattva*.[137] Writers in Arabic frequently included Būdhāṣaf within the category of false or pseudo-prophets. Al-Masᶜūdī knew Būdhāṣaf as 'the first of the Sabians'; he had appeared in the land of India 'and was Indian' (*wa-kāna hindiyyan*), but left his native land for the western regions in the early days of the reign of Ṭahmūrath (or Jam, according to another account). He laid false claims to prophetic status and presented himself as a link between God and His creation (*tanabbaᵓa wa-zaᶜama annahu rasūl Allāh wa-annahu wāsiṭa bayna llāh wa-bayna khalqihi*), and he ordered people to pursue the path of 'renunciation of the world' (*al-zuhd fī hādhā l-ᶜālam*). He also renewed the worship of idols, and encouraged people to practise such worship through 'an assortment of stratagems and deceptions' (*wa-qarraba li-ᶜuqūlihim ᶜibādatahā bi-ḍurūb min al-ḥiyal wa-l-khudaᶜ*).[138] Similarly, the scientist and polymath al-Bīrūnī, in *al-Āthār al-bāqiya ᶜan al-qurūn al-khāliya* ('The Remaining Traces from Past Ages'), describes Būdhāṣaf as 'the first of the pseudo-prophets to be remembered' (*awwal al-madhkūrīn minhum [min al-mutanabbiᵓīn]*), and states that he appeared in the reign of Ṭahmūrath.[139] As Patricia Crone has suggested, the name Būdhāṣaf and the Arabic *Kitāb Bilawhar wa-Būdhāṣaf* ('Book of Bilawhar and Būdhāṣaf', a widely transmitted story derived from Indian legends of the life of Gautama Buddha)[140] are likely to have originated in eastern Iran; it was probably also in this region that the figure of Būdhāṣaf became linked to the Pishdadi king Ṭahmūrath, in whose reign he is commonly said to have appeared.[141]

If authors in Arabic understood Būdhāṣaf to be a human being, their conceptions of *al-budd*, especially in the plural form *bidada*, not infrequently emphasised iconographic rather than biographical or spiritual dimensions. The secretary al-Khwārazmī, who may have hailed from Balkh, dedicated his encyclopaedic *Mafātīḥ al-ᶜulūm* ('Keys of the Sciences') to Abū l-Ḥasan ᶜUbayd Allāh al-ᶜUtbī, vizier under Nūḥ II b. Manṣūr (r. 366–87/976–97); the work includes glosses and interpretations of numerous technical terms, and for the term *al-budd*, al-Khwārazmī adopted the Arabic *ṣanam*, 'image' or 'idol'.[142] ᶜUmar b. Sahlān al-Sāwī (d. *c.* 540/1145),[143] a judge, philosopher and the compiler of the *Mukhtaṣar Ṣiwān al-ḥikma* ('Epitome of the Bookcase of Wisdom'), an abbreviated version of the lost collection of philosophical materials known under the title *Ṣiwān al-ḥikma* ('Bookcase of Wisdom'), also described *al-budd* as an image (*ṣanam*) worshipped by Indians.[144]

Ibn al-Nadīm provided a full account of Buddhism that, he specifies, drew on three distinct sources. His first source was an account in the hand of 'a man from Khurasan' of a composition entitled *Akhbār Khurāsān fī l-qadīm wa-mā ālat ilayhi fī l-ḥadīth* ('Reports of Ancient Khurasan and That Which Derives from It in the Present'). Ibn al-Nadīm read this text, which, he reports, resembled the *dustūr*, presumably the model on which it was based. From this source Ibn al-Nadīm asserts, 'the prophet of the Sumaniyya was Būdhāṣaf; most of the people of Transoxiana followed this path (*madhhab*) before Islam and in antiquity'.[145] His second source was a copy, dated 249 /863 and in the hand of the scientist and philosopher al-Kindī, of the report of the vizier Yaḥyā b. Khālid al-Barmakī's envoy, dispatched to India in search of medicinal plants and briefed to supply an account of the religions of the Indians. On the basis of the envoy's report, Ibn al-Nadīm discussed places set aside for religious devotions, houses (of worship) (*buyūt*) and the condition of the *bidada*; he described the *bidada* housed within such *buyūt* and the precious substances out of which they had been formed.[146] His references to *buyūt lil-ᶜubbād wa-l-zuhhād*, 'houses for worshippers and renunciants' in the vicinity of Balkh and elsewhere are likely to indicate Buddhist monasteries.[147] From a third, different but otherwise unidentified source, Ibn al-Nadīm then addressed conceptual dimensions of *al-budd* (*al-kalām ᶜalā l-budd*). Indians disagree on the matter, he writes; one group (*ṭāʾifa*) considers him, or it, to be the form or image (*ṣūra*) of the Creator; another group considers him the form or image of His prophet to them. They differ further in that one group consider the prophet to be an angel, another consider the prophet to be a human being, another an *ᶜifrīt*, another the form of Būdhāṣaf the sage (*Būdāsaf al-ḥakīm*), who came to them from God. Each group has its way of worshipping and exalting him; a reliable source, he avers, reports that each community (*milla*) among them has its own image to which they return in worship and veneration.[148] Ibn al-Nadīm does not attempt to reconcile these various reports, the last of which leaves it somewhat unclear whether he, or his source, understood *al-budd* to denote an image or a person. Every writer understood Būdhāṣaf to have been a human being, whether a prophet, a pseudo-prophet or a sage. Some of the points ascribed to Ibn al-Nadīm's final source resemble the account of al-Maqdisī, who composed his encyclopaedic *al-Badʾ wa-l-taʾrīkh* ('The Creation and History') in Sistan in 355/966. On the authority of a *Kitāb al-Mamālik* ('Book of Kingdoms'), perhaps the work associated with al-Jayhānī, al-Maqdisī reported having read that the Sumaniyya consisted of two sects (*firqatāni*), one of whom claimed that *al-budd* was a sent prophet (*kāna nabiyyan mursalan*), while the other regarded him as the Creator (*al-bāriʾ*) rendered visible to humankind in this form (*turāʾiyan lil-nās fī tilka l-ṣūra*).[149] He perhaps refers to the Hinayana (or Theravada) and Mahayana branches of Buddhism. In *Taḥqīq mā lil-hind* ('Verification of That Which Pertains to India'), al-Bīrūnī identifies *al-budd* as the author of a book concerning 'knowledge of the unseen' (*ʿilm al-ghayb*) and founder of the 'wearers of red, the Shumaniyya' (*ṣāḥib al-muḥammara al-shumaniyya*); even he, however, devotes most attention to *al-budd* in his chapter concerning the origins of idolatry, where he concentrates his attention on images.[150] Ibn al-Nadīm, al-Maqdisī and al-Bīrūnī knew *al-budd* to have been a human being, even if they display a preoccupation with Buddhist iconography. Not surprisingly, their representations of reputed Buddhist phenomena and concepts reflect interference from Muslim theological categories.

Pseudo-Māwardī was in no doubt as to the humanity of *al-budd*, to whom he refers to the exclusion of any invocation of Būdhāṣaf or attention to idolatry. He cites wise utterances ascribed to *al-budd* in three instances. In one instance, he identifies *al-budd* as 'the leader of the Indians' (*zaʿīm al-hind*). The term *zaʿīm*, sometimes neutral, quite frequently denoted a leader of a 'false' religious community.[151] Pseudo-Māwardī, however, knew *al-budd* to be a leading sage revered for his wisdom among Indians. *Naṣīḥat al-mulūk* belongs to a different literary genre than the descriptive and encyclopaedic works of al-Masʿūdī, al-Maqdisī, Ibn al-Nadīm and al-Bīrūnī; although it has encyclopaedic elements, it is primarily a work of advice. Pseudo-Māwardī had no occasion to furnish a description of Buddhism, and, in the absence of such an account, his understanding of the religion cannot be assessed. But his incidental references suggest an understanding of the person and significance of the Buddha that differed in kind from that of many of his contemporaries, including, for example, al-Masʿūdī, who referred to the spiritual teachers of the Indians and Chinese, worshippers of idols and the heavenly bodies, as *ḥukamāʾ*, sages or wise philosophers, but evinced little awareness of the person of the Buddha. Pseudo-Māwardī's acquaintance with and esteem for *al-budd* is likely to have derived from more direct contact with Buddhist culture, at least its material and imaginative remnants, than that reflected in the materials related to Būdhāṣaf, shaped, apparently, elsewhere in eastern Iran.

Pseudo-Māwardī's citations of the Buddha, alongside those from other authoritative sources of human wisdom, find a parallel perhaps only in the previously mentioned *Kitāb Bilawhar wa-Būdhāṣaf*, in which *al-budd* appears solely in the second part. Pseudo-Māwardī knew the Buddha as an Indian sage, whose wise sayings he reproduces in the same way that he cites comparable utterances ascribed to Aristotle, Luqmān, Ardashīr, Sābūr (Shāpūr), the Indian king Sāb.t.r.m and other exemplary figures. The textual sources from which the utterances ascribed to the Buddha derived remain to be established, but at least one of them appears in *Bilawhar wa-Būdhāṣaf*, where other similar, but not identical, passages exist. The later tenth-century writer al-ᶜĀmirī (d. 381/992), a student of Abū Zayd al-Balkhī and author of *al-Iᶜlām bi-manāqib al-Islām* ('Proclamation of the Virtues of Islam'), possibly composed in Nishapur, repeated, without attribution, one of the quotations ascribed to the Buddha in *Naṣīḥat al-mulūk*.[152] Perhaps in Tukharistan such materials circulated in forms that retained their associations with the Buddha, since in this region Buddhism, especially in its substantial material vestiges, remained a visible presence, and commerce and a degree of intellectual exchange provided continued contact with Indian communities.

Arezou Azad has recently indicated the continuing sanctity attached to Balkh's ancient sacred sites among its Muslim inhabitants.[153] Pseudo-Māwardī provides evidence of a parallel phenomenon: a continuing appreciation of the region's rich legacy of wisdom. Significantly, al-Masᶜūdī reports the account by an individual involved in 'transmission and examination' (*wa-qad dhakara baᶜḍ ahl al-riwāya wa-l-tanqīr*) that he had read above the door of the Nawbahār an inscription in Persian. Translated, the text read: 'Būdhāṣaf said: The gates (or courts) of kings require three qualities (in persons who frequent them): intellect, patience and wealth' (*qāla Būdāsaf: abwāb al-mulūk taḥtāju ilā thalāth khiṣāl ᶜaql wa-ṣabr wa-māl*). Beneath this inscription, an individual had added, in Arabic, 'Būdhāṣaf lied: it is incumbent on the free (noble) man (*al-ḥurr*), if he possesses even one of these three qualities, that he eschew the court of the authorities' (*kadhaba Būdāsaf: al-wājib ᶜalā al-ḥurr idhā kāna maᶜahu wāḥida min hādhihi l-thalāth al-khiṣāl an lā yalzama bāb al-sulṭān*).[154] Even though the Persian inscription is attributed to Būdhāṣaf rather than the

Buddha, al-Masᶜūdī's report is suggestive. If the author's physical environment indeed contained such inscriptions in Persian or Arabic, they attest to the continued circulation of wise sayings associated with Buddhist figures in the region of Balkh. They supplement the several Buddhist or Buddhist-associated inscriptions, including examples of Aśoka's edicts, present in the larger material culture in scripts and languages that had long since ceased to be legible or comprehensible to the local population.[155] Further material evidence of wise inscriptions, though not originally associated with Buddhism, survives in the Delphic maxims incised at Aï Khanom.[156]

In addition, Balkh enjoyed a high reputation for its religious scholarship, including jurisprudence and rational theology. As previously noted, al-Iṣṭakhrī, quite probably drawing on the account of Abū Zayd al-Balkhī, praised the people of Balkh and Marv as exceptionally distinguished in jurisprudence, religion, rational speculation and dialectical theology, and, according to Shaykh al-Islām Vāᶜiẓ, 'scholars and jurists' referred to Balkh as *dār al-fuqahā*, 'the abode of jurists'.[157] Of particular significance in the context for *Naṣīḥat al-mulūk*, the city produced and enjoyed the simultaneous residence of two leading intellectual figures and men of letters, the philosopher and polymath Abū Zayd al-Balkhī (d. 322/934), and the Muᶜtazilite theologian Abū l-Qāsim al-Kaᶜbī (d. 319/931).

Most sources agree that Abū Zayd al-Balkhī died in 322/934, at which date he is reported by Yāqūt to have been eighty-seven or eighty-eight years old; he would thus have been born in about 235/849–50.[158] He is said to have travelled to Iraq, and to have studied there with al-Kindī (*c.* 183–256 /800–70), whose presence at the Abbasid court spanned several decades of the earlier and mid-ninth century.[159] Al-Kindī associated with Caliph al-Maᵓmūn and especially Caliph al-Muᶜtaṣim, to whose son Aḥmad he was appointed tutor.[160] (Al-Maᵓmūn and al-Muᶜtaṣim, as Chapter 1 indicated, receive particularly laudatory treatment in Pseudo-Māwardī's account of exemplary rulers.[161]) If he was a student of al-Kindī's – Franz Rosenthal regards the relationship as improbable 'in any literal sense'[162] – Abū Zayd al-Balkhī would have had to have travelled to Iraq as a very young man, as, according to Yāqūt, he in fact did.[163] As Hans Hinrich Biesterfeldt observes, whether he spent his years in Baghdad as a direct student of al-Kindī or not, al-Balkhī belonged to al-Kindī's circle.[164] Al-Balkhī is reported to have spent eight years in Iraq and to have visited neighbouring countries as well.[165] He almost certainly made the pilgrimage to Mecca, perhaps more than once, and his composition of a work devoted to the superiority of Mecca to all other places, entitled *Faḍāᵓil Makka ᶜalā sāᵓir al-biqāᶜ* ('The Superior Virtues of Mecca Over All Other Places'), is perhaps related to his visit(s) to the city and sanctuary.[166] At an unknown date, he returned to his native Balkh.[167] There, he continued the method and teachings of al-Kindī across a spectrum of disciplines, transmitted Kindian approaches and doctrines to his students, notably al-ᶜĀmirī (d. 381/992) and Ibn Farīghūn, author of *Jawāmiᶜ al-ᶜulūm* ('Compendium of the Sciences'), and facilitated the broad diffusion of the 'Kindian tradition' 'from Baghdad to Bukhara'.[168]

Abū l-Qāsim al-Kaᶜbī, associated with the theology of the Muᶜtazilites of Baghdad, pursued his studies of *ᶜilm al-kalām* in that city under Abū l-Ḥusayn al-Khayyāṭ (d. *c.* 300/913), but returned to spend most of his life in his native Khurasan.[169] There he became the primary figure in the development of Baghdadi Muᶜtazilism, a designation that, as his example demonstrates, no longer corresponded to the geographical location in which this body of doctrine thrived. Amongst its most distinctive teachings was the doctrine of *al-aṣlaḥ*, 'the optimal', which held that God, in His justice, was compelled to act in the way that was most conducive to well-being (*ṣalāḥ*) for each of His creatures; the Basran Muᶜtazila of this period dissented from this view, even though earlier Muᶜtazilites of Basra, including the littérateur and polymath al-Jāḥiẓ (*c.* 160–255/776–868), had subscribed to it. Al-Kaᶜbī lived at a time in which, following the eclipse of the Abbasids' promotion of the inquisition (*miḥna*), rationalist theologians struggled to maintain their standing, in social and intellectual terms, against the increasing predominance of the specialists in ḥadīth (*ahl al-ḥadīth*).[170] Al-Kaᶜbī belonged to a family with a record of administrative experience. His father, as previously noted, had served under the Tahirids, and al-Kaᶜbī had found employment as a secretary for Muḥammad b. Zayd al-Dāᶜī (d. 287/900), the Zaydī ruler of Tabaristan.[171] When the *dihqān* and military commander Aḥmad b. Sahl (d. 307/920) was appointed governor of Khurasan in 306/918, he offered the post of vizier to Abū Zayd al-Balkhī, who refused it. Aḥmad then offered the position to al-Kaᶜbī, who assumed the office of vizier, and composed, perhaps during this period, a book entitled *Tuḥfat al-wuzarāᵓ* ('Gift of Viziers').[172]

Abū Zayd became secretary under al-Kaᶜbī, who made over a portion of his salary for his friend's benefit.[173] As later chapters will demonstrate, the current study finds that the milieu that supported the two intellectuals and friends also produced *Naṣīḥat al-mulūk*.

The proposal that Pseudo-Māwardī wrote against a Tukhari background finds some support, I suggest, in the local knowledge implied in the author's mention of Balkh, in his references to images carved into the mountains and rocks, and paintings in buildings and residences (or palaces), and in his adducing of the Buddha as a lasting source of human wisdom. Tukharistan provided a meeting ground and central point for material and cultural exchanges in every direction.[174] As Volume II will demonstrate, *Naṣīḥat al-mulūk* is replete with pseudo-Aristotelian materials, and with materials associated with an Indic provenance. Several aspects of *Naṣīḥat al-mulūk*, then, support the hypothesis that Pseudo-Māwardī resided and wrote in Balkh. It remains to consider one other possible location that, despite the absence of a reference in the text, is consistent with a significant number of its characteristics.

A Samarqandi Provenance

Although *Naṣīḥat al-mulūk* lacks a specific reference to Samarqand, some of the characteristics of Balkh that render it a plausible location for the text's genesis apply also to the former Samanid capital. A Samarqandi location perhaps finds further support in the author's continuing attachment to Isḥāq b. Aḥmad I, who enjoyed strong support in the city of which he was governor in the later ninth and early years of the tenth century.

Like Balkh, Samarqand was situated at the intersection of trade routes that linked it with India and Afghanistan (via Balkh and Tirmidh), and to the east with the Turkish steppes and China. These connections gave their names to the city's four main gates: Bāb al-Ṣīn ('The China Gate'), Bāb Bukhārā, Bāb al-Nawbahār and Bāb al-Kabīr ('The Great Gate') or Bāb Kishsh.[175] Like Balkh, Samarqand enjoyed multiple associations with antiquity. It too was reputed to have been built by Alexander, and in addition Tubbaᶜ, the title employed in Arabic sources to denote the Himyarite rulers of south-western Arabia from the late third to the early sixth centuries, appears in accounts of the city's construction.[176] Samarqand also retained specimens of ancient epigraphy in scripts illegible to the contemporary inhabitants.[177] In an indication of its significant contact with China, Samarqand was the site of the earliest production of paper (*kāghidh*) for markets to the west, and in the tenth century the city remained an important centre for its production.[178] Several of the ᶜulamāᵓ of Samarqand bore the *nisba* al-Kāghidhī,[179] and the city possessed a commercial area (*khān al-kawāghidhīn*) designated for persons involved in producing and trading in the commodity.[180] Again like Balkh, Samarqand's cosmopolitanism found expression in the multiplicity of its religious communities. As its Bāb al-Nawbahār suggests, Samarqand too had a Buddhist history, although Xuanzang's silence regarding its Buddhist sites suggests the religion's diminished presence in the city and its environs by the early seventh century; a century later, Huichao reported a single Buddhist monastery and a single monk.[181] Other religious communities remained more numerous and more visible. Al-Iṣṭakhrī reports on a settlement for Christians in the vicinity of Samarqand,[182] and Ibn Ḥawqal described the city's sizable and long-standing Christian population; a Nestorian bishopric established there in the sixth century had been superseded by the city's elevation to a metropolitan see in the early eighth century.[183] Other Christian communities also lived in the city, the material remains of which suggest a high degree of inter-confessional contact.[184] Zoroastrians involved in the maintenance of the irrigation system on which the area's abundant agricultural production depended were exempt from the poll-tax (*jizya*) on account of their indispensable services.[185] Towards the end of the tenth century, the unidentified author of *Ḥudūd al-ᶜālam* mentioned a convent of Manichaeans (*khānagāh-i Mānaviyān*) at Samarqand, and knew them as 'auditors' (*nighūshāk*).[186] Al-Muqaddasī, also in the later tenth century, associated Samarqand with *ahl jamāᶜa wa-sunna*, 'people of the whole community and [the Prophet's] normative practice',[187] but well into the tenth century the city evidently retained a diverse population and a consciousness of its rootedness in antiquity. Pseudo-Māwardī lived in a milieu that possessed these characteristics, as his countless references to *milal* (religious communities), *adyān* (religions) and *diyānāt* (religions or religious paths) suggest. A Samarqandi location is also compatible with Pseudo-Māwardī's attention to the proper treatment of the *dhimmī* communities, communities of non-Muslims to whom security and protection were extended and who were liable to the poll-tax.[188] Pseudo-Māwardī's linking of religious movements with instability finds a plausible context in Samarqand, where a dissident religious community known by their distinctive clothing as the 'Wearers of White' (*mubayyiḍa*), led by 'the Veiled One', al-Muqannaᶜ, had taken control of the city, and where the governor of Samarqand, Jibrāᵓīl b. Yaḥyā, had assisted in suppressing the revolt during the caliphate of al-Mahdī (r. 158–69/775–85). The tenth-century geographers reported the continued existence of communities of *mubayyiḍa* in the region.[189]

Samarqand's distinctive religious and scholarly cultures similarly provide a compatible setting for the composition of *Naṣīḥat al-mulūk*. In the later ninth and early tenth centuries, numerous religious scholars, most of them connected loosely or, later, more formally with Ḥanafī and Māturīdī orientations and groupings, lived, taught and practised in Samarqand; the city's thriving religious culture is amply documented in *Kitāb al-Qand fī maᶜrifat ᶜulamāᵓ Samarqand* and *Fażāᵓil-i Balkh*. In these decades, legal, theological and sectarian boundaries were movable and imprecise, and the fluidity and creativity of the Samarqandi religious environment stimulated the emergence of distinctive approaches to religious questions. The Ḥanafī theologian al-Māturīdī, for whom death dates of 332/943, 333/944 and 336/947 are recorded, stemmed from the Maturid quarter of the city, and Abū l-Layth Naṣr b. Muḥammad al-Samarqandī (d. 373/983), the Ḥanafī jurist, theologian and Qurᵓān commentator, also hailed from the city. Both al-Māturīdī and Abū l-Layth al-Samarqandī were accorded the honorific title *Imām al-hudā*, 'the Imam of Guidance', an appellation bestowed on highly esteemed scholars. As Fuᵓād ᶜAbd al-Munᶜim Aḥmad has made clear, the author of *Naṣīḥat al-mulūk* appears to have followed Ḥanafī perspectives in his treatment of legal matters.[190] Pseudo-Māwardī's strong support for the role of rational speculation, to which he commonly refers as *naẓar*, and the exercise of judgement, or *raᵓy*, is compatible with a Ḥanafī–Māturīdī and Samarqandi as well as a Muᶜtazilite provenance. In the course of the tenth and eleventh centuries, the theological doctrine of the Ḥanafī–Māturīdī scholars of Samarqand would spread throughout Transoxiana, eastern Khurasan, Balkh, and among the newly converted Turks in the Karakhanid territories of Central Asia.[191] The teachings of al-Māturīdī and his followers within or alongside a broadly Ḥanafī orientation linked Balkh with Transoxiana, and with Samarqand in particular.

The scholarly culture of Samarqand found expression not only in works of theology, jurisprudence and exegesis, but also in homiletic and edificatory works. Significantly, Abū l-Layth al-Samarqandī combined his religious scholarship, especially in the fields of *fiqh* and *tafsīr*, with writings, probably intended for a broad audience, devoted to moral exhortation (*mawāᶜiẓ*) and the cultivation of moral characteristics (*akhlāq*).[192] Among these writings was *Tanbīh al-ghāfilīn* ('The Alerting of the Negligent'), a collection that provides a number of suggestive parallels with *Naṣīḥat al-mulūk*. It consists largely of Prophetic ḥadīth, but also includes utterances of the early caliphs and other revered figures, such as the Egyptian mystic Dhū l-Nūn (*c.* 18–246/796–861) and the previously mentioned renunciant Shaqīq al-Balkhī, and unspecified persons referred to by the term 'sage' (*ḥakīm*), occasionally in Persian ('a sage said in Persian', *qāla ḥakīm bi-l-fārisiyya*).[193] The book is arranged in thematic chapters devoted to virtues and vices, death and the afterlife, the rights of parents, children, relatives and neighbours, religious and ritual duties, spiritual practices and their merits, and similar matters. Towards the end, Abū l-Layth includes a chapter of admonitions which appear without attributions, followed by several chapters of stories (*ḥikāyāt*) and, finally, prayers of petition and praise (*bāb al-duᶜāʾ wa-l-tasbīḥāt*). Van Ess comments of this work, which, in an indication of its popularity, was translated into Persian, that it 'comes close to the spirit of Iranian *andarz* literature'.[194] While Samarqand was hardly unique in its fostering of such a homiletic culture, this prominent aspect of the city's character contributes to its plausibility as a location for *Naṣīḥat al-mulūk*'s composition.

Most importantly, numerous and varied contacts provided close links between the cities of Balkh and Samarqand in the later ninth and early tenth centuries. Several characteristics of Samarqand's religious culture extended to Balkh as well, and a number of scholars moved between the two cities. Abū l-Layth al-Samarqandī, for instance, studied in Balkh with the Ḥanafī jurist Abū Jaᶜfar Muḥammad al-Hinduwānī (d. 362/973), and left intellectual descendants in both cities. The extensive connections between the two commercial and cultural centres permit the hypothesis that Pseudo-Māwardī participated most directly in the intellectual–cultural mentality of Balkh, but that he also engaged in the wider dialogues and debates current in Transoxiana, and especially Samarqand.

PART II

GOVERNANCE AND SOCIETY

3

Kingship and Governance: Concepts and Terminology

The two chapters in Part I of this volume addressed the situation of Pseudo-Māwardī's *Naṣīḥat al-mulūk* in time and place. In those chapters I sought to establish that the book is a product of the first half of the tenth century and the Oxus regions, and I suggested more precisely that it was written during the reign of Naṣr II in the vicinity of Balkh. In what follows, I attempt to read *Naṣīḥat al-mulūk* in the context and as a product of this distinctive milieu. Chapters 3 and 4 undertake such a reading with regard to Pseudo-Māwardī's presentation of kingship and governance.

Mirrors for princes frequently display perspectives that differ considerably from the approaches characteristic of juristic and theological writings.[1] Their authors possessed diverse professional backgrounds, and accordingly mirrors encompass a broad range of points of view and intersect with various specialised strands of discourse. Among the earlier examples in Arabic are secretaries' and administrators' compositions, often dedicated to particular topics or written to address a particular situation or occasion; the 'testaments' of rulers and governors, addressed to their successors or to their subjects; the testaments or edificatory writings of religious figures, addressed sometimes to an individual and frequently to a broader public; and texts of varied length that set forth, often in language that recalls materials assimilated into Arabic from Middle Persian and, to some degree, Greek, Syriac and Sanskrit sources, principles of royal governance, wise maxims, practical advice and regulations for the king's officials and for persons in attendance at the court.[2] By the eleventh and twelfth centuries, mirrors in Arabic and Persian had grown considerably in length and scope, and, while retaining a high degree of flexibility, the genre, now often in the form of a book for presentation, had acquired several characteristics. Mirrors of this period address well-known themes, such as royal justice and clemency, the dangers of acting in anger or haste and the necessity of consultation. The specific import of authors' treatments of these topics is often obscured by their deployment of an established repertoire of Qur^ʾānic verses, Prophetic ḥadīth, utterances ascribed to named or, perhaps more commonly, generic and deliberately decontextualised figures ('a king', 'a vizier', 'a sage'), narratives and anecdotes, verses of poetry, aphorisms and proverbs.

Pseudo-Māwardī wrote at a particular moment in the generic history of the Arabic mirror, and *Naṣīḥat al-mulūk*, among the earliest book-length mirrors in Arabic, contributed to the mirror's continuing expansion. Its closest predecessor in length is probably *Akhlāq al-mulūk*, known as *Kitāb al-Tāj*, the contents of which, however, are largely restricted to the customs and conduct appropriate to the royal court. *Naṣīḥat al-mulūk*, it might be said, possesses the expansive scale of *Akhlāq al-mulūk* (*Kitāb al-Tāj*), and recapitulates some of its themes and contents. Pseudo-Māwardī combines these characteristics of *Kitāb al-Tāj* with the philosophical treatise of the Kindian tradition, and the edificatory and exhortative discourse of the testament (*waṣiyya*). *Naṣīḥat al-mulūk* anticipates, in different ways, the eleventh-century mirrors of al-Thaʿālibī, Kaykāʾūs, Pseudo-Ghazālī and Niẓām al-Mulk; the writings of moral philosophers such as Miskawayh (d. 421/1030) and Naṣīr al-Dīn Ṭūsī (597–672/1201–74); and the homiletic writings of preacher-advisers such as the Ḥanbalī jurisconsult, historian and polymath Ibn al-Jawzī (510–97/1126–1200) and the judge ʿAbd al-Raḥmān al-Shayzarī (d. 589/1193).[3]

In an attempt to integrate Pseudo-Māwardī's voice into the better-known source material for the Samanid period, this study offers an interpretation of *Naṣīḥat al-mulūk* that links it to the immediate environment in which it was written. Mirrors for princes provide historians with exceptionally rich materials, explicit and implicit, for studies of the conceptual aspects of power, as well as its expression in rhetoric and ceremony. As I shall demonstrate in this chapter, Pseudo-Māwardī articulates a particular understanding of a rightful order in the cosmos, in which kings functioned as intermediaries between the divine and mundane realms. This conception reflected the cultural and intellectual discourses that prevailed in Pseudo-Māwardī's milieu; it also shaped his perception and analysis of the political and social conditions that he observed and experienced in the Oxus regions of the early tenth century.

The King and the Cosmic Order

In continuity with ancient conceptions of sovereignty, Pseudo-Māwardī portrays the ruler's position in an exalted, somewhat sacralised fashion. He depicts the king's status as an intermediate one between the ranks of the angels and prophets, on the one hand, and the human, animal and mineral kingdoms, on the other. He opens his second chapter, devoted to 'The virtues of kings in the grandeur of their stations, and the cultivation of virtues and avoidance of vices incumbent upon them', with the following words:

> As for God's – great and glorious[4] – preferring (*tafḍīl*) of humankind over the other animals, and His preferring (*tafḍīl*) of animals over plants and minerals; and God's – great is His mention – subjugation (*taskhīr*) to humankind of everything in the created world, whether in the sky or on earth, and that which lies between them among the constituents of His creation and the species of His creatures – in (these matters) no doubt should arise among people of intelligence (*ahl al-ᶜuqūl*), nor any controversy or argument, and no rejection of the universal witnessing to it, the general observation of it, or the agreement of the intelligent on it. For God, great is His mention, has said, 'He has subordinated (*sakhkhara*) to you that which is in the heavens and that which is in the earth, all of it, from Him' (45: 13).[5] He said, 'He has subordinated (*sakhkhara*) to you the sun and the moon, (they being) persistent; and He has subordinated (*sakhkhara*) to you the night and the day. He has given you of everything that you have asked Him for, and if you were to count the bounty (*niᶜma*) of God you could not reckon it' (14: 33, 34). He has said, 'We have ennobled the Children of Adam; We have carried them on the land and the sea, We have sustained them with good things, and We have preferred them greatly (*faḍḍalnāhum . . . tafḍīlan*) over many of those whom We have created' (17: 71).
>
> Next, God, great is His mention, gave precedence (*faḍḍala*) to kings (*mulūk*) over the categories of humanity (*ṭabaqāt al-bashar*) in the same way that He preferred humanity over the other kinds and species of creation, in several respects, by manifest indications, and evidentiary testimonies

> present and known both to the intellect (by reason) and by hearing (of the divine revelation) (*li . . . dalāʾil mawjūda wa-shawāhid fī l-ʿaql wa-l-samʿ jamīʿan ḥāḍira maʿlūma*).[6]

Pseudo-Māwardī introduces in this passage some of the leading themes and concepts of his mirror. The principle of *tafḍīl*, God's preferment or privileging of some parts of His creation over other parts, in an infinitely differentiated order illustrates the rational nature of divine action and provides proof of the divine wisdom; *tafḍīl* and its antonym, *taskhīr*, subordination, recur in this passage. The concepts of favour (*niʿma*), on the one hand, and gratitude (*shukr*), on the other, grounded in scripture, evoke relationships of reciprocity.[7] These linked ideas formed part of a widely shared mentality. Pseudo-Māwardī's contemporary in the nearby town of Tirmidh, the mystic al-Ḥakīm al-Tirmidhī (d. *c.* 295–300/905–10), evoking the concept of subordination (*taskhīr*) conveyed in Pseudo-Māwardī's Qurʾānic passages, began his *Kitāb al-Riyāḍa wa-adab al-nafs* ('Book of the Discipline and Training of the Self') with the statement, 'God the Exalted created human beings for His service (*khidma*), and created everything else in subjugation to them . . . and in every subjugated thing He made that which was needful and beneficial to these servants' (*fa-jaʿala fī kull musakhkhar mā yaḥtāju ilayhi hāʾulāʾi l-khadam wa-mā yarjiʿu nafʿuhu ilayhim*).[8] Pseudo-Māwardī, in a manner characteristic of his outlook and method, emphasises the harmonious evidences of observation (*mushāhadat al-jamīʿ iyyāhu*) and scripture, of reason and revelation (*al-ʿaql wa-l-samʿ*).

In a similar passage at the beginning of his sixth chapter, 'On the governance of the élites' (*fī siyāsat al-khāṣṣa*), Pseudo-Māwardī develops further his presentation of the divinely ordained hierarchical order. In this location, he explicitly likens the king's relationship to his subjects to God's relationship to His creation when he urges the king to follow the divine example in the selection and training of the privileged persons who compose his *khāṣṣa*, the members of the élites that surrounded him:

> It is incumbent on the virtuous king that his *khāṣṣa* should be his first priority, and his attention to them most frequent, general and extensive. He should train them so intensively that no one among the people of his kingdom or within his dominion will be quicker in obedience to him or

further from disobedience to him, nor stronger in determination to help him, nor more observant in his service to him (*aḥsan adaban fī khidmatihi*) than they are, in accordance with the emulation of God, glorious and exalted, and the imitation of His likeness among His creation. For God, exalted and glorious, when He created His creatures and mandated in His wisdom that which He commanded for them and prohibited from them (*awjaba fī ḥikmatihi amrahum wa-zajrahum*), and subjected them according to that which was most in accordance with their well-being (*taᶜabbadahum bi-mā huwa aṣlaḥ lahum*), and arranged for their affairs in their religion and their concerns in this world, in their afterlife and their first (mundane) life, He chose among them angels, whom He made into armies (*junūd*) over His creation, charged with the affairs of His creatures;[9] and assistants (*aᶜwān*) to the people of His summons [to religious belief] (*li-ahl daᶜwatihi*).[10] He made them the nearest of creatures to Him in station and the closest of them, by His favour, in rank. He chose them from among those whom He knew would not disobey Him in what He commanded them; rather, they would glorify Him night and day without lapsing into weariness or slander. In addition, He made them the longest in endurance, the most forceful in the strength of their obedience to Him (*aqwāhum ᶜalā ṭāᶜatihi quwwatan*), and the most extensive in their power (*qudra*) to execute His commands and convey His messages (*risālāt*) in His earth and His heavens.

Then He chose messengers among the people, and made them stewards (*umanāʾ*) over His creation. He made His messengers from those whom He knew were the strongest of His creatures in resolve, the furthest of them in perspicacity, the greatest of them in obedience, and the least of them, after the angels, in disobedience to Him. He knew that from them there would issue no major sin (*kabīra*) that would evict them from His friendship (*wilāya*), nor, in enmity (*ᶜadāwa*) to Him, would they engage in unlawful acts, nor would they incur suspicion in discharging His message and establishing His religious community (*milla*), His religion (*diyāna*), His religious law (*sharīᶜa*) and His order (*ṣanᶜa*). Rather, He made them trustworthy (*umanāʾ*), noble, wise, learned, virtuous, beneficent, godly (*atqiyāʾ*), generous and strong, in accordance with that which He has made

> clear in this regard in His Book (*kitāb*) and clarified in His address (*khiṭāb*) when He said, 'God is most knowing with regard to where He places His message' (22: 75) . . . Then He assisted them all by His granting of success, protected them (*ᶜaṣamahum*) by His guidance, strengthened them with His help, exalted them by His assistance to victory, and supported their insights by His favour and His might.[11]

In these passages, Pseudo-Māwardī conveys his conception of the degrees of the divinely ordained cosmos. The ruler is situated in a category of his own between, on the one hand, the realms of God's chosen angels and prophets, with whom He communicates His will for His creation, and, on the other hand, the lower ranks of being, the management of whose welfare He delegates to kings. The graded arrangement of the various categories of beings, in Pseudo-Māwardī's rationalist perception, reflects God's wisdom; the divinely ordained hierarchy of the created world conforms to reason and revelation, which correspond to one another in fully harmonious fashion. In this conception Pseudo-Māwardī echoes the outlook associated with al-Kindī and his intellectual descendants.[12] His remarks also allude to a number of specifically Muᶜtazilite points of view. His portrayal of God's imposition of commands and prohibitions as an expression of His wisdom, and as a means of promoting the well-being of His creatures, reflects a point of view common to the Muᶜtazila. Pseudo-Māwardī's reference to God's ordering of the creation in accordance with the 'optimal' (*al-aṣlaḥ*), that is, that which best promotes the well-being (*ṣalāḥ* or *maṣlaḥa*) of His creatures, alludes to a specifically Baghdadi Muᶜtazilite doctrine.[13] In assuming the precedence of angels over prophets, Pseudo-Māwardī again articulates a view common to most of the Muᶜtazila, but disputed among non-Muᶜtazilite theologians.[14] In the last sentence reproduced in the above passage, Pseudo-Māwardī refers to the concept of *ᶜiṣma*, God's granting of protection from the commission of sin. In this instance, Pseudo-Māwardī observes that God extends this protection to prophets. He has already stated that God selects as His prophets human beings who, in His omnipotence He already knows, will never commit a major sin (*kabīra*). In Pseudo-Māwardī's lifetime and milieu, prophets' protection from the commission of major and minor sins (*kabāʾir* and *ṣaghāʾir*, respectively) was a matter of discussion and debate; indeed, Abū

Zayd al-Balkhī composed a treatise entitled *Kitāb ᶜIṣmat al-anbiyāʾ* ('The Immaculate Quality of the Prophets').[15] Pseudo-Māwardī's non-Muᶜtazilite contemporaries, such as the theologian al-Ashᶜarī (d. 324/935–6), tended to attribute more limited *ᶜiṣma* to prophets. (Eventually, comprehensive conceptions of prophetic *ᶜiṣma* would become widespread.) Pseudo-Māwardī's mention of prophets' abstention from the commission of major sins leaves unaddressed the disputed topic of the full scope of prophetic *ᶜiṣma*, and the issue of whether their state of divine protection characterised prophets' entire lives or began only after their calling to their prophetic mission.[16] A related theological question concerns the impact of sin on the individual's status as a believer. Pseudo-Māwardī makes it clear that commission of a major sin (*kabīra*) occasioned expulsion from God's friendship (*wilāya*) and the incurring of His enmity (*ᶜadāwa*). This position is consistent with Muᶜtazilite doctrine according to which God's 'promise [of heavenly reward] and threat [of punishment]' implied His permanent assignment of individuals to their deserts in the afterlife; only repentance and abandonment of sin mitigated this outcome.[17] It might be added that Pseudo-Māwardī alludes to God's bestowal of *ᶜiṣma* not only on prophets, but also, subject to His will, on other human beings; his treatment of the exceptional virtue of the Umayyad caliph ᶜUmar b. ᶜAbd al-Azīz illustrates this theological point.[18]

In the second of the two passages cited in the preceding pages, Pseudo-Māwardī introduces another central theme of his mirror: that the order that God had instituted throughout creation provided a model for the order that the king should strive to institute in his kingdom. The notion presupposes the ruler's detachment from the categories (in Pseudo-Māwardī's phrase, *ṭabaqāt al-bashar*) that comprised the social hierarchy. In his pioneering study of social bonds and loyalties in the Buyid period, Roy Mottahedeh demonstrated that the king's status as an outsider was understood as an integral element in the maintenance of the political and social order.[19] This conception, to which Sasanian antecedents contributed, found wide expression in several genres of Arabic and Persian literature over many centuries.[20] The idea's associations with antiquity enhanced its meaning for Pseudo-Māwardī and the contemporaries who shared his mentality. In formulations associated with Iranian, Greek and Indian authorities, the notion of the ruler's exalted and separate station co-existed with an insistence on the interconnected nature of the various components of the kingdom. The image found its quintessential articulation in the various formulations, known as 'circles of justice', that asserted the interdependence of sovereignty and the principal functional groupings among the king's subjects, particularly the soldiery who defended his territories and the producers of the wealth that funded his campaigns; the entire system required the balance that only the ruler, by virtue of his exceptional and detached status, was able to effect through his just governance.[21] Several circles of justice in Arabic formulations appear in attributions to the paradigmatic Sasanian monarchs Ardashīr and Anūshīrvān, the founder of the dynasty and its most celebrated member, respectively. Pseudo-Māwardī ascribes a circle of justice to the latter figure: 'Anūshīrvān said: Sovereignty subsists by means of armies (*al-mulk bi-l-junūd*), armies by wealth, wealth is extracted from the lands, the lands flourish by virtue of prosperity, and prosperity cannot endure other than by justice'.[22] This compound understanding of the king's position, at once unparalleled and contingent, informed the evolving political culture of the early centuries and continued to find expression in numerous Arabic, Persian and Turkish writings over the course of a millennium.[23] Among these writings, *Naṣīḥat al-mulūk* illustrates the continued meaningfulness of these enduring conceptions, which shaped Pseudo-Māwardī's understanding and articulation of the conditions of his particular time and place.

Central to the social relationships presupposed in *Naṣīḥat al-mulūk*, as several passages adduced in this chapter will demonstrate, is the concept and practice of *khidma*, literally 'service', but in many cases substantially devoid of servile connotations.[24] Likened, as al-Ḥakīm al-Tirmidhī's previously mentioned formulation indicates, to the relationship between God and His creation, *khidma* in the human realm at once presupposes a deeply hierarchical form of social organisation and illustrates the contingency of the ruler's power. If, as Jürgen Paul has indicated, in conceptual terms the relationship of *khidma* evoked an institution similar to slavery, this evocation was largely metaphorical.[25] The practice of *khidma* embraced slave- and freeborn men alike; indeed, persons of illustrious lineage and high status, even members of dynastic families, entered into relationships of *khidma* with the ruler. The relationship involved reciprocal obligations: the 'servant' (*khādim*), in a formal ceremony, pledged obedience and loyalty to the recipient of service (*makhdūm*), who thereby incurred the responsibility for 'protection' and the provision of appropriate 'benefits' (*niᶜam*), also expressed in favourable treatment or 'kindness' (*iḥsān*). At least in design, each party's repeated fulfilment of these expectations reinforced the strength of the bond between them. The practice also carried with it the expectation of 'increase', namely, that the demonstrations of loyal service, on the one hand, and generous remuneration, on the other, would not remain constant but would rise in a continual fashion. Exponents of this expectation found support for it, as Pseudo-Māwardī would later in his second chapter, in the Qurʾānic text, 'If you are thankful, I shall give you more' (*la-in shakartum la-azīdannakum*) (14: 7). It was partly in this subtle balance between *khidma* and *niᶜma* that the risk of damage to the delicate relationship of *khādim* and *makhdūm* was located.[26]

Naṣīḥat al-mulūk supplies an exceptionally full description and analysis of *khidma*. The principal passage appears after Pseudo-Māwardī's discussion of various terms related to sovereignty, and is presented towards the end of the present chapter. The eleventh-century Persian *Siyar al-mulūk* ('The Ways [or Conduct] of Kings') of Niẓām al-Mulk reflects the importance of the concept and practice of *khidma*, the origination and model enactment of which the vizier often associates with the Samanid court.[27] The replication of the system, by virtue of which the ruler's *khādim* was also a *makhdūm* in relation to his subordinates, fostered the creation of networks. For example, according to al-Iṣṭakhrī and Ibn Ḥawqal, the people of Transoxiana were 'the most obedient of people to their superiors and the most willing of them in service to their overlords' (*wa-hum . . . aḥsan al-nās ṭāᶜatan li-kubarāʾihim wa-alṭafuhum khidmatan li-ᶜuẓamāʾihim*).[28] As Paul has argued, given the geographers' remarks elsewhere concerning the people's proclivities to revolt, they probably referred in this statement to the people's loyalty to persons beneath the level of dynastic or even local rulers; in this case their 'obedience' and 'service' perhaps applied to leaders of groups, whether defined in religious and juristic terms (*madhāhib*), or in terms of residential quarters.[29]

Several passages in *Naṣīḥat al-mulūk*, particularly in its second and sixth chapters, reflect the importance of *khidma*, which, like the related word *khadam* (sometimes 'servants', but sometimes persons, whether servile or free-born, bound by relationships of *khidma*), figures prominently in the author's depiction of governance and society. Like other designations for social categories, the word *khadam* carried many meanings. The term *khādim* sometimes denoted a eunuch; it is perhaps on account of this association that Ibn Khaldūn (732–84/1332–82), the fourteenth-century North African historian and philosopher, disparaged *khidma* and considered it contrary to manly virtue.[30] In the description of al-ᶜĀmirī (d. 381/992), a continuator of the Kindian tradition in Khurasan in the second half of the tenth century, the *khadam* constituted one of fourteen essential categories among the ruler's *aᶜwān*, his 'assistants' or 'aides', and they appear to have performed services related to the care of the king's person.[31] Indeed, the term *khadam* appears frequently in conjunction with the plural term *aᶜwān*, another category that appears to denote different types of people in different contexts. In Abbasid contexts, the term *aᶜwān* often designated notables involved in the collection of taxes, persons, as Ira Lapidus has written, 'who were not subordinates, who could not be given orders, but whose cooperation had to be enlisted nonetheless'.[32] These *aᶜwān* perhaps became identified with the office of the *maᶜūna*, which involved responsibility for the maintenance of law and order as well as broader fiscal, and perhaps other civil, duties.[33] The erudite littérateur Ibn al-Muqaffaᶜ (*c*. 102–39/720–57), translator of several Middle Persian texts into Arabic and important contributor to the formation of Arabic literary prose, links rulers (*wulāt*) with their *aᶜwān* in *al-Risāla fī l-ṣaḥāba* ('Epistle on the [Caliph's] Companions'), a text in which he advised the caliph regarding his choice of fit companions and a variety of political, religious and social issues.[34] In this context, the *aᶜwān* appear as a category of individuals close to the ruler at the royal court, probably members of the ruler's retinue.[35] In his eleventh-century Persian chronicle of the Ghaznavids, the secretary and historian Bayhaqī pairs the *aᶜwān* with 'performers of service', *khidmatkārān*.[36]

In the case of *khadam*, *aᶜwān* and other terms that appear frequently in Arabic writings of the first centuries, it is difficult to assess when, and to what degree, the Arabic words render terms that had been employed in Middle Persian, Parthian and Sogdian contexts, and still more difficult to determine the extent to which the functions of the persons described by these categories might have resembled or differed from those of earlier societies.[37]

New Persian usages, such as *chākar* (servant) and *bandeh* (servant or bondsman), present the same questions. De la Vaissière has indicated two distinct connotations of the Persian term *chākar*, one deriving from Persian usage and suggesting the status of the servant or apprentice, the other deriving from Sogdian usage and connoting the distinctive Sogdian military institution of the *chākar*, the personal soldier-retainer who guarded his master, a king or member of the nobility, at all times, and whose service included, but was not limited to, the functions of the ruler's bodyguard.[38] Accordingly, the terms *chākar* and *bandeh*, like the Arabic *khadam*, embraced a conjunction of bondage or servitude, rhetorical or actual, and personal privilege. In one example, the mid-tenth-century preface appended to certain manuscripts of the *Shāhnāmeh* ('Book of Kings', completed in about 400/1010) of Firdawsī describes Abū Manṣūr al-Maᶜmarī, the leading administrator or *dastūr* of the governor of Nishapur, as the governor's (metaphorical) servant (*chākar*).[39] In another example, even after he had defeated him, the victorious Amir Ismāᶜīl b. Aḥmad used the language of *bandeh*, 'servant' or bondsman' and *khudāvand*, 'lord', to describe, and effect a restoration of, his relations with his brother Naṣr.[40] In this case, Ismāᶜīl, a member of dynastic family, enacted the renewal of his ties of *khidma* to his older brother and lord. The term *bandeh* represents linguistic continuity with the Middle Persian *bandak*, whose status also varied greatly according to context.[41] The linguistic and conceptual similarity that such cases suggest need not imply direct evolution or indirect continuity with earlier patterns and practices. In some cases, indeed, the resemblances in terminology are likely to co-exist with, and perhaps mask, shifts in practice and association.[42]

In the case of the *khidma* to which Pseudo-Māwardī and Niẓām al-Mulk refer, the relationship found expression in the concept of a 'contract' or 'covenant' (*ᶜahd*, pl. *ᶜuhūd*), under which both parties acknowledged mutual obligations. When the ruler failed to honour the covenant to which he had pledged agreement, the *khādim*'s duty of obedient service lapsed. The principal elements in the covenant were the *khādim*'s obligation to render *khidma* and the ruler's corresponding duty of *wafāᵓ*, a term that connoted loyalty, trustworthiness, the honouring of expectations and being true to one's word. *Wafāᵓ* often took the form of material generosity, through the bestowal of 'favour' (*niᶜma*) or the demonstration of 'benevolence' or 'kindness' (*iḥsān*).

According to the ninth-century *Akhlāq al-mulūk* of al-Taghlibī, 'The honouring of people entitled to loyalty is among the characteristics of the king' (*min akhlāq al-malik ikrām ahl al-wafāʾ*), the term *akhlāq* (pl. of *khulq* or *khuluq*, a moral characteristic) indicating the moral, as well as the practical or pragmatic, force of the concept. Indeed, al-Taghlibī states explicitly that *wafāʾ* involved not only verbal gratitude (*shukr al-lisān*), but also, in addition to the expression of gratitude in oral and practical terms ('by the tongue and the limbs'), in the case of benefactors other than the ruler, the recognition in the royal presence of the person who has bestowed favour (*man anʿama ʿalayhi*), the equal sharing of benefits, in terms of wealth and possessions, with the person's companion or adherent (*ṣāḥib*), and the protection of the individual's descendants and family.[43] *Naṣīḥat al-mulūk* includes an eclectic choice of *akhbār*, narrative accounts, especially in the epilogue, that reinforce the concepts of *khidma* and *wafāʾ*. Pseudo-Māwardī, who chose to leave his royal audience with instructive examples of these moral and practical imperatives, adduced pertinent maxims attributed to, in one case, an envoy to the Umayyad court in Damascus and in another, the 'books of the ancients':

> Al-Wāqidī (d. 207/822) said: A royal envoy (*baʿḍ rusul al-mulūk*) died in Damascus in the time of ʿAbd al-Malik b. Marwān [r. 65–86/685–705]. In his pocket was found a golden tablet, on which three lines appeared: 'When loyalty disappears, tribulation descends; when protection dies, revenge lives; and when treacheries appear, blessings are made light of' (*idhā dhahaba l-wafāʾ nazala l-balāʾ wa-idh māta l-iʿtiṣām ʿāsha l-intiqām wa-idhā ẓaharat al-khiyānāt ustukhuffat al-barakāt*).[44]

> Al-Madāʾinī (*c.* 135–215 or 228/752–830 or 843) mentioned that among that which was found in the books of the ancients (*kutub al-awwalīn*) pertaining to the qualities that constitute the pillars of authority were these words: 'Nothing occasions the demise of sovereignty like negligence (*ihmāl*), nothing rewards exertion like judgement (*raʾy*), nothing promotes the derivation of judgement like consultation, nothing reduces the enemy (*qalla al-ʿadūw*) like justice (*ʿadl*), nothing brings about victory like restraint (*kaff*), nothing strengthens bonds of favour (*niʿma*) like beneficence (*muʾāsāt*), nothing repays kindness (*iḥsān*) like (good) intention

(*niyya*), nothing adorns high status like humility (*tawāḍu*ᶜ), and nothing earns hatred like pride (*kibr*)'.[45]

As a pair, Pseudo-Māwardī's examples depict the theme of *wafā*ᵓ, associated with *ni*ᶜ*ma* and *iḥsān*, as timeless and universal: inscribed on a golden tablet and in ancient books, the principle's immutable significance finds recognition in permanent physical form. In what follows, I shall refer to several examples that illustrate the intertwined themes of *khidma* and *wafā*ᵓ, and provide context for the author's insistence throughout his mirror on the ruler's obligation to observe the 'rightful claims' (*ḥuqūq*) of his *khadam*.[46]

A Decentralised and Cooperative Model of Governance

Writings produced at a physical or social remove from the court, among them several works of local history and geographical sources, confirm through illustration Pseudo-Māwardī's emphasis on the conceptual and practical limits of royal power. As the studies of Jürgen Paul in particular have demonstrated, the governmental functions of the Samanid amirate depended less on central control than on a decentralised model of cooperation.[47] Power was dispersed among a number of élite groupings, which, subject to their own internal dynamics, reproduced themselves in ways that promoted stability in local environments even as power at the centre passed from one amir, and even one dynasty, to another. Members of the élites mediated between the changing rulers and the local populations, and the cooperation of these intermediaries with the dynasty was essential to the functioning of the Samanid system. The members of the categories that performed this mediating function were tied to the amirs, or to their immediate overlords, not by virtue of simple dependency, but through bonds of obligation and loyalty that required both parties' attention and maintenance. The relationship of *khidma* represents a ceremonial manifestation of a system that is likely to have operated with varying degrees of formality beyond the court as well as within it. The result was a practice of governance and social control that functioned through networks of individuals who negotiated among groups at the same time that they were responsible for and to the groupings in which they participated. This devolved system, in which local leaders and communities exercised considerable autonomy and interacted in limited ways with more distant political authorities, appears quite continuous with the evidence for the early Abbasid period reflected in the previously cited corpora of documents, in Arabic and Bactrian, analysed by Geoffrey Khan and Nicholas Sims-Williams.[48] As this chapter will show, Pseudo-Māwardī perceived a system of hierarchically arranged loyalties and obligations that sustained the polity in which he lived. He depicted the proper functioning of this system with reference to the groups that he observed in his milieu, in accordance with his theological–philosophical disposition to perceive rationality in the divinely ordained and 'natural' order, and in accordance with the inherited understandings of his ancient regional culture.

Among the individuals involved in the upper segments of this cooperative model of political management were members of the Samanid dynastic family and the ruler's extended household, members of co-existing dynastic families whose bases of power were encompassed within or adjacent to the Samanid domains, and members of established landowning regional families. The Samanids accommodated certain members of other dynastic families within their domains; the Khalafid line of the Saffarid dynasty, for example, dominated Sistan for a large portion of the Samanid period.[49] From these free-born élites and, increasingly over the course of the tenth century, from the ranks of his personal extended household of slaves and slave-born élites (*mamālīk*), the senior amir appointed persons to military governorships and other eminent positions in the administration of his kingdom. The governors of regions and major cities were leading military commanders – governors of Khurasan characteristically bore the Persian title *isfahsālār* (or *sipahsālār*), 'commander-in-chief'[50] – who possessed the capacity to mobilise and equip sizable contingents of personal troops. Such individuals, who accordingly presided over large numbers of persons, some of them bound in dedicated service, exercised considerable autonomy in their established positions. At this level of power, the maintenance of equipoise between the satisfaction of these leading figures' acknowledged interests (in the language of the prevailing political culture, their *ḥuqūq* or 'rightful claims') and the preservation of the king's exceptional position required careful attention.[51] Disturbance of this balance risked the ruler's forfeit of the individual's services, on which he depended for various types of assistance, including the conduct of his military campaigns. The maintenance of the social equilibrium involved, on the ruler's part, the liberal fulfilment of the claims (*ḥuqūq*) of his governors, appointees and vassals, and the avoidance of acts that might alienate them or tempt their ambitions. By virtue of the related concept of 'increase' (*mazīd* or *ziyāda*), loyal service, as described in the preceding section, entitled the *khādim* to further marks of favour. As a result, the system was liable to escalation, and disappointed expectations sometimes prompted the direct challenge of revolt. Contemporaries and later historians often described the rejection of suzerainty that resulted from disappointment as *tawaḥḥush* or *istīḥāsh*, terms that implied a sense of alienation.[52] While these interconnected themes recur in mirrors for princes, *Naṣīḥat al-mulūk*, as this chapter will show, includes an unusually full treatment of the arrangement. Pseudo-Māwardī, in keeping with the specifications outlined in *Akhlāq al-mulūk*, clarifies that the ruler's obligation to protect and care for persons pledged to him encompassed their entire households, composed of relatives by birth and by marriage and of affiliated persons.

The senior amirs depended on their networks of governors and military commanders for the governance of their kingdoms, and when faced with external and internal threats. In an indication of the relative nature of the senior amir's power, other members of the dynastic family established lasting bases of personal power in the cities under their governance, and developed extensive and substantial networks parallel to those of the senior amir. A prominent example lies in the familial branch of Isḥāq b. Aḥmad, who had held a number of governorships before his appointment to Samarqand, from whence he launched his two contests for the senior amirate. The substantial and enduring power and prestige attached to Isḥāq are evident in the continuing political roles and activities of his sons. In Farghana, where Isḥāq had previously held the post of governor, his son Muḥammad succeeded him; father and son possessed sufficient autonomy to mint their own coins, in Samarqand and Farghana, respectively, in 294/906–7 and 299/911–12.[53] According to Gardīzī, at the end of Ismāᶜīl's reign, another son of Isḥāq, Manṣūr, assumed the governorship of Rayy, where he appointed the free-born commander and *dihqān* Aḥmad b. Sahl as his chief commander (*sarhangī*).[54] In 298/910–11, Aḥmad II sent the experienced and long-serving (free-born) general Ḥusayn b. ᶜAlī al-Marwazī (sometimes al-Marwarrūdhī) to lead a major campaign against Sistan. After Ḥusayn had brought the province under Samanid suzerainty, Aḥmad, in 299/911, appointed Manṣūr b. Isḥāq to the governorship of the province.[55] Manṣūr proved to be highly unpopular with the population, to whom, in a breach of *wafāʾ*, he failed to honour his promises ('When he came to Sistan, he spoke extremely favourably to the people and made generous promises, which he did not fulfil' (*chūn bi-Sīstān āmad mardumān-rā besyār nīkūʾī guft va-vaᶜd-hā-yi nīkū kard va-ānrā vafā nakard*)).[56] The people's resistance found expression in a Kharijite-led revolt in support of a member of the Saffarid family, in the course of which Manṣūr was deposed and imprisoned in the citadel.[57] Aḥmad II responded by sending Ḥusayn b. ᶜAlī, at the head of a large army, back to Sistan. Ḥusayn laid siege to Zaranj, overcame the revolt and secured Manṣūr's release, whereupon the latter departed for Nishapur to take up the governorship of Khurasan, and Aḥmad, in 300–1/913–14, appointed the *mamlūk* Sīmjūr, who had entered the Samanids' service as a client (*mawlā*) of Ismāᶜīl b. Aḥmad, to govern Sistan.[58]

Aḥmad's repeated appointments of Manṣūr indicate the importance to the early tenth-century Samanid polity of the cooperation of collateral branches of the dynastic family. Through the power that they exercised in cooperation with or opposition to the senior amir, the sons of Isḥāq and their allies evidently controlled large areas of Khurasan for considerable periods of time.[59] During Naṣr II's reign, Ilyās, another son of Isḥāq, launched a series of revolts in the area of Farghana. Ilyās's challenge won the support of, on one occasion, the general Muḥammad b. Ḥusayn b. Mutt (known as al-Isfījābī), with a large Turkish army (*jamᶜ min al-turk*), and on another, Abū l-Faḍl b. Abī Yūsuf, governor of Shash.[60] In the course of these events, Naṣr installed in the governorship of Farghana Abū Bakr Muḥammad b. al-Muẓaffar Chaghānī (d. 329/940–1) of the important regional family, the Āl-i Muḥtāj of Chaghaniyan, which lay across the River Oxus from Balkh. Abū Bakr Muḥammad defeated Ilyās's third revolt and engaged Ilyās in negotiations, which resulted in Ilyās's summons to Bukhara.[61]

In a striking pattern, in the aftermath of internal revolts, the amirs of the earlier Samanid period frequently re-appointed rival members of the Samanid dynastic family, and sometimes members of other powerful families and prominent commanders who had rebelled against them, to their former positions. Aḥmad II reinstated his uncle Isḥāq, after his first resistance, as governor of Samarqand; and Naṣr II, following the mediation of Abū Bakr Muḥammad Chaghānī, invited Ilyās b. Isḥāq, who had launched three revolts against him, to Bukhara, where the amir pardoned him and gave him a relative in marriage.[62] This phenomenon attests to the inescapable sharing of power at even the highest levels within the Samanid domains, and the strategic importance of the ceremonial renewal of *khidma*. The political culture assumed the senior amir's 'favour' of, and dependence on, highly placed members of the dynastic families. Accordingly, the amirs' restoration to prominence of individuals whose services were indispensable not only accrued to their reputations for clemency, a virtue emphasised in mirrors, but also assisted the return to equilibrium, for which the ceremonial enactment of *khidma* provided a mechanism, and on which the cooperative model of governance depended. Military governors and members of powerful families, such as Abū Bakr Muḥammad Chaghānī, and high-ranking members of the courtly élite, such as the viziers Jayhānī and Balᶜamī, frequently brokered the restoration of ties.[63] Despite this phenomenon, Treadwell has suggested that the pattern of revolts initiated among collateral branches of the dynasty and the significant support that they were able to attract from the Samanids' leading military commanders and local vassals may have prompted the amirs to discontinue the practice of appointing family members to the principal provincial governorships in eastern Transoxiana and Khurasan, and to turn instead to free-born amirs, such as Abū Bakr Muḥammad, and increasingly to *mamlūk*s, such as Sīmjūr, who had risen through *iṣṭināᶜ*, the 'fosterage' and 'nurturing' of their royal masters, to elevated positions in the Samanids' service. Some of these appointments proved to be hereditary: Sīmjūr was the first of a line of military governors who bore the *nisba* Sīmjūrī,[64] and Abū Bakr Muḥammad's son Abū ᶜAlī Aḥmad Chaghānī (d. 344/955) succeeded his father as governor of Khurasan in 327/938–9.[65]

The fluctuating and contingent nature of the amirs' power finds further demonstration in the shifting alliances among their powerful 'servants', the retention of whose loyalty required, among other factors, accurate gauging of and proper attention to their 'rightful claims'. An example of proper conduct is that of Ismāᶜīl b. Aḥmad, who reputedly cared extremely well for his clients (*mawālī*), including his father's *mawlā* Sīmāᵓ al-Kabīr.[66] Other cases, as the following pages will show, offer a contrast to this acclaimed behaviour.

Two leading figures of the early Samanid period, both free-born and both of whom, having served successive Samanid amirs, had attained positions of power and privilege, rebelled during the reign of Naṣr II. The first was the previously mentioned general Ḥusayn b. ᶜAlī al-Marwazī, whom Aḥmad II had dispatched to subdue Sistan and secure the release of Manṣūr b. Isḥāq, Aḥmad's Samanid governor in Zaranj. At the same time that Manṣūr, freed from captivity, left for Khurasan, Aḥmad II recalled Ḥusayn b. ᶜAlī, who had, in fact, entered into negotiations with the leaders of the revolt that had evicted Manṣūr. But instead of appointing Ḥusayn, whose experience encompassed decades of service to the Samanid family, to the governorship of Sistan, Aḥmad appointed the *mamlūk* Sīmjūr. The historian Gardīzī described Ḥusayn, who reportedly felt entitled to the governorship of Sistan in exchange for his successful restoration of the province to Samanid suzerainty, as *mutavaḥḥish*, 'alienated' or 'disaffected',[67] and the historian Ibn al-Athīr (555–630/1160–1233) described his reaction to the amir's perceived breach of his obligation by the related term *istīḥāsh*.[68] Ḥusayn manifested his disaffection when in 302/914–15, shortly after the assassination of Aḥmad II, Manṣūr b. Isḥāq joined his father's revolt against the accession of Naṣr, and Ḥusayn, in accordance with their previous agreement, joined forces with Manṣūr in Khurasan, and went on to assume the leadership of the rebels after Manṣūr's death.[69] At some point, for reasons that might or might not have borne a relationship to his political ambitions, Ḥusayn b. ᶜAlī became a leading figure among the Ismaᶜiliyya, a major branch of the Shiᶜa that in the tenth century mounted a sustained challenge to Abbasid authority and to the power of regional rulers, and established, among other polities, the Fatimid dynasty (297–567/909–1171) in North Africa, Egypt and Syria. Ḥusayn assumed leadership of the Ismaᶜili *daᶜwa*, the missionary movement that summoned individuals to faith and allegiance, in Khurasan from about the early 320s (that is, from approximately 932 onwards).[70]

Naṣr II entrusted the suppression of Ḥusayn's rebellion to the second, previously mentioned figure, Aḥmad b. Sahl b. Hāshim al-Kāmkārī (d. 307 /920), another distinguished commander who had served under Ismāᶜīl b. Aḥmad and Aḥmad b. Ismāᶜīl as well as Naṣr b. Aḥmad. Aḥmad b. Sahl belonged to a prominent family of *dihqāns* whose lands lay in the vicinity of Marv. He had governed Marv under the Saffarids before, having endured imprisonment at the hands of ᶜAmr b. al-Layth, he transferred his support to the Samanid dynastic family.[71] Numismatic evidence establishes his governorship at Balkh; coins were minted in his name in Tukharistan, especially Andarab, between 303 and 307 (*c.* 914–19).[72] Sent against Ḥusayn b. ᶜAlī, Aḥmad entered Nishapur in 306/918–19, and defeated Ḥusayn in the same year. Ḥusayn was imprisoned in Bukhara, until, in another instance of the reparable potential of ties of *khidma*, the vizier Abū ᶜAbdallāh al-Jayhānī secured the general's release, and Ḥusayn subsequently returned to the service of Naṣr.[73] Immediately after this episode, however, Aḥmad b. Sahl himself rebelled in Khurasan, and settled in his ancestral lands of Marv. Naṣr sent first his general Qarategin, Amir of Gurgan, against him, and later another general, Ḥamūya b. ᶜAlī, who defeated Aḥmad just outside the city. Aḥmad fled until his horse could carry him no further. He requested a safe conduct (*istaʾmana*), but Ḥamūya b. ᶜAlī captured him in 307/919–20. Whereas the rupture in Ḥusayn b. ᶜAlī's relationship with Naṣr proved reparable, Aḥmad's relationship with the Amir appears to have been permanently severed; he died in captivity in Bukhara in the same year (307/920).[74]

Designations of Holders of Power in *Naṣīḥat al-mulūk*

Fluctuations in power, negotiated among multiple individuals at a high level in the polity, found expression in the fluidity of titles by which they were identified. A number of titles, depending on the context in which they appear, denoted individuals at differing levels of authority. Jürgen Paul's analysis of the titles used in geographical writings, which, since they were often produced apart from the courtly milieu, were less likely to impose the distorting perspective of the central state, bears comparison with the evidence of *Naṣīḥat al-mulūk*.[75]

Naṣīḥat al-mulūk supplies an extensive treatment of the terms used to designate holders of authority. Pseudo-Māwardī gives priority to the term *malik*, which he discusses with reference to the Qurʾān as well as contemporary usage in his environment. This discussion occurs in his second chapter, which, as shown above, opens with the author's assertion of God's privileging of humanity over the rest of the animal kingdom, and His preferring of the animals over the kingdoms of the plants and minerals.[76] Pseudo-Māwardī advances this observation as a premise for his later assertion, namely, God's privileging of kings over the categories of humankind. His explication of this proposition, represented in the passage rendered below, concludes with Pseudo-Māwardī's statement that he has decided to use the term *malik* in his book, since it is the clearest term and the one most commonly used in his environment:

> (Among the proofs of the proposition that God has privileged kings over humankind is the fact that) God, great and glorious, has ennobled kings by the epithet by which He has described Himself, for He has called them 'kings' and He has called Himself a 'king'. He has said, 'Possessor of the Day of Judgement (*mālik yawm al-dīn*)' (1: 4); and 'For God is exalted, the true king (*al-malik al-ḥaqq*)' (23: 116; 20: 114). In describing the kings of humankind, He has said, 'And God has sent to you Saul as a king' (2: 247), and 'When He made prophets among you and made you kings' (5: 20). In commending to humankind the concept (*ma*ᶜ*nā*) by which a human being might merit to be called a 'king', and His choosing of the epithet for Himself and His praise by it, He has said: 'Who possesses sovereignty on this day? It belongs to God, the One, the All-Powerful' (40: 16). He said, 'Say, O God, possessor of sovereignty, You bestow sovereignty on whom You will, and You take sovereignty away from whom You will' (3: 26). He said, 'David slew Goliath, and God gave him sovereignty and wisdom (*al-mulk wa-l-ḥikma*)' (2: 251). He said, 'And We brought them a great kingdom (*mulkan* ᶜ*aẓīman*)' (4: 54). God has granted the king the use of this epithet (*ṣifa*) as He has bestowed upon him the name (*ism*) with which He was content for Himself, by which He praised Himself to His creation, and which He then bestowed upon them (His creatures). He clarified their precedence (*faḍl*) in it when He said, 'We have apportioned among them their livelihood in the life of the world, and We have raised some of them above others in degrees, so that some of them may take others in subordination' (43: 32). No one subject to this expression (*fī ḥukmi hādhā l-lafẓ*) is prior in excellence (*awlā bi-l-faḍl*), nor more abundant in his allotment (*ajzal qisman*), nor higher in degree (*arfa*ᶜ *darajatan*) than kings, since humanity is subjected to them, bound to toil in their service (*khidma*) and to act in accordance with their command and prohibition (*fī amrihim wa-nahyihim*).[77]

The passage demonstrates Pseudo-Māwardī's repeated technique of proceeding from a divine name or attribute to its applicability to kings. In extending divine sovereignty to the realm of earthly kings, he implies a relationship of *khidma* that ties the entirety of humanity to the kings whom God has placed over them. The replication of the relationship across vertically arranged categories of being illustrates, for Pseudo-Māwardī, the wisdom and rationality of the divinely created order. The passage foreshadows the extended presentation of the *khidma* relationship, reproduced below, that follows later in his chapter.

Pseudo-Māwardī continues to discuss other terms that he regards as subsumed within the term *malik* or synonymous with it. These designations include *rāᶜin*, *sāʾis*, *rabb al-arḍ* and *raʾs*:

> Among other proofs is that God has made kings His deputies (*khulafāʾ*) in His lands, His stewards (*umanāʾ*, pl. of *amīn*) over His servants, the executors of His ordinances (*aḥkām*) among His creation (*khalīqa*) and of His statutes (*ḥudūd*) among His (human) creatures. In this way it has been said, 'The *sulṭān* is the shadow of God on earth', because it is part of His due claim (*ḥaqq*) that His model (*mithāl*) should be followed in the earth and His regulations (*rusūm*) kept alive among its denizens. This responsibility conforms with His having made them the cultivators of His lands, and having named them shepherds (*ruᶜāt*, pl. of *rāᶜin*) to His servants, likening them to the shepherds who care for livestock and cattle, and comparing their relationship to their subjects to that between the shepherd and his flock. In this sense the philosophers (*al-ḥukamāʾ*) have called them 'trainers' [of animals] (*sāsa*, pl. of *sāʾis*), for their place in relation to those under their governance (*maḥalluhum min masūsīhim*) resembles the place of the trainer (*sāʾis*) in relation to his cattle and riding animals, whose condition is deficient. He trains (*yasūs*) them, in terms of taking responsibility for their affairs, knowing that which is in their interests (*maṣāliḥ*, pl. of *maṣlaḥa*) and that which is to their detriment (*mafāsid*). Furthermore they (the philosophers) have called the activities that are particular to kings 'governance' (*siyāsa*).[78]

In this passage, which further evokes the orderly patterning that illustrates the divine wisdom, Pseudo-Māwardī portrays the relationship between God and the king as a reciprocal one, in which God, having favoured kings, possesses rightful claims against them. The pattern of reciprocity is recapitulated in the relationship between the king and his subjects: the king is entitled to his subjects' obedience and service, and the subjects who render their obedience and service to the ruler thereby acquire rights against him. The usage of *sāsa* in his environment is attested in the *Kitāb Ṣūrat al-arḍ* ('The Form of the Earth') of Ibn Ḥawqal; in his introduction, Ibn Ḥawqal describes the contents of his geographical work as comprising knowledge of interest to *al-mulūk al-sāsa*, 'governing kings', a phrase that appears frequently in *Naṣīḥat al-mulūk*, as well as to *ahl al-murūʾāt*, 'persons of manly virtues', and *al-sāda min jamīᶜ al-ṭabaqāt*, 'the leaders among all the social categories'.[79]

When Pseudo-Māwardī refers to the use of the term *sāsa* among *al-ḥukamāʾ*, he almost certainly includes within the ranks of the latter, in conformity with the common usage of the eastern regions, the sages and philosophers of the past and their intellectual descendants in the present.[80] The noun *sāʾis*, as he explains, is related to *siyāsa*, customarily employed to designate governance; in some contexts, the term carries the more specific connotation of discipline.[81] Pseudo-Māwardī's association of the term *siyāsa* with the philosophers quite possibly suggests his familiarity with the Kindian tradition, in which the subject appears to have occupied an important place. Several figures involved in the tradition's establishment associated with the court and with powerful individuals. As previously noted, the philosopher al-Kindī, perhaps already prominent at court during the caliphate of al-Maʾmūn, served as tutor to Aḥmad, son of Caliph al-Muᶜtaṣim; al-Kindī's student Aḥmad b. al-Ṭayyib al-Sarakhsī (d. 286/899) was a tutor to the future Caliph al-Muᶜtaḍid, a boon companion (*nadīm*) at the caliphal court, and appointed to the office of *ḥisba*, supervision of the markets and of public morality (he was, however, dismissed and died, or was executed, in prison). Abū Zayd al-Balkhī, another illustrious student of al-Kindī, avoided the circles of the powerful, with the exception of his service under the governor Aḥmad b. Sahl; he was nevertheless knowledgeable regarding the financial administration of Khurasan (*kāna aᶜlam bi-dawāwīn Khurāsān*).[82] Regardless of the degree of their participation in activities related to governance, all three philosophers composed treatises on the subject of *siyāsa*.[83] It is quite likely that it is to these representatives of the Kindian tradition that Pseudo-Māwardī alludes in his reference, in relation to *siyāsa*, to the *ḥukamāʾ*. In another suggestive passage, the anonymous author of a compilation of philosophical texts, probably a member of the circle of the moral philosopher and historian Miskawayh (d. 421/1030), wrote, 'If he [the individual] possesses the capacity to improve himself (*idhā qadara ^{c}alā istiṣlāḥ nafsihi*), he [also] possesses the capacity to improve persons other than himself, and he is thus called "governing" and that action of his is called "government".'[84]

Pseudo-Māwardī continues:

> Similarly the past communities of bygone days (*al-umam al-māḍiya fī l-ayyām al-khāliya*), and the Arabs especially, used to call them 'lords of the earth' (*arbāb al-arḍ*, pl. of *rabb al-arḍ*) – 'lords' both in an absolute and a limited sense, since they used to regard them with dread and hope, in that they would execute God's ordinances, carry out His statutory penalties, uphold His precepts (*farā$^{\circ}$iḍ*) and precedents (*sunan*), and investigate their interests (*maṣāliḥ*) and needs, and that which would harm and benefit them, so that they (the 'lords of the earth') would represent among their subjects, in the visible realm (*fī l-shāhid*), the Lord, blessed and glorious, to whose perception and beholding there is no path (*alladhī lā sabīla ilā idrākihi wa-mushāhadatihi*).[85]

Having evoked kings' intermediary position between God and their subjects, Pseudo-Māwardī develops his theme of affinity with the pre-Islamic past. He cites al-Nābigha al-Dhubyānī and ^{c}Adī b. Zayd (d. *c.* 600), poets at the courts of the Ghassanids and Lakhmids, Arab dynasties whose lands in the northern regions of the Arabian peninsula had bordered on Byzantine and Sasanian territories. Of ^{c}Adī, he cites the celebrated verse in which the poet alluded to the Lakhmid ruler Nu^{c}mān as *rabb al-khawarnaq*, after the lavish palace that he had had constructed in the vicinity of al-Hira; Pseudo-Māwardī's audience would have associated the verse with the story of Nu^{c}mān's subsequent turn from worldliness to contemplation of life's brevity and the fleeting nature of royal power.[86]

Although his mirror is not a theological treatise, Pseudo-Māwardī repeatedly assumes or invokes Mu^{c}tazilite doctrines in his arguments. In this passage, he alludes to the theological question of the impossibility of perceiving or beholding God ('the Lord . . . to whose perception and beholding there is no path'). His assertion that neither is possible coincides with the theological position of the Muᶜtazilite theologian al-Kaᶜbī, who held that vision (*ruʾya*) in any context presupposed corporeality, and could not therefore be applied to God. Al-Kaᶜbī, who was resident and teaching in Khurasan at the time when Pseudo-Māwardī wrote, reasoned that vision constituted perception (*idrāk*), which was accordingly also impossible in the case of God.[87] The theologian al-Māturīdī, who lived in Samarqand in the same period and directed most of his criticism of the Muᶜtazilites against specific doctrines under debate in that city, argued against al-Kaᶜbī in this matter; he asserted that vision was not of a single kind and that the meaning of perception was 'comprehension of the limits (or definitions) of things' (*al-wuqūf ᶜalā ḥudūd al-shayʾ*).[88] The issue proceeds in part from the interpretation of Moses' Qurʾānic prayer, 'O my Lord! Show me (your self), so that I might look upon You' (*rabbi arinī anẓur ilayka*) (7: 143).[89] Pseudo-Māwardī's presentation of the Arabs' 'lords of the earth' illustrates his engagement in the theological controversies of his milieu; his language in this passage, as in several other instances, demonstrates his alignment with the doctrines of al-Kaᶜbī.

Pseudo-Māwardī continues:

> On account of the grandeur of the state of kings, the lexicographers (*ahl al-lugha*) have called the king a 'head' (*raʾs*), since they liken his place in relation to his subjects to the place of the head in relation to the body: all the limbs are subordinate (*musakhkhara*) to it and prepared to carry it; and because the body cannot survive without it and cannot stand upright other than with it; and because it is the part of the body in which the senses are combined, and without which the animal could not survive, there being no difference between the living animal and the dead, or the world of (inanimate) minerals, other than through the senses. The head is the source of the intellect and discrimination (*maᶜdan al-ᶜaql wa-l-tamyīz*),[90] by which God has favoured (*faḍḍala*) human beings over other animals.
>
> On this matter, the poet [ᶜAlī b. Jabala al-ᶜAkawwak, 160–213/776–828], praising Ḥumayd b. ᶜAbd al-Ḥamīd [al-Ṭūsī, d. 210/825],[91] said:
>
> > Men are a body; the Imam of Guidance[92]
> > Is a head, and you are the eye in the head.
>
> Another said:

> If the head were sound and straight, then
> Every foundation would stand on justice.

> A virtuous king of India said in a testament (*ᶜahd*) that he composed for his son, 'Know, O my son, that this testament (*waṣiyya*) of mine to you, and this charge (*ᶜahd*) of mine to you, offers the similitude of a man, alive and upright. His head is you, O ruler (*ayyuhā l-wālī*); his heart is your vizier, his hands your assistants (*aᶜwān*), his legs your subjects. The spirit (*rūḥ*) that supports you is your justice (*ᶜadāla*), so protect this man as you protect yourself, and seek the well-being (*istaṣliḥ*) of his members as you seek the well-being of the limbs of your body.'[93]

In this section, Pseudo-Māwardī invokes the ancient and ubiquitous metaphor of the human body to describe the body politic.[94] The term *raʾs* resonates with the designation *raʾīs*, and finds a parallel in the English 'head' or 'captain'. The author's concern in this context is partly lexicographical; in the tenth and eleventh centuries the term *raʾīs* often denoted a leader of local stature, frequently a leading notable in a city or urban neighbourhood, rather than a figure at the highest level of power.[95]

Pseudo-Māwardī continues:

> An indication of the lofty stature of the king is that he has been called, in the terminology of religion and lexicography (*fī l-dīn wa-l-lugha*), *sulṭān*. The word *sulṭān*, in linguistic terms, denotes proof (*ḥujja*); God, may He be exalted and glorified, has said, 'Or have you a clear authority (*sulṭānun mubīnun*)? Then produce your writing, if you are truthful' (37: 156, 157); and [Solomon's speech, when he gathered the birds and found that the hoopoe was absent] 'I shall punish him most severely, or I shall slaughter him, unless he brings me a clear excuse (*bi-sulṭānin mubīnin*)' (27: 21). So God, blessed and mighty, made the just among kings a proof (*ḥujja*) over His creation. Similarly, the Imamiyya [also known as the Ithnā ᶜAshariyya or 'Twelvers', the major branch of the Shiᶜa] apply that which is related from the Prophet – 'The earth shall never be devoid of a proof (*ḥujja*)'[96] – to the immaculate imam (*al-imām al-maᶜṣūm*), on whom they call and to whose remembrance they are devoted. And on account of the lofty state of kings, the Muslims have called the most glorious authority in Islam

> (*al-sulṭān al-ajall fī l-Islām*) an imām, for he is among those whose example must be followed, whose action must be emulated, and whose command must be carried out.
>
> These paramount concepts (*hādhihi l-maᶜānī al-jalīla*) constitute the indications of the noble names by which kings are distinguished. We have chosen, however, in this book of ours, among all of these names, to designate the ruler by the term 'king' (*malik*), since it is the most prevalent and common, and the most lucid and straightforward name.[97]

Pseudo-Māwardī begins this section with a discussion of the term *sulṭān*, which he occasionally employs, albeit less frequently than *malik*, *amīr* and *sāʾis*, as a designation of highest office as well as in the abstract sense of 'power' or 'authority' in the course of his book.[98] It is possible that these usages reflect a later recension of the text, especially since Pseudo-Māwardī's explication of the term suggests its abstract meaning rather than its (later) application to a specific individual. His train of thought moves from *sulṭān* to another term that carried abstract and personified meanings, *ḥujja*, 'proof', and from this term he moves to the term *imām*. His acknowledgement of the Imami Shiᶜite concept of the *imām maᶜṣūm*, divinely preserved from sin and error, is notable. From the Imamiyya's understanding of the term *imām*, Pseudo-Māwardī passes to its general meaning for the Muslim community as a whole. Possibly in a reflection of his Muᶜtazilite perspective, he interprets the term in an abstract sense, as 'the most glorious authority in Islam', and does not identify it with a particular individual, family or group. It is striking that while he refers to individual caliphs, he devotes no attention, at any point in his mirror, to the office of the caliphate.

Contemporary and later writers employed the term *ḥujja* when they sought to emphasise the divinely sanctioned nature of political authority. The poet Rūdakī (d. 329/940–1), who enjoyed the patronage of several rulers, including Naṣr II, and was Pseudo-Māwardī's contemporary, composed a Persian panaegyric in praise of the Saffarid Abū Jaᶜfar Aḥmad b. Muḥammad (r. 311–52/923–63), whom he lauded with the claim *ḥujjat-i yektā khudāy va-sāyeh-yi ūst*, 'He is proof of [the existence of] the One God, and he is His shadow', and to whom, moreover, he declared obedience to be a religious requirement.[99] Niẓām al-Mulk would also invoke humanity's need for a proof or authority, and employ the religiously laden term to emphasise the subjects' duty of obedience.[100]

Pseudo-Māwardī concludes the passage reproduced above with the indication that in his milieu, at least in Arabic, *malik* was the most commonly employed designation for the ruler(s) with whom he was concerned. His observation finds copious attestation in contemporary sources. The anonymous author of *Ḥudūd al-ᶜālam* and al-Bīrūnī referred to the Samanid rulers as *mulūk Khurāsān*. The use of the term *malik* was not restricted to the Samanid amirs, however; the author of *Ḥudūd al-ᶜālam* refers not only to the 'King of the East' (*malik-i mashriq*), by whom he intended the '[a]mīr of Khurasan', but also to the contemporary *mulūk-i aṭrāf*, rulers of the provinces.[101] Paul found that the titles *amīr*, *sulṭān*, *malik* and *pādshāh* (Persian, king) might all apply to the Samanid senior amirs, for whom, significantly, no title or designation was exclusively reserved; at the same time, the titles *amīr*, *sulṭān*, *malik* and *dihqān*, and in Persian also *pādshāh* and *mihtār*, were employed to designate local potentates and princes.[102] The fluidity amongst these terms reflects the fluidity of power, variously shared and negotiated among persons at different social levels and different degrees of removal. Narshakhī states that after his victory over ᶜAmr and the expansion of the Samanid territories to encompass Khurasan, Transoxiana, Turkistan, Sind va-Hind and Gurgan, Ismāᶜīl appointed an amir to each of his cities.[103] Pseudo-Māwardī evokes, as a model for his royal audience, the figure of the exemplary ruler, to whom the text refers as, in a majority of instances, *al-malik* (frequently in such formulations as *al-malik al-ḥāzim*, 'the resolute king', and *al-malik al-fāḍil*, 'the virtuous king'). Pseudo-Māwardī also employs the term in the plural, especially to refer to kings of the past (*al-mulūk al-awwalūn*, *al-mulūk al-mutaqaddimūn*), and in a contemporary context in the term *abnāᵓ al-mulūk*, the 'sons of kings', a term likely to encompass not only the ruling king's children, but also the offspring of local dynastic families. In a clear indication that the term was in use in his immediate environment, he refers to '. . . the kings of our own time among the people of our religious community, the rulers of the people of our *qibla*' (that is, the people who pray in the direction of Mecca, or co-religionists) (*mulūk zamāninā hādha min ahl millatinā wa-wulāt ahl qiblatinā*).[104] This passage suggests that Pseudo-Māwardī intended his book to reach the 'kings of our time', and it is likely that he included in this group the Samanid family, especially Amir Naṣr II, and, as a secondary audience, the provincial rulers, the *mulūk al-aṭrāf.*

It is directly after this inventory of terms related to the exercise of power that Pseudo-Māwardī situates and describes the principle and practice of *khidma*. His extended presentation of the topic proceeds from his discussion of the king's relationship to his subjects:

> It is part of the grandeur of kings' condition, and an element of their precedence over their subjects and over the various categories of people (*ṭabaqāt al-nās*), that all of the subjects under the king's authority, while they are of a kind with him in form (*ṣūra*) and resemble him in nature (*khilqa*),[105] and while he is not burdened with their acquisition or purchase, their station in relation to him is in many respects that of chattels (*maḥall al-mamlūkīn*). Pertinent to this matter is what God, great and glorious, has said in the story of Sheba: 'I found a woman ruling them (*tamlikuhum*), and she has been given (a generous portion) of all things, and she has a great throne' (Q. 27: 23). For 'to rule' is derived etymologically from 'property' (*milk*), and not from 'sovereignty' (*mulk*). Furthermore, the subjects can be divided into two parts: those whose place in relation to the king is that of a material (*mādda*), and those whose place in relation to him is that of a tool (*āla*). He uses the latter to work the material according to whatever he wants, desires, wishes and envisages. Then he produces from the material a form (*ṣūra*) that reflects his work according to the measure of his skill in the craft and his ability to accomplish his purpose (*gharaḍ*) and intention (*niyya*).
>
> This is what God has made obligatory on all people regarding prompt obedience to the just ruler (*al-imām al-ʿādil*) and the virtuous king: sincere support and respect for his exalted position, and refraining from opposition to him, as long as he obeys God and adheres to His precepts (*farāʾiḍ*) and statutes (*ḥudūd*). For He has said, 'O you who believe! Obey God, obey the Messenger, and those in authority among you' (Q. 4: 59). And the Prophet (upon whom be peace) said, 'Obey the imam, even if he is an Ethiopian slave, as long as he obeys God among you'. He also said, 'He who strives to subdue a *sulṭān* will himself be subdued by God'.
>
> These are a few of the many ways by which God has elucidated the virtues of kings, the elevation of their stations, the exaltedness of their ranks, the

loftiness of their standing, the extent of their gravity, the greatness of God's favours (*ni*ᶜ*am Allāh*) to them, and the varieties of His bounties (*funūn ayādīhi*) to them. So it is incumbent in all categories of cases that no one should be more thankful towards God, more attentive in upholding the execution of His precepts and commands, in caring for that which has been vouchsafed to his care and protecting that which has been entrusted for his protection, than kings should be – since this behaviour constitutes the contractual part (*al-ma*ᶜ*hūd*) of their actions to those of their bondsmen and servants over whose affairs God has placed them in control (*al-ma*ᶜ*hūd min af*ᶜ*ālihim bi-man mallakahum Allāhu umūrahum min* ᶜ*abīdihim wa-khadamihim*).

They should also be most thankful because, if they remember God's bounties (*ni*ᶜ*am Allāh*) to the weakest of His creatures and His kindness (*iḥsān*) to the least of His bondsmen, they will not find a favour that approaches it in worth in the kindness that creatures display one to another, nor any favour comparable in value. Moreover when kings give to their subjects, they give them the wealth of others as a trust (*wadī*ᶜ*atan*) to them, or they grant them a share in authority over others as a loan (ᶜ*āriyatan*), placed temporarily in their hands. Indeed, kings' gifts are quick to decline and rapidly disappear; sometimes they harm their recipients, and in any case they bring them no benefit; and sometimes they entail their perdition in the world and in religion, at their end and their beginning. Moreover kings are not satisfied with them unless the occasions for their favours towards them increase in number, the grounds for their benefits become more apparent, and their subordinates become ever more thankful and quicker in their obedience to them. They should undergo greater ordeals, become more punctilious in upholding kings' rights (*ḥuqūq*), and in observing their orders and prohibitions. At the same time kings consider that whoever falls short in a matter, or alters, exchanges or is ungrateful for a benefit (*man qaṣṣara fī shay*ʾ*in minhu aw ghayyara aw badala aw kafara ni*ᶜ*matan*) or belittles a favour (*ghamaṭa ṣanī*ᶜ*atan*) deserves their dislike, deprivation, punishment and abandonment, especially anyone who persists in such behaviour, and commits disobedience in an open fashion. This is a balance (*mīzān*) in which the intelligent person should weigh that which occurs between himself and his Creator, and a model (*mithāl*) that he should emulate, since it is in the visible realm (*fī l-shāhid*) according to that which we have mentioned, and their treatment of those beneath them is according to that which we have clarified.

If kings are mindful of God's bounties to them, His benefits to them in exalting their status and magnifying their authority, His delegating to them the governance (*siyāsa*) of His servants and the cultivation of His lands, His assigning them to lasting dominion and endless felicity, with the generality of His bounties (*ᶜāmmat niᶜamihi*) the number of which cannot be counted, and their distinguishing quality of (*khāṣṣat[u]hā*) the grandeur of which cannot be described – it is incumbent upon them that they should fear the consequence of ingratitude (*kufrān*) and the recompense of disobedience (*ᶜiṣyān*). It is furthermore incumbent on the subject who craves increase (*ziyāda*), desires the overlooking (*ihmāl*) (of his shortcomings) and a reprieve (*mudda*), and wishes for excellent success (*ḥusn al-tawfīq*) and assistance (*al-maᶜūna*) in this world and a fine reward in the world to come, that he should persevere and strive in rendering gratitude and obedience, and shun ingratitude and disobedience; for the recompense of thankfulness is kindness and increase (*al-iḥsān wa-l-mazīd*), while the recompense of ingratitude is punishment, rejection (*tankīr*), abandonment and reproach. This (point) becomes firmly impressed upon persons who know God (*hādhā alladhī yalzamu l-ᶜārifīn bi-llāh*), and it is indispensable for persons who are brought close to Him and who are mindful of His bounties (*ᶜalā l-muqarrabīn bihi wa-l-dhākirīn li-ālāʾihi*), and persons who confess the truth of His Book and His Verses, for God, great and glorious, has said: 'If you are grateful, I shall give you more, and if you are ungrateful, then my punishment is severe' (14: 7); and He said, 'God does not change a people's state until they change that which is in themselves' (13: 11). He said, 'We exchanged for their two gardens two gardens bearing bitter fruit (*akl khamṭ*), the tamarisk and a small amount of the lote-tree (*sadr*). In this way, We recompensed them [the people of Sheba] for their ingratitude. Do We punish any other than the ungrateful?' (34: 16, 17).[106]

While emphasising the common humanity of king and subjects, Pseudo-Māwardī proceeds with his lexicographical exploration of royal stature. His likening of the subjects to objects in the king's possession is reminiscent of certain passages ascribed elsewhere to Sasanian provenance; the Arabic rendering of the Sasanian *ᶜAhd Ardashīr* instructs its audience that the ruler's authority lies over the subjects' bodies rather than their hearts; the littérateur Ibn Qutayba (213–76/828–89) adduces a quotation from a 'Book of *Āʾīn*', a book that detailed appropriate conduct and derived from a Middle Persian model, in which an unidentified Persian king declaims that he owns his subjects' bodies, not their intentions.[107] Pseudo-Māwardī makes clear, however, that the ruler's 'possession' of the subjects involves inalienable responsibilities that amount, in effect, to limits of his power. God has placed kings in authority over their subjects, but their authority consists of an entrustment, not an entitlement, and still less the disposition of ownership. Invoking the vocabulary of rightful claims, already employed in reference to God, he proceeds to describe the reciprocal obligations of king and subjects. Kings are entitled to their subjects' obedience, but only if they are just, and only if obedience to them conforms to the prior claims due from each human being, including the king, towards God. In accordance with Muᶜtazilite teachings, the absolute claim of obedience to God circumscribes the obedience to which kings can lay claim from their subjects, who, if they exercise reason, will weigh the demands of each 'king' in the balance. When Pseudo-Māwardī cites the well-known ḥadīth concerning the ruler's right to obedience, he adds the qualifying requirement that the ruler obey God.[108] Developing the associations of his recent reference to *rabb al-khawarnaq*, he emphasises the ephemeral and contingent nature of royal power. Kings are temporary custodians of wealth and favours, themselves fleeting, and their value lessened if, when bestowed, they entail a moral risk for the beneficiaries.

The language of favour (*niᶜma, iḥsān*), bestowed on the *khādim* by the person served by him, the *makhdūm*, in exchange for obedience, figures prominently in Pseudo-Māwardī's depiction of the relationship between kings and God on the one hand, and subjects and kings, on the other. It is a mark of divine favour to be 'brought close' to Him, and the same term, in this context, evokes the spatiality of courts in which, in a mark of royal favour, persons placed closest to the king possessed the highest rank. From the *khādim*'s point of view, the appropriate response to the bestowal of favour is gratitude (*shukr, shukrān*); ingratitude (*kufr, kufrān*) incurs the withdrawal of benefits, and risks severing the relationship altogether.[109] Pseudo-Māwardī's quotation of Q 34: 16–17 is particularly apt, since it refers to the divine punishment that met the ungrateful people of Sheba, who rejected God's prophets and in consequence suffered a deluge that occasioned the destruction of their dams. As Pseudo-Māwardī explains, the relationship of *khidma* also carried with it the expectation of 'increase' (*ziyāda*); both parties anticipated as a corollary of the constant renewal of the relationship a constant increase in the satisfaction of their rightful claims, the king by means of demonstrations of loyalty and gratitude. Pseudo-Māwardī's use of the term *maᶜhūd* evokes the concept of the obligation or covenant (*ᶜahd*); related meanings of the root *ᶜ-h-d* recur in the Qurᵓān, and contributed substantially to the evolution of the vocabulary of social relationships.[110] In specifically political contexts, Niẓām al-Mulk would employ terms such as *naw-ᶜahd*, for those newly pledged to obedience, and *bad-ᶜahdī*, for breach of pledged obedience.[111]

Throughout this eloquent presentation of the reciprocal responsibilities of kings and their subjects, Pseudo-Māwardī portrays the ruler–subject relationship as a replication of the divine–royal relationship. The theme of the ruler's duty to emulate the divine model provides a comprehensive conceptual foundation for *Naṣīḥat al-mulūk* in many respects. Pseudo-Māwardī articulates the relationship between the ruler and his subordinates with references to scriptural categories. The divinely ordained and natural order is also, however, comprehensible to reason and perceptible to the senses. As a result, Pseudo-Māwardī's exposition proceeds according to an independent logic in which he describes the social and political patterns of his environment. His description of the mutual obligations and expectations of *khidma* illuminates the conceptual as well as the social–cultural context in which Ḥusayn b. ᶜAlī and Aḥmad b. Sahl, powerful figures whose service to the Samanid amirs had endured over decades, eventually rebelled. The ties of *khidma* required continual renewal; Naṣr II, in the estimation of these long-standing 'servants', had failed to maintain them. If the balance of *khidma* and *niᶜma* was disturbed, the bond lost its compelling force.[112]

The Title 'Amir'

In his presentation of the language associated with the royal office, Pseudo-Māwardī, somewhat surprisingly, does not use the term *amīr*. The omission is the more striking since he employs the term quite frequently, especially in the plural form *umarāʾ*, in the course of his book. He often uses it as an apparent synonym for *malik*, as in the phrase, 'the wealth of God that is in the hands of kings and amirs' (*al-mulūk wa-l-umarāʾ*).[113] In another instance, Pseudo-Māwardī avers that he has located numerous apposite sayings from kings, caliphs and amirs to support the arguments of his book.[114] A similar association, in which amirs appear among the holders of authority whose examples are instructive and worthy of imitation, occurs in his discussion of the divisions of the religious sciences, where he adds to his description of the transmission of Prophetic materials knowledge of the foundations of the religious community and the established practices (*sunan*) of its caliphs, the governance of its amirs and the teachings of its scholars (*sunan khulafāʾihā wa-siyāsat umarāʾihā wa-aqāwīl ʿulamāʾihā*).[115] Elsewhere, Pseudo-Māwardī mentions 'the virtuous kings, intelligent imams and trustworthy amirs' (*al-mulūk al-fuḍalāʾ wa-l-aʾimma al-ʿuqalāʾ wa-l-umarāʾ al-umanāʾ*), who provide a model (*qudwa*), and whose pronouncements (*aqāwīl*) and paths (*madhāhib*) constitute a proof (*ḥujja*) for those who wish to follow.[116] Where in this fashion he groups amirs with kings and caliphs, it is probably the senior amirs and other leading members of the dynastic family, such as Isḥāq, that he intends.

In another set of examples, Pseudo-Māwardī uses the term *amīr* with particular reference to Khurasan. When, as indicated in Chapter 1, he turns from his discussion of selected caliphs to rulers who held authority in the eastern regions, he refers to the latter as *al-umarāʾ min wulāt Khurāsān*.[117] With explicit reference to the Samanid context, he describes Naṣr I b. Aḥmad, as previously indicated, as 'one of the religiously observant and austere *umarāʾ*'.[118] In most cases, Pseudo-Māwardī appears to use the term *amīr* in reference to the senior members of the Samanid dynastic family. In one instance, he observes that adjudication in matters of religious law falls among the responsibilities of the amir: 'Sometimes the amir is required to lead the prayer, or receives a written enquiry regarding one of the obligatory and voluntary charitable taxes (*zakawāt* and *ṣadaqāt*), or matters of marriage and matrimony are brought up to him, or sales and inheritances, and the remaining types of ordinances (*sāʾir funūn al-aḥkām*)',[119] a description that is compatible with the public involvement in the religious life of the Muslim community evident among Pseudo-Māwardī's favoured generation of Samanid amirs, the sons of Aḥmad b. Asad. In these more specific usages of the term *amīr*, Pseudo-Māwardī probably intends the leading Samanid amirs, including those who held major regional and city-based appointments. His application of the term is consistent with Paul's observation that the title *amīr* embraced the Samanid senior amir, local rulers and municipal authorities; in its application to individuals other than the senior amir, it connoted limited dependence on the central power.[120]

This chapter, the first of a pair that seek to relate Pseudo-Māwardī's depiction of kingship and governance to other contemporary and near-contemporary portrayals across a range of genres, has concentrated on his explication of terms and his conception of the place and role of kings in a cosmos that reflects the wisdom of its Creator. By integrating Pseudo-Māwardī's voice into the existing corpus of materials germane to the earlier Samanid period, I seek to convey his participation in the multifaceted discourse of his time and region. In a study of Pseudo-Māwardī's presentation of the social and political mechanisms by which the king effected his rule, Chapter 4 continues in this endeavour.

4

Intermediaries and Networks

In continuation of Part II's examination of the composition and character of the Samanid state, this chapter explores Pseudo-Māwardī's presentation of social groupings beneath the level of kings, amirs and their immediate servants and assistants. It considers Pseudo-Māwardī's explicit and implicit treatment of the constituent categories among the *khāṣṣa* and the *ᶜāmma*, the élites and the common people, the king's inner and outer public,[1] and seeks to convey his perception of their relationships to royal sovereignty and their mediating functions in a diffuse political system. The most pertinent discussions fall in Pseudo-Māwardī's sixth and seventh chapters, devoted to the governance of the *khāṣṣa* and *ᶜāmma*, respectively. Incidental information appears throughout the book, and materials drawn from more than one chapter will be addressed.

The Samanid dynasty's ability to endure depended on the periodically active support and participation of the region's multiple communities and constituencies. The maintenance of this support, whether active or implicit, entailed, beneath the levels of central and regional dynastic power, the engagement of a diverse set of localised holders of authority, who performed the functions of intermediaries between the rulers and the populations in given localities. While hierarchical in appearance, the Samanid system of rule depended on the networks of these local figures, whose episodic challenges to Samanid authority the amirs were only partially and on some occasions able to accommodate and contain. Jürgen Paul has argued that for long periods of time, it was such intermediaries, with their associates and extended families, who possessed and exercised power; the Samanids, and the Abbasid caliphate in Baghdad still more remotely, represented, at most, a symbolic power.[2]

Social Categories and Office Holders in *Naṣīḥat al-mulūk*

Pseudo-Māwardī, in his chapter devoted to governance of the *ᶜāmma*, describes the relationship of royal sovereignty to the multiplicity of groupings among the subjects in the following terms:

> It should be known that the king's adornment lies in the well-being (*ṣalāḥ*) of the subjects. The more affluent and distinguished the subjects, and the nobler their condition in terms of religion and the world, and the more prosperous and extensive his kingdom (*mamlaka*), the greater in power (*aᶜẓam sulṭānan*) and the more illustrious in repute (*ajall shaᵓnan*) the king; whereas the more base in state and dejected in mind the subjects, the more negligible in sovereignty, the more insignificant in income and demeaned in reputation is the king. For it is not suitable for the governing king to seek the prosperity of his station (*manzila*) by ruining the stations (*manāzil*) of the subjects, nor to amplify the contents of his treasuries (*khazāᵓin*) and the repositories of his wealth (*buyūt amwālihi*) by depleting and diminishing the houses (*buyūt*) of the common people.[3]
>
> His adornment and magnificence lie as much in the prosperity of the kingdom (*mamlaka*), the plenty of its revenue, the abundance of its wealthy (*aghniyāᵓ*), elders (*mashāyikh*), *dihqān*s (*dahāqīn*), scholars (*ᶜulamāᵓ*), jurists (*fuqahāᵓ*), men of (political) opinions (*dhawū l-ārāᵓ*),[4] its notables (*sarawāt*), judges (*ḥukkām*), ascetics (*nussāk*), philosophers (*ḥukamāᵓ*), and the categories of office holders and members of respected families (*aṣnāf dhawī l-marātib wa-l-manāqib*) among them, as in the prosperity of his castles (*quṣūr*), the lavishness of his palaces (*dūr*), the abundance of his horses, his troops (*junūd*), his servants (*khadam*) and his furnishings (*athāth*).
>
> Moreover, the might that he possesses against his enemies, derived from his subjects, who hear and obey him, are bound in love to him and defend him, is no weaker than the strength that he acquires through his assistants (*aᶜwān*) and troops (*junūd*) (*wa-laysa ᶜizzatuhu ᶜalā aᶜdāᵓihi bi-raᶜiyyatihi al-sāmiᶜa al-muṭīᶜa al-muḥibba lahu al-dhābba ᶜanhu bi-awhā min quwwatihi bi-aᶜwānihi wa-junūdihi*). The fear that he might harbour towards his enemies, those who are external to his kingdom as well as those who

> oppose him in his particular religious community (*milla*) and the community at large (*umma*), should be no more acute than his fear of the opposition of his subjects' hearts. Rather, the occasions for fear that reach him on account of his subjects are more extensive, more far-reaching, more consequential and more decisive.[5]

In this passage, Pseudo-Māwardī, in an evocation of the contingency of the king's power, divides the constituencies of the kingdom into two contrasting sets. The division corresponds to categories of persons directly dependent upon the ruler and subject to his command, on the one hand, and categories whose service was primarily voluntary and negotiable, on the other. The first category, the *khāṣṣa*, enjoyed the privileges that accompanied a relationship with the king, but were subject to its constraints. The second category, the *ᶜāmma*, encompassed categories of various economic and social levels, united in their lack of direct dependence on the king (they were, of course, involved in other relationships of dependency). Pseudo-Māwardī impresses on his royal ruler that the second set of persons were no less vital to his enduring sovereignty and the stability of the polity than the first.

Pseudo-Māwardī presents two versions of his binary division, represented in the second and third paragraphs of the translation. In his first version, he constructs a first set of the king's *junūd*, 'troops', and his *khadam*; in the second iteration, he constructs a parallel set of the ruler's *aᶜwān*, 'assistants' and *junūd*. Jointly, then, Pseudo-Māwardī links the king's troops, *khadam* and *aᶜwān* (the substitution of *aᶜwān* for *khadam* in this second passage suggests that the terms are virtually synonymous in this instance). In an idea similar to that explored in his discussion of *milk*, Pseudo-Māwardī describes these groupings as 'his', and he mentions them, in the first instance, in the same set as the ruler's horses, palaces and royal furnishings.

The second set of categories consists, in Pseudo-Māwardī's first iteration, of the wealthy (*aghniyāʾ*), elders (*mashāyikh*), *dihqān*s (*dahāqīn*), scholars (*ᶜulamāʾ*), jurists (*fuqahāʾ*), political advisers (*dhawū l-ārāʾ*), notables (*sarawāt*), judges (*ḥukkām*), ascetics (*nussāk*), philosophers (*ḥukamāʾ*), and persons 'possessed of ranks' (office holders) and meritorious status (persons of illustrious lineage) (*aṣnāf dhawī l-marātib wa-l-manāqib*). In his second iteration of the two contrasting groups, Pseudo-Māwardī does not list categories, but describes the groups to which he refers as the ruler's subjects, who heed his word, obey him, love him and defend him. This second set consists of categories that are separate and apart from the king's troops and *khadam*, and largely independent of his direct control; Pseudo-Māwardī presents these groups as 'belonging' not to the king, but to the kingdom. In this set, the list of categories on whose well-being and cooperation the king depends consists of persons whose status derives from wealth, inherited status, status acquired through learning and the cultivation of the intellect, esteemed ways of life and outlooks, and professional rank. They include, probably, the governors of cities and their subordinates; the principal members of local landowning families, including the still prominent and self-conscious group of *dihqān*s (pl. *dahāqīn*); the leading religious scholars, judges and other prominent members of the urban élites; by inference, if Pseudo-Māwardī's *dhaw[ū] . . . l-manāqib* correspond to the senior members of eminent families, the leading representatives of ᶜAlid families, whose social stature had risen throughout the ninth century;[6] and ascetics, who enjoyed high esteem among broad segments of the population. These groups functioned as intermediaries between the agents of royal authority and the population. Some of these categories, such as judges, held appointments, but required the consensus of the population in order to discharge their duties in an effective manner; others, such as ascetics, held no official appointment, but possessed authority on the basis of their standing in their communities and the loyalty of the local people.[7] The very length of Pseudo-Māwardī's list of categories whose cooperation the king requires suggests the broad diffusion of authority among a diverse and inclusive set of constituencies.

Categories Bound in Personal Service to the Ruler

Pseudo-Māwardī's first set of categories, distinguished from the longer lists of groups with whom the ruler did not interact in a direct manner, comprised the *khadam*, *a*ᶜ*wān* and *junūd*, troops. Since Chapter 3 included some discussion of the ruler's *khadam* and *a*ᶜ*wān*, it is the ruler's *junūd* that receive primary attention in the ensuing section. The soldiers who constituted the Samanid armies reflected several of the diverse groupings within the Samanid polity. Over the course of the Samanid era, the amirs' personal and standing troops comprised increasing numbers of *mamālīk*, from whom the rulers commanded personal loyalty as part of the system of mutual rights and obligations described in Chapter 3.[8] Most examples of this shift demonstrate its prevalence among the highest ranks of the amirs' military appointees; the extent to which the lower levels of the soldiery changed in composition is less evident.[9]

The most striking indications of change appear among the amirs' appointments to the highest ranks of their military and governmental staff. Among the ranks of the governors, by the mid-tenth century, the amirs had replaced, or attempted to replace, members of the Samanid dynastic family and other leading families with *mamālīk*. In the following century, Niẓām al-Mulk would cite with approval the words of an unidentified Persian poet:

> One obedient slave is better than thirty thousand sons;
> For the latter seek the death of the father, while the former seeks the glory of his lord.[10]

Paul has suggested that Ismāᶜīl b. Aḥmad already sought to diminish his dependence on the *dahāqīn*, whose service, as their inclusion in Pseudo-Māwardī's second set of groupings implies, was voluntary, by building an army led by his personal retainers.[11] Aḥmad II's appointment of the *mamlūk* Sīmjūr to the province of Sistan represents one of the earlier instances of this trend. Naṣr II, as previously mentioned, appointed the free-born Muḥtājids of Chaghaniyan to the governorship of Nishapur; but Naṣr's successor Nūḥ I b. Naṣr (r. 331–43/943–54) endeavoured to replace Abū ᶜAlī Chaghānī with Ibrāhīm b. Sīmjūr, and elicited the vigorous resistance of Abū ᶜAlī. The contest that ensued, in which Abū ᶜAlī was ultimately successful, illustrated the vying for status among the free-born commanders who belonged to leading local families and the ruler's *mamālīk*, as well as the limits of Nūḥ's power.[12] The amirs' increasing appointments, by the middle of the century, of *mamālīk* to positions of high rank initiated the process whereby, in the later Samanid period, Turkish *mamlūk*s would eventually seize control of the polity and inaugurate a succession of Turkish-led dynasties in the eastern regions.[13]

The geographers al-Iṣṭakhrī and Ibn Ḥawqal, whose reports reflect conditions roughly contemporary with the proposed dating for *Naṣīḥat al-mulūk*, remarked in an instructive manner on distinctive aspects of the Samanid military forces. According to their observations, whereas most armies scattered in times of defeat or crisis, with the result that it was extremely difficult to reassemble them, the Samanid armies did not disperse. The geographers attributed this distinguishing quality of the Samanid armies to their being composed of two groupings: 'Turkish slaves, acquired by the kings' wealth and purchased from their regions', and free men and *dihqāns*, whose residences, lands, families and neighbours were well known (and thereby traceable) (*fa-inna juyūshahum al-atrāk al-mamlūkūn riqqan bi-mālihim wa-sharwā manāṭiqihim wa-min al-aḥrār wa-l-dahāqīn man yuᶜrafu dāruhu wa-makānuhu wa-āluhu wa-jīrānuhu*), so that even if they dispersed, they returned to a single, and known, place.[14] Al-Iṣṭakhrī's and Ibn Ḥawqal's characterisations of the Samanid armies suggest that in the first half of the tenth century, the contributions of free men and *dahāqīn* in the Samanids' armies remained substantial. The text of *Naṣīḥat al-mulūk*, which mentions the ruler's *junūd* in a separate category from the *dahāqīn*, suggests a similar stage in the shifting composition of the amir's forces. Pseudo-Māwardī refers frequently to the king's *junūd*, but almost never mentions his *mamālīk*. When on one occasion he refers to the latter category, it is in the context of the education of the king's *ghilmān*, with whom Pseudo-Māwardī linked the *mamālīk*; this linking is consistent with accounts of the assassination in 301 /914 of Aḥmad II, in which the terms *mamālīk* and *ghilmān* are used. Despite this occurrence, Pseudo-Māwardī provides no indication of the potential intervention of *mamālīk* or *ghilmān* in political affairs.[15]

In the second iteration of the categories bound in personal service to the ruler, Pseudo-Māwardī refers to the ruler's *aᶜwān* and *junūd*. He invokes this pairing on repeated occasions throughout his text, including, as noted in Chapter 3, in the context of God's appointment of His angels.[16] When Pseudo-Māwardī applies the same language to designate primary categories within the ranks of the ruler's *khāṣṣa*, he uses this resonance to evoke their distinction and proximity, in spatial and metaphorical terms. Pseudo-Māwardī contrasts these two categories with the king's 'subjects', who are bound to heed and obey him, but also 'love and defend' him. He avers that the subjects, under these conditions, contribute no less substantially to the king's might against his 'enemies' (external or internal) than his professional armies. Pseudo-Māwardī's reference to the subjects' willingness to provide military defence on the king's behalf, when need arises, out of 'love', suggests the voluntary nature of their service. Unlike these categories, the passage implies, the *a*ᶜ*wān* and *junūd* are obliged to serve by virtue of their relationships with the ruler; their services formed part of the ruler's rightful claims over them.

In *Naṣīḥat al-mulūk*, the term *a*ᶜ*wān*, literally 'assistants', usually appears in contexts that suggest closeness to the ruler. As in the case of the terms *khadam*, *chākar* and *bandeh*, reviewed in Chapter 3, the term *a*ᶜ*wān* invites consideration of possible continuities with late antique Iran and western Asia.[17] The term frequently appears in Arabic renderings of Middle Persian texts, and suggests a group closely associated with the king's person; examples appear in the ᶜ*Ahd Ardashīr* ('Testament of Ardashīr'),[18] the *Āʾīn* ('[Book of] Customs' or 'Regulations') of Ardashīr[19] and the ᶜ*Ahd Sābūr* ('Testament of Shāpūr'), all of which evoke the Sasanian period.[20] The continuing use of the term in the context of the courts of the early Islamic centuries is likely to reflect, if not a seamless continuity in practice, the degree to which the Iranian cultural heritage shaped the political culture and individuals' perceptions of their environment. In *Naṣīḥat al-mulūk*, the *a*ᶜ*wān* often appear, as in the current instance, with the *junūd*; elsewhere in the mirror, they appear with the *wuzarāʾ*. On one occasion, Pseudo-Māwardī quotes Ibn al-Muqaffaᶜ: 'Affairs cannot be conducted without viziers and assistants (*al-wuzarāʾ wa-l-a*ᶜ*wān*). Viziers and assistants are of no use without love and sincere counsel (*al-mawadda wa-l-naṣīḥa*), and love and counsel are of no use without sound judgement and probity' (*al-raʾy wa-l-*ᶜ*afāf*).[21] The passage confirms the associations of these *a*ᶜ*wān* with proximity to the king's person. Pseudo-Māwardī's pairings of the *a*ᶜ*wān* with *junūd*, on the one hand, and *wuzarāʾ*, on the other, implies the fluidity of 'military' and 'civilian' functions. This perception is consistent with Samanid conditions, in which viziers participated in campaigns and often supported large military contingents; a diverse set of individuals who were not professional soldiers took up arms on occasion, sometimes in defence of their cities and towns.[22]

Although he refers to historical incidents, including one that he describes as 'recent',[23] Pseudo-Māwardī supplies little information regarding the composition of the Samanid armies. He mentions neither *ribāṭāt*, the military outposts located at the margins of the steppe, nor 'volunteers'.[24] When he addresses military matters, it is in the context of his ninth chapter, devoted to 'the management of enemies and criminals' (*tadbīr al-aᶜdāᵓ wa-ahl al-jināyāt*). In this context, after a preface in which he emphasises the divine prohibition against bloodshed among God's creatures (*al-khalīqa wa-l-bashar*) and against the infliction of harm upon any person (*aḥad min al-nās*), Pseudo-Māwardī addresses the cases of the three Qurᵓānic categories of 'polytheists' (*mushrikūn*), rebels (*bāghūn*) and 'those who obstruct the roads'.[25] With regard to these categories, Pseudo-Māwardī notes the range of juristic opinion; to a large extent the effect of his discussion is to discourage, as far as possible, responses that would involve injury or the loss of life; as he writes elsewhere, 'kindness is more effective than violence'.[26] In treating the distinctions among the different categories of the king's enemies and the responses appropriate in different cases, he cites numerous maxims from Aristotle's correspondence with Alexander, several verses of poetry, and the precedents established by the Prophet's *sunna* and the actions recorded for the early caliphs. Especially with regard to the second category, that of rebels, it is above all ᶜAlī's actions to which Pseudo-Māwardī, like numerous other authorities, refers.[27] He discusses ᶜAlī's struggles against the Companions Ṭalḥa and al-Zubayr, both killed in the Battle of the Camel in 36/656, who, together with the Prophet's widow ᶜĀᵓisha (d. 58/678), challenged his leadership and suffered defeat; the Kharijites, who after initial support of ᶜAlī withdrew their allegiance in the face of his perceived willingness to compromise; and Muᶜāwiya, the governor of Damascus, positioned to avenge his kinsman ᶜUthmān's murder and become the first caliph of the Umayyad dynasty.[28] These historical figures represent different forms of rivalry and disobedience, and provide not merely illustrative examples but also conceptual tools for Pseudo-Māwardī's analysis. Like other commentators on the duties of the royal office, Pseudo-Māwardī holds the king responsible for external and internal defence, and criminal justice. As Volume II will show, he emphasises the conditions and limits that circumscribed the king's legitimate use of force, and he encourages restraint in a systematic manner. He instructs the king in explicit terms that neither he nor his representatives possessed the right to molest *ahl al-milla wa-l-dhimma*, the Muslim and non-Muslim communities who together comprised his subjects.[29]

Categories Whose Support of the Ruler was Voluntary

The categories of civilian and military were somewhat indeterminate during the Samanid period; especially in Transoxiana, cities, regions and even private individuals appear to have disposed of the means to assemble relatively large numbers of armed persons.[30] The early Samanid amirs depended extensively on the military support of these varied constituencies in order to augment their own troops. The capacity and readiness to provide material or moral support for the amir's campaigns, to represent him in matters of local governance, and to facilitate the collection of taxes probably all informed Pseudo-Māwardī's's second set of groupings.

Pseudo-Māwardī begins his enumeration of groups whose contentment and resultant cooperation were essential to the ruler with 'the wealthy' (*al-aghniyāʾ*).[31] Importantly, the term connotes financial means and, in a general sense, independence of need. According to al-Iṣṭakhrī and Ibn Ḥawqal, the wealthy people (*ahl al-tharwa, ahl al-amwāl*) of Transoxiana were distinctive in the largesse that they expended not for their own amusements, but for the numerous *ribāṭāt* and public works associated with *jihād*.[32] In some cases these projects are quite likely to have proceeded apart from Samanid sponsorship. The leadership and allegiances of groups involved in military undertakings in the Samanid era varied; the Samanid amirs inaugurated several campaigns, but the military activities of their subjects were not limited to these initiatives. It is likely that Pseudo-Māwardī's mention of 'the wealthy' early in his list arises in part from his perception of the Samanids' dependence on their economic power for the campaigns that they initiated. The 'wealthy people' who, according to the geographers' accounts, perhaps contributed to the funding for independent initiatives were also in a position to provide material support and recruits for the ruler's military undertakings.

Directly after the 'wealthy', Pseudo-Māwardī mentions the *mashāyikh*, a term that applied to loose groupings of distinguished persons, often elders or senior figures, particularly in urban settings. Pseudo-Māwardī's inclusion of these individuals as a category among the urban élites conveys their periodic assembly for specific reasons. The effectiveness of their mediation and endorsement in situations of great variety rendered their cooperation essential to the amirs. Narshakhī refers to *jamāʿatī az mashāyikh-i Nīshāpūr*, 'a group of the elders of Nishapur', whom ᶜAmr sent to Ismāᶜīl apparently in an effort to avoid hostilities.[33] The historian Ibn Ẓāfir reports that upon learning of the death of Aḥmad II, the *mashāyikh* of Samarqand supported Isḥāq b. Aḥmad's bid for the amirate and pledged allegiance to him. In another context, the same author refers to *al-mashāyikh al-ᶜaskariyya wa-l-muṭṭawwiᶜa*, translated by Treadwell as 'the generals among the standing army and the militia'.[34] In his *Tārīkh-i Bayhaq* (completed in 563/1167), a later work informed extensively by earlier sources, Ẓahīr al-Dīn ᶜAlī b. Zayd Bayhaqī, known as Ibn Funduq (*c.* 490–565/1097–1169) invokes the 'elders, notables and scholars of Khusrawjird' (*mashāyikh va-aᶜyān va-ᶜulamā-yi Khusrawjird*).[35] Al-Thaᶜālibī relates an episode in which the *mashāyikh* of Nishapur, including members of the wealthy and prominent Mīkālī family, who traced their lineage back to the Sasanian monarchs, responded to the discontent of the Amir Abū l-Ḥasan Ibn Sīmjūr, who oscillated between obedience and disobedience when instructed to travel to Fars.[36]

Pseudo-Māwardī's reference to the *dihqān*s early in his second set of social groupings attests to their prominence in the polity and their continuing particularity as a group. It supports the conjecture that he wrote *Naṣīḥat al-mulūk* in the earlier rather than the later part of the tenth century, and confirms his residence in the eastern rather than the western parts of Iran. The *dihqān*s, landed gentry or village landlords commonly described as having comprised the 'base' or 'backbone' of the Sasanian social structure, had survived the conquests of the seventh century and emerged as indispensable intermediaries between the local population and the ruling élite of the new polity, for which they performed essential administrative and fiscal functions.[37] In the eighth and ninth centuries, the *dihqān*s of Sogdia often appear as a distinctive group. Étienne de la Vaissière has found that Sogdians remained a substantial presence in Marv in the eighth century,[38] and the historian al-Yaᶜqūbī (d. 292/905 or later) attests to the numerous Sogdians engaged in commercial activities in Baghdad in the second half of the eighth century.[39] The Sogdians had also played a significant military role in the Abbasid state, especially under Caliph al-Maʾmūn.[40] Attesting to their identity as a distinct grouping, al-Iṣṭakhrī and Ibn Ḥawqal report that al-Marzubān b. T.r.k.s.fā was summoned to Iraq among 'a number of *dihqān*s from Sogdia' (*jumlat dahāqīn al-Sughd*).[41] Although the *dihqān*s lost their high status in Iraq and western Iran in the course of the ninth century, in the north-eastern regions they remained important actors in a variety of political, military, social and cultural functions at least throughout the first half of the tenth century, 'vigorous, powerful, well entrenched',[42] 'numerous and influential to an extent unknown in parts of the Islamic world further west'.[43]

In an indication of the prestige still attached to the designation in the lifetime of Pseudo-Māwardī, the Persian poet Rūdakī (d. 329/940–1), in a celebrated ode, described a banquet held at Naṣr II's court. Among the eminent persons assembled, Rūdakī distinguished an individual *dihqān*, Pīr-i Ṣāliḥ, who was seated with the free-born men of status (*ḥurrān*) in the presence of the amirs and the vizier Bal^camī.[44] *Dihqān*s appear among the religious scholars and transmitters of ḥadīth listed in *al-Qand fī dhikr ^culamā^ɔ Samarqand*.[45] Even the frequent association of the *dahāqīn* (pl. of *dihqān*) with arrogance, perpetuated in a ḥadīth that circulated in Transoxiana, perhaps attests in a pejorative fashion to their visibility and status.[46] Al-Tha^cālibī not only referred to the *dahāqīn* as a recognisable grouping, but also identified *dahqana*, the quality and function of the *dihqān*, alongside the functions of *salṭana* (authority), *tijāra* (commerce) and *imāra* (command, rulership).[47] Persons described as *dihqān*s exercised a lesser degree of independence than persons described by the title of *malik* or *amīr*, but still included on occasion individuals also described as 'kings of the provinces' or margraves (*mulūk al-aṭrāf*).[48] In early and even later tenth-century Nishapur, the status of *dihqān*, especially in combination with other factors, contributed significantly to the estimation of high social rank, as the examples of the Maḥmī family, who combined descent from Caliph ^cUthmān with the status of landed *dihqān*s, and the Ṣā^cidī family, who combined government service and scholarship with attachment to a *dihqān* family, demonstrate.[49] *Naṣīḥat al-mulūk* reflects a moment at which the *dahāqīn* still occupied a prominent and distinctive position in the polity and society.

Pseudo-Māwardī's inclusion of the *dahāqīn* in the set of groupings whose cooperation the ruler required, but could not compel is likely to connote in part their potential contributions to military campaigns. As locally established landowning families, the *dihqān*s were in a position to muster significant numbers of troops. Al-Iṣṭakhrī and Ibn Ḥawqal, in another pertinent observation, emphasised the *dahāqīn*'s importance as commanders of troops, and praised their loyal service.[50] Treadwell has stated that such references usually apply to 'client princes who fought for the Samanids and the other noblemen of high status, both Persians and Arabs, who led the free soldiers (as opposed to slaves) in the Samanid ranks'.[51] The long-standing nature of the *dihqāns*' connection with their lands also rendered them custodians of regional lore and customs. The preservation of ancient wisdom constituted a principal component in the cultural repertoire associated with the *dahāqīn*. In Volume II, I shall suggest that the *dihqāns*' cultural prominence contributed to the context that produced *Naṣīḥat al-mulūk*.[52]

Both of these characteristics, the military and the cultural, find an illustration in the first half of the tenth century in the previously mentioned figure of Aḥmad b. Sahl, who, according to the historian Gardīzī, belonged to the *dihqāns* of Jiranj, among the larger villages in the environs of Marv, where a particularly red breed of rose was named after his grandfather Kāmgār. Aḥmad participated extensively in the maintenance and governance of the Samanid domains. Gardīzī, who devotes a substantial portion of his account of the Samanid era to Aḥmad, reports that the *dihqān*, whose forefathers had served the Tahirids, under whom the Samanids had held office and whose customs they perpetuated when they reached their turn in power, served the successive amirs Ismāᶜīl, Aḥmad and Naṣr, and won victories on their behalf. Gardīzī further remarks on Aḥmad's noble Persian lineage (*az aṣīlān-i ᶜajam būd*, 'he was of noble Persian descent'), reputedly from Yazdagird-i Shahriyār (= Yazdagird III), last of the Sasanian kings, as well as his personal qualities: he was a man of sound judgement (*mardī bā-raʾy*), on whose advice Ismāᶜīl reportedly depended heavily and to whom he entrusted important matters.[53] In a suggestion of his involvement in the renewal of his region's Persian culture, it is reported that Aḥmad b. Sahl commissioned a certain Āzādsarv to collect the stories of the epic hero Rustam.[54] His brothers were skilled in the secretarial arts and astrology.[55] As noted in Chapter 3, between 303/914 and 307/919, Aḥmad governed in Balkh,[56] and it is quite likely that Abū Zayd al-Balkhī and Abū l-Qāsim al-Kaᶜbī associated with Aḥmad during these years, which preceded the latter's appointment as governor of Khurasan. A number of narratives convey the cordial relationship between Abū Zayd al-Balkhī and Aḥmad b. Sahl; in one example, the governor is favourably impressed by the philosopher's tact and good manners in using only his *kunya*, Abū Zayd, and avoiding the articulation of his own name, Aḥmad b. Sahl, in the ruler's presence, since the two men shared it.[57] It is possible that Pseudo-Māwardī was a member of this circle and acquainted with Aḥmad b. Sahl as well. He perhaps heard Aḥmad's accounts of the earlier Samanid amirs, and envisaged relationships such as that between Ismāʿīl and Aḥmad when he encouraged the ruler to consult selected members of his *khāṣṣa*, and to employ them as intermediaries in his contacts with the *ʿāmma*.[58]

Having, at Naṣr's request, subdued Ḥusayn b. ʿAlī's rebellion against Samanid authority, Aḥmad, as already said, also rebelled. Like Ḥusayn, Aḥmad, after decades of loyalty to the Samanid amirs, eventually considered his bond of obligation to have been severed. In Ibn al-Athīr's language, Naṣr had 'assured him of things that he did not fulfil' (*ḍamina lahu al-amīr Naṣr ashyāʾ lam yafi lahu bihā*).[59] In an indication of the sundering of his obligations to Naṣr, who had violated the principle of *wafāʾ*, Aḥmad omitted Naṣr's name from the oration (*khuṭba*) in the Friday prayer in Nishapur.[60] The episode perhaps marks the incipient change in the standing of the *dihqān*s in Khurasan and Transoxiana in the later Samanid period, when, due to deteriorating economic conditions in the rural areas, on the one hand, and the rise of Turkish *mamlūk*s, on the other, they appear in some cases to have become impoverished, and to have left their lands and fled to the cities.[61] The gradual disappearance of the title of *dihqān* from writers' accounts, however, did not necessarily indicate a thorough social and economic eclipse.[62] Recent research suggests that the heirs of the *dahāqīn*, under other titles, continued to exercise many of the social functions of their predecessors.[63]

Also included in Pseudo-Māwardī's list of categories among the *ʿāmma* are scholars and ascetics (*nussāk*). Not infrequently, individuals who belonged to these categories came from wealthy and highly regarded families, and their authority and standing were enhanced by intermarriage with similarly notable families. The renunciant Shaqīq al-Balkhī (d. 194/810), for example, was exceedingly wealthy: he owned 300 villages in Balkh, and possessed a fortune of 600,000 dirhams.[64] Scholars and renunciants (*zuhhād*, pl. of *zāhid*),[65] not always clearly distinguishable, increased their stature through their participation in networks supported through ties of marriage, study and association. The family members and students of Shaqīq, Ibrāhīm b. Adham (d. 166 /777–8) and Ḥātim al-Aṣamm (d. 237/851–2), all renunciants from Balkh, provide examples of such interconnections, which continually reinforced the standing of persons affiliated with the network.[66] Renunciants also derived authority and status from the loyalty and esteem that some of their members enjoyed among local populations. These individuals could make use of their social capital in a variety of arenas and for a variety of functions. Religious scholars possessed the authority to confer legitimacy on the ruler's undertakings, including his military campaigns; they also shaped the culture of the frontier and the broader society through their transmission of Prophetic ḥadīth related to *ghazw*, the episodic campaigns at the frontier, and cognate issues, such as death in battle and the afterlife.[67] Although numbers of 'volunteer' *ghāzī*s drawn to the frontier joined Samanid campaigns, it appears that religious scholars and renunciants (*zuhhād*), in a demonstration of the individually motivated pious behaviour for which Ibrāhīm b. Adham, as Chapter 5 will describe, provides an emblematic case, sometimes led *ghāzī* activities apart from Samanid leadership.[68] Their partially independent functions in a variety of military-related activities rendered the ruler's cultivation of these broader groupings essential for the maintenance of his rule. Scholars and renunciants could, moreover, turn the community's loyalty in various directions, including in public prayer on behalf of the ruler and his dynasty or, in occasional expressions of protest, in public prayer for the removal of a vizier, a ruler or a dynasty.[69] Their functions are also likely to have included fiscal responsibilities.

Pseudo-Māwardī refers to a category of *sarawāt* (pl. of *sariyy*), persons of high rank, possibly a reference to the *nuqabāʾ* (pl. of *naqīb*), leaders, of the ᶜAlid families,[70] and local leaders at the municipal level.[71] Treadwell has indicated that the amirs on occasion enlisted the military contributions of urban militias; the assistance of the *sarawāt* might perhaps have been required in such situations.[72]

Pseudo-Māwardī mentions *ḥukkām* (pl. of *ḥākim*), a term that might extend to local holders of power, but which in Pseudo-Māwardī's usage seems to suggest the primary meaning of 'jurists' or 'judges'. Ibn Funduq, who uses the term *ḥākim* in both its political and its juristic senses, employs the phrase 'the house of the Ḥākimīs', *khāndān-i Ḥākimīyān* (or *Funduqīyān*) to describe his own ancestors, who held judgeships and some other positions and bore the title of *Ḥākim*.[73] Paul, furthermore, notes the use of the term *ḥākim* for an individual, possibly in conjunction with or dependent on a judge, involved in compiling records regarding the distribution of water and taxation.[74]

Among the other groupings included in Pseudo-Māwardī's set of categories on whose voluntary cooperation the ruler depended are 'groups of those possessed of ranks and meritorious status' (*aṣnāf dhawī l-marātib wa-l-manāqib*). The *dhaw[ū] l-marātib* probably connoted office holders, including, perhaps, persons involved in the collection of revenue. Pseudo-Māwardī's term *dhawū l-manāqib* is likely to have designated members of the Prophet's lineage, and especially the ᶜAlids, descendants of the Prophet through Fāṭima and ᶜAlī. As Bulliet has stated, the ᶜAlids, by the late ninth century a prominent local élite in the cities of Khurasan, constituted 'a blood aristocracy without peer'; as the example of the Āl Zubāra of ninth-century Nishapur illustrates with particular clarity, the family of the Prophet enjoyed a widespread and increasing respect and veneration that transcended religious or political affiliations.[75] In Nishapur, Hamadan, Qum, Rayy and Samarqand, ᶜAlid families frequently combined their Prophetic genealogy with other kinds of social capital, such as marriage relations, wealth and scholarship.[76]

A Multi-confessional Society

A final aspect of the passage reproduced in the preceding pages concerns the relationship of the listed categories to confessional groups. A possible allusion to the multi-religious nature of the subject population appears in Pseudo-Māwardī's frequent pairing of the terms *milla* and *umma*. If the pairing sometimes arises from Pseudo-Māwardī's copious use of parallelism, it often seems that it connotes, or at least evokes in an abstract fashion, a distinction between the specifically Muslim community (the *milla*), on the one hand, and the multi-confessional community as a whole (the *umma*), on the other. Such a distinction would follow the inclusive sense of the term *umma* evident in certain Qurᵓānic passages, and in the Constitution of Medina, the document designed to govern the composite community formed after the *hijra*, or emigration of the Prophet and his followers from Mecca to Medina in 622.[77] Especially relevant, in view of the broad dissemination and continuous development of Ḥanafī teachings in Pseudo-Māwardī's region, is the conception of inter-confessional affinity associated with Abū Ḥanīfa (d. 150/767). The Ḥanafī text entitled 'The Learned and the Learner' (*al-ᶜĀlim wa-l-mutaᶜallim*), attributed to Abū Ḥanīfa, records the words: 'God Almighty sent His Prophet as a mercy (*raḥmatan*) to bridge separateness (*li-yajmaᶜa bihi al-furqa*) and to promote harmony (*li-yuzayyida l-ulfa*), not to divide allegiances (*li-yufarriqa l-kalima*) and instil discord'. In one version, the continuation of this text presents it as a reference to intra-Muslim relations; in another version, the passage appears without restriction to a particular group.[78] *Al-ᶜĀlim wa-l-mutaᶜallim* continues:

> Do you not know that the prophets, God's benedictions and peace be upon them all, were not committed to different religions (*ᶜalā adyānin mukhtalifa*)? Not every prophet among them ordered his people to abandon the religion of the prophet who was before him, because their religion was one (*li-anna dīnahum kāna wāḥidan*). Every prophet called (the people) to his own religious law (sharīᶜa) and forbade the law of the prophet who was before him, because their laws were many and various (*li-anna sharāʾiᶜahum kathīra mukhtalifa*); on this matter God Almighty said, 'We have made for each of you a religious law (*shirᶜa*) and a path (*minhāj*); and had God willed, He would have made you one community' (*la-jaᶜalakum ummatan wāḥidatan*) (5: 48) [that is, (according to) a single religious law (*sharīᶜa wāḥida*)]. He commended them all to uphold religion, which is affirmation of the divine unicity (*awṣāhum jamīᶜan bi-iqāmat al-dīn wa-huwa al-tawḥīd*), and not to divide [in this matter], because He made their religion a single religion.[79]

Abū Ḥanīfa, then, is reported to have distinguished between a single and unifying religion (*dīn*) and a plurality of religious laws; he expressly equates *dīn* with *tawḥīd*. The dual categories of *umma*, the inclusive whole, and *milla*, the specific confessional community, persist in the religious discourse of Pseudo-Māwardī's environment, in which the development of Ḥanafī teachings, as the juristic content of *Naṣīḥat al-mulūk* reveals, were deeply imprinted.

Also noteworthy in Pseudo-Māwardī's enumeration of constituent social categories is his use of terms that avoid religiously exclusive connotations. For example, the term *nussāk* (pl. of *nāsik*), ascetics, did not connote a particular religious community, whereas the term *zuhhād* had become predominantly identified in the author's time and place with Muslim figures. As Chapter 5 will indicate, numerous figures in Balkh and Samarqand bore the epithet *al-Zāhid*; *al-Nāsik*, by contrast, almost never appears. At the same time, the term *nāsik* appears frequently in non- or pre-Islamic contexts; it appears in *Kalīla wa-Dimna*, *ᶜAhd Ardashīr* and al-Taghlibī's *Akhlāq al-mulūk*, and Aristotle is described as *nāsik mutaᶜabbid*, 'a religiously observant ascetic'.[80] Pseudo-Māwardī also employs the term *ḥukkām*, 'judges', in preference to the term *quḍāt* (pl. of *qāḍī*), which applied exclusively in a Muslim context. Pseudo-Māwardī's choice of vocabulary that carried inclusive rather than specific connotations is consistent with the religious diversity of his society and his strong sense of the continuing instructiveness of the experience of earlier communities.

In conclusion, it is appropriate to cite a second, similarly evocative, passage of social description that appears subsequently in Pseudo-Māwardī's seventh chapter:

> The king should know the categories of the people and their ranks, including the sons of kings, the nobles, those possessed of lineage and prestige and their children (*abnāʾ al-mulūk wa-l-ashrāf wa-dhaw[ū] al-ansāb wa-l-aḥsāb wa-awlād[u]h[u]m*); the scholars and ascetics and their relatives (*al-ᶜulamāʾ wa-l-nussāk wa-dhaw[ū]h[u]m*); the wealthy (*al-aghniyāʾ*),[81] the owners of estates and lands (*arbāb al-ḍiyāᶜ wa-l-araḍīn*); the merchants, artisans and tradesmen (*al-tujjār wa-l-ṣunnāᶜ wa-l-mahana*); and those of high standing (*aṣḥāb al-aqdār*) among them. He should order them in their ranks and place them in their stations, and furnish each category among them with its due (*fa-yuwaffira ᶜalā kulli ṭabaqatin minhum ḥaqqahum*), according to the measures of their resources (*ᶜalā maqādīr asbābihim*) and their ranks among humankind, and the degree to which they are brought into the ruler's proximity, bound to him in attachment and appointed to stations (*[ᶜalā] marātibihim min al-bashar wa-l-taqrīb wa-l-irfāq wa-l-tartīb*). This strategy will induce them to strive for precedence in seeking the good and to compete with one another in the attainment of excellence in whatever concern or activity is theirs. This practice becomes a causative factor in the sound arrangement of their affairs, the harmonious equilibrium of their states, and the pleasant nature of their persons.[82]

This passage supplements the impression of governance and society under the earlier Samanids that emerged from the previously studied section. Pseudo-Māwardī presents the social groups whom the king should 'know', assign properly to their appropriate stations, and whose rightful claims he should fulfil. The theme of maintaining the social hierarchy by ensuring that individuals remain in the positions appropriate to them, and are not elevated or demoted other than in accordance with established and predictable patterns, is a staple among authors of mirrors. The author's reference, once more, to the rightful dues, *ḥuqūq*, of individuals and groups, and the ruler's obligation to honour these claims, reveals further the centrality of this institution in the maintenance of social and political stability. This passage demonstrates explicitly that the claims of members of the higher categories included their families, for whom the ruler was equally responsible: status was invested not only in the individual, but also in his household.

In this passage, Pseudo-Māwardī groups the various social categories into five sets. In the first set, the 'sons of kings' (*abnāʾ al-mulūk*) appears to refer, without differentiation, to members of the ruler's extended family and other dynastic families, perhaps including the provincial *mulūk al-aṭrāf*. The linking of these *mulūk* with the persons of noble and respected descent, together with the emphasis on their children and successors, suggests the hereditary nature of their status. Included in this set, designated under the rubric of *ashrāf*, are, certainly, the ᶜAlid families. The second grouping to which the author refers consists of persons whose social status derives from their learning and the moral quality of their lives, the religious scholars and ascetics (*nussāk*). (As in the previously cited passage of social description, the author employs the term *nussāk* rather than *zuhhād*.) Again, the reference is not only to the individuals, but also to their relatives who acquired special status by virtue of their kinship with such persons. The third cluster of groups is the wealthy, notably those whose wealth derives from their possession of land. It is likely that the author included the more prominent *dihqān*s in this set; there is no evidence in *Naṣīḥat al-mulūk* to suggest that he also referred to members of prominent military families of *mamlūk* background, such as the Sīmjūrīs, who, a little later in the century, acquired vast estates.[83] Fourth in Pseudo-Māwardī's list are urban groupings, whose wealth and livelihood derived from commerce, manufacturing and other occupations. His fifth group, 'persons of high standing' (*aṣḥāb al-aqdār*), perhaps connotes office holders. After enumerating these social categories and urging the king to acknowledge their dues, Pseudo-Māwardī warns his audience against the perils of alienating them.

The extracts studied in Chapter 3 and this chapter attest to, on the one hand, the semi-sacralised representation of kingship and the exclusive place reserved for kings in the divine order, and, on the other hand, the indirect nature of governance in the period of the earlier Samanid amirs. Notwithstanding the intensely hierarchical portrayal of the ruler's relationship to the population, Pseudo-Māwardī describes the ruler's dependence on the cooperation of multiple, specifically identified social groups. These groups occupied differing levels in the social and political order. Pseudo-Māwardī distinguishes between groups composed of individuals bound to him in personal loyalty and obligation, and categories of persons whose voluntary cooperation and support the ruler was compelled to cultivate. His depiction of the social groups whose satisfaction was essential to the ruler's sovereignty suggests the importance for political and social stability of individuals at secondary levels of power. The centre of the Samanid polity exerted limited control over governmental matters. Significant authority lay with networks of individuals, bound within and across categories through codes of conduct and carefully maintained relationships. Pseudo-Māwardī's language for such relationships invokes 'love', namely, individuals whose positive cooperation was voluntary rather than coerced. As Volume II will show, it was this phenomenon that stimulated his own offering of advice to the ruler.[84]

PART III

THE RELIGIOUS LANDSCAPE

5

Multiplicity and Rhetoric

Part III of this volume, in four chapters, studies the religious-political context for Pseudo-Māwardī's *Naṣīḥat al-mulūk*, and explores the textual indications of his philosophical-theological disposition and his religious sensibility. The chapters address the confessional composition of the Samanid domains and some of the varied discourses related to religion that flourished in the tenth-century *mashriq*. These discourses accommodated inclusive, pluralistic and exclusionary aspects: they assumed and acknowledged, often without evaluative rhetoric, the polity's religious diversity; they also refuted religiously identified groups, and located the potential for political instability in particular forms of religious interpretation. In Pseudo-Māwardī's conception, the 'protection' of religion was among the king's principal responsibilities. Part III explores Pseudo-Māwardī's understanding of the relationship between religion and kingship, and the factors that contributed to his perception, perhaps shared by numbers of his contemporaries, that the Samanid polity had fallen into incipient crisis.

Pseudo-Māwardī foreshadows the theme of religious divergence in a fleeting reference to 'pseudo-prophets' (*mutanabbiʾūn*) in his preface. In that context, Pseudo-Māwardī states that just as God sent His prophets to kings rather than to individuals, so pseudo-prophets had directed their attention towards kings, since subjects follow the path (*madhhab*) of their leaders.[1] Placed prominently at the opening of *Naṣīḥat al-mulūk*, the remark is likely to allude to the circumstances of the Samanid court at the time of the mirror's composition. The purpose of the present chapter is to explore the religious landscape of the period and the religious–intellectual culture that shaped Pseudo-Māwardī's perception and his articulation of religious arguments. Chapter 6 addresses the governance and behaviour of the Samanid amirs, and especially the amirs likely to have coincided with Pseudo-Māwardī's lifetime, with regard to the religious culture of their domains. Chapter 7 presents Pseudo-Māwardī's analysis of the 'corruption' that he perceived in the kingdom, and Chapter 8 offers a summary of Pseudo-Māwardī's location in the religious context of his milieu.

Western Central Asia had a long history of religious multiplicity. The region's location occasioned the convergence of numerous cultural currents, and facilitated the interaction of a profusion of religious orientations and communities. The Arab-Muslim armies encountered 'a mosaic of religions' in the area,[2] where archaeological investigations have uncovered indications, similarly attested in the eighth-century Bactrian and Arabic documents,[3] of a population that professed local forms of Zoroastrianism, Christianity and Buddhism, as well as a variety of religious systems that focused on specific divinities and sacred phenomena.[4] Though reduced and transmuted in the course of the ninth and tenth centuries by the rapid rate of conversions to Islam, especially among the Turkic populations of the steppe, communities of Zoroastrians, Buddhists, Jews, Christians and Manichaeans, their boundaries not always clearly demarcated, continued to live within and in proximity to the Samanid domains, and had left deep and durable impressions in the regional culture. The appearance of figures, movements and writings not easily situated within any of these religious traditions but suggesting contact with many of them was a distinctive feature of the region's history.[5]

Inner Khurasan's population, incorporated into the lands of the caliphate in the seventh century, was probably predominantly Muslim by the early tenth century. Cities, however, acquired Muslim majorities much faster than the lands that surrounded them, and the impression given by the written sources, composed overwhelmingly in urban areas and for urban populations, may obscure the continuing presence of large non-Muslim communities in rural areas.[6] Geographical writings, especially those based on the first-hand observations of authors and their informants, provide something of a corrective to this impression, and suggest in several areas a mixed religious landscape.[7]

In the Samanids' central territory of Transoxiana, with its borders facing the lands of Inner Asia, Islamisation had a more attenuated history. The campaigns of the early amirs and the simultaneous travels and transactions of Iranian merchants brought about an intensification of contacts towards and beyond the steppe, yet substantial religious pluralism remained.[8] Such multiplicity was perhaps still more pronounced in Tukharistan and the regions bordering on India. At least in Kabul, which had a Muslim governor,[9] and Ghur, Muslims appear to have represented a minority.[10] According to al-Iṣṭakhrī and Ibn Ḥawqal, the Muslims of these localities resided among non-Muslims who 'lived peaceably' with them (*musālimūn*).[11] Conditions differed considerably in different environments, and did not remain constant. In the late tenth century, al-Muqaddasī reported numerous manifestations of intense factional attachments, *ᶜaṣabiyyāt*, among the groupings of the Muslim population and sometimes directed towards other confessional groups; he mentions Balkh and Samarqand specifically as sites of 'factional attachment at the expense of persons outside the religious path' (*ᶜaṣabiyyāt ᶜalā ghayr al-madhhab*).[12] The report perhaps suggests the continuing presence of sizable non-Muslim communities in these cities at a date when the populations of other major urban centres in the region had become predominantly Muslim.[13]

Naṣīḥat al-mulūk provides no indication of such inter-confessional strife in Pseudo-Māwardī's milieu. The region's intellectual culture, furthermore, continued to reflect, among other sensibilities, Abū Ḥanīfa's conception of a single religion and a plurality of religious laws; according to this perspective, the adoption of distinctive laws created the boundaries of specific religious communities that shared a common foundation in belief.[14] From its title, the treatise *Sharāᵓiᶜ al-adyān* ('The Laws of the Religions') of the early tenth-century Kindian polymath Abū Zayd al-Balkhī seems likely to have reflected this outlook.[15] As the Ḥanafī text *al-ᶜĀlim wa-l-mutaᶜallim*, cited in Chapter 4, indicated, the recognition of a diversity of religious communities found a conceptual and scriptural frame of reference in the Qurᵓānic 'Had Your Lord willed, He would have made humankind a single community, yet they do not cease to differ' (11: 118). Works of Qurᵓānic commentary report several interpretations that include the 'People of the Book' (*ahl al-kitāb*) among the believers.[16] Pseudo-Māwardī shared this conception of a plurality of religions, all of which possessed a common foundation, and a corresponding multiplicity of religious communities, each of which was distinguished by its own law. His vocabulary is replete with the pluralities of *adyān* (religions), *umam* (religious communities or nations), *milal* (religious communities), *diyānāt* (religions or religious paths) and *sharāᵓiᶜ* (religious laws). Al-Maqdisī, who shared Pseudo-Māwardī's perspective in many respects, would employ the same plural terminology in his twenty-two-volume *Kitāb al-Badʾ wa-l-taʾrīkh* ('Book of the Creation and History'), composed in Bust in the third quarter of the tenth century.

This inclusivity appears to have thrived in many tenth-century intellectual environments, but it is perhaps particularly distinctive of the encyclopaedists of the period. Al-Masʿūdī, al-Maqdisī and Ibn al-Nadīm,[17] all of whose writings possessed encyclopaedic aspects, provided accounts of older religions that were largely devoid of evaluative judgements.[18] In a striking example, Ibn al-Nadīm composed an unusually long, detailed and straightforward account of the life and teachings of Mānī.[19] Works that reflect an acquaintance with *falsafa*, especially those associated with Ismaʿili circles, such as the *Kitāb* or *Rasāʾil* ('Epistles') of the Ikhwān al-Ṣafāʾ ('Brethren of Purity' or 'Sincere Brethren', the name adopted by the philosophers who composed the encyclopaedic collection of fifty-odd thematic epistles), recognise the plurality of religious laws and link them to the differences among human communities.[20] To a significant degree, Pseudo-Māwardī, followed by al-Maqdisī and Abū Zayd al-Balkhī's student al-ʿĀmirī, participate in this inclusive discourse.[21] Each of these authors drew attention to areas of agreement among religions. Al-Maqdisī and al-ʿĀmirī, whose works reveal similarities with, but differed in genre and purpose from, Pseudo-Māwardī's mirror, also explored the differences among them.[22] Even al-ʿĀmirī, in his ostensibly polemical *al-Iʿlām bi-manāqib al-Islām* ('Declaration of the Excellent Qualities of Islam'), assigned to Mazdaeans (*al-majūs*) and Manichaeans (*al-thanawiyya*) an intermediate theological position between persons whose stance he described as *mushrik* ('associative', that is, of 'partners' with God) and persons whose position he termed *kitābī* ('scriptural'), in other words, peoples of the book.[23] For all these writers, the *ahl al-dhimma* ('People of the Pact') belonged among the *ahl al-sharāʾiʿ* ('People of the Religious Laws'), acknowledged, as will be seen below, in the Muʿtazilite theologian al-Kaʿbī's formulation *al-muslimūn wa-ahl al-sharāʾiʿ* ('Muslims and People of the Religious Laws').[24] Pseudo-Māwardī, moreover, in keeping with his references to 'religions' and 'religious communities', reminds the king of his responsibilities towards the *ahl al-dhimma* as well as his duties towards the Muslim community.[25] His approach suggests a mentality that envisaged, in Guy Monnot's phrase, 'a living symbiosis' between Islam and the earlier religions.[26]

The same trio of writers also shared the principle of ranking, expressed elsewhere in *Naṣīḥat al-mulūk* by the term 'preference' or 'preferment', *tafḍīl*. The principle, while highly flexible, supported the notion of a multi-confessional structure in which Islam represented the highest point. This perspective accommodated religious difference, but also provided a conceptual framework for a flourishing literature of refutation. Most of the titles of refutations listed in Ibn al-Nadīm's *al-Fihrist* were directed towards Christianity, Judaism and Zoroastrianism and their respective adherents.[27] More distant or sparsely represented religions attracted localised refutation. Where it survived, or was suspected to have survived in disguised form, Manichaeanism elicited perhaps a particularly virulent strain of polemic. Not only writers who acknowledged common beliefs and principles among religions, but also authors who placed a high value on the intellectual accomplishments and wisdom of the peoples of the past engaged in the production of refutations. For example, al-Kindī, who expressed his impartial appreciation for the cumulative knowledge attained and transmitted from earlier peoples, also wrote refutations of religious groups, including the Manichaeans.[28] His student Abū Zayd al-Balkhī, in Pseudo-Māwardī's immediate environment, composed a *Kitāb al-Radd ᶜalā ᶜabadat al-aṣnām* ('Refutation of the Worshippers of Idols')[29] and al-Kaᶜbī, leading representative of the Baghdadi branch of the Muᶜtazila in Khurasan in the early tenth century, wrote in an authoritative manner on the subject of Indian religions.[30]

It was particularly the specialists in theological argument, the *mutakallimūn*, who produced a prolific literature of refutation, directed sometimes against non-Muslim religious groups and sometimes against Muslims who held opposing points of view. The polemical attacks against many philosophers and theologians, especially Muᶜtazilite figures, undoubtedly stimulated their assiduity in this regard.[31] Abū Zayd al-Balkhī and al-Kaᶜbī, exceptionally well versed in the diverse religious cultures of their region, both faced charges of religious dissidence: when Abū Zayd was attacked for atheism (*ilḥād*), al-Kaᶜbī defended his credentials as a *muwaḥḥid*, yet al-Kaᶜbī too faced accusations of *zandaqa* in his native city of Balkh.[32] The point is pertinent to the pronounced attention to heterodoxy in *Naṣīḥat al-mulūk*, which displays affinities with the Kindian tradition and with Muᶜtazilite theology. Al-Kaᶜbī composed a number of works that engaged critically with the doctrines of individuals or groups within the Muslim community.[33] Amongst al-Kaᶜbī's writings is a work that bears the title *al-Naqḍ ᶜalā al-Rāzī fī l-ᶜilm al-ilāhī* ('Criticism of al-Rāzī on the Subject of Divine Knowledge'), apparently a disputation with the eminent physician Muḥammad b. Zakariyyāᵓ al-Rāzī (*c.* 250–313 or 323/854–925 or 935). According to ᶜAbd al-Jabbār al-Hamadhānī (d. 415 /1024–5), chief judge at Rayy and the most prominent theologian of the later Basran Muᶜtazilite school, when the ruler of Balkh (*sulṭān Balkh*) fell ill, he summoned al-Rāzī. The physician took the opportunity to propose a disputation with al-Kaᶜbī, whereupon the latter castigated him for his alleged denial of prophethood, among other tenets held by *al-muslimūn wa-ahl al-sharāᵓiᶜ* ('Muslims and the People of Religious Laws').[34] In a particularly polemical example, in *Tathbīt dalāᶜil al-nubuwwa* ('Consolidation of the Proofs of Prophecy', composed 385/995), ᶜAbd al-Jabbār engaged in a comprehensive refutation of non-Muslim religions, Greek and Muslim philosophy and Ismaᶜili and Imami Shiᶜism; the Prophet, he claimed, had exposed the error and unbelief of the religions of the Jews, Christians, Byzantines, Persians, Majūs (Zoroastrians), Indians, Quraysh and the Arabs.[35]

Al-Māturīdī, a leading theologian in Samarqand, where the emerging grouping of theologians would come to be named after him, was as energetic in his refutations of Muslim and non-Muslim groups alike as his Muᶜtazilite contemporaries. In a reflection of the religious and cultural–intellectual diversity of his environment, al-Māturīdī refuted the views of Christians, Jews, Zoroastrians, materialists (*dahriyya*), Buddhists (*sumaniyya*), sophists (*sūfisṭāᵓiyya*), Bardesanites, Marcionites, 'dualists' (*thanawiyya*, that is, individuals who acknowledged two opposed forces rather than a single divinity) and, above all, Manichaeans, who, in Guy Monnot's analysis, constituted one of his 'obsessions'.[36] He also refuted the Karrāmiyya, a Muslim group named after Ibn Karrām of Sistan, who died in 255/869 in Jerusalem; a popular and ascetically inclined movement, the Karrāmiyya were widespread in the central and eastern regions, especially Khurasan, in the later ninth and tenth centuries. Al-Māturīdī also argued against the Ḥashwiyya, a derogatory term applied to scholars who, because of the importance they attached to ḥadīth and their antipathy to rational interpretation, accepted the reliability of reports that reflected anthropomorphic conceptions of the divine; and against the Imami Shiᶜa and the Ismaᶜilis, who, as will be seen, were active in Transoxiana in his lifetime.[37] Among his most sustained and detailed criticisms were his arguments against individual Muᶜtazilites, especially his contemporary al-Kaᶜbī.[38] The emerging Samarqandī–Māturīdī discipline of theological argument found vigorous continuation in the *Tabṣirat al-adilla fī uṣūl al-dīn* ('Explication of Proofs in the Principles of Religion') of Abū l-Muᶜīn al-Nasafī (d. 508/1114). In this work, al-Nasafī devoted a chapter to the criteria for assessing the truth or falsehood of religions (*ṣiḥḥat al-adyān wa-fasāduhā*),[39] and refuted the Majūs (Zoroastrians), the Thanawiyya, Buddhists (*sumaniyya*), the 'Brahmans' (*barāhima*), the Karrāmiyya, the Ashᶜariyya and especially the Muᶜtazila, among whom he too engaged in particular disputes against al-Kaᶜbī.[40]

In a milieu characterised by religious multiplicity and competing theological perspectives, Pseudo-Māwardī, like al-Kaᶜbī and al-Māturīdī, attached great importance to effective religious argumentation. A Muᶜtazilite whose approach and doctrines situate him in the Baghdadi branch associated in his vicinity with al-Kaᶜbī, Pseudo-Māwardī urges the ruler to equip himself to participate in such arguments; he is quite likely to have engaged in disputation himself. *Naṣīḥat al-mulūk* is neither a theological treatise nor a work of refutation, yet it reflects a mentality in which dialectical argument provided a means of defence for an embattled religious-political concord. Although, as his treatment of al-Maᵓmūn showed, he refers to communities' competition for excellence, Pseudo-Māwardī, unlike al-Māturīdī, pays less attention to communities outside the Islamic fold than to the internal divisiveness that he imputes to unspecified groups of *ahl al-ahwāᵓ* ('adherents of heterodoxies', 'free-thinkers'), *ahl al-baghy* ('rebels'), *munāfiqūn* ('hypocrites') and *mulḥidūn* ('heretics', 'atheists').[41] His observation of religious dissent's links with political ambition on the one hand and of the attacks against philosophers and rational theologians on the other, it is proposed, contributed to his writing of *Naṣīḥat al-mulūk*. Al-Maqdisī, a Muᶜtazilite who wrote some two decades after Pseudo-Māwardī, echoed his predecessor; although, like Pseudo-Māwardī, he abstained from identifying particular groups, he described his composition as his response to his patron's demand for a book that would 'stand up for and safeguard religion, defend the core of Islam and refute the trickery of its enemies' (*munāḍalatan ᶜan al-dīn wa-ḥtiyāṭan lahu wa-dhabban ᶜan bayḍat al-Islām wa-raddan li-kayd munāwīhi*), who despised 'divine laws' (*sharāᵓiᶜ*) and 'religions' (*adyān*).[42]

In his concentration on divisions within the religious community as opposed to parallel communities apart from it, Pseudo-Māwardī resumes a concern already articulated some decades earlier by the religious scholars of Transoxiana, who sought to define the boundaries of the community in the theological tract known as *al-Sawād al-aᶜẓam*, 'The Great Multitude'.[43] Prepared in Arabic under the auspices of Amir Ismāᶜīl b. Aḥmad (r. 279–95 /892–907), who, in response to the concerns of the religious scholars, convened a group of them for the purpose of composing the treatise, *al-Sawād al-aᶜẓam* was later translated into Persian under Nūḥ II b. Manṣūr (r. 365–87/976–97) and adopted as the 'official catechism' of the Samanid realm.[44] In its Persian translation, *al-Sawād al-aᶜẓam* opens with the statement that the reason for its composition was 'that misguided people, innovators and heretics (*bīrāhān va-mubtadiᶜān va-havādārān*) had become numerous in Samarqand, Bukhara and Transoxiana'.[45] Their appearance had caused the religious leaders, jurists and scholars (*aʾimmeh va-fuqahā va-ᶜulamā*) of those localities to reflect on how their forefathers had adhered to the *ṭarīq-i sunnat va-jamāᶜat*, 'the way of normative practice and the (majority) community', whereas now various forms of religious aberration (*havā*) had appeared. These religious scholars informed the Amir of Khurasan, Ismāᶜīl b. Aḥmad, who ordered ᶜAbdallāh b. Abī Jaᶜfar and other jurists (*fuqahā*) to elucidate the 'correct path and the way of normative practice and the community' (*madhhab-i rāst va-ṭarīq-i sunnat va-jamāᶜat*), 'the one that our forefathers pursued'. They turned to Abū l-Qāsim Isḥāq Samarqandī (d. 342/953), who would become judge of Samarqand, to explicate the correct path, 'the one that the Prophet pursued'.[46] Samarqandī wrote the (perhaps collective) text in Arabic, and it was brought to Ismāᶜīl; the amir and the scholars unanimously approved of it, and agreed that it represented 'the correct path of the *sunna* and *jamāᶜa*'.[47] Subsequently, Nūḥ II ordered its translation into Persian, so that the common people, like the élites, should have access to it, benefit from it, gain knowledge of the path, and remain distant from heterodoxy (*havā*) and innovation (*bidᶜat*).[48]

Despite the sense among the Samarqandī scholars that the region's production of heterodoxies represented a departure from an earlier 'correct' form of religious belief and practice, a form they considered to have been embodied in their authoritative forefathers and before them in the Prophet, their efforts to define and advocate the parameters of such religious rectitude suggest an initiative to attract and compel the political support of the Samanid amirs in the face of actual or potential rivals for status and privilege. The scholars undertook these efforts in a context in which significant portions of the population had only recently adopted a certain, perhaps minimal, level of Islamisation, and the numbers of new affiliates to the *dār al-Islām*, some of whom would attain high status, continued to rise.[49] It is possible that the scholars sought to direct the new Muslims' allegiance towards a particular inflection of Islamic religious culture as a defensive measure against the similar efforts of rival groupings, whose increasing numbers of adherents represented a challenge to their authority and prestige. The urban contexts of the pre-eminent scholars and the strength of local religious cultures in rural settings are likely, moreover, to have generated an associated, possibly class-related, set of concerns. In its demarcation of the boundaries of the 'correct path', *al-Sawād al-aᶜẓam* lists seventy-three sects that the authors identified with the Prophetic ḥadīth, according to which all were bound for hell except for the *madhhab-i sunnat va-jamāᶜat*.[50] The tract refutes specific doctrines associated with a number of groups, whom it identifies by name. It treats Muᶜtazilite doctrines with considerable antipathy,[51] and evinces a marked hostility towards the Karrāmiyya; in one instance, it declares them the worst and most ignorant of all the seventy-two (errant) *millat*.[52] The Karrāmiyya thrived amongst people of relatively humble background in urban and rural settings, and it is likely that fears of revolt, a theme already pronounced in Sasanian writings and perhaps in continuity with them, contributed to the apprehensions and hostility of the urban élites.[53] Under Ismāᶜīl, in any event, a number of groups elicited the apprehensions of the scholars of the *ahl al-sunna wa-l-jamāᶜa*, the non-Shiᶜite majority who affirmed the importance of normative custom, especially that of the Prophet, and would eventually become known as Sunnis, of Transoxiana.[54] For later writers, such as Niẓām al-Mulk, the sense of threat had as its central focus the *bāṭiniyya*, a term used to describe groupings that sought to uncover the 'inner' (*bāṭin*) dimension of religious teachings in addition to, or in preference to, their exterior or outer (*ẓāhir*) meanings, and a term that in the course of the tenth century came to connote above all the Ismaᶜili Shiᶜites.

As Ḥasan Anṣārī has already proposed, it was probably in the last decade or so of Naṣr II's reign that Pseudo-Māwardī composed his mirror, in which he warned the king against the logical sequence that linked religious movements with political reversal.[55] To whom did Pseudo-Māwardī allude in his references to *ahl al-baghy* and *ahl al-ahwā*ʾ, rebels and free-thinkers or heretics? Unlike the authors of *al-Sawād al-aᶜẓam*, Pseudo-Māwardī refrains from identifying the groups to whom he alludes. In a single instance, he refers to the *zanādiqa*, in the phrase 'the enemies of sovereignty and religion among the *zanādiqa* and the atheists (or heretics)' (*aᶜdāʾ al-mulk wa-l-dīn min al-zanādiqa wa-l-mulḥidīn*).[56] The term *zanādiqa* (pl. of *zindīq*), like the term *bāṭiniyya*, did not designate a specific group. It was a highly adaptive label, and in particular contexts it acquired contemporary connotations. Its associations with Manichaeanism, presented in an array of late antique writings as the quintessential expression of religious subversion, rendered it applicable to a variety of forms of dissent. The early Abbasid period had witnessed numerous allegations of *zandaqa*, portrayed as a pervasive phenomenon to which members of the intellectual and cultural élites, especially figures, such as Ibn al-Muqaffaᶜ (d. *c.* 139/757) and Abān al-Lāḥiqī (d. 200/815), involved in the translation of Middle Persian literature and the transmission of late antique culture and learning, were particularly disposed.[57] In the course of the eighth and early ninth centuries, such charges became increasingly potent, and by the time of the reign of al-Mahdī (r. 158–69/775–85) they had produced systematic repression. In tracing its connotations for Pseudo-Māwardī's audience, it is instructive to consider the associations that the label *zandaqa* had come to bear.

Manichaeanism and *Zandaqa*

Despite their broad geographical dispersal from North Africa to south-eastern China, Manichaeans usually constituted small and persecuted communities, and represented 'the outsider par excellence'.[58] The territories of the Muslim sphere were no exception to this experience. In the aftermath of persecution, according to Ibn al-Nadīm, the leadership of the Manichaean community had transferred its centre from Iraq to Samarqand, where the ruler of 'China' (*malik al-Ṣīn*) (that is, the Uighur kingdom, the single polity in which, in 763, Manichaeism had been adopted as the established religion) sent word to an unidentified but hostile ruler of Khurasan (*ṣāḥib Khurāsān*) that unless the latter refrained from violence against and provided legal protection for Manichaeans within his domains, the king would inflict violent punishment on the more numerous Muslims within his territories.[59] As indicated in Chapter 2, a community of Manichaeans and a Manichaean monastery (*khāngāh*) still existed during al-Māturīdī's lifetime in tenth-century Samarqand.[60] In the following century, al-Bīrūnī (362–after 442/973–after 1050) reported that remnants of Mānī's followers continued to survive and were dispersed throughout the lands, but gathered in the territories of Islam only in Samarqand, where they constituted a 'sect' (*firqa*) known as the Sabians.[61] Abū l-Maᶜālī Muḥammad b. ᶜUbaydallāh, who wrote in Ghazna under Jalāl al-Dīn Masᶜūd ᶜAlāᵓ al-Dawla (r. 482–92/1089–99), reported the existence in that city of a Manichaean manuscript.[62]

A dominant strand in Arabic and Persian writings of the tenth century and later identified Mānī as a *zindīq*, and located the origination of this disparaging epithet with him. Most authors who commented on the term related it to the *Zand*, commonly (if erroneously) conceived of as a body of allegorical interpretation for the *Avesta*.[63] Al-Masᶜūdī observed that the terms *zandaqa* and *zindīq* first appeared in the time of Mānī. Zoroaster, he explained, had brought to the Persians a book in Old Persian called the *Avesta* (*Bastāh*). Given the linguistic difficulty of the *Avesta*, he prepared a work of exegesis (*tafsīr*), which was called the *Zand*, and a further commentary (*sharḥ*) on the *Zand* (*tafsīr al-tafsīr*) called the *Bāzand*. In one place, al-Masᶜūdī describes the *Avesta*'s contents as matters pertaining to the promise and threat (of the afterlife), command(s) and prohibition(s), and other religious laws and acts of worship.[64] A little later, he describes the *Zand* as an elucidation of the allegorical interpretation (*taᵓwīl*) of the *Avesta*. Accordingly, whenever anyone 'introduced into their religious law (*sharīᶜa*) anything that conflicted with the revelation (*al-munzal*), namely the *Avesta*, and deviated towards the allegorical interpretation, namely the *Zand*, the Persians called him a *zandī*', which term became in Arabic *zindīq*.[65] ᶜAbd al-Jabbār states that since no one understood the language of the *Avesta* in Mānī's time, he was able to produce a purported *tafsīr* of it, by which he attracted the common people.[66] Over a century later, the twelfth-century genealogist ᶜAbd al-Karīm al-Samᶜānī (506–62/1113–66) claimed that Mānī was a *majūsī* (Magian or Zoroastrian) who sought fame (*ṣīt*) and reputation (*dhikr*). To that end he founded a path (*waḍaʿa ṭarīqatan*) and assembled a book that he called *Sāburqān* (*Shābuhragān*); he claimed that his *Sāburqān* was the *zand*, meaning *tafsīr*, of the Book of Zoroaster, and for this reason he was called a *zindīq*.[67]

These accounts illustrate the association of figurative scriptural interpretation with strategic designs to undermine an established religious law and attain social and perhaps political status. The elision of these elements becomes more pronounced in the several treatments of *zandaqa* that link Mānī with the later figure of Mazdak. Towards the end of the tenth century, the Samanid secretary al-Khwārazmī, in his compendium of technical terms *Mafātīḥ al-ʿulūm* ('Keys of the Sciences', *c.* 387/977), ascribed the phenomenon of *zandaqa* to Mazdak, who brought forth a book that he called the *Zand*. Mazdak, according to al-Khwārazmī, reportedly claimed that his *Zand* contained the allegorical interpretation (*taʾwīl*) of the *Avesta*, and accordingly his followers assumed the name *zandī*.[68] These accounts converged with and supported the association, a feature of Sasanian discourse and well established in late antiquity, of religious dissent with political subversion. The association of these ideas, as Chapter 7 will demonstrate, is prominent in *Naṣīḥat al-mulūk*. It reaches perhaps its fullest development in the eleventh-century *Siyar al-mulūk*, in which, as part of his narrative of Mazdak's revolt, Niẓām al-Mulk reported that according to the *mōbads*, certain parts of the *Avesta* and *Zand* could bear ten meanings, and every *mōbad* and learned person (*dānā*) explained and interpreted them differently.[69]

Al-Bīrūnī remarked explicitly on the metaphorical uses of the term *zanādiqa* when he observed that the remnants of Mazdak's supporters following his execution were known as the Mazdakiyya and the Khurramdīniyya in terms of their religion and group (*nisbatan ilā dīnihim wa-madhhabihim*), and as *zanādiqa* with regard to interpretation, since they held the *Zand* to constitute *tafsīr*, and the *Bāzand* to constitute *taʾwīl*. The term *zanādiqa*, he wrote, extended to the Manichaeans 'in a figurative and metaphorical sense' (*ʿalā ṭarīq al-majāz wa-l-istiʿāra*), and to 'the *bāṭiniyya* in Islam' by way of drawing a parallel with them (*tashbīhan lahum*).[70] Al-Bīrūnī's statement is borne out by the presentations, explicit or implicit, of a host of tenth- and eleventh-century writers, for whom the term *zandaqa*, with its full set of acquired associations, stretched into the past as far as Mānī and Mazdak and, after periodic repetitions, manifested itself in the subversive activities of the contemporary *bāṭiniyya*.

The Conflation of *Zanādiqa* and *Bāṭiniyya*

The terms *zindīq* and *bāṭinī*, both associated with allegorical or esoteric interpretations of scripture, provided tenth- and eleventh-century authors with a flexible set of applications. If *zandaqa* conveyed, in certain contexts, 'dualism', it also connoted less specific forms of heterodoxy. Above all, perhaps, the term carried the paired associations of intellectual élitism and political subversion. Accordingly, it provided a vehicle for the identification of contemporary *bāṭinī* heterodoxies with the stereotyped models of the past, and the accompanying transfer of the ominous trajectories of the latter to the former. It was *zandaqa* of which members of the intellectual and secretarial élites at the Abbasid court, among them Ibn al-Muqaffaᶜ, Abān al-Lāḥiqī and the Barmakids, had been accused. As Julie Scott Meisami and Elton Daniel have observed, the connotations of the term were not lost on Samanid audiences: when the opponents of the viziers al-Jayhānī and Abū l-Ṭayyib Muḥammad b. Ḥātim al-Muṣᶜabī, the latter appointed to the vizierate no later than 330/941, referred to them each as *zindīq*, they implicitly equated these individuals with similarly accused persons, charged with subversion, at the Abbasid court. Abū ᶜAlī Balᶜamī, vizier under ᶜAbd al-Malik I b. Nūḥ (r. 343-50/954-61) and his successor Manṣūr I b. Nūḥ (r. 350-65/961-76), provides a striking example when in 352/963 he received the Amir's commission to adapt al-Ṭabarī's 'History' into Persian.[71] In the resulting *Tārīkhnāmeh*, Abū ᶜAlī Balᶜamī depicted the *zanādiqa* of the Abbasid era as nominal Muslims who in actuality denied the Prophet's status, made light of prescribed religious rituals, and engaged in licentious sexual practices; when he further observed that 'most of them belonged to the upper classes and were distinguished either by their rhetorical or poetical abilities, or by their high intelligence and wisdom', his description reminded his audience of the contemporary Ismaᶜili presence among the intellectual élites.[72] These associations grew more explicit in the following century. In a chapter devoted to religions that had preceded Islam, Abū l-Maᶜālī included a section devoted to 'the path of the *qarmaṭīs* [pl. *qarāmiṭa*, Carmathians] and *zindīqs*' (*madhhab-i qarāmiṭa va-zanādiqa*). The term *qarāmiṭa* is linked with the early Ismaᶜili leader Ḥamdān Qarmaṭ (d. 321/933), who was active in southern Iraq;[73] the name subsequently became extended to the Isma^c^iliyya in general. Abū l-Ma^c^ālī found no difference among groups identified as *qarāmiṭa*, *zanādiqa* or *ibāḥatīyān*, the 'permissive'.[74] The clusters of ideas with their contemporary implications would become yet more marked in the Seljuk period, when Niẓām al-Mulk, with unmistakable implications, presented an extended narrative in which a sequence of heretics appear,[75] and the historian Ibn al-Balkhī, who completed his *Fārsnāmeh* ('Book of Fars') during the reign of the Seljuk Muḥammad (Tapar) b. Malikshah (r. 498–511/1104–17), drew an elaborate analogy between 'Mānī the *zindīq*' (*Mānī-yi zindīq*) and the *mulḥidān* of the present.[76]

Pseudo-Māwardī wrote considerably earlier than these writers, but it seems likely that his reference to *zanādiqa* would have connoted for his audience first and foremost the Isma^c^iliyya, reports of whose prominence at the court of Naṣr II circulated in the region's cities.[77] In an environment in which many types of perceived heterodoxies prospered, and a number of violent uprisings were associated with religious claims, it is quite likely that Pseudo-Māwardī, who presents his advice as universal, imagined a wider audience for his cautionary treatise, and considered it suitable for rulers in regional locations as well.

Before turning to the Isma^c^ili *da^c^wa* in the Samanid domains during Pseudo-Māwardī's lifetime, it is instructive to consider a further element likely to have shaped his perception of the nature of heterodoxy and, by extension, the Isma^c^iliyya. As indicated in Chapter 2, Pseudo-Māwardī lived in a region deeply shaped by a Buddhist heritage. Transoxiana and parts of Tukharistan were the regions that had experienced the movement and uprising of al-Muqanna^c^ and his followers, a movement that, as Patricia Crone has demonstrated, reflected contact with the distinctive form of Sogdian Buddhism that had devotion to Maitreya, the Buddha of the future, at its centre.[78] Sogdian Manichaeans sometimes identified the Buddha Maitreya with Mānī.[79] The significance of al-Muqanna^c^, who eventually immolated himself in a conflagration in 163/779–80 or 166/782–3,[80] to later portrayals of heterodoxy, is evident in his inclusion, in later sources, in the lines of religious subversives that prefigure current conditions. For Niẓām al-Mulk, al-Muqanna^c^ joins the panoply of case studies adduced to prove that heterodoxy never changes.[81] Al-Bīrūnī, somewhat differently, detailed the histories of the pseudo-prophets and the peoples whom they had 'duped' (*tawārīkh al-mutanabbiʾīn wa-umamihim al-makhdūʿīn ʿalayhim*). His list begins with the figure of Būdhāṣaf, 'the earliest of the pseudo-prophets' (*awwal al-madhkūrīn minhum*), and continues with Mānī, Mazdak, Musaylima, Bihāfarīd (b. Māhfarvardīn, an eighth-century Zoroastrian figure whose religious experience and teachings reflect the adoption of certain Islamic principles),[82] al-Muqannaʿ, al-Ḥallāj (244–309/857–922, the mystic, executed in Baghdad, reputedly on account of his ecstatic utterances) and Ibn Abī Zakariyyāʾ (al-Ṭammāmī) who had appeared in 319/931, probably during Pseudo-Māwardī's lifetime.[83]

For Pseudo-Māwardī, however, al-Muqannaʿ and his followers, described as the 'Wearers of White' (*al-Mubayyiḍa* or *Sipīdjāmagān*) because of their white clothing, are likely to have appeared not merely as an abstract illustration of a principle, but as a more specific example and memory. In Transoxiana and to a degree in Tukharistan, traces and impressions of al-Muqannaʿ's movement remained. According to *Tārīkh-i Bukhārā*, al-Muqannaʿ's father, Ḥakīm, hailed from Balkh, and had served as a commander (*sarhangī*) under the Amir of Khurasan during the reign of al-Manṣūr.[84] Al-Muqannaʿ, apparently named Hāshim, appears to have worked as a secretary and possibly as a soldier in the employ of Abū Dāʾūd Khālid b. Ibrāhīm al-Dhuhlī (d. 140 /757), the Abbasid missionary (*dāʿī*) and general who was appointed governor of Khurasan after the execution in 137/755 of the architect of the Abbasid revolution and millennial figure Abū Muslim.[85] (As indicated in Chapter 2, Pseudo-Māwardī mentioned Khālid b. Ibrāhīm in connection with Balkh in his treatment of textual portents.[86]) According to *Fażāʾil-i Balkh*, that city included a mosque known as 'the Mosque of al-Muqannaʿ', after an individual of that name who had erected the walls (whether this Abū ʿAbdallāh [al-]Muqannaʿ, who lived long after Hāshim, was in any way related to him remains uncertain).[87] The residents of Balkh do not appear to have joined al-Muqannaʿ's movement in significant numbers, but surrounding districts, including Chaghaniyan, figured prominently in his proselytising and military activities.[88] During the fourteen years of his revolt, al-Muqannaʿ and his followers controlled much of Sogdia. Although the movement was especially strong in rural areas,[89] al-Muqannaʿ also seized the city of Samarqand, where he minted coins,[90] activities that demonstrated an explicit challenge to the power and legitimacy of the existing authorities. In addition, he appears to have adopted certain titles that suggested claims to temporal authority, as well as to religious status.[91]

Notably, it was authors contemporary with Pseudo-Māwardī who produced many of the accounts of al-Muqannaᶜ, a point that indicates the significance and interest of his movement in the period in which he wrote *Naṣīḥat al-mulūk*. Narshakhī, who completed the original Arabic *Taᵓrīkh Bukhārā* in 332/943–4, included an exceptionally full account of al-Muqannaᶜ and the Mubayyiḍa; the surviving Persian version describes the movement as a *fitneh* (Persian form, 'sedition'), and associates it with extreme violence and destruction.[92] Abū ᶜAlī Balᶜamī evinces no interest in the movement's religious character and concentrates instead on its conflict with the authorities and its territorial expansion, achieved by means of a series of ruses (*ḥiyal*, sing. *ḥīlat*).[93] In further gestures towards his political importance, Balᶜamī refers to al-Muqannaᶜ as 'King of Sogdia' (*malik-i Sughd*) and 'Muqannaᶜ Khāqān'.[94] Abū Tammām, a tenth-century Ismaᶜili missionary and disciple of the missionary (*dāᶜī*) and philosopher Muḥammad b. Aḥmad al-Nasafī (Nakhshabī) (executed in 332/943), produced an account that drew in part on personal observation.[95] Abū Tammām lived and wrote in Khurasan during Pseudo-Māwardī's lifetime,[96] and is among the writers who drew extensively, directly or indirectly, on the *Maqālāt* ('Doctrines') of al-Kaᶜbī, although not, it would seem, in his reports regarding the Mubayyiḍa of his time.[97]

The Mubayyiḍa evidently attracted the attention of Pseudo-Māwardī's contemporaries, and it is likely that their reports contributed to his understanding of the relationship between religious dissent and political challenge. In addition, several sources attest to the continuing presence of Mubayyiḍa in certain localities during and, indeed, after the lifetime of Pseudo-Māwardī. Abū Tammām reports having encountered and engaged in debate with many Mubayyiḍa (*la-qad raᵓaytu minhum khalqan kathīran wa-nāẓartuhum*, 'I encountered a large group of them and debated them'). Apart from the most learned among them, he found, they evinced no knowledge of the principles of their religion and no familiarity with al-Muqannaᶜ or his time. But they eschewed prayer, fasting and washing in cases of major ritual impurity, practised dissimulation, married only amongst themselves while they lived in the midst of Muslims, permitted access to their women, but were nevertheless trustworthy (*lahum ma*ᶜ*a hādhā kullihi amāna*), never engaged in deceit, theft or harm of other people, and avoided bloodshed except in cases in which they committed themselves to revolt or to seek revenge.[98] Qubāvī, the adapter into Persian of Narshakhī's *Ta*ʾ*rīkh Bukhārā* in 522/1128–9, added that 'that *qawm*', meaning the followers of al-Muqannaᶜ, were present in Kishsh, Nakhshab and some of the villages of Bukhara.[99] Al-Muqaddasī wrote, 'In the rural districts (*rasātīq*) of Hayṭal are groups called "white-clad" (*aqwām yuqālu lahum bayḍ al-thiyāb*) whose teachings (*madhāhib*) approximate to *zandaqa*'; and al-Thaᶜālibī observed that the Mubayyiḍa were still active in Transoxiana during his lifetime.[100] In another suggestive indication, Ibn al-Nadīm reports on the authority of Abū l-Qāsim al-Kaᶜbī that some people called al-Muslimiyya (after Abū Muslim) were in fact al-Khurramdīniyya, literally 'adherents of the joyous religion';[101] and that he had heard that a community (*jamā*ᶜ*a*) of these persons lived 'among us in Balkh' in a village called Ḥarsād and Yaljānī.[102]

Pseudo-Māwardī lived, then, in a locality that had experienced the mission and revolt of al-Muqannaᶜ, and continued to bear their imprint. Groups associated with the Mubayyiḍa still existed in his milieu. Several of his contemporaries recorded versions of al-Muqannaᶜ's beliefs and the history of his uprising. Al-Muqaddasī would liken their religious disposition to *zandaqa*, and Niẓām al-Mulk would claim, apparently conflating reports, that prominent Ismaᶜili members of the Samanid court under Amir Manṣūr I (r. 350–65/961–76) enlisted the support of the 'Wearers of White' (*Safīdjāmagān*) of Farghana, Khujand and Kasan in order to mount an insurrection.[103]

The Paradigm of Heterodoxy

Representations of heterodoxies in late antiquity, and in Arabic and Persian writings of the middle centuries, frequently possess a paradigmatic quality. Authors deploy *topoi*, often of considerable antiquity, which link each occurrence of heterodoxy with a series of familiar antecedents. Of the several elements that contribute to this stereotyped mode of presentation, Pseudo-Māwardī adopts, as Chapter 7 will demonstrate, the association of divergent scriptural interpretations with religious division; the association of religious dissent with political subversion; the linking of religious dissent with antinomianism and the pursuit of pleasure; and the deployment of deliberate strategies of deceit. Wilful falsehood constitutes a major element in the prevalent depictions of pseudo-prophets, held to proclaim false doctrines and employ deceitful stratagems, by means of which they encouraged vice and licentiousness, in order to seduce the credulous and eventually seize power. The established Zoroastrian authorities of the later Sasanian period promoted this cluster of associated ideas, which appears in the 'Letter of Tansar', the 'Testament of Ardashīr' and other documents. The lexicon pervades the writings of ninth-, tenth- and eleventh-century writers across numerous literary genres. In *al-Masālik wa-l-mamālik*, al-Iṣṭakhrī used the verb *istaghwā*, to deceive, in connection with the mystic al-Ḥallāj, whose pronouncements, the geographer reported, attracted a group among the viziers (*jamāᶜa min al-wuzarāᵓ*), several ranks among the ruler's retinue (*ṭabaqāt min ḥāshiyat al-sulṭān*), the governors of the major urban centres (*umarāᵓ al-amṣār*), the 'kings' of Iraq, al-Jazira, the Jibal and the regions adjacent to them, and engendered the fear that many of the people of the palace, such as the chamberlains, *khadam* and others, would be deceived.[104] ᶜAbd al-Jabbār's polemical refutations of Muslim and non-Muslim groups are replete with accusations and insinuations of duping the gullible, seeking leadership under the guise of assisting the masses towards truth, and abandoning and denying the religious law.[105]

The Ismaᶜili *Daᶜwa*

As *al-Sawād al-aᶜẓam* reflects, the proliferation of heterodoxies in the later ninth and early tenth centuries produced a somewhat generalised unease amongst the custodians of established religious forms. Like al-Māturīdī, the authors of the tract expressed more intense hostility to some groups than others, but still directed their disquiet towards a plurality of groups. The prevalence of religious dissenters had not yet induced the focused anxiety directed towards the Ismaᶜiliyya in the tenth and eleventh centuries.[106] Already in the later ninth century, however, the Ismaᶜiliyya were growing in strength in widely dispersed locations. As early as 270/883, the Ismaᶜili *daᶜwa* had passed from Yemen to India, where the original teaching was maintained into the tenth century.[107] The Fatimids, who had taken control of North Africa (Ifriqiya) from 297/909, would take Egypt in 358/969, and the Qarmaṭīs established their kingdom in al-Baḥrayn, to which location they took the

Black Stone of the Kaᶜba in 317/930. In Rayy, Abū Ḥātim al-Rāzī (d. 322/934–5), who became an Ismaᶜili missionary (*dāᶜī*) in approximately 300/912, reportedly secured the conversion of, among other prominent figures, the governor, Aḥmad b. ᶜAlī al-Marwazī (d. 311/924), whose brother, the general Ḥusayn b. ᶜAlī al-Marwazī, would assume the leadership of the *daᶜwa* in Khurasan.[108] In the Caspian provinces, Abū Ḥātim's mission appears to have attracted, at least for a time, the interest of Asfār b. Shīrūya of Daylam (d. 318/930–1), another general in the Samanid armies, and Mardāvīj b. Ziyār of Gilan (r. 319–23/931–35), who seized many of the northern territories in the wake of the former's revolt, although he later turned against the Ismaᶜilis.[109] The *daᶜwa* was particularly active and successful, however, in Khurasan and Transoxiana. Missionaries had been active in the Samanid domains since the late ninth century, and were well enough established to be able to produce several treatises in these regions.[110] Ismaᶜili uprisings are reported from as early as 295/907, the end of the reign of Ismāᶜīl b. Aḥmad; according to Niẓām al-Mulk, Ismāᶜīl acted forcefully against the Ismaᶜilis when the governor of Herat informed him of the success of their proselytising activities.[111] The *daᶜwa*, simultaneously active in areas far apart from one another, was not a single or uniform entity. It appears that the Ismaᶜili movement in Khurasan began before the rise of the Fatimid dynasty in North Africa and independently of it, although the *dāᶜīs* perhaps maintained intermittent contact with the Fatimids after their rise to power.[112] Like al-Maqdisī and the anonymous author of *Ḥudūd al-ᶜālam*, Pseudo-Māwardī is likely to have known of the *daᶜwa* active in Sind, where Multan became a leading centre for the Ismaᶜiliyya; one of the local rulers adopted the creed and the *khuṭba* was read in the name of the Fatimid imam.[113]

Unlike the Karrāmiyya, who represented a movement rooted in an appeal to the poor, the Ismaᶜiliyya appear to have appealed equally to persons of status and prestige. If the Karrāmiyya evoked a fear of an uprising from the lower classes, it was the perceived or actual social and political prominence of persons attracted to *bāṭinī* teachings that aroused apprehension among representatives of urban constituencies. Almost certainly in an allusion to the contemporary Ismaᶜiliyya, ᶜAbd al-Jabbār observed the success of the *zanādiqa* and *mulḥida* (heretics, atheists) in deceiving, and thereby gaining the support of a certain group (*qawm*) among the municipal leaders (*ruʾasāʾ*),

secretaries (*kuttāb*) and viziers (*wuzarāʾ*) in a seditious uprising (*fitna*).[114] It is possible, perhaps on account of the strength of the Ismaʿili presence at the court of Naṣr II, that the associations of Ismaʿilism with the more prosperous urban notables and with members of the ruling élites were particularly strong in the eastern regions.[115] *Al-Qand fī dhikr ʿulamāʾ Samarqand*, substantially replicating the report of ʿAbd al-Jabbār, mentions the positive response to the Ismaʿilis' teachings among the leaders of localities, the regional rulers, the *dahāqīn* and the notables among the administrative staff of the Samanid domains (*ajāba daʿwatahum ruʾasāʾ al-bilād wa-l-salāṭīn wa-l-dahāqīn wa-aʿyān al-kataba fī l-dawāwīn*).[116]

As indicated previously, according to Niẓām al-Mulk, the governor of Rayy, Aḥmad b. ʿAlī al-Marwazī and his brother, the Samanid general Ḥusayn b. ʿAlī al-Marwazī, both became Ismaʿilis, apparently at a relatively early date. In 287/900, the year that Ismāʿīl b. Aḥmad received the caliphal patent of investiture in Bukhara, Ḥusayn occupied Nishapur and Herat and brought both cities under Samanid control.[117] In the reign of Aḥmad II, Ḥusayn conquered Sistan for the Samanids, but, as mentioned in Chapter 3, he rebelled against Samanid rule in the reign of Aḥmad's successor Naṣr II. After the suppression of his revolt by Aḥmad b. Sahl in 306/918–19, Ḥusayn was seized and imprisoned in Bukhara, but he was later released and returned to Naṣr's service.[118] The date of Ḥusayn's adoption of Ismaʿilism is unknown, but at some point between 318/930 and 327/939, during which period the previous *dāʿī*, Abū Saʿīd al-Shaʿrānī, died, Ḥusayn assumed the leadership of the Ismaʿili *daʿwa* in Khurasan.[119] His high rank, long experience and proximity to the Samanid ruling dynasty equipped him to continue the approach of his predecessor in seeking the conversion of the political élite.[120] According to Niẓām al-Mulk, who provided a full, if problematic, account of the activities of the *daʿwa* in the Samanid domains, Ḥusayn facilitated the conversion to Ismaʿilism of several people in Taliqan, Maymana, Faryab, Gharchistan and Ghur.[121] Niẓām al-Mulk further asserts that when Ḥusayn in turn passed on his leadership of the Ismaʿili mission in Khurasan to his deputy (*nāʾib*), the previously mentioned Muḥammad b. Aḥmad Nakhshabī (= Nasafī), he urged him to go to Bukhara and Samarqand in order to convert their citizens, and to attend in particular to the notables at the court of the Amir of Khurasan (*aʿyān-i ḥażrat-i amīr-i Khurāsān*), Naṣr b. Aḥmad.[122] The instruction pre-figures the adoption of Isma^cilism among members of the king's *khāṣṣa*, and on the part of Amir Naṣr II b. Aḥmad himself.[123]

According to Niẓām al-Mulk, the *dā*ᶜ*ī* Nasafī's converts at the Samanid court included two of the Amir's boon companions (*nadīms*), one of whom, Ashᶜath, was also Naṣr's private secretary (and related to Naṣr by marriage); Abū Manṣūr Chaghānī, whom he describes as head of the military department (ᶜ*āriż*), who was married to Ashᶜath's sister; and Aytash, the amir's private chamberlain (*ḥājib-i khāṣṣ*).[124] A succession of Naṣr's viziers reportedly held heterodox beliefs, and at least two of them are likely to have been Ismaᶜilis. Ibn al-Nadīm described Naṣr's first vizier (Abū ᶜAbdallāh Muḥammad b. Aḥmad) al-Jayhānī, vizier from approximately 301–13/914–25, as a dualist (*wa-kāna al-Jayhānī thanawiyyan*).[125] Two subsequent viziers from the Jayhānī family are reported to have been Ismaᶜilis: Abū ᶜAlī Muḥammad b. Muḥammad, vizier to Naṣr from approximately 326–30/937–41, and Abū ᶜAbdallāh Aḥmad b. Muḥammad Jayhānī, vizier under Amir al-Manṣūr b. Nūḥ (r. 350–65/961–76).[126] Abū ᶜAlī Muḥammad b. Muḥammad was succeeded in the office no later than 330/941–2 by Muḥammad b. Ḥātim al-Muṣᶜabī, also an Ismaᶜili. According to al-Thaᶜālibī, it was al-Muṣᶜabī, in collaboration with a *dā*ᶜ*ī* known as Ibn Sawāda al-Rāzī, who orchestrated Naṣr's conversion.[127]

The Ismaᶜili *da*ᶜ*wa* was also active in Sistan, where it perhaps provides some of the context for al-Maqdisī's composition of his encyclopaedic *al-Bad*ᵓ *wa-l-ta*ᵓ*rīkh*. After the execution of the Ismaᶜili missionary Muḥammad b. Aḥmad al-Nasafī in Bukhara in 332/943, Abū Yaᶜqūb Isḥāq b. Aḥmad al-Sijistānī, *dā*ᶜ*ī* for the Fatimids, carried the mission into Sistan.[128] According to some accounts, the previously mentioned Saffarid Abū Jaᶜfar Aḥmad (r. 311–52/923–63), who ruled Sistan during the reign of Naṣr II and was widely known for his involvement and interest in the philosophical sciences, was also an Ismaᶜili. His son Abū Aḥmad Khalaf b. Aḥmad (r. 352–73/963–83, 373–93/983–1003), the possible recipient of al-Maqdisī's *al-Bad*ᵓ *wa-l-ta*ᵓ*rīkh*, appears to have promoted a mainstream interpretation of Sunni Islam, and is likely to have been responsible for the eventual execution of Abū Yaᶜqūb al-Sijistānī.[129]

The Ismaᶜiliyya elicited the full array of negative stereotypes among the writers whose texts dominate the surviving literature. In continuity with the representations of Mazdak and al-Muqannaᶜ, accounts of the Ismaᶜiliyya included prominent charges of calculated deceit, contempt for established religious forms and licentious behaviour. In the later tenth century, Ibn al-Nadīm reported that when in [2]87/900 the Fatimid Imam ᶜUbaydallāh (r. 297–322/909–34) sent Abū Saᶜīd al-Shaᶜrānī to Khurasan, the *dāᶜī* 'beguiled many'; at a later date, al-Nasafī 'duped' Amir Naṣr b. Aḥmad.[130] Ibn al-Nadīm also referred to the Ismaᶜili followers of the Fatimid Imam al-Qāʾim bi-Amr Allah (r. 322–34/934–46) as 'making light of the sharīᶜa and the establishment of prophecy' (*al-istikhfāf bi-l-sharīᶜa wa-l-waḍᶜ lil-nubuwwa*).[131] Al-Thaᶜālibī and Niẓām al-Mulk would also deploy the themes of deception and antinomianism.[132] As the following chapters will demonstrate, Pseudo-Māwardī anticipates these representations of heterodoxy in *Naṣīḥat al-mulūk*, where, without explicit identification of his intended referent, he equates pseudo-prophets with deceit, associates the corrupt élites with *al-istikhfāf bi-l-dīn*, 'making light of religion', and with permissive conduct and political ambitions.

Authors of advisory texts produced some of the most hostile treatments of heterodoxy in general and of the Ismaᶜiliyya in particular. It is notable that of the three surviving accounts of Naṣr's conversion, which most historians of the Samanid era passed over in silence, two appear in works of advice: the *Ādāb al-mulūk* ('Manners and Customs of Kings') of al-Thaᶜālibī and the *Siyar al-mulūk* of Niẓām al-Mulk. Denise Aigle has observed the frequent development of mirrors in times of political crisis.[133] For al-Thaᶜālibī and especially Niẓām al-Mulk, the story of Naṣr demonstrated the inevitable compounding of religious dissent with political instability. Yet, as Neguin Yavari has recently shown, the mirror-writers' forceful warnings against heterodoxy accompanied invocations of ancient wisdom and appeals to the ruler to exercise reason in the religious sphere.[134] These features are especially marked in *Naṣīḥat al-mulūk*, in which exclusionary assertions are to some extent counterbalanced by their placement in an inclusive framework. As Chapter 7 will demonstrate, *Naṣīḥat al-mulūk* anticipated the later mirrors of al-Thaᶜālibī and Niẓām al-Mulk, and its treatment of these themes illuminates the mentality and discourse that shaped the writings of Pseudo-Māwardī's successors.

6

Religion and the Samanid Amirs

Written in the oblique third-person mode of address, *Naṣīḥat al-mulūk* is intended for 'the kings of our religious community in this time of ours'. Pseudo-Māwardī urges these unidentified kings to prepare themselves, through study and the development of their rational faculties, to participate in and, when necessary, to intervene in the kingdom's religious sphere. In order to situate and interpret Pseudo-Māwardī's advice in this regard, it is instructive to survey the orientations and practices of the Samanid amirs, which provide a context for his attitude and response in *Naṣīḥat al-mulūk*.

Over the course of the Samanid era, the amirs' involvement in religious life and in the kingdom's religious affairs reflects considerable change. In the later ninth and early tenth century, the sons of Aḥmad I cultivated religious scholars, engaged in the hearing and transmission of ḥadīth and participated in *jihād*. Their religious style, which evinces considerable continuity with Tahirid practices, appears to have linked them with a strong current in the prevailing culture, in which austerity (*zuhd*), often coupled with study and emulation of the example of the Prophet, constituted a prominent component. Later amirs acted in the context of a quite different political configuration. The Karakhanids, a large tribal confederation probably related to the Karluks, adopted Islam in the middle years of the tenth century, when their head Satuq Bughra Khān assumed the name ᶜAbd al-Karīm; his grandson Hārūn, or Ḥasan Bughra Khān, would occupy Bukhara in 382/992 and initiate the formation of the Karakhanid dynasty (382–609/992–1212) in Transoxiana.[1] Accordingly, in the latter half of the tenth century, the steppe lands to the north and east of the Samanid domains ceased to represent a religious frontier. At the same time, the Buyids, from their centres in Iraq and western Iran, mounted repeated challenges for control of contested territories in northern and central Iran. The later amirs directed much of their attention towards these challenges. The amirs of the later tenth century also presided over a more extensive administrative apparatus, and they appear to have maintained greater distance from most of their subjects, including the ᶜulamāᵓ. Nevertheless, the later amirs chose to promote a distinctive interpretation of Sunni Islam through a variety of means, including the 'translation' or adaptation of prestigious works of religious scholarship, notably the *Tafsīr* of al-Ṭabarī, from Arabic into Persian and the promulgation in Persian of the theological tract *al-Sawād al-aᶜẓam*.[2]

Pseudo-Māwardī almost certainly composed *Naṣīḥat al-mulūk* during the reign of Naṣr II b. Aḥmad, which in many respects marks a hiatus between the earlier and the later divisions of the Samanid period. If, as the evidence of the text suggests, Pseudo-Māwardī wrote his mirror in significant measure in response to reports of the amir's incipient or actual conversion to Ismaᶜilism, it is quite likely to date from the last decade or so of Naṣr's reign, that is, roughly 321–31/933–43.[3] In *Naṣīḥat al-mulūk*, I suggest, Pseudo-Māwardī in effect urges the amir to consider the merits of the style and practices of the sons of Aḥmad I, namely, Naṣr I, Isḥāq and Ismāᶜīl. It was this generation whose conduct shaped Pseudo-Māwardī's conception of good governance, a governance that he regarded as conducive to the social and moral well-being (*ṣalāḥ* or *maṣlaḥa*) of rulers and subjects alike. The purpose of the present chapter is to explore the Samanids' dispositions and practices in matters that involved religion, in order to establish the context for Pseudo-Māwardī's portrayal of the ills that beset kingdoms and their remedies, the subject of Chapter 7 below, and to suggest the character of the governance that he admired and advocated.

The Early Samanid Amirs

The Samanid amirs who governed Bukhara and Samarqand up until the reign of Aḥmad II participated actively in the public religious sphere. They undertook various religiously associated activities and expended substantial efforts in the cultivation of mutually supportive relations with the religious scholars in their cities. Their involvement in the public religious arena is evident in various respects.

In several cases, the early amirs attended the funerals of prominent religious scholars and on a number of occasions they led the funeral prayers.[4] Attendance at funerals and participation in the rites of burial constituted a *farḍ kifāya*, that is, an obligation that fell upon the community in its entirety and that required the active performance of at least some of its members. It was customary for a near relative to lead prayers at the grave of the deceased. In the case of the deaths of particularly respected individuals, however, a prominent figure unrelated to the deceased might lead the funeral prayers, an arrangement that suggested the prestige of the deceased and cast a favourable reflection on the individual honoured to lead the prayers. In such cases, as Muhammad Qasim Zaman has demonstrated, the governor or local representative of the political authorities was often eager to lead the funeral prayers in order to advertise the state's patronage of widely admired figures.[5] In 211/826–7, Aḥmad b. Asad led the prayer for Abū ᶜUthmān Salm b. Ḥafṣ al-Fazārī al-Samarqandī, who had held the judicial office (*qaḍāʾ*) of Samarqand for many years.[6] In 231/846, Aḥmad's son Naṣr conducted the prayers at the funeral of Saᶜd b. Naṣr al-Zāhid al-Wāᶜiẓ (the renunciant and preacher) al-Samarqandī.[7] On another occasion, the reports of which circulated among the scholars of ḥadīth, Naṣr accompanied a funeral on foot. In a demonstration of the behaviour that earned him his reputation for religious observance and austerity, Naṣr, walking through the mud, said, '[God's] claims are fulfilled only through hardship' (*lā tuqḍā l-ḥuqūq illā bi-l-mashaqqa*).[8] Naṣr's brother and successor Ismāᶜīl b. Aḥmad led the prayer for the ḥadīth scholar Abū Tawba Saᶜīd b. Hāshim b. Ḥamza al-Kāghidhī al-Samarqandī, who died in Samarqand in 259/873.[9] Another brother, Amir Yaᶜqūb b. Aḥmad (I), prayed over Abū Saᶜīd b. Dāʾūd al-Warrāq al-Samarqandī at the latter's death in 282/895.[10] The early amirs' practice of attending scholars' funerals demonstrated their attentiveness to a prevalent strand of the contemporary regional religious–political culture. Members of the Tahirid dynastic family had engaged in the same activity,[11] and in another example, Dāʾūd b. al-ᶜAbbās al-Bānījūrī (d. 259/873), the governor of Balkh (*amīr-i Balkh*), recited the funeral prayers over the learned jurist Muḥammad b. Mālik b. Bakr (d. 244/858–9), who commanded a vast following.[12] Although they did not originate the practice of participation in the funeral rites of leading scholars, the early Samanid amirs below the rank of senior amir or before they attained it appear to have pursued it in a particularly deliberate fashion. During their absences, they delegated these responsibilities to their deputies. When in 235/849–50 a judge died during Naṣr's absence on a campaign, the amir's deputy (*khalīfa*) read the funeral prayers; and at the death in 248/863 of Zibrak al-Aᶜraj, who transmitted ḥadīth related to *hijra* and *jihād* and also led an army of fighters (*ghuzāt*, pl. or *ghāzī*) in Samarqand, Naṣr's deputy al-Ḥasan b. Hilqām prayed over him.[13]

The case of the esteemed ḥadīth scholar Abū Muḥammad ᶜAbdallāh b. ᶜAbd al-Raḥmān al-Dārimī (181–255/797–869) provides an illuminating example of the religious culture of Samarqand during this period. Al-Dārimī was noted for his intellect, gravity, austerity and religiosity, and for his knowledge of jurisprudence, the abundance of the materials that he had committed to memory and his knowledge of scriptural interpretation (*kāna fī ghāyatin min al-ᶜaql wa-l-razāna wa-l-zuhd wa-l-diyāna wa-l-fiqh wa-l-ḥifẓ wa-l-tafsīr*), and it was he who promoted most conspicuously the science of the 'traditions' (authenticated transmitted reports of the sayings and practices) of the Prophet and his Companions (*huwa alladhī aẓhara ᶜilm al-ḥadīth wa-l-āthār wa-l-sunna*) at Samarqand. Many of the compilers of the Prophet's *sunna*, including al-Bukhārī (194–256/810–70), Muslim (d. 261/875) and al-Bukhārī's student al-Tirmidhī (210–79/825–92), all of whose collections were classified among the 'six books' regarded as authoritative among Sunni Muslims, related ḥadīth from al-Dārimī.[14] The Samanids' conciliatory approaches notwithstanding, al-Dārimī declined the office of judge in Samarqand; in the face of their insistence, he consented to judge only a single case.[15] Despite, or perhaps in respectful acknowledgement of, his detachment from worldly power, when al-Dārimī died in 255/869, Aḥmad b. Yaḥyā b. Asad, the Amir of Samarqand, prayed over him. Instances of close contact among amirs and scholars continued into the early tenth century. Among those who transmitted from al-Dārimī was Abū Naṣr al-Fatḥ b. Qurra of Baghdad, who settled in Samarqand and became a trusted figure (*amīn*) close to Ismāᶜīl b. Aḥmad; in turn, the leader of the army in Samarqand, Abū Isḥāq Ibrāhīm b. Aḥmad, transmitted from Abū Naṣr.[16]

Like the Tahirids, the Samanid amirs of this period also participated directly in the acquisition and promotion of religious scholarship.[17] The pattern is already apparent in the figure of Aḥmad (I) b. Asad, governor of Samarqand until his death, when the city passed to his son Naṣr (I) b. Aḥmad. Aḥmad, according to Narshakhī, was 'learned and pious' (*ᶜālim va-pārsā*), and according to Ibn al-Athīr, he was religiously observant (*dayyin*), rationally intelligent (*ᶜāqil*) and composed fine poetry (in Arabic).[18] At least four of his sons – Naṣr (I), Isḥāq, Yaᶜqūb and Ismāᶜīl – heard and transmitted ḥadīth, which they related on the authority of several transmitters, including their father.[19] They belonged to the socially and professionally diverse groupings of persons who, while not specialists in the transmission of the Prophetic *sunna*, devoted a portion of their time to the activity.[20] Prominent among the subjects of the ḥadīth related by the early amirs are the themes of *ghazw*, justice and respect for scholars.[21] In this generation, the amirs and several leading scholars participated in a common religious–political culture supported and reinforced by a network of ties that connected the two spheres.

Tellingly, a secretary in the service of Naṣr I transmitted a ḥadīth that endorsed association with the ruler.[22] The subject of association with the authorities was actively debated during the earlier Samanid period; the extant writings of al-Kaᶜbī demonstrate the prominence of the question,[23] and Pseudo-Māwardī devoted a section in his final chapter, in which he addressed a sequence of matters of controversy, to the permissibility or otherwise of working for an unjust ruler.[24] The ḥadīth scholar Abū l-Faḍl al-ᶜAbbās b. Maḥmūd b. ᶜAbd al-Raḥmān (d. 321/933), who held the office of chief of police (*ṣāḥib shuraṭ*) in Samarqand, found the assembly (*majlis*) of Naṣr I 'crammed full of scholars, commanders and elders of the city' (*ghāṣṣ bi-l-ᶜulamāᵓ wa-l-quwwād wa-mashāyikh al-balad*).[25] Ismāᶜīl b. Aḥmad's secretary or vizier (*kātib*), was among the individuals who transmitted from him,[26] and a family of scholars served in high administrative positions under successive Samanid amirs, beginning with Ismāᶜīl.[27] Isḥāq appears in a chain of transmitters (*isnād*), the mechanism that authenticated the reliability of a ḥadīth;[28] and ᶜAwaḍ b. Muḥammad al-Hilqāmī, Isḥāq's deputy (*khalīfa*) and chief of police in Samarqand, related ḥadīth and delivered the *khuṭba* during Ramadan.[29]

Again following the example of the Tahirids, celebrated for their cultivation of poetry, the amirs of Naṣr I's generation combined their pursuit of religious studies with an interest in Arabic literary culture. ᶜAbdallāh b.

Ṭāhir, trained in literary and religious culture, *adab* and *fiqh*, was especially noted for his poetry and prose. When he became ill, he repented, shattered his musical instruments (he delighted in music and song, and was skilled in composition) and freed prisoners.[30] Pseudo-Māwardī, who cites ᶜAbdallāh's poetry, observes Isḥāq b. Aḥmad's devotion to religious knowledge (*ᶜilm*) and to literary culture (*adab*), his love (*maḥabba*) for the persons who pursued these subjects, and his frequent and attentive contact with them.[31] Ismāᶜīl likewise attained a degree of learning in both the religious and the literary branches of knowledge. According to a report related on the authority of Naṣr II's vizier Abū l-Fażl Balᶜamī, Ismāᶜīl stated that the first book pertaining to *adab* that he had committed to memory was the *Adab al-kātib* ('Good Conduct of the Secretary') [of the littérateur Ibn Qutayba], and next the *Gharīb al-ḥadīth* ('Obscure Parts of the Ḥadīth') of Abū ᶜUbayd [al-Qāsim b. Sallām, d. *c.* 224/838];[32] he then embarked on the study of ḥadīth and *ādāb* (pl. of *adab*). Al-Nasafī reported further that Ismāᶜīl was proficient in Arabic grammar and inflexion (*iᶜrāb*), and well versed in the differences of legal interpretation (*kāna . . . yaᶜlamu l-ikhtilāfāt*).[33]

Furthermore, it is indicative of the religious culture in which the early amirs participated that Ismāᶜīl experienced more than one vision of the Prophet in his dreams. Dream visions of the Prophet, according to several ḥadīth and a widely shared understanding, could only be veridical.[34] (In an illustration of the significance attached to dreams, visions of the Qurʾānic figure al-Khiḍr also occurred frequently in Samarqand, and sometimes in the *ribāṭ*s at the frontier.[35]) In addition to the dream in which the Prophet predicted his ascendancy over Isḥāq, Ismāᶜīl recounted a dream in which he saw the Prophet, with Abū Bakr on his right, ᶜUmar on his left and ᶜAlī standing behind his back. Ismāᶜīl, in a milieu noted for devotion to ᶜAlī, had held Shiᶜite beliefs in his youth. The vision reportedly left him ill for several months, until his brother Naṣr wrote to him and advised him to turn in repentance (of his convictions) towards God and His Prophet. Ismāᶜīl subsequently abandoned his Shiᶜism and is said to have regained his health.[36]

The early generation of amirs was also distinguished by personal engagement in warfare. Their participation in military activities in the borderlands linked them to a distinctive religious culture that thrived at the frontier. Numbers of individuals undertook the journey to the Byzantine or Central

Asian frontiers. The renunciant Ibrāhīm b. Adham (d. 166/777–8) of Balkh, in a particularly celebrated example, reportedly fought and died in battle at the Byzantine frontier.[37] Later hagiographies lend a symbolic significance to the practice, and the journey to the borderlands, associated with figures such as Ibrāhīm b. Adham, became a *topos*.[38] In Central Asia, as attested by the previously noted passage in *Tārīkh-i Sīstān*, the early amirs' participation in *ghazw* and *jihād* involved them in the culture of *zuhd*, austerity, which had accompanied the religious–military life in the *ribāṭāt* along the Central Asian frontier since the eighth century.[39] (It also, of course, brought material benefits, as indicated in Chapter 1.) The prominence of volunteers (*mutaṭawwiᶜa*) among the soldiers at the frontier suggests a dispersed and varied constituency of individuals, whose support the early Samanid amirs perhaps hoped to secure through their personal leadership in campaigns of *ghazw*.[40] Pseudo-Māwardī associated Naṣr I with the qualities of religious observance and austerity, *ᶜibāda* and *zuhd*,[41] topics to be explored further in the following pages; these qualities found expression in, among other settings, the culture associated with the frontier.

Of all the amirs, it is Ismāᶜīl whose military endeavours left the most marked impress on his lasting reputation. In his campaign against Talas in 280/893, Ismāᶜīl brought the ruler and many *dihqān*s into Islam, converted a church into a mosque, had the *khuṭba* read in the name of Caliph al-Muᶜtaḍid, who had invested him with the governorship (*ᶜamal*) of Transoxiana, and returned to Bukhara with much booty.[42] As indicated in Chapter 1, Pseudo-Māwardī reports the personal participation in military activities of Caliph Hārūn al-Rashīd and Caliph al-Muᶜtaṣim, and also notes Ismāᶜīl's well-publicised participation in *ghazw*.[43] Al-Nasafī describes Ismāᶜīl in the following terms: 'He was among the most virtuous of amirs, [in that he] acted justly in his ordinances and was compassionate towards his subjects; he became proverbial for (his) fine moral character and companionship, and (his) enthusiasm for *jihād* and the killing of infidels; and he possessed a large army'.[44] During Ismāᶜīl's reign, his nephew Aḥmad b. Naṣr [I], whom Ismāᶜīl had appointed (presumably to Samarqand) after his father's death, followed the example of his father and uncles by his engagement in *ghazw*.[45] After the reign of Ismāᶜīl, however, the Samanid amirs appear to have discontinued the practice of active participation in warfare. Against persons who sought to dissuade the king from personal participation in warfare, as well as several other royal activities, Pseudo-Māwardī conveys his opinion that such personal engagement befitted the ruler's office.[46]

Various other reports indicate the early amirs' sustained efforts to promote a cooperative relationship with the ᶜulamāᵓ in their cities. Ismāᶜīl responded to the appeal of the scholars of Transoxiana by providing full support for the production of the boundary-setting tract, *al-Sawād al-aᶜẓam*.[47] Pseudo-Māwardī lists among Ismāᶜīl's virtues his public and visible commitment to religious observance and the upholding of the religious law.[48] The Samanids are particularly noted for having exempted the ᶜulamāᵓ from the ritual kissing of the ground before the ruler (*taqbīl al-arḍ*).[49] Ismāᶜīl and Isḥāq each bestowed an annual gift of 4,000 dirhams on the Shāfiᶜī scholar Muḥammad b. Naṣr al-Marwazī (202–94/817–906), and Isḥāq's subjects in Samarqand did likewise, perhaps an illustration of Pseudo-Māwardī's reiterated point that subjects imitate the conduct of their ruler.[50] As this example demonstrates, the Samanids' preferential treatment of the ᶜulamāᵓ was not limited to scholars of the Ḥanafī *madhhab*, despite the latter's predominance among the Samanid élite.[51] Al-Nasafī confirms this impression in his report that Ismāᶜīl did not display obvious partiality towards one grouping (*farīq*) over another.[52] The striking narrative of Ismāᶜīl's predictive dream, in which the Prophet attributes his triumph over Isḥāq to his deference to Muḥammad b. Naṣr and Isḥāq's withholding of respect from the scholar, underlines the central importance of the cultivation of the ᶜulamāᵓ in the construction of legitimacy.[53]

The tenor of Pseudo-Māwardī's ideals of governance and leadership is fully compatible with the hypothesis that he wrote within memory of the period represented by Naṣr I, Ismāᶜīl I and Isḥāq. The evidence of *Naṣīḥat al-mulūk* coincides with and supplements the impressions furnished in other near-contemporary sources regarding the religious culture of the early Samanid period. Pseudo-Māwardī's depiction of the conduct and disposition of these early amirs suggests a high level of contact and cooperation between the early amirs and the leading ᶜulamāᵓ.[54] Like the caliphs whom the author extolled earlier in his historical section, the early Samanid amirs are praised for their display of a distinct set of religiously associated virtues: austerity; godliness; religious observance; cultivating religious learning; seeking the companionship of men of learning and extending generosity towards them; and upholding the outer meanings of the religious law.

Furthermore, Pseudo-Māwardī's appeal to his royal audience is consistent with the impression that the Samanids' involvement in the religious culture of their subjects, including the nurturing of personal relationships with the leading ᶜulamāᵓ in their cities, decreased markedly during the first half of the tenth century. Paul has concluded that the solicitous and mutually supportive relationship between the amirs and the mainstream ᶜulamāᵓ weakened following the reign of Ismāᶜīl, after which time the amirs' participation in *jihād* and *ghazw*, in the transmission of ḥadīth, and at the funerals of scholars appears to have ceased.[55] This shift is likely to have intensified during the reign of Aḥmad II. At the beginning of his reign, Aḥmad II received scholars, such as the ḥadīth scholar Abū ᶜĀṣim ᶜAmr b. ᶜĀṣim al-Marwazī, who visited him, apparently in Samarqand, in 295/907–8.[56] Although al-Muqaddasī reported that the Samanid amirs consistently selected the most learned and upright jurist of Bukhara, elevated him, promulgated his judgement, fulfilled his needs and governed the districts according to his word (*wa-yakhtārūna abadan afqaha man bi-Bukhārā wa-aᶜaffahum fa-yarfaᶜūnahu wa-yaṣdarūna ᶜan raᵓyihi wa-yaqḍūna ḥawāᵓijahu wa-yuwallūna l-aᶜmāl bi-qawlihi*),[57] accounts of personal interaction decline in frequency in later years. Pseudo-Māwardī, I suggest, perceived these changes, which grew more pronounced in the aftermath of Aḥmad II's assassination, and his experience of earlier patterns shaped his response to the conditions he observed during Naṣr's reign.

Concepts of *ᶜIbāda* and *Zuhd*

A signal feature of the cultural milieu and mentality that engendered *Naṣīḥat al-mulūk* is a linked pairing of religious–cultural virtues, *zuhd*, or austerity, and *ᶜibāda*, or devotion, to the fulfilment of religious obligations. These qualities appealed to numerous constituencies among the populations of western Asia in the late antique and early Islamic eras. As Leah Kinberg has shown, the concept of *zuhd* embraced a spectrum of meanings, many general in scope and connoting strong moral engagement, and some evoking specific forms of disciplined behaviour.[58] Interest in austerity, which for many people betokened moral excellence, flourished particularly in Baghdad, where large numbers of renunciants (*zuhhād*) settled in the course of the ninth century. The appeal of *zuhd* manifested itself in, for example, the proliferation of a literature devoted to the topic. Among the *zuhhād* of Baghdad, Ibn Abī l-Dunyā (208–81/823–94) composed a treatise on the subject of *zuhd*, and another on the subject of *taqwā*, or 'godliness',[59] and al-Ḥārith b. Asad al-Muḥāsibī (d. 243/857–8) composed 'many books on the subject of austerity'.[60] The breadth of the subject's interest finds further attestation in the oeuvres of the ninth-century littérateurs al-Jāḥiẓ and Ibn Qutayba, each of whom included a *Kitāb al-Zuhd* in their respective works *al-Bayān wa-l-tabyīn* ('Clarity and Clarification') and *ᶜUyūn al-akhbār* ('Choice Accounts').[61] The topic's appeal also produced a flourishing literature of *zuhdiyyāt*, 'poems on the theme of austerity', which gradually developed into a distinct poetic genre.[62] Indeed, Pseudo-Māwardī cited (without always identifying the poet) several verses of Abū l-ᶜAtāhiya (d. *c.* 210/825), whose prodigious output of literary exhortations in this genre, popular with the people of Baghdad, struck some of his contemporaries and rivals as being at odds with his behaviour.[63]

The qualities of *zuhd* and *ᶜibāda* also shaped the lives of countless individuals in the towns and villages of ninth-century eastern Iran and Transoxiana. The renunciant Bishr (al-Ḥāfī, 'the bare-foot') b. al-Ḥārith (al-Marwazī) (150–227/767–841), born near Marv although he settled in Baghdad, is identified as *al-ᶜābid al-zāhid*, 'devoted to worship and austerity'; he too composed a book on the subject of austerity.[64] The mystic al-Ḥakīm al-Tirmidhī, probably an older contemporary of Pseudo-Māwardī, spent much of his life in his native city of Tirmidh, but was summoned to neighbouring Balkh in about 261/874 on charges of heretical teachings; his intellectual activity included the study of ḥadīth, and he provided a model of a life of religious devotion coupled with personal humility and poverty.[65] The topic appears as a distinct category in the collections of ḥadīth compiled by Muslim, Ibn Māja (209–73/824 or 825–87), al-Tirmidhī and al-Dārimī, all of whom lived in the *mashriq*.[66]

The practice of austerity was a marked feature in the public cultures of Balkh and Samarqand.[67] Pseudo-Māwardī's inclusion of *nussāk* among the categories of persons whose cooperation was indispensable in governance attests to the social prominence and persuasive power of renunciants in his milieu.[68] His presentation is consistent with the evidence of al-Nasafī's *al-Qand fī dhikr ᶜulamāᵓ Samarqand* and *Fażāᵓil-i Balkh*, which indicate that the qualities of *zuhd* and *ᶜibada* earned their practitioners not only respect and admiration, but also status and prestige in this pair of cities. Amongst the notable inhabitants of these cities, the epithets *al-zāhid*, *al-ᶜābid* and also *al-ḥakīm* ('the wise' or 'the sage', an honorific mode of address for a respected religious authority) appear, singly and in combination, with considerable frequency.[69] In another suggestion of the early date of *Naṣīḥat al-mulūk*, Pseudo-Māwardī similarly refers to practitioners of *zuhd* and *ᶜibāda*, but not *taṣawwuf*; by the end of the tenth century Ibn al-Nadīm would group individuals under the rubric of 'worshippers, renunciants and Sufis' (*al-ᶜubbād wa-l-zuhhād wa-l-mutaṣawwifa*).[70]

In Samarqand, Naṣr I b. Aḥmad appears to have promoted and participated in an austere religious culture, in which the inspiration of Prophetic example, expressed in the hearing and transmission of ḥadīth, and a deferential approach towards leading figures among the ᶜulamāᵓ, demonstrated on ceremonial occasions, constituted prominent characteristics. According to several accounts, Ismāᶜīl too exhibited *zuhd* in his manner of governance.[71] In this setting, persons committed to lives of austerity quite frequently occupied prominent positions in the public sphere. As his *nisbas* indicate, the previously mentioned Saᶜd b. Naṣr al-Zāhid al-Wāᶜiẓ al-Samarqandī, who died in 231/846, practised austerity and performed the public functions of preaching and exhorting the population.[72] Abū Naṣr Khushnām b. al-Miqdād al-ᶜĀbid, who died in Samarqand in 271/884, also bore the *nisba* 'the Renunciant' (al-Zāhid); that he too enjoyed a position of social prominence is to be inferred from the report that a son of Naṣr I and member of the Samanid dynastic family, Luqmān b. Naṣr b. Aḥmad al-Amīr, prayed over him at his funeral.[73] In another example, Abū l-Qāsim al-Ḥakīm al-Samarqandī (d. 342/953), the leading scholar involved in the production of *al-Sawād al-aᶜẓam* in the reign of Ismāᶜīl, is identified in the introduction to the Persian translation, *Tarjameh-yi al-Sawād al-aᶜẓam*, as *khvājeh imām-i zāhid* ('the distinguished renunciatory imam').[74] As the examples of al-Ḥakīm al-Samarqandī and al-Ḥakīm al-Tirmidhī illustrate, sometimes conjoined with these epithets is the designation *ḥakīm*, often included in the honorific titles of eminent and esteemed figures in the *mashriq*; this term connotes learning and wisdom, especially a superior understanding of religious truth, and appears frequently among individuals disposed to the interior life.[75]

Fażāʾil-i Balkh reflects the equal prominence of renunciants in that city's public culture, and its author availed himself of, among other sources, the *Kitāb al-Zuhd* of ᶜAbbād b. Kathīr in the preparation of his work.[76] As Bernd Radtke has indicated, the renunciants Shaqīq al-Balkhī, Ibrāhīm b. Adham and Ḥātim al-Aṣamm (d. 237/852), as well as Ḥātim's student Aḥmad b. Khiḍrawayh (d. 240/854–5), and Ibn Khiḍrawayh's students Abū Bakr al-Warrāq (d. 280/893) and Muḥammad b. al-Faḍl (d. 317/929), all of whom hailed from or lived in Balkh, were related by birth or marriage to established families of the élite.[77] The examples of Ibrāhīm b. Adham, Shaqīq al-Balkhī and Ḥātim al-Aṣamm are particularly noteworthy, since they reflect the interconnected cultural networks of Balkh and Samarqand: Shaqīq came to Samarqand, where he related from Abū Ḥanīfa; Ibrāhīm b. Adham and his son, as well as Ḥātim al-Aṣamm, related in turn from Shaqīq.[78] Shaqīq, moreover, owned large areas of land in the vicinity of Balkh, and had acquired a large fortune, in part as a result of his commercial activity.[79] *Al-Qand fī dhikr ᶜulamāʾ Samarqand* and *Fażāʾil-i Balkh* both attest to the high status of these three figures, and to the relationships among their students and associates.[80] The attribute of *zuhd*, it should be added, was not restricted to males; *Fażāʾil-i Balkh* records accounts of a woman renunciant, a *Ḥakīma Zāhida*, wife of Ibn Khiḍrawayh.[81]

The high status and economic means of religious scholars (*ᶜulamāʾ*) and ascetics (*nussāk*) provide context for Pseudo-Māwardī's advice to his royal readership regarding the necessity for harmonious and cooperative relations with these categories.[82] Their social standing rendered them well situated to assist him if he won their support. It also permitted them to challenge and resist the initiatives and demands of governmental power. Bernd Radtke, on the basis of the evidence of *Fażāʾil-i Balkh*, has noted the recurrence of such conflicts in that city. Most of the documented incidents occurred during the early Abbasid period, but a particularly notable case took place during the Samanid period. In this example, Abū Bakr Muḥammad b. Saᶜīd al-Balkhī (d. 328/939–40), the forty-fifth shaykh (in chronological order) of the city,[83] considered the demands placed on a village to be wrongful. Ḥasan b. Abī l-Ṭayyib al-Muṣᶜabī, the deputy's official (*yekī az ᶜummāl-i khalīfeh*) responsible for raising revenue, engaged in a disputation with the scholar. Perhaps the son of the Samanid vizier Abū l-Ṭayyib al-Muṣᶜabī, this Ḥasan b. Abī l-Ṭayyib asked the shaykh Abū Bakr if he had forgotten the fate of his teacher (*ustādh*), the forty-fourth shaykh Abū l-Qāsim Ṣaffār (d. 326/937–8). Abū Bakr asked in rejoinder whether Ḥasan remembered the fate of his *ustādh*, Abū l-Ṭayyib al-Muṣᶜabī, who 'belonged to the Qarāmiṭa' (*az aṣḥāb-i qarāmiṭeh būd*).[84]

Given the likely dating (*c*. 326–8/937–40) and location of the case, it is possible that Pseudo-Māwardī observed the unfolding of these events. Furthermore, it seems probable that the Qarmaṭī al-Muṣᶜabī to whose fate the shaykh Abū Bakr alluded was the vizier who reportedly induced Naṣr's conversion.[85] The account indicates that it was possible to conceive of explicitly articulated resistance to political authority in Pseudo-Māwardī's immediate milieu. His act of literary intervention, it would seem, was not an altogether isolated event, but took place in a context in which individuals, albeit exceptionally, might take it upon themselves to challenge the agents of the political authorities. Whereas the shaykh Abū Bakr engaged in direct confrontation, Pseudo-Māwardī adopted a posture of 'love' when he offered a discursive treatise grounded in rational argument and literary dexterity.

The case of the shaykh Abū Bakr also sheds light on another aspect of Pseudo-Māwardī's composition. As Chapter 7 will suggest, Pseudo-Māwardī appears to have been aware of the presence of Ismaᶜilis among the courtly élites, and to have known that the amir either had, or might become, an Ismaᶜili himself. His decision to intervene permits the inference that Pseudo-Māwardī thought it possible that the king might 'repent'. Two accounts of Naṣr's conversion state that he did, in fact, experience a kind of repentance. Ibn al-Nadīm, who provides the earliest of the accounts, wrote that Naṣr repented after his adoption of Ismaᶜilism.[86] Al-Thaᶜālibī, who provides a fuller narrative of the amir's conversion, including its prelude and aftermath, stated that Naṣr experienced a period of intense repentance and fear of death before he succumbed to the comforting doctrines of the Ismaᶜili missionaries. During this period, the amir had repented of drinking and shedding blood, had devoted himself to pious observance, secluded himself in prayer and weeping, and feared death intensely (*kāna yakhlū bi-l-duᶜāʾ wa-l-bukāʾ wa-yakhāfu l-mawt ashadda al-khawf*). This fragile state, in al-Thaᶜālibī's account, had predisposed him to the deceptive teachings of al-Muṣᶜabī – the vizier to whom, probably, the shaykh Abū Bakr referred as a *qarmaṭī* – and Ibn Sawāda. These two Ismaᶜili missionaries had, in al-Thaᶜālibī's portrayal, persuaded Naṣr to their doctrine by promoting the notion that pleasure would relieve the rational soul (*al-nafs al-nāṭiqa*) of its troubles in the physical world.[87] These reports (the accuracy of which, of course, cannot be assessed) suggest that the possibility of repentance featured in significant fashion in contemporary reports of Naṣr's attraction to Ismaᶜilism. *Naṣīḥat al-mulūk* emphasises the right of the individual to 'repent', that is, to reconsider his action and change his behaviour; among other examples, in his oration, Yazīd III had requested the caliph's right to acknowledge and amend his shortcomings.[88] It was in this context, perhaps, that Pseudo-Māwardī raised the topic of abandoning one religious affiliation for another. Whether Naṣr indeed renounced his allegiance to the Ismaᶜiliyya remains unknown.

The Reign of Naṣr

Already in the early decades of the tenth century, the amirs who succeeded Ismāᶜīl developed different styles of leadership, and interacted less closely with the ᶜulamāᵓ. If this shift occasioned a growing estrangement between the religious scholars and the court, the identification of the highest ranks of the Samanid court with Ismaᶜilism during the reign of Naṣr exacerbated their alienation.[89] A number of scholars died in a phenomenon that al-Nasafī described as *taᶜaṣṣub al-qarāmiṭa*, 'the factional activity of the Carmathians', possibly an uprising.[90] As the incident involving the shaykh Abū Bakr al-Balkhī's resistance to the deputy's tax-collector indicates, the ᶜulamāᵓ did not uniformly acquiesce in the face of the increasing prominence of Ismaᶜilis among the élites. According to Niẓām al-Mulk, news of the amir's attachment to Ismaᶜilism spread amongst the religious scholars and judges of the capital city and the regions (*ᶜālimān va-qāżiyān-i shahr va-navāḥī*), who assembled, and presented their displeasure to the commander of the army, the leading officers of which likewise opposed the amir's support for the Ismaᶜili missionaries.[91] In an especially notable example, this time explicitly directed against the vizier Abū l-Ṭayyib al-Muṣᶜabī, on 27 Ramadan in an unspecified year the ḥadīth scholar Abū Yaᶜlā ᶜAbd al-Muᵓmin b. Khalaf al-ᶜAmmī (259–346/873–957) prayed publicly for the perdition of the vizier, whom he accused of *zandaqa* and *ilḥād*, and for that of the *qarāmiṭa*, among whom, like the shaykh Abū Bakr, he included al-Muṣᶜabī. On the same occasion he prayed for the release of the scholar and *raʾīs* of Nasaf Abū ᶜUthmān Saᶜīd b. Ibrāhīm (al-Raʾīs al-Nasafī), whom the vizier had summoned to the court in connection with *taᶜaṣṣub al-qarāmiṭa*.[92]

As Chapter 7 will demonstrate, Pseudo-Māwardī, like some of his fellow citizens, was aware of the prominence of Ismaᶜilis in the amir's *khāṣṣa*. He feared the king's susceptibility to the élites' powers of persuasion, and, if the amir had already succumbed, he sought to induce him to renounce his new allegiance.

It was probably in the last decade of his reign that Naṣr turned towards Ismaᶜilism.[93] On the basis of numismatic evidence, Crone and Treadwell have concluded that in 329–30/940–1, his son Nūḥ (r. 331–43/943–54) rebelled against his father; it is less certain that Naṣr's adoption of Ismaᶜilism prompted Nūḥ's revolt, despite the construction of events relayed in the sources.[94] A possible indication that Naṣr's conversion was a significant factor in Nūḥ's rebellion is the latter's appointment, following his accession in 331 /943, of the highly regarded Ḥanafī scholar and judge of Bukhara Abū l-Faḍl Muḥammad b. Aḥmad al-Sulamī al-Marwazī as his vizier. In a similar case, the governor Ibn Farīghūn appointed the judge Abū ᶜUmar ᶜAbd al-Waḥīd b. Aḥmad (d. 368/978–9) to the vizierate, in which capacity the judge served for many years.[95] Furthermore, it was towards the beginning of the reign of Nūḥ b. Naṣr, in the year 333/944–5, that the 'leader (*zaᶜīm*) of the Ismaᶜilis' affair', Muḥammad b. Aḥmad al-Bazdawī (= al-Nasafī/Nakhshabī) and his associate Muḥammad b. Saᶜīd b. Muᶜādh al-Manādīlī al-Bukhārī al-Ṣabbāgh were killed.[96] Later phases in the reign of Nūḥ saw further actions against the Ismaᶜilis, although even then several Ismaᶜilis (or persons accused of Ismaᶜilism) remained in high office.[97] It is likely that unrest continued in provincial locations, but, as Crone and Treadwell have shown, Niẓām al-Mulk's report of a second set of events involving Ismaᶜilis at the court of Manṣūr I (r. 350–65/961–76) probably arose from his conflation of accounts pertaining to local uprisings during the reign of ᶜAbd al-Malik (r. 343–50/954–61) with the events of Naṣr's reign.[98]

The overtly didactic nature of the two fullest accounts of Naṣr's conversion, those of al-Thaᶜālibī and Niẓām al-Mulk, complicates efforts to reconstruct and interpret his reign. Other accounts present quite different aspects of his interests and activities. A prominent line of historiography, especially in Persian, presents Naṣr II b. Aḥmad in positive terms. This Persian discourse presents Naṣr as the just monarch who presided over a resplendent court and as the patron of Rūdakī, associated with the beginnings of Persian poetry. In an early example, Narshakhī, a supporter of Ismāᶜīl's line, states that he was a just king (*pādshāh-i ᶜādil*), indeed more just than his father, and that he possessed many splendid qualities, too many to enumerate (*shamāᵓil-i ū besyār būdeh ast*).[99] In an apparently isolated but precisely dated account, set at the Samanid court in 327/939, Naṣr b. Aḥmad appears in the role of defender of the realm and opponent of religious dissent. In that year, Naṣr reportedly acceded to the request of Abū Ḥafṣ Aḥmad b. Muḥammad Ibn al-Zaburqān, the jurist (*faqīh*) of Bukhara and 'adviser of the kingdom' (*mushīr al-mamlaka*) that the amir grant him access to a Nishapuri man said to have been a materialist (*min al-dahriyya*).[100] This individual had reportedly employed techniques of deception and trickery in an attempt to incite a Chinese invasion of the Samanid (and Muslim) domains, and he was accused of heresy and the denial of the divine attributes (*al-ilḥād wa-l-taᶜṭīl*).[101] In his efforts to deter a Chinese campaign, Naṣr was able to summon, alongside his generals (*ḥujjāb*) and military slaves (*ghilmān*), large numbers of voluntary forces composed of *ghuzāt* (pl. of *ghāzī*), *ᶜayyārūn* (independent fighters) and *mashāyikh* to appear with him in Bukhara.[102] In this report, Naṣr appears not as a heretic, but as an effective opponent of a significant military threat instigated by a heretic's politically motivated falsehood.

In several regards, the reign of Naṣr b. Aḥmad contrasted with both the era of the earlier amirs, who cultivated a relatively austere style of life and granted extensive precedence to the ᶜulamāᵓ, and the era of the later amirs, who exhibited greater detachment from their subjects, but actively promoted a religious disposition, articulated in Persian, that underpinned their legitimacy.[103] His receptivity to alternative religious paths was by no means, however, discordant with the royal culture of eastern Iran during his lifetime. Naṣr was contemporary with, and reportedly admired, the Saffarid ruler of Sistan, Abū Jaᶜfar Aḥmad, who likewise ascended to power at a very young age, and for whom Rūdakī composed one of his most celebrated odes. Accounts of the reigns of Abū Jaᶜfar and his son and successor

Khalaf b. Aḥmad (r. 352–73/963–83, 373–93/983–1003) suggest a shifting intellectual–cultural outlook, and mirror the more pronounced contrast drawn in comparisons between Naṣr and his son and successor Nūḥ. Abū Jaᶜfar, like Naṣr, ruled during a period in which the Ismaᶜili *daᶜwa* was active in his region. Sometimes reported to have been an Ismaᶜili, he was, as previously mentioned, exceptionally involved in the promotion of philosophy, patron of the great philosopher Abū Sulaymān al-Sijistānī (d. *c.* 374/985), and convener of an illustrious and convivial court.[104] His son Khalaf, by contrast, was ostentatious in his deference to religious scholars: he 'put aside military dress and donned the clothing of scholars and jurists', held sessions for the discussion of religious learning, 'cultivated the ᶜulamāᵓ and despised fools', was familiar with all the sciences but gave precedence to the religious ones, and dedicated a session to ḥadīth and disputation (*munāẓareh*) every night, with the result that the ᶜulamāᵓ from far and wide sought his proximity.[105] Khalaf also garnered much praiseworthy attention for his commissioning, at great expense, of an ambitious multi-volume commentary on the Qurᵓān; according to one account, he expended 20,000 dirhams on the project.[106] It was probably Khalaf, moreover, who ordered the execution of the Ismaᶜili missionary Abū Yaᶜqūb al-Sijistānī.[107]

Pseudo-Māwardī, I suggest, composed *Naṣīḥat al-mulūk* when the model of the early amirs remained in living memory. At that time of competing religious persuasions, the Ismaᶜiliyya were just beginning to attract the concentrated attention of scholars and other defenders of a cultivated religious–political symbiosis; in the following century, Niẓām al-Mulk, in hindsight, would consider them the quintessential political–religious dissidents of the age. When Pseudo-Māwardī wrote *Naṣīḥat al-mulūk*, reports of the growing strength of the Ismaᶜili *daᶜwa* at Naṣr's court had reached the provincial cities and elicited apprehension among prominent sections of the population. Writing at a moment when the *daᶜwa* seemed poised to transform the Samanid polity, Pseudo-Māwardī believed that subjects followed their kings, and that it was in kings' opportunity to set an example that their real power resided. Through the complex hierarchical networks that connected the various social categories, each individual responded to his superior and became a model for those beneath his ranks. Disengaged from the court, and perhaps fearing a more radical dismantling of their networks, certain scholars and intellectuals of the early tenth century remembered the unusual efforts of the earlier amirs to foster an extensive cooperation between the leading scholars and the dynastic family. This cooperation, in their view, conformed to the model of religion and state prescribed in the late Sasanian texts that had, in significant measure, shaped an intellectual and scholarly mentality in early tenth-century Balkh and Transoxiana, and furnished a language that was both familiar and authoritative for the analysis of local struggles for power.

7

The Afflictions of the Kingdom and their Remedies

In the third chapter of *Naṣīḥat al-mulūk*, Pseudo-Māwardī describes a sequence of developments that result, he argues, in the ruin of the kingdom and the loss of first the king's legitimacy and eventually his power. He also prescribes measures for the avoidance and correction of these developments. This section of *Naṣīḥat al-mulūk* immediately precedes Pseudo-Māwardī's chronologically arranged presentation of prophets, caliphs and kings who combined their exercise of temporal authority with the discharge of their religious and moral responsibilities and whose collective example provided instructive and persuasive models for the amirs of the present. The following pages offer a translation and discussion of most of this section of Pseudo-Māwardī's third chapter. A particularly prominent point of reference in this chapter is *ᶜAhd Ardashīr*, which, with other legacies of the late antique heritage, contributed deeply to the shaping of Pseudo-Māwardī's mentality.

Pseudo-Māwardī opens his discussion with an assertion of the similarities among communities, which share many characteristics. Given this affinity, contemplation of the experience of earlier kingdoms proves highly instructive:

> We say: The conditions of the communities (*umam*, pl. of *umma*) whose accounts are well known, of the kingdoms (*mamālik*) whose reports are famous, and the kings (*mulūk*) the beginnings and ends of whose days have been transmitted to us are similar and akin to one another. On this subject it has been related from our Prophet that, in describing the condition of his *umma*, he said: 'By all means follow the customary practices of those who came before you in a completely identical manner (feather for feather and

> shoe for shoe), so that were someone among them to enter a lizard's hole, then you too would enter it.'[1] (He said this) even though God distinguished this *umma* by the existence of truth in it until the Day of Resurrection, and made its consensus a proof against any areas of disagreement that remain (*jaʿala ijmāʿahā ḥujjatan ʿalā mawāḍiʿ ikhtilāfihā mā baqiyat*), and promised it support and assistance until the end of time and the passing of the duration of the world.
>
> In the course of the affairs of the world and the unfolding of the practices of communities (*umam*), it has become apparent that there has been no kingdom that has not had as its foundation (*uss*) a religious tradition (*diyāna min al-diyānāt*), and as its root (*aṣl*) a (religious) community (*milla min al-milal*), on which its regulations (*sharāʾiṭ*) and precepts (*furūḍ*) have been built, and according to which its ordinances (*aḥkām*) and statutes (*ḥudūd*) have proceeded.[2] There has been no religion, ancient or modern, that has not had as its first principle the summons to knowledge of God (*al-duʿāʾ ilā maʿrifat Allāh*), the Great and Glorious, and His unity; encouragement of the obedient and observant (*al-targhīb . . . lil-muṭīʿīn al-mutadayyinīn*) to seek the abundant reward and generous recompense that He holds for them; the urging of people to amass provisions for the Abode of Repose and Permanence; and austerity (*tazahhud*) in the Abode of Transience and Passing Away.[3]

In these opening remarks, Pseudo-Māwardī employs language reminiscent of the initial section of the 'Testament of Ardashīr':

> Know that kingship and religion are twin brothers, neither one of which can be maintained without the other. For religion is the foundation of kingship, and kingship is the guardian of religion. Kingship cannot subsist without its foundation, and religion cannot subsist without its guardian.[4]

Pseudo-Māwardī's linkage of the themes of kingdom (*mamlaka*), foundation (*uss*) and religion (*diyāna*) would have evoked for his audience the widely disseminated principle, articulated in this passage from the *ʿAhd Ardashīr*, of the partnership between sovereignty and religion; he cites this passage with explicit attribution at the end of his chapter.[5] The allusion to and direct citation of Ardashīr's formulation, at the beginning and end of his chapter, respectively, attest to the continuity and universalism that shaped

Pseudo-Māwardī's perception of history. Throughout his mirror he impresses upon the king his responsibility to heed the lessons conveyed in the wisdom transmitted from the past, regardless of its provenance.[6] His emphasis on the universal applicability of his opening statements also reflects an affinity with the Kindian tradition.[7] From *umam*, complex communities composed of multiple groups, Pseudo-Māwardī proceeds to *milal*, distinct communities associated with specific religions.[8] Later in the tenth century, al-ᶜĀmirī, a student of Abū Zayd al-Balkhī and participant in the Kindian tradition, would echo Pseudo-Māwardī's approach to his subject in a similarly analytical survey of 'the paths to the calamities that ensue continually among religions (*adyān*) and religious communities (*milal*); they are not restricted to the religion of Islam, rather they comprehend them all'.[9] The significant role of Muᶜtazilite doctrines in shaping Pseudo-Māwardī's exposition probably underlies his equation of 'knowledge of God' (*maᶜrifat Allāh*) with the divine unicity (*tawḥīd*) and his emphasis on God's reward for obedience to His commands and prohibitions.[10]

In an elaboration of the invariable patterns discernible in the workings of religion and sovereignty, Pseudo-Māwardī continues:

> If the kingdom's law-bringer (*al-ātī bi-sharīᶜatihā*) and founder of the pillars of its community (*al-wāḍiᶜ li-arkān millatihā*) departs from its midst (*kharaja . . . min baynihā*), whether to do so constitutes truth or falsehood, he sows difference (*ikhtilāf*) among his (larger) community (*umma*) and conflict among the people of his (specific) religious community (*milla*). Sometimes that eventuality arises out of (or takes the form of) rivalry in leadership (*munāfasatan fī l-riʾāsa*), and sometimes it appears as (or arises out of) opposition in religion (*mukhālafatan fī l-dīn*). Then the difference that has arisen among the people carries them unceasingly towards factionalism (*taᶜaṣṣub*) and leads them towards partisanship (*taḥazzub*). The days follow one another incessantly and time grows long, until their covenants (*ᶜuhūd*) become distant from the root of the religion and they forget much of that of which they have been reminded. Sometimes the coffers of this world are opened for them and they are inclined towards them, until with the passing of the days their kingdom becomes a world of vanity (*dunyā tīh*) passed from hand to hand by mortals (*tatadāwalahā aydī abnāʾihā*),[11] and

> their governance (*siyāsatuhum*) [becomes] one of appetites (*shahwāniyya*) coveted by the lower selves of those who seek it (*anfus ṭullābihā*), contested amongst its masters (*arbābuhā*). Something of this kind is related concerning ᶜUmar b. al-Khaṭṭāb, may God be pleased with him: when he was brought the spoils of al-Qadisiyya [a battle in which the Muslim armies defeated the more numerous forces of the Sasanians in 15/636 or 16/637, and which led to the conquest of Iran], he began to examine them, and as he beheld them, he wept. [The Prophet's Companion] ᶜAbd al-Raḥmān b. ᶜAwf [d. *c.* 31/652] said to him, 'O Commander of the Faithful! This is a day of happiness and joy.' He [ᶜUmar] replied, 'Indeed, yet no people (*qawm*) has ever been brought this [kind of booty] without it bequeathing them enmity and hatred.'[12]

Having asserted the structural features common to all kingdoms and religions, Pseudo-Māwardī describes the common patterns that give rise to religious–political dissent and conflict. The law-bringer who secedes from an existing law, whether the religion in question is 'true or false', generates difference and strife. His dissent generates opposition in matters of religion and political leadership (*riʾāsa*), and as the zealous attachments among the population mount, the established order falls into disarray. The seductive appeal of wealth exacerbates the dangers of division. To describe these processes, Pseudo-Māwardī employs the conspicuous idioms *al-ātī bi-sharīᶜatihā*, 'the law-bringer' and *al-wāḍiᶜ li-arkān millatihā*, 'founder of the pillars of the religious community'. These expressions evoke the similar phrase *wāḍiᶜ al-sharīᶜa*, 'founder of the law', which appears frequently in the discourse of the *falāsifa*, and especially in the writings of his contemporary al-Fārābī.[13] In accordance with Pseudo Māwardī's discursive method, his adoption of such language avoids identification with a particular religion. Furthermore, his explicit statement that his description applies to all religions, whether old or new, true or false, develops the brief anticipatory statement in his preface, according to which prophets and pseudo-prophets adopt the same approach in their proselytising activities.[14] His use of the term *taᶜaṣṣub*, 'factionalism' or intense attachment to a group, is likely to have connoted for his audience the potential for communal strife, including the episodes to which al-Nasafī referred as *taᶜaṣṣub al-qarāmiṭa*.[15]

After citing the predictive insight of ᶜUmar, who, invoking the universal experience of every people, foresaw the divisive effects of riches among his community,[16] Pseudo-Māwardī describes the consequences that ensue when kings pass on their kingdoms to their inexperienced and untested sons:

> Sometimes kings have made their kingdoms a bequest that descendants inherit from their predecessors, sons from fathers, and the young from their elders. Some kings designate (*yaᶜhadu*) a son to succeed them without examining him for his intellect (*min ghayr imtiḥān lahu fī ᶜaqlihi*), without knowledge of his excellence (*faḍl*), and without enquiry into his knowledge (*ᶜilm*) of the affairs of religion (*umūr al-diyāna*) that are the root and foundation of the kingdom, and without attention to the substantive matters of sovereignty (*asbāb al-mulk*) that constitute its branches (*furūᶜ*)[17] and custodians (*ḥurrās*). When an inexperienced person (*ghirr*) finds himself in this position, exposed (*mumtaḥan*) to the intoxication of youth and wealth (*sukr al-shabāb wa-l-tharwa*), the intoxication of might, the kingdom, leisure and power (*sukr al-ᶜizz wa-l-mamlaka wa-l-farāgh wa-l-qudra*), and sees that there is no restraining hand, no watchful eye, and no forceful strength above him – he will feel secure against the vicissitudes of time, lulled into delusion by the good fortune of his days. In times of security (*amn*), he will not remember fear, nor in his turn in power (*dawla*) will he remember its transience, nor in safety and health (*al-salāma wa-l-ṣiḥḥa*) will he remember disease and illness; might (*ᶜizz*) will not render him mindful of humility, nor wealth (*ghinā*) of poverty, nor victory (*ẓafar*) of defeat. He will imagine the entire world as one of pure happiness and absolute pleasure. Consequently he will pursue the world's pleasures and give preference to his desires, and he will forget what God performed with those of his kind who came before him, including those who possessed greater power and larger forces than he does. He will be blind to the events of the age and to the occurrences that he witnesses day and night during his days and hours. He will not recall that which the ancient kings said: 'He who goes astray in his authority will be humbled in his might.'[18]
>
> If he develops in this way, then, in the exercise of sovereignty, he will aspire only to enjoyment, whether licit or illicit; his objective in the exercise of power will become domination and duration (*al-tasalluṭ wa-l-taṭāwul*),

> whether rightful or false. He will set aside the ordinances related to this world (*aḥkām al-dunyā*), and ignore the statutory limits of governance (*ḥudūd al-siyāsa*). His governance will become an amusement (*ᶜabath*), his custodianship a diversion (*lahw*). Eventually, it is this that he will leave behind as an inheritance, and as an established custom (*sunna*) among his followers. At the same time, among his subjects the oppressors and the oppressed will multiply, and likewise the unjust and the unjustly treated. They will imitate their kings in abandoning the lower self (*nafs*) to its pleasures and the fulfilment of its desires, sprung from the animal appetites (*al-shahawāt al-ḥayawāniyya*) that repel the directives of rational intellects.[19]

Maintaining the abstract tone of his observations, Pseudo-Māwardī addresses the perils of kings' passing on their kingdoms to their untested sons. An inexperienced and unprepared king, lacking in intellect, virtue and knowledge, is easily beguiled by the lures of power and wealth, and pays no heed to the examples of those whom God fashioned before him. Pseudo-Māwardī's formulation is again reminiscent of Arabic renderings of Middle Persian antecedents. This corpus of literature includes several instances in which the appeal and danger of power are likened to a state of intoxication. *Bilawhar wa-Būdhāṣaf* opens with reference to 'the intoxication of power, the intoxication of youth, the intoxication of pride and the intoxication of desires' (*sukr al-sulṭān wa-sukr al-shabāb wa-sukr al-ᶜujb wa-sukr al-shahawāt*).[20] Ibn al-Muqaffaᶜ, deeply familiar with this literature and a leading purveyor of it into Arabic, had warned in *Kitāb Ādāb al-kabīr* against *sukr al-sulṭa wa-sukr al-ᶜilm wa-sukr al-manzila wa-sukr al-shabāb* ('the intoxication of power, the intoxication of knowledge, the intoxication of status and the intoxication of youth').[21] Most strikingly, Pseudo-Māwardī's formulation recalls the opening sections of the 'Testament of Ardashīr', which begins with mention of 'the intoxication of power, which is greater than the intoxication of wine' (*sukr al-sulṭān alladhī huwa ashaddu min sukr al-khamr*).[22] Shortly after this passage, the 'Testament' continues:

> Those who preceded us said: 'It is when things appear to be going well (*ᶜinda ḥusn al-ẓann bi-l-ayyām*) that reversals (of fortune) occur'. There were among those [ancient] kings those whose might reminded them of humiliation, their security of fear, their merriment of calamity and their

> power of helplessness (*wa-qad kāna min ūlāʾika l-mulūk man yudhakkiruhu ᶜizzuhu al-dhulla wa-amnuhu al-khawfa wa-surūruhu al-kaʾāba wa-qudratuhu al-maᶜjaza*).[23]

The passage provides another example of the degree to which Pseudo-Māwardī's acquaintance with *ᶜAhd Ardashīr* informed his conceptual world and his articulation of it. The allusion in his presentation to the intoxicating potential involved in the combination of power and youth would not have been lost on his audience. Later in *Naṣīḥat al-mulūk*, Pseudo-Māwardī cited a related passage, this time with explicit acknowledgement, from the opening sections of *ᶜAhd Ardashīr*, with the comment that it too expressed the points that he sought to convey:

> Ardashīr has mentioned many of these concepts (*hādhihi l-maᶜānī*) in the opening section (*awwal faṣl*) of his 'Testament', where he said, 'The forms (*ṣiyagh*) of kings are not the forms of the subjects. Kingship by its nature consists in might (*ᶜizz*), security (*amn*), merriment (*surūr*) and power (*qudra*), according to the qualities of pride, audacity, arrogance and amusement. As the king increases in life by the drawing of breath, and as he becomes more secure in his sovereignty, he experiences an increase in these four qualities, until the increase transports him to the intoxication of power, which is stronger than the intoxication of wine. He will forget the adversities, the mistakes, the reversals and the misfortunes, the abomination of the dominion of the age, the vileness of the triumph of the time. Accordingly he will let loose his hand and his tongue in speech and action.'[24]

The interplay of allusions and explicit quotations illustrates the foundational role of the Middle Persian repertoire, in its Arabic versions, in the intellectual and cultural world of Pseudo-Māwardī and his audience. The conceptual and lexicographical components of this repertoire informed Pseudo-Māwardī's articulation of his arguments in a manner that was familiar and comprehensible to his contemporaries in the upper Oxus regions; explicit attribution of such elements was unnecessary. It is perhaps significant that a century later, al-Thaᶜālibī knew the statement, 'The intoxication of power is stronger than the intoxication of youth', as a proverb.[25]

Pseudo-Māwardī continues:

> People's sentiments (*ahwā*ᵓ) towards him will become divided, and opinions (*ārā*ᵓ) of him will differ. The sons of this world, those who grant it precedence and are desirous of it, will seek to approach kings with counsels (*naṣā*ᵓ*iḥ*) intended largely for their own benefit, and consultations designed to yield fruit for their own good. Accordingly wicked viziers (*wuzarā*ᵓ *al-sū*ᵓ) and oppressive assistants (*a*ᶜ*wān al-ẓalama*) will multiply. They will force the kings to swallow deceit (*ghishsh*) in morsels of counsel (*nuṣḥ*); they will show them error (*ḍalāl*) in the form of guidance (*hudan*); they will propose transgression (*ghayy*) to them in place of uprightness (*rushd*). They will conceal them (*ḥajjabūhum*) from wise counsellors (*al-nuṣaḥā*ᵓ *al-ḥukamā*ᵓ);[26] they will intervene between them and virtuous scholars (*al-*ᶜ*ulamā*ᵓ *al-fuḍalā*ᵓ): they will err and lead others astray; they will perish and cause others to perish.

> If they behave in this way, then the wise (*ḥukamā*ᵓ), the learned (ᶜ*ulamā*ᵓ) and those who perceive defects in their outward forms (*al-buṣarā*ᵓ *bi-l-*ᶜ*uyūb fī ṣuwarihā*) and faults in their inner qualities (*al-madhāmm bi-a*ᶜ*yānihā*), find themselves caught between alternatives: the position of the person who is cowed and abased or impeded and rejected; the person who refrains from coming to the king because his religion prevents him from doing so, and the wise philosopher (*ḥakīm*) who deems himself too elevated to associate with him, or the fearful person who recognises that if he confronts the king with advice that addresses his well-being (*ṣalāḥ*) and brings him counsel (*nuṣḥ*), if he presents him with advice conducive to his deliverance and right guidance, the king will punish him for it with the most intense punishment and will castigate him with the most painful chastisement – because the truth is bitter, and the counsel of someone who forbids the pursuit of passion is onerous, except for the person of consummate intellect (*al-*ᶜ*āqil al-kāmil*), and for the virtuous and resolute person (*al-fāḍil al-ḥāzim*).[27]

Employing a set of images and a vocabulary familiar to his audience, Pseudo-Māwardī describes the danger of self-interested persons' exploitation, for their own purposes, of royal negligence and distraction. Pseudo-Māwardī's disquisition with regard to 'wicked viziers' permits the displacement of criticism from the monarch to his counsellors and companions, a common strategy among writers of mirrors. The figure of the duplicitous and ill-intentioned vizier, already a *topos* in *Kalīla wa-Dimna*, becomes a staple of later advisory writings (most striking is the story of Rāst-ravishn, the predatory and self-interested vizier of the Sasanian king Bahrām-i Gūr (Bahrām V), in the eleventh-century Persian *Siyar al-mulūk*).[28] The trope of the wicked vizier who exploits his sovereign's inattentiveness conveys the contrast, central to the logic of *Naṣīḥat al-mulūk*, between sincerity and deception, *naṣīḥa* and *ghishsh*.

Pseudo-Māwardī also evokes the vulnerable position of the well-intentioned counsellor, who risks rebuke and punishment if he dares to offer advice.[29] Although fear of royal reprisal required no explanation, Pseudo-Māwardī's reference to the dangers of punishment in the wake of the king's displeasure brings to mind the portrayal of Amir Naṣr in some near-contemporary sources. The secretary and historian Abū l-Fażl Bayhaqī had read in the 'Accounts of the Samanids' (*dar akhbār-i Sāmānīyān*) of Naṣr's quickness to anger and his tendency to deliver hasty and harsh punishments. At his accession, this prince had possessed all the requisite royal attributes (*bar hameh-yi ādāb-i mulūk savār shod*), but he also displayed an extreme propensity to spite, maliciousness, violence and anger (*dar vay sharāratī va-za*ᶜ*āratī va-saṭvatī va-ḥashmatī bi-ifrāṭ būd*).[30] According to Bayhaqī's narrative, Naṣr realised that his conduct was unpopular, and enlisted the aid of his vizier Balᶜamī and his chief administrator (*ṣāḥib-dīvān*) Muṣᶜabī, here portrayed in a positive light, in rectifying the flaw.[31]

Pseudo-Māwardī concludes this part of his discussion with the following remark:

> Many of these problems (*abwāb*) have afflicted (*nāla*) the kings of our time amongst the people of our religious community (*min ahl millatinā*) and the rulers of our co-religionists (the people of our *qibla*) (*wulāt ahl qiblatinā*).
>
> These are all types of corruption (*abwāb al-fasād*) that arise from the love of positions of authority, the sensual appetites and the eager desire to fulfil them (*min jihat ḥubb al-riyāsāt wa-l-shahawāt wa-l-tashāḥḥ* ᶜ*alayhā*).[32]

Although he refrains from identifying individuals, Pseudo-Māwardī's characteristic movement from the universal and timeless to the particular and actual could hardly take a more pointed form. He explicitly brings to his audience's attention the immediate applicability of the recurrent patterns that he has sketched. However non-specific his language, his audience would have understood that Pseudo-Māwardī's remarks regarding, for example, kings' promotion of their children to the throne alluded to the case of Naṣr II. The extant sources place considerable stress on Naṣr's youth – he was reportedly eight years old – at the time of his contested succession, and Pseudo-Māwardī's laudatory remarks regarding Isḥāq, the senior member of the Samanid dynastic family, may suggest that he considered him a worthier successor to Ismāᶜīl and to Ismāᶜīl's son Aḥmad than Naṣr. That the matter of Naṣr's youth evoked controversy in Pseudo-Māwardī's milieu is apparent in the work of the historian Ibn Ẓāfir (d. 613/1216), who, in contrast to the overwhelming preponderance of surviving accounts, reported that Naṣr acceded to the throne at the age of twelve. Ibn Ẓāfir reports further that, following his father Aḥmad's assassination, Muḥammad b. Aḥmad, the governor of Bukhara, consulted the leading jurists and traditionists as to which of the late amir's sons should succeed him, and, having pledged allegiance to Naṣr, announced to the people of Bukhara that the young amir was 'sound of mind, has the Qurᵓān by heart, knows the religious duties and is well educated'.[33] Ibn Ẓāfir's account suggests that the notables of Bukhara who supported Naṣr's claim felt compelled to address criticisms with regard to their candidate's age, experience and religious knowledge, precisely the matters raised in Pseudo-Māwardī's analysis.

Another probable example of Pseudo-Māwardī's allusions to contemporary circumstances lies in his antipathy towards viziers and 'assistants'. Partly because of his youth and inexperience, the young king, Pseudo-Māwardī avers, was particularly dependent on these figures and susceptible to their manipulation. His criticism perhaps embraced the viziers of the Jayhānī family, many of whom, as previously noted, were associated with heterodoxy of one sort or another. Abū ᶜAbdallāh Muḥammad b. Aḥmad al-Jayhānī, reportedly a dualist (*thanawī*),[34] appears to have attracted remarkable ill-will, to the extent that, according to Ibn Ẓāfir, the people of Bukhara stoned his coffin and refused to pray over him.[35] Abū ᶜAlī Muḥammad b. Muḥammad al-Jayhānī, as indicated above, is likely to have been an Ismaᶜili. The unpopularity of Muḥammad b. Muḥammad's successor Abū l-Ṭayyib al-Muṣᶜabī among the citizenry of Balkh, apparently on account of his allegiance to the Ismaᶜiliyya, has already been observed.[36] Alternative discourses, especially in Persian, presented favourable images of these figures: Gardīzī described Jayhānī as learned, intelligent, excellent and perspicacious in all matters (*mardī dānā būd va-sakht hūshyār va-jild va-fāżil va-andar hameh chīzhā baṣārat dāsht*), and Bayhaqī made no distinction in merit between Muṣᶜabī and Balᶜamī, who jointly undertook the delicate matter of managing the erratic and often unpopular orders that issued from the young amir.[37] In keeping with the authority that he invested in the inherited wisdom of past peoples, Pseudo-Māwardī portrays these figures, by implication, as agents of subversion. His charge against the 'wicked viziers' that they 'induce them [kings] to swallow deceit in the guise of counsels, show them deviance in the form of guidance, display error in the semblance of uprightness, keep them from wise counsellors, and intervene between them and virtuous learned men, so that they go astray and lead others astray, perish and cause others to perish' recapitulates a *topos* grounded in perennial wisdom. Perhaps this sentiment contributed to his contemporary ᶜAbd al-Muᵓmin b. Khalaf's public call for al-Muṣᶜabī's downfall.[38] Pseudo-Māwardī's composition of a mirror represented a considerably less confrontational approach than the direct challenge articulated by the ḥadīth scholar, who, incidentally, had refused to greet al-Kaᶜbī when the latter paid him a visit;[39] the accusations of irreligion advanced against rationalist theologians, it is proposed, form part of the context for Pseudo-Māwardī's treatment of heterodoxy.

Despite his careful and consistent emphasis on the timeless applicability of his critical analysis and his marked avoidance of explicit identifications, it is not difficult to imagine the implications of Pseudo-Māwardī's presentation: the settling of the line of succession among Ismāᶜīl's descendants had yielded less qualified rulers; in particular, the eight-year-old Naṣr had succumbed to the manipulations of his viziers, who had encouraged the amir's dedication to pleasure, deterred him from the pursuit of learning, excluded him from governance, kept him at a distance from his subjects, transformed the courtly culture, impeded the access of learned and wise persons capable of delivering sound advice, and sought to enlist him in their political ambitions. Throughout *Naṣīḥat al-mulūk*, Pseudo-Māwardī identifies kings' principal weakness in their susceptibility to pleasure, and viziers' principal instrument in their tempting of rulers to devote themselves wholeheartedly to its pursuit. The portrayal finds an echo in al-Thaᶜālibī's later account of al-Muṣᶜabī's and Ibn Sawāda's success in deflecting Naṣr from his 'repentance' by urging him to alleviate the burden of his moral suffering by means of dedication to pleasure (*ladhdha*).[40]

In *al-Iᶜlām bi-manāqib al-Islām*, al-ᶜĀmirī presented a similar analysis of religious conflict. Using, like Pseudo-Māwardī, universal terms, al-ᶜĀmirī declared difference (*ikhtilāf*) a cause of dispute (*mumārāt*), dispute an opening to hostility (*taᶜādin*), hostility a staircase to communal attachment (*ᶜaṣabiyya*), and *ᶜaṣabiyya* a chronic affliction (*al-dāʾ al-ᶜuḍāl*).[41] Differences in religion manifested themselves in the formation of groups, which, particularly in the face of opposition, persisted through the determined adherence of their members. Al-ᶜĀmirī imputes internal religious conflicts (*al-ikhtilāfāt fī bāb al-diyānāt*) to a number of causes, among them the deliberate undermining of religion by persons whose intention is 'to show the religion to be false and weaken its foundation' (*tazyīf al-dīn wa-tawhīn asāsihi*). Such persons, according to al-ᶜĀmirī, undertook such sabotage out of attachments grounded in the claims of power or kinship (*immā li-taᶜaṣṣub malakī aw li-taᶜaṣṣub nasabī*),[42] the compulsive attraction of licentiousness (*li-sawas al-khalāᶜa*), or a preference for the ways of wanton behaviour (*li-īthār ṭuruq al-majāna*). Among their methods was the concoction of forged reports (*akhbār muzawwara*) falsely attributed to authoritative figures, such as leading scholars of Prophetic tradition (*aʾimmat aṣḥāb al-ḥadīth*) or a leader of the population (*aḥad ruʾasāʾ al-ᶜāmma*). This technique caused the weak (-minded) to imagine that certain defects were part of the foundation of the religion (*asās al-milla*).[43] Al-ᶜĀmirī's description of the techniques employed in the subversion of religion echoes the analysis of Pseudo-Māwardī, as the following section will demonstrate.

The Corruption of Kingdoms

As he states in several places in *Naṣīḥat al-mulūk*, Pseudo-Māwardī, following the view of late Sasanian *andarz*, regards sovereignty and religion as inseparably linked.[44] Problems in the kingdom were likely to manifest themselves in religious forms, and, as he proceeds to explain, religious movements were a potential source of political instability. Having addressed the interconnections between kingship and religion, Pseudo-Māwardī turns to the sphere of religion specifically, and offers an explanation for the appearance of dissension and difference that will, in his analysis, eventually result in political challenge:

> As for the category (of corruption) whose path is the path of religion specifically, it is that the speech (*kalām*) of every scripture (*kitāb*) and the reports (*akhbār*) of every prophet (*nabī*) carry the possibility of different interpretations (*taʾwīlāt mukhtalifa*), because that (potential) is present in the nature of speech itself (*dhālika mawjūd fī l-kalām bi-nafs ṭibāʿihi*). It is well known that the more eloquent, articulate, beautifully formed and broadly expressive the speech is, the more it is receptive to the various arts of interpretation and methods of exegesis (*funūn al-taʾwīlāt wa-ḍurūb al-tafāsīr*).
>
> There is no speech that possesses more of these qualities than that of God, exalted is His mention, for it is the most eloquent, concise, allusive speech (*idh kāna afṣaḥa l-kalām wa-awjazahu wa-aktharahu rumūzan*), combining more than any other a multiplicity of meanings with a limited number of letters ([*kāna*] . . . *ajmaʿahu lil-maʿānī al-kathīra wa-l-aḥruf al-yasīra*).[45] Our Book, which is the Qurʾān, is primary among scriptures and the most distinguished among them for these (ample) meanings, for the language in which God revealed it is the most eloquent of languages, and it is a scripture the composition of which He made an authoritative proof (*ḥujja*) for His people (*ʿalā qawmihi*) and a sign to His Prophet (*ʿalam li-nabiyyihi*).
>
> Necessarily in religion, events (*ḥawādith*) occur that require rational speculation (*naẓar*), and specific cases (*nawāzil*) for which scholars are obliged to derive (*istikhrāj*) responses; nor can scholars avoid the need (to investigate) a narrative account (*khabar*) of ambiguous meaning, or a tradition (*athar*) for which interpretations (*taʾwīlāt*) differ as to its purport according to the passage of time. If they insist (in their interpretations), opinions will differ over particular (legal or theological) questions (*ikhtalafat al-ārāʾ fī l-masāʾil*) and subjective perceptions will divide over specific cases (*tafarraqat al-ahwāʾ fī l-nawāzil*). For every point of view (*li-kull raʾy*) there will be followers (*tabaʿ*), legislators (*musharriʿūn*), leaders (*aʾimma*) and persons led by example (*muʾtammūn*). Over the course of time the adherents (*anṣār*), partisans (*mutaʿaṣṣibūn*), supporters (*aʿwān*) and defenders (*muḥāmūn*) of each point of view will increase, and this development leads

to disagreement within religious communities (*ikhtilāf al-umam*) and their conflict with one another.[46]

Pseudo-Māwardī's account of the genesis of schisms through the inevitable multiplicity of interpretations of revealed scripture evokes contemporaneous conceptions of *zandaqa*, associated, as observed in Chapter 5, with alternative, usually figurative or metaphorical, interpretations, initially of the *Avesta*.[47] Although he mentions neither Mānī nor Mazdak, Pseudo-Māwardī perhaps alludes to them when he refers to 'every scripture and . . . every prophet without exception'. His observation pre-figures Niẓām al-Mulk's report that the *mōbad*s of the time of Mazdak acknowledged that certain parts of the *Avesta* and *Zand* could support ten meanings, and that every *mōbad* and scholar or learned person (*dānā*) explained and interpreted them differently.[48] Although Pseudo-Māwardī articulates his analysis in an abstract fashion and refrains from evaluative assessments of different types of interpretation, it is likely that his audience would have inferred an allusion to the various groupings of *bāṭiniyya*, who distinguished between exterior (*ẓāhir*) and interior (*bāṭin*) levels of meaning and in some contexts privileged the latter over the former. This supposition finds support in the writings of Pseudo-Māwardī's contemporary al-Māturīdī, who similarly located the proliferation of religious schisms in the phenomenon of allegorical interpretation, and criticised the groups that, in his view, interpreted scripture on the basis of the meanings they wished to find rather than a critical reading of the text.[49]

In the passage cited above, Pseudo-Māwardī employs the terms *taʾwīl* and *tafsīr* without obvious evaluative differentiation. His usage of the terms probably resembled that of al-Māturīdī, who named his work of exegesis *Kitāb Taʾwīlāt al-Qurʾān* ('Book of Interpretations of the Qurʾān'); according to this understanding, *tafsīr* (exegesis) involved the attachment of a definitive meaning to a text, a task for which only the Prophet's Companions were qualified, whereas *taʾwīl* involved the identification of all the possible meanings of a text, an activity that was open to all.[50] Many later writers would associate *taʾwīl* with exclusively figurative or esoteric, *bāṭinī*, techniques of interpretation and a concomitant rejection of *ẓāhirī* meanings, especially in matters related to the religious law.[51] The scholar and theologian ʿAbd al-Qāhir al-Baghdādī (d. 429/1037), who was educated in Nishapur and taught there for part of his life, regarded the symbolic interpretation (*ta*ʾ*wīl*) of the *bāṭiniyya* as tantamount to rejection of the sharīʿa,[52] and for the Muʿtazilite ʿAbd al-Jabbār, any person who claimed that for the mandatory religious duties and prohibitions there was a *bāṭin* and a *ta*ʾ*wīl* had manifestly left Islam: the *bāṭiniyya* had rejected the practice of both the *fuqahā*ʾ and the *ʿāmma* in their insistence that for every *ẓāhir*, including acts of worship, there was a *bāṭin*.[53]

Pseudo-Māwardī opens his analysis with reference to the 'nature' of speech, and particularly sacred speech. 'Nature' is a term that he employs frequently in *Naṣīḥat al-mulūk*; his use of the category perhaps suggests an involvement in the speculation regarding the 'natures' (*ṭabā*ʾ*i*ʿ) of things evident in the Kindian tradition, among certain groups among the Muʿtazila and in the writings of al-Māturīdī.[54] Moving from the universal to the particular, Pseudo-Māwardī proceeds from his analysis of the genesis of schisms to a discussion of the particular qualities of the Arabic language. This subject had generated a substantial literature that embraced numerous genres. Al-Kindī, for example, discussed the ambiguity of language and the need for interpretation in his treatise 'On the Prostration of the Outermost Sphere' (*al-Ibāna ʿan sujūd al-jirm al-aqṣā*), in which he offered an explication of the Qurʾānic verse 55: 6, *al-najm wa-l-shajar yasjudāni* ('And the stars and the trees prostrate themselves').[55] Like Pseudo-Māwardī, al-Kindī observes that multi-valence and ambiguity are common to all languages, but especially characteristic of Arabic.[56] Moreover, in his treatment of prophecy, presented in his 'Treatise on the Quantity of Aristotle's Books' (*al-Risāla fī kammiyyat kutub Arisṭāṭālīs*), al-Kindī contrasts 'divine knowledge' (*al-ʿilm al-ilāhī*), that is, the knowledge of prophets vouchsafed to them through revelation, to that attainable through philosophy, or 'the human sciences' (*al-ʿulūm al-insāniyya*). He identifies the qualities of *wijāza*, *bayān*, *qurb al-sabīl* and *iḥāṭa bi-l-maṭlūb* (concision, clarity, accessibility and comprehensiveness) inherent in divine speech, and observes the multiple meanings that a single Arabic word often carries.[57] Pseudo-Māwardī's near-contemporary Abū l-Layth al-Samarqandī (d. 373/983), whose theological outlook appears to have resembled that reflected in *al-Sawād al-aʿẓam* more closely than that of the Māturīdiyya, amongst whose first generation he is often counted,[58] likewise insisted on the necessity of sensitivity to the nuances of the Arabic language for persons engaged in interpretation (*tafsīr*). Abū l-Layth argued that to deny the permissibility of interpretation would negate the Qurʾān's status as a definite proof (*ḥujja bāligha*, cf. Q 6: 149) for God's creatures, and that its interpretation was therefore permitted for persons who 'knew the Arabic lexicon and the circumstances of the revelation' (*jāza li-man ᶜarafa lughāt al-ᶜarab wa-ᶜarafa shaʾn al-nuzūl*).[59]

Given his several references to the external manifestation of the religious law (*iẓhār al-sharīᶜa*), Pseudo-Māwardī perhaps inclined towards the interpretative approach of Abū Zayd al-Balkhī, who, in his *Naẓm al-Qurʾān* ('The Order of the Qurʾān'), 'avoided (*kāna yatanazzahu*) what is said about the Qurʾān except the literal meaning (*ẓāhir*), free of explanation (*tafsīr*), interpretation (*tawʾīl*), and ambiguity (*mushkil*)'.[60] The tenth-century littérateur and philosopher Abū Ḥayyān al-Tawḥīdī (*c.* 315–411/927–1023) praised the same work, and declared of Abū Zayd that 'no one else has managed to combine wisdom (or philosophy, *ḥikma*) and the sharīᶜa as he has'.[61] In his continuation of the Kindian tradition, al-ᶜĀmirī, in a similar vein, wrote, 'It is known that between that which is established by proof and necessitated by the intellect, and that which the true religion requires, there can be neither conflict (*mudāfaᶜa*) nor opposition (*ᶜinād*)'.[62]

Pseudo-Māwardī continues:

> No religion and no religious community has been without its hypocrites and opponents (*lā yakhlū dīn min al-adyān wa-lā milla min al-milal min munāfiqīn fīhā wa-muᶜādīn lahā*). When they find their community divided, at variance and in conflict, these individuals manifest their secret ruses and their hidden invectives, and insinuate them into their religious paths (*madhāhib*); they contrive deceptive inventions (*ikhtaraᶜū ikhtirāᶜāt kādhiba*) and insert them into their accounts (*akhbār*). By these means the common people[63] among them are seduced and the inexperienced among them corrupted. Next they aim at the kings, who are devoted to knowledge of the world, disinclined to the principles of the religious law, living in opulence and luxury, their desires directed towards the enjoyment of pleasures, their hopes expended on the gratification of appetites, their aspirations consisting of liberty (*ḥurriyya*), licentiousness (*khalāᶜa*), and departure from obedience (*al-murūq ᶜan al-ṭāᶜa*). They entice them with distractions and

> entertainments (*al-malāhī wa-l-malā*ᶜ*ib*),[64] and press upon them the use of flutes and stringed instruments (*al-mazāmīr wa-l-ma*ᶜ*āzif*);[65] they present to them things that mar their reputation, undermine their manly virtue (*muruwwa*), ruin the kingdom, deaden religion, sow opposition among the inclinations of the subjects (*ahwā*ᵓ *al-ra*ᶜ*iyya*) and alter the indications of the law (*amārāt al-sharī*ᶜ*a*). Kings accept these things from them, since they are consonant with their desires (*ahwā*ᵓ) to make light of religion (*al-istikhfāf bi-l-dīn*) and cast off its burden.[66]

Pseudo-Māwardī's reference to individuals who insinuate their falsehoods among the common people and among kings, who practise deceit, beguile the common people, permit the illicit and promote unrestrained indulgence in pleasure reflects the paradigmatic representation of heterodoxy. His exposition remains abstract; his most direct reference to a particular heterodoxy is Pseudo-Māwardī's single mention of *zanādiqa*, itself a generic category, albeit one that was acquiring particular connotations.[67] Writing later in the century, al-ᶜĀmirī similarly associated licentiousness (*khalā*ᶜ*a*) with *zanādiqa*, persons who 'hunt' people of weak intelligence, one by one, by misrepresenting the teachings of the ancient philosophers and exploiting their prestige.[68] Early in the following century, al-Thaᶜālibī, whose early life spanned the latter part of the Samanid period, who in *Ādāb al-mulūk* drew largely on examples from the Samanid era and whose treatment of Naṣr's attraction to Ismaᶜilism is reminiscent of Pseudo-Māwardī's portrayal of antinomian heterodoxy, was explicit in his association of 'liberty' (*ḥurriyya*) and 'making light of Islam' (*al-istikhfāf bi-l-Islām*) with the Ismaᶜiliyya of the Samanid era.[69] It is likely that in his repeated references to heterodox groups, whom he depicted as dangerous and opportunistic, Pseudo-Māwardī had in mind a range of movements, but especially groups that valued esoteric over exoteric meanings in relation to the religious law. For his audience, his 'hypocrites' and 'opponents', who conducted their subversive activities within religious communities, were likely to encompass his 'ill-intentioned viziers' (*wuzarā*ᵓ *al-sū*ᵓ), such as al-Muṣᶜabī, who took advantage of their opportunity to induce the sovereign to reject the roots of the law (*uṣūl al-sharī*ᶜ*a*) and to alter the (outer) signs of the law (*amārāt al-sharī*ᶜ*a*). Perhaps in a riposte to claims that the spiritually initiated had transcended the need for the observance of exterior forms, Pseudo-Māwardī affirms more than once the comprehensive nature of the law, which embraced the ruler, the élites and the common people.[70] In devoting extensive attention to legal questions germane to kingship in the final three chapters of his book, his purpose was perhaps to engage the rational participation of his audience in matters of religious laws.

Pseudo-Māwardī's description of hypocrites (*munāfiqūn*) evokes a Qur'ānic category and is, at the same time, reminiscent of a passage in the 'Testament of Ardashīr':

> Among the subjects there is a kind of people who outwardly display humility (*tawāḍu*ᶜ), but are inwardly filled with pride (*kibr*). A man of this type exhorts kings and upbraids them with admonition, since he finds this method the easier of the two ways of injuring them . . . These persons are the enemies of dynasties (*a*ᶜ*dā*' *al-duwal*) and the misfortune of kings (*āfāt al-mulūk*).[71]

The confluence between the outlook evident in the 'Testament' and the mentality of Pseudo-Māwardī's milieu facilitated the impression of the universality of hypocrites' efforts to ruin kings and exercise power for their own purposes.[72] Tarif Khalidi points out that Pseudo-Māwardī's contemporary al-Masᶜūdī's description of the history of ancient nations, particularly those of India and China, reflects a similar perspective: after an initial period of wisdom, these societies had lapsed into ignorance, marked by the prevalence of doubts, lethargy, the pursuit of pleasure and the adoption of blind imitation, all of which had rendered them susceptible to false religions.[73]

Pseudo-Māwardī continues:

> When the matter of kings becomes like this, they being the persons whose actions are imitated and whose reported conduct (*āthāruhum fī siyarihim*) is emulated, then the persons close to them in privilege and the persons bound to them in service (*khawāṣṣuhum wa khadamuhum*) adopt the same path. For every person of privilege, there is someone who is more privileged than he is (*li-kull khāṣṣ khāṣṣ*), and for every follower, there is someone who is followed (*li-kull muqtadin muqtadan bihi*). In this situation lies the clashing of swords.

> The people who adhere to religions (*ahl al-adyān*) will resolve to revolt against the king and his followers (*al-khurūj ʿalā l-malik wa-atbāʿihi*), against the authorities and their partisans (*wa [ʿalā] al-sulṭān wa-ashyāʿihi*). They will hold it lawful to bring an end to his power (*yastaḥillūna izālat yadihi*). The people of the world (*ahl al-dunyā*) will not heed any claim on his part, nor acknowledge any virtue in him without calculating their own advantage (?),[74] and will not hold obedience to him to be binding upon them (*lā yūjibūna lahu ṭāʿatan tulzimuhum*). Instead, they will hold the view that the king has become someone who, though great, has resorted to stealing (*ṣāra man ʿazza bazza*), or someone who vanquishes and then plunders (*man ghalaba salaba*).[75] And so rebels (*khawārij*) will multiply, kingdoms will be destroyed, the subjects will be ruined, acts of disobedience and indecency will become widespread (*tashayyaʿa al-maʿāṣī wa-l-fawāḥish*). (Demands for) provisions (*muʾan*) will increase, and the king will need large numbers [of troops] and ample supplies of equipment. It might happen that the wealth of the kingdom will prove too tightly strained to supply the provisions due to the king's assistants and retinue (*muʾan al-aʿwān wa-l-ḥāshiya*). That situation leads to unrest in the army (*shaghab al-jund*) and the forming of factions among the allegiances of the king's assistants (*taḥazzub ārāʾ al-aʿwān*). The king is oblivious of the hardship and the excessive burden that he has brought upon the subjects, and the subjects cease to pay attention to their obligation to him. If they obey, their obedience is forced and coerced; and if they revolt and triumph, they are excused before God, and before the people of religion, intellect, judgement and excellence. In their own estimation, they are to be thanked as well as pardoned. In due course, his [the king's] enemies will covet his sovereignty and his opponents will seek to eliminate the religion.[76]

It is not difficult to recognise in this forceful passage an allusion to the increasing prevalence of heterodoxy among the élites that surrounded Naṣr II and the deteriorating condition of the population that Pseudo-Māwardī regarded as its result. He describes the progressive assimilation of individuals to heterodox groupings as a product of the vertical networks through which persons followed, through loyalty and emulation, the commands of the individuals to whom they were bound ('for every privileged person, there is a person more privileged than he is; and for every follower, there is someone who follows him'). Among the members of the élite to whom Pseudo-Māwardī alluded, perhaps, was Ḥusayn b. ᶜAlī al-Marwazī, who reportedly occasioned the affiliation with the Ismaᶜiliyya of large numbers of people in the vicinities in which he exercised greatest authority.[77]

Pseudo-Māwardī describes the reactions of the subjects to such developments at the centre of the polity. First he notes the resistance of persons committed to religions (*ahl al-adyān*). As the examples addressed in Chapter 6 indicated, certain religious figures, some of them probably known to Pseudo-Māwardī, did not flinch from expressing their resistance ('they will hold it lawful to bring an end to his power'). But Pseudo-Māwardī also describes the disaffection of *ahl al-dunyā*, the worldly, who will cease to recognise the amir's claims to their loyalty and cease to feel bound in obedience to him. During his reign Naṣr II faced numerous rebellions, some led by members of the Samanid dynastic family, and some by other high-ranking figures, such as the military commander and *dihqān* Aḥmad b. Sahl.[78] The motivations of these figures, the *ahl al-dunyā* of the author's description, probably owed little to matters of religious difference, but in the face of breach of loyalty (*wafāʾ*), vassals who had served the amirs for decades and eventually rebelled might have perceived the ruler as having 'resorted to stealing'. Faced with rebellions on the part of the religious and the worldly, *ahl al-adyān* and *ahl al-dunyā*, the ruler, in Pseudo-Māwardī's analysis, will find himself in ever greater need of troops, whom he will not be able to pay. Increasing numbers of his subjects will grow disaffected and consider their duty of obedience to be annulled. He warns that this growing dissatisfaction will result either in the ruler's deposition, which many of his subjects will regard as justified, or, at best, in his extorting of obedience solely by force.

In this passage, Pseudo-Māwardī engages the controversial question of whether and under what circumstances open opposition to the ruler might be permissible. The issue received considerable attention during the Samanid period. *Al-Sawād al-aᶜẓam*, not surprisingly, asserts the mandatory nature of obedience, and the permissibility of praying for the amir whether he is just or unjust.[79] Pseudo-Māwardī, by contrast, implies that in cases of extreme harm, rebellion (*khurūj*) becomes legitimate. In this regard he represented the dominant Muᶜtazilite position in the matter.[80] Most of the Muᶜtazila considered rebellion against the unjust or sinful *sulṭān* to be permissible or even mandatory, but they qualified this view with the requirement that the imam, the legitimate ruler, be present (*lā yakūnu l-khurūj illā maᶜa imām ᶜādil*).[81] In Pseudo-Māwardī's immediate milieu, al-Kaᶜbī dedicated a section of his *Maqālāt* ('Doctrines') to the 'rebellion of the people of justice' (*khurūj ahl al-ᶜadl*), that is, the Muᶜtazila.[82] Al-Kaᶜbī devoted the better part of this section of his treatise to the Umayyad Caliph Yazīd's overthrow of his cousin al-Walīd and his subsequent speech, similarly reproduced in full in Pseudo-Māwardī's enumeration of virtuous rulers.[83] Pseudo-Māwardī warns his royal audience that if the king alienates the 'people of religion' and the 'people of the world', many of his subjects will consider his deposition to be justified. His reproduction a few pages later of the speech of the Umayyad caliph Yazīd III, which concluded with the pronouncement, 'Obedience is not incumbent upon the creature if it involves disobedience to the Creator' (*lā ṭāᶜata li-makhlūq fī maᶜṣiyat al-khāliq*),[84] and his ascription to Yazīd's predecessor al-Walīd of oppression, injustice, heresy (*ilḥād*) and unbelief (*kufr*), illustrated and developed his point. Al-Kaᶜbī, in a different genre, followed his transcription of Yazīd's oration with the report that ᶜAmr b. ᶜUbayd (80–144/699–761), the ascetically inclined figure whom Pseudo-Māwardī cites in numerous places, supported the right to rebellion in this instance and considered Yazīd's overthrow of his cousin to be lawful.[85] Especially when regarded in conjunction with al-Kaᶜbī's *Maqālāt*, *Naṣīḥat al-mulūk* prompts the speculation that during the reign of Naṣr the permissibility of rebellion received discussion in at least one provincial city. If it is correct to infer that such discussions took place, they provide a further context, apart from the context provided by the politics of the court, for Nūḥ's seizure of power from his father in 331/943.

In his next section, Pseudo-Māwardī moves explicitly from his still largely abstract and allusive depiction of the ills of kingdoms to 'the conditions of our community' (*aḥwāl ummatinā*). After the Prophet, the Rāshidūn had 'seen in the caliphate only a means to promote the revival of religion, and in the office of the ruler (*imāra*) only a means to ensure the well-being (*ṣalāḥ*) of the Muslims':

> They were people who displayed kindness to the believers. Their conduct constituted justice, their words virtue, their judgement truth, and their speech honesty . . . They defeated armies, subdued tyrants and killed pharaohs,[86] and they manifested (*aẓharū*) the light of the truth in the west and in the east. Their exterior (*ẓāhir*) was humility and their interior (*bāṭin*) obedience towards God. Their desire was for the world to come, and [their disposition] contempt for this world, which they positioned beneath their feet, since they knew it truly (*idh ᶜarafūhā ḥaqqa maᶜrifatihā*) and placed it in its proper station, as the Prophet said . . . when he passed a pile of rubbish, 'He who delights to gaze upon the world in its entirety must also look squarely at this' . . . [87]

> ᶜUmar b. al-Khaṭṭāb used to say to his officials, 'We are not appointing you over the heads and bodies of the Muslims. We are appointing you merely that you should uphold the prayer among them and instruct them in knowledge and the Qurʾān.'[88]

In this section, Pseudo-Māwardī implies a contrast between the Rightly Guided Caliphs' 'belittling of the world' (*al-istikhfāf bi-l-dunyā*) and the disdain for or making light of religion (*al-istikhfāf bi-l-dīn*) imputed to the Umayyad caliphs who succeeded them. Nevertheless, he avoids the trope of the shift from 'caliphate' (*khilāfa*) to 'kingship' (*mulk*) common in Abbasid historiography; indeed, he employs the terms *khalafa* and *khalaf*, related to the term *khilāfa*, in connection with the Umayyads, whom he also cites individually:

> Then there came successors [*khalafa min baᶜdihim khalaf*] who desired this world, preferred it, pursued it and granted it precedence, took pleasure in it, appropriated the wealth of God and took the servants of God as chattels, and left their subjects abject – except for those among them whom God protected (from such behaviour) (*illā man ᶜaṣama Allāhu minhum*).[89]

In this passage Pseudo-Māwardī refers, as he had in previous contexts, to God's extension of *ᶜiṣma*, divine protection, to individuals whom He chooses.[90] He illustrates his point with reference to examples drawn from the historical past, the instructive nature of which he impresses upon his audience.

In a transitional passage, Pseudo-Māwardī concludes this section of his exposition and proceeds from the causes of corruption to their remedies:

> The factors that we have mentioned in this chapter ruin kingdoms, corrupt religions, arouse covetousness among the enemies of kings and cause the clashing of swords, as we have enumerated and mentioned. For every one of these sicknesses there is a remedy by which health is restored, and for every corruption (*fasād*) a way that brings about well-being (*ṣalāḥ*), and an opportunity to avert harm for whoever wishes to take precautions and to guard against these dangers for whoever is inclined to success.[91]

Pseudo-Māwardī reiterates his observation that after the leadership of the Prophet and his upright Companions in the beginning of his community (*fī ṣadr ummatihi*), leaders had succumbed to 'a hardening of hearts, and delusion and deception by this world', and he proceeds from diagnosis to treatment:

> As for . . . the age of the Prophet and his righteous Companions in the beginning of his community, until the time when hearts hardened, and worldly delusion (*ightirār bi-l-dunyā*) and deception (*al-inkhidā*ᶜ *lahā*) set in: the accounts concerning them (the figures of the early period) remain vibrant and alive, even if their bodies have vanished, and the reports of them are present and actual, even if their persons are absent. It is proper for the resolute king and determined ruler that he pledge his heart to hearing their [the Prophet's and his righteous Companions'] traditions (*āthār*), and to reading the reports of their conduct (*siyar*), the historical accounts (*akhbār*) concerning them and their guidance (*hady*); and he should reflect on the cautionary signs (*min dalā*ʾ*ilihi al-wā*ᶜ*iẓa*) and evidentiary indications (*wa-[min] a*ᶜ*lāmihi al-shāhida*) that God, great and glorious, has established in His earth and His heaven. He should also reflect on the past kings who have preceded him, so that he should learn thereby about his condition and see himself (in the mirror of their experience). For they are evident before his eyes; they address him even though they lack the faculty of speech, and exhort him even though they lack the faculty of hearing. We shall devote a separate chapter to admonitions immediately after this one, and we shall mention in it that which we deem useful and pertinent, if God wills.[92]

Remedies for the Kingdom's Ills

In the remainder of this section of his chapter, Pseudo-Māwardī addresses particular dilemmas and instructs his audience with regard to their solutions:

> As for averting the damage of free-thinking people (*aṣḥāb al-ahwāʾ*), those who defame religion and seek to deceive other people away from [the religious community, *milla*] by duplicitous tactics and deceptive falsehoods (*al-ḥiyal al-ghārra wa-l-abāṭīl al-khādiʿa*), the precaution against it is rational enquiry into the discourse of theologians who defend the principles of religion (*al-naẓar fī kalām al-mutakallimīn al-dhābbīna ʿan uṣūl al-dīn*), and are practised in debating with atheists (or heretics) and opponents (*al-mutadabbirīn bi-munāẓarat al-mulḥidīn wa-l-mukhālifīn*); to gather them together, hear them and listen to the interpretation of traditions (*taʾwīl al-āthār*), the explanation of accounts (*tafsīr al-akhbār*), and the meanings of Qurʾānic verses (*maʿānī l-āyy*). For whoever enquires into these meanings (*man naẓara fī hādhihi l-maʿānī*) will know (*ʿarafa*) the excellence (superiority) (*faḍl*) of the sciences of Islam over other sciences, the strength (*quwwa*) of this religion over other religions, the superiority of this sharīʿa in goodness (*ḥusn*) and strength over every other sharīʿa and religious community (*milla*) to which a community (*umma*) is linked and a sect (*firqa*) affiliated.
>
> If no astute religious specialist (*al-mutakallim al-ḥādhiq*) or incisive scholar (*al-ʿālim al-ṣārim*) is present, then he should read their books composed in support of religion, in demonstration of its fine qualities (*iẓhār maḥāsinihi*) and interpretations (*taʾwīlāt*), and the occasions for historical accounts (*ʿilal al-akhbār*). He should devote some of his times of leisure and solitude to this occupation; the opportunity to do so will not elude the king if he wishes it, nor will it escape him if he seeks it.[93]

An important element in Pseudo-Māwardī's *Naṣīḥat al-mulūk* is his repeated assertion of the importance and efficacy of *naẓar*, rational speculation or enquiry.[94] As this passage indicates, he regarded intellectual exertion as a means to the attainment of knowledge, *maʿrifa*. Pseudo-Māwardī's perspective is consistent with the teaching of al-Kaʿbī, who regarded *naẓar* as *ṣaḥīḥ*, a means to true knowledge, of a kind that transcended convictions held on account of familiarity (*ilf*) or communal attachment (*ʿaṣabiyya*).[95] At its highest level, in Pseudo-Māwardī's view, such intellectual activity is the preserve of theologians, the *mutakallimūn* who, central in the resolute king's arsenal against subversion, 'defend the principles of religion' against attack. As indicated in Chapter 5, in Pseudo-Māwardī's lifetime the *mutakallimūn*, themselves often accused of irreligion, engaged in theological debates and, in significant measure in self-defence, produced a copious literature of refutation.[96] Under their instruction and by means of the rational speculation in which they excel, the king will learn that 'this sharīʿa' is not only superior to that of any other *umma*, but also to that of any other sect (*firqa*).[97] Pseudo-Māwardī's language consistently assumes religious plurality and heterogeneity. Should the king lack opportunities to associate with religious specialists, he adds, he should apply himself to the private study of their books. It is likely that Pseudo-Māwardī addressed this contingency in the light of scholars' increasing absence from Naṣr's court, a development to which he refers in the passage that follows.

In his next section, Pseudo-Māwardī discusses the remedy for the supremacy of 'evil viziers' and the resulting alienation of persons of wisdom and rational intellect, probably a reference to philosophers and theologians. To combat this problem, the ruler should uphold the highest standards in his personal life and in his governance:

> As for the triumph over the king of wicked viziers (*wuzarāʾ al-sūʾ*) and seekers of this world, and the flight of the wise and intelligent (*al-ḥukamāʾ wa-l-ʿuqalāʾ*) from him, the way of precaution against these problems is to exhibit (*iẓhār*) trustworthiness (*amāna*), modesty (*ʿiffa*) and justice (*ʿadl*) among the subjects, to show compassion and kindness towards them, and to open the gates of counsels (*fatḥ abwāb al-naṣāʾiḥ*) among them. If he does this, every one of them will exhibit (*aẓhara*) that which is concordant with his king's inclinations and resembles the opinion of his leader (*raʾīs*), whether he acts out of belief or hypocrisy, or is sincere or dissembling (*murāʾin*). The people of religion, wisdom, trustworthiness, fear of God and sincerity of intention (*ahl al-dīn wa-l-ḥikma wa-l-amāna wa-l-khashya wa-l-ṣidq fī l-niyya*) will approach him, make haste to come to him, and will

> indicate to him the truth, guide him towards uprightness, restrain him from corruption, present him with counsels, and dissuade him from wrongful acts (*qabāʾiḥ*), 'for the *sulṭān* is a market, and to every market is brought only that which sells well in it'.[98]

Pseudo-Māwardī's advice amounts to a reversal of the process of imitation that brought about, in his analysis, the problem of corruption. The king should make a virtue of the fact that the people in his presence, for reasons of self-interest, will always wish to please him. If he changes his behaviour – and such a change lies within his capacity – the persons who surround and depend upon him will change their behaviour accordingly. Whether they do so out of conviction or hypocrisy is immaterial; the important point is that their changed behaviour will be imitated in turn. By changing himself, the king wrests power from the wicked viziers and incidentally earns the affection of his subjects. By manifesting good behaviour, in the form of trustworthiness, modesty or temperance, justice, compassion and kindness, and accepting counsels, the king will induce other people to heed his example and likewise improve their conduct, since to do so would please the monarch and thereby serve their self-interest. The likening of the king to a marketplace, a well-known metaphor, implies that it is in the king's power to create demand for a commodity, which his subjects will then strive to supply, since only if they respond to the market's demand will their wares be received and rewarded. As Pseudo-Māwardī suggests repeatedly, the king's greatest power lies in his ability to compel by example, and he is therefore obliged, as a matter of ethical principle, to set a high standard in his behaviour and speech.

Pseudo-Māwardī instructs the king that he must restrain his subjects from delving into topics that lead them to schism and factionalism, according to God's command and the example of the kings of the past:

> As for guarding against difference in the subjects' hearts and the division of the common people's inclinations (*ahwāʾ*) concerning religion, the way to manage and arrange this matter entails various approaches. Among the appropriate courses of action is this: That he should induce the people to cease plunging into matters that will lead them into division (*tafarruq*) and summon them to factionalism (*taḥazzub*). To do so is in accordance with

God's command to His servants, and with His Prophet's practice (*sunna*), which He has confirmed upon them, and with the governance of the resolute kings before him ... He said, 'This is My straight path, so follow it, and do not follow other ways, lest you become separated from His way' (6: 153). He forbade them from division and factionalism in many verses. The Prophet said, 'God has mercy on him who renounces argument, even if he is in the right.'[99] He also said, 'Do not differ in (your) ranks, lest you should differ in your hearts.'[100] [The first caliph] Abū Bakr al-Ṣiddīq, may God have mercy upon him, said to Salmān al-Fārisī [Salmān 'the Persian', a Companion of the Prophet, reported to have died in Madaʾin in 35 or 36/655 or 656],[101] on the subject of debate (*kalām*) – and he was in the right in it – 'Desist from debate, for I fear lest the Companions of the Prophet of God should fall into disagreement.' There are many proverbs of this kind.[102]

This approach is the established method for stemming the causes of disagreement. The strategy is, firstly, that the king should recite among the people the verses and traditions (*āthār*) in which concord (*iʾtilāf*) is ordered and division and difference are forbidden. Then he should discipline himself, and reprimand, rebuke and punish anyone who initiates an innovation (*aḥdatha bidʿatan*) or deviates in a practice (*alḥada fī sunnatin*).

If this course of action is not feasible, and if difference and dissension have become general, having preceded the king's lifetime and advanced before his reign, then the way to proceed is that he should not permit an originator (*muḥdith*) to initiate [an innovation] in his own time, especially if it entails opposition to the outer meaning of the law and the root of the religious community (*wa-lā siyyamā idhā kānat mukhālafatan li-ẓāhir al-sharīʿa wa-aṣl al-milla*); and he should manage it according to the first procedure.

If this course of action is not feasible – and it is extremely difficult and hard, indeed the resolute kings before us, solicitous of the affairs of religion and sovereignty, undertook it and exerted themselves in it, and for them too it was not always feasible to achieve that which they desired, and it was difficult to attain that which they wished – then there are two possible courses:

> One of them comprises anticipation of the next life, directing his aspiration towards it, and seeking that which God holds in store for those who are sincere in His religion and those who exert themselves in the perception of His truth (*idrāk ḥaqqihi*). If he chooses this path and if, by way of balanced rational speculation (*al-naẓar al-ᶜadl*) and listening to propositions (*samāᶜ al-aqāwīl*), the truth, with regard to matters over which the community (*umma*) differs, becomes firmly established in his view, then he should summon people and show gentleness in disseminating and promulgating it, by bringing people close to the true path (*madhhab al-ḥaqq*), supporting those who summon people to it (*al-duᶜāt ilayhi*) and those who enquire into it in a rational manner (*al-nāẓirīn fīhi*). He should exercise oversight (*ḥisba*) with regard to everything that proceeds from his authority in that respect. In this course of action lie a great recompense and an abundant, noble reward. It is the way of the prophets … and the path of the friends (*awliyāʾ*) (of God), the righteous, the rightly guided leaders of the people of our summons (to faith) (*ahl daᶜwatinā*), and of those who were before us …
>
> The second course of action is that convinced in the truth, he should proclaim in manifest fashion (*yuẓhir*) the sum (*jumla*) of that on which the people of his religious community are in agreement and over which his co-religionists (*alsun ahl daᶜwatihi*) are in concord. He should exert himself in seeking knowledge (*maᶜrifa*) of that body of agreed upon matters with certainty and soundness. Next he should uphold the religious laws (*qāma bi-l-sharāʾiᶜ*), implement the ordinances (*aḥkām*), spread justice and beneficence (*al-ᶜadl wa-l-iḥsān*), and banish injustice and hostility (*al-jawr wa-l-ᶜudwān*). He should not engage in any matters over which people differ beyond knowledge of the sum (*jumla*) (of matters on which they agree), since there is no expectation of uniting the inclinations (*ahwāʾ*) of the people in one single view (*ᶜalā raʾy wāḥid*), especially after long periods of time have elapsed and succeeded one another, and after difference has already set in.[103]

This section offers counsels for the avoidance and treatment of the communal fragmentation and potential for political upheaval that, Pseudo-Māwardī held, accompanied disagreements within religious communities. Still signalling at every turn the universal nature of his observations, Pseudo-Māwardī juxtaposes his appeals to the experience of the past with references specific to the *milla*. He presents the king with two alternatives: he may either attempt, by means of disciplined rational enquiry, to achieve personal conviction in the matters over which the community is divided, and then seek to propagate his point of view; when he associates this path with the worthy rulers of the past, within and beyond the *milla*, his audience perhaps imagined Ardashīr and al-Maᵓmūn, although his insistence on the gentle dissemination of a conviction, as well as the need for oversight, expressed the limits of the ruler's activity in this regard; or, accepting the inevitability of religious differences, he may confine his efforts to affirming the community's core beliefs and practices, avoiding controversial issues and upholding the agreed-upon parts of the religious law.

This passage is one of several that indicate Pseudo-Māwardī's familiarity with the theological concept of the 'sum' (*jumla*), a set of basic principles, on which all members of the community should agree. He appears to have adhered to the doctrine of the *aṣḥāb al-jumal*, 'minimalists', with whom al-Kaᶜbī appears to have been aligned.[104] According to this view, the common people were exempt from the obligation to reflect on specific dogmatic issues; for them, a general knowledge of doctrine sufficed, and in matters of detail, *taqlīd*, uncritical acceptance of a point of view was acceptable.[105] Al-Kaᶜbī held that knowledge of theological details constituted a *farḍ kifāya*, a collective obligation (as opposed to a *farḍ ᶜayn*, an individual obligation), and was not obligatory upon the *ᶜāmma*.[106] In this regard he departed from the opinion of other Muᶜtazilite writers, such as ᶜAbd al-Jabbār of the Basran branch, for whom the common people were not exempt from intellectual exertion and who rejected *taqlīd*.[107] Pseudo-Māwardī appears to have agreed with al-Kaᶜbī, since he did not believe that all members of the community should be encouraged to pursue rational speculation into religious matters that lay beyond the minimal set of principles; on the contrary, he regarded it as a path to division and fracture. Al-Maqdisī, like Pseudo-Māwardī, would argue that people should be dissuaded from engaging in controversies on matters of theological detail.[108] The concept of a core set of religious principles appears also in the writings of the Māturīdiyya; Abū Salama al-Samarqandī, who in the mid- to late tenth century transmitted teachings of al-Māturīdī, composed a *Jumal uṣūl al-dīn* ('Sums of the Principles of Religion'), which amounts to a concise summary of the doctrines of his predecessor.[109]

Pseudo-Māwardī's advice that the king should promote a minimal sum of beliefs and discourage his subjects from engaging in divisive theological disputes also reflects his affinity with the 'Testament of Ardashīr', which similarly locates the appearance of dissident groupings in the proliferation of differing interpretations of sacred texts. In a manner reminiscent of the 'Testament', Pseudo-Māwardī advised the king to prevent the entanglement of the common people in matters of disagreement that might engender rebellion and civil strife. The 'Testament' goes further, and, in an example of Pseudo-Māwardī's first alternative, urges the ruler to promote a single interpretation:

> In the past before us there have been kings [each] one of whom would impose the interpretation on the totality [of the people] (*yataᶜahhadu al-jumla bi-l-tafsīr*) and the instruction on the community (*wa-l-jamāᶜa bi-l-taḥṣīl*), and (assign) tasks to the idle (*wa-l-furrāgh bi-l-ashghāl*); just as he would maintain his body by cutting the excessive parts of his hair and nails and by thorough washing away of dirt.[110]

The 'Testament' connects the dangers of religious dispute with lack of occupation, and proposes that the king secure uniformity of interpretation by ensuring that the subjects are fully employed:

> Know that the demise of polities begins with the neglect of subjects who lack known occupations and recognised forms of work; for if inactivity becomes widespread among the people, it allows them to reflect on affairs and to ponder fundamental matters (*uṣūl*). When people reflect in this way, they reflect according to their different natures, and consequently the paths (*madhāhib*) among them become different. The differences of their schools engender their hostility towards and resentment of one another; yet despite their differences they are united in their dislike of kings.[111]

Other passages of *Naṣīḥat al-mulūk* suggest that Pseudo-Māwardī shared the Testament's apprehensions with regard to subjects' inactivity.[112]

Pseudo-Māwardī's urging of his royal addressee to assume leadership in religious matters recapitulates the perspective of Ibn al-Muqaffaᶜ, who in *al-Risāla fī l-ṣaḥāba* envisaged and promoted 'the vision of a determinate religious establishment working as part of the administrative bureaucracy, somewhat in the ancient Persian tradition'.[113] Pseudo-Māwardī's 'path of truth' (*madhhab al-ḥaqq*), identified with 'the people of our summons [to faith]' (*ahl da^c watinā*), co-existed with and faced competition from other *da^c awāt*. In this situation, the king's responsibility required him to investigate religious matters himself and to establish the principles on which the people of his *da^c wa* agreed. Further, he should publicise his support for this minimal sum of agreed upon matters, and recognise the lack of communal agreement beyond it. In urging the king to resist 'innovations' that ran counter to the external aspects of the sharī^c a, Pseudo-Māwardī distinguished between *ẓāhirī* and *bāṭinī* understandings of legal topics, an allusion to groups, like the Isma^c iliyya, who explored the interior and hidden dimensions of the law. Pseudo-Māwardī's advice that the ruler should uphold the *ẓāhir* and resist the *bāṭin* entailed an implicit, perhaps defensive assertion of his own stance, a reflection of the dominant Mu^c tazilite view of faith.[114]

Next, Pseudo-Māwardī turns to the means of averting the ambitions of enemies. The proposed strategy involves both the king's just and virtuous treatment of his subjects, and his cultivation of personal virtue and self-restraint:

> As for the stratagem (*ḥīla*) for eliminating his enemy's ambitions against him, there are various ways:
>
> The first and most direct path is that which we have already set forth regarding the sowing of mutual affection in the hearts of the subjects (*i^ɔ tilāf qulūb al-ra^c iyya*) and uniting them with justice (*^c adl*), equity (*inṣāf*), favour (*faḍl*) and beneficence (*iḥsān*), the cultivation of the kingdom through these measures, and the fair discharge of the land-tax (*kharāj*) and revenues (*ghallāt*) by these means.
>
> The second is [that he should] cleanse himself of base cravings (*al-maṭāmi^c al-daniyya*), reprehensible characteristics (*al-akhlāq al-dhamīma*), succumbing to desires (*ittibā^c al-shahawāt*) and indulgence in pleasures (*al-istihtār bi-l-ladhdhāt*), especially in matters that God has forbidden and prohibited; and rise to the acquisition of virtues (*nayl al-faḍā^ɔ il*) and the attainment of fine qualities (*darak al-manāqib*), including knowledge (*^c ilm*), religion (*dīn*), justice (*^c adl*), kindness (*rifq*) and the other attributes of excellence.

> Whoever examines these stations (of achievement), ponders their implications and finds that he lacks their imprint and is bereft of their adornment will be unable to control the cravings of his carnal self (*nafs*) and will risk abasement (*dunūʾ*) on account of his desires.[115]
>
> Next among the proposed strategies are good administration in affairs and consultation of persons of good sense, judgement and experience(s) (*dhaw[ū] al-albāb wa-l-raʾy wa-l-tajārib*), as it has been said, 'Outwit your enemy by rectifying your faults.' On this subject Aristotle wrote to Alexander, 'Improve yourself (by demonstrating) that which prompts the subjects to affirm your claim (to their obedience). Display gifts and fine conduct among your subjects, for these things will cause your subjects to prosper, and humble your enemies and those who defy you.' He also said, 'Improve yourself for your own sake, and the people will follow you.'[116]
>
> Next are the gathering of selected forces and a chosen retinue (*jamᶜ al-junūd al-mukhtārīn wa-l-ḥāshiya al-muntakhabīn*), skilled in battles and wars and the use of stratagems; and striving to unite their favourable opinions of him and their hearts (*istijmāᶜ ārāʾihim wa-qulūbihim*) by exercising justice among them, rewarding him who does good for his beneficence and requiting him who does wrong for his wickedness, and ample bestowal of their allowances (*idrār arzāqihim*), according to the recommendations that we shall mention in the chapter on governance of the élite if God wills.[117]

According to Pseudo-Māwardī, the king's best defences against the hostility of his enemies are, in turn, to treat his subjects with justice and benevolence, and thereby win their loyalty and affection; to rectify himself through the cultivation of virtue; to govern well and merit his subjects' obedience; and to assemble, in readiness, his most able soldiers, whose loyalty he must earn by means of fairness and generosity. The passage provides an example of his consistent, if in this case implicit, urging of the king to avoid conflict unless he is certain that no alternative remains.

In a direct reference to the conditions of his time, Pseudo-Māwardī proceeds to address the appearance of injustice in the kingdom and the means to avert it:

As for guarding against an occurrence that, it has been observed, has afflicted the kings of the time, namely the appearance of corruption, the altering of (established) affairs, kings' appropriation of the possessions of the subjects, and the manifest appearance of injustice and inclination towards this world, and things of this sort, there are several methods:

Firstly, attentiveness to God, great and glorious, and the knowledge that God is the first to be followed, and the prophets are the most deserving of persons to be emulated; and that he should know that God, great and glorious, recompenses each soul for that which it has earned: 'No burdened soul shall bear the load of another' (35: 18).

Next, by his aspiration he should rise to be most excellent (*afḍal*) before God and in the sight of the intelligent, and of highest station (*arfaᶜ manzilatin*) in the sight of the wise among them. Kings are especially suited for this distinction and the most likely of people to cultivate this attribute of high aspiration, because they are not content unless they are higher in rank than their equals and their peers among the people of their kind (*li-annahum lam yarḍaw illā an yakūnū fawqa ashkālihim wa-nuẓarāʾihim min ahl nawᶜihim darajatan*), above them in terms of glorious deeds (*aᶜlā minhum manqabatan*) and more conspicuous in terms of virtue (*aẓhar minhum faḍīlatan*). If the king is not (already) so disposed, then he should adhere to (the path of) the virtuous among the kings; for kings compete with one another in excellence in the noble qualities that they possess. It is incumbent on the excellent king that he emulate the most virtuous of kings rather than the base among them, and that he imitate their examples in their virtues to the exclusion of their vices. For there has been no community (*lam takun umma min al-umam*) whose kings have not included monarchs who were resolute, effective, wise and devout (*ḥazama wa-sāsa wa-ḥukamāʾ wa-mutadayyinūn*). Indeed, the people of religion had regard only for persons who adopted this path, for whoever opposed it, diverged from it and deviated from it, his kingship (in their view) was the kingship of the stealing oppressor and the foreign usurper. In addition, a single king varies and differs in his actions, in goodness and wickedness, and virtues and vices. It is incumbent on the king of far aspiration who considers adopting a model to emulate that he ensure that in being in turn emulated, his practice (*sunna*) followed and his conduct imitated, it is in his good actions and not in his bad actions, and in his most virtuous aspects and not in his vices.[118]

For we have related from the Prophet: 'Do not be opportunists (*immaᶜa*) who say that if the people behave well then we shall behave well, and that if they behave badly then we shall behave badly. Rather, adjust yourselves so that if the people behave well you behave well too, but if they behave badly, do not become oppressive.'[119] A wise philosopher said, 'If you see the people involved in (acts of) goodness, then compete with them in it, and if you see them in (acts that lead to) perdition, leave them alone; they choose only for themselves.'[120] God, great is His mention, said, 'O you who believe: You are responsible for your own selves. He who goes astray cannot harm you if you are rightly guided' (5: 105). They used to say that a man once lamented the corruption of the age to a sage, and the sage said to him, 'You are the age; if you behave well, the age will be good, and if you behave badly, then it will be corrupt.'[121]

This set of quotations concludes Pseudo-Māwardī's presentation of the ills of the kingdom and their cures. He impresses upon the king the impact of his conduct; he should adopt the most excellent model for himself and ensure that he provides his subjects with a virtuous example, since they will, for better or worse, imitate him. He adduces a Prophetic hadīth narrated on his own authority (*wa-qad rawaynā ᶜan al-nabī*), a saying of 'a philosopher', a Qurᵓānic verse (5: 105) and an unattributed utterance in wide circulation (*wa-qālū*). Pseudo-Māwardī then turns to the chronological section of his chapter.

In sum, Pseudo-Māwardī's treatment of the ills that beset kingdoms suggests that the king faced challenges to his power articulated in terms of *riyāsa*, political leadership, and *diyāna*, religious allegiance. When, in his analysis, the latter developed into, or masked, the former, it constituted a critical challenge to the ruler's authority and the polity's stability. Like several of his near-contemporaries, Pseudo-Māwardī envisages a multi-communal polity in which the various communities observed different religious laws. These co-existing communities differed, of course, in their proximity to the truth: he asserts the superiority of 'this *milla*', 'our *milla*' and 'our religion' over their counterparts, and describes the ruler's role as that of 'defender of the domain of religion', 'responsible for the affairs of the Muslims' (*al-dhābb ᶜan ḥawzat al-dīn wa-l-qāʾim bi-umūr al-Muslimīn*).[122] At the same time, faced with the fluid contours of contemporary religious movements, Pseudo-Māwardī strives to define the borders of the *milla*, in a manner that still allowed for considerable internal difference. The establishment of these borders of the 'true path' required rational speculation (*naẓar*). When in a later section Pseudo-Māwardī describes the religious education necessary to the king, he situates the need for such training in part in the defence of religion and the protection of the *milla*.[123]

The Circumstances of Pseudo-Māwardī's Composition

Pseudo-Māwardī's treatment of the dangers to which polities are subject, and his advice for the avoidance or rectification of these calamities, are consistent with the hypothesis that he wrote his book relatively late in Naṣr's reign, during the period in which the amir and several eminent members of his court espoused the teachings of the Ismaʿiliyya. While it seems probable that Pseudo-Māwardī's allusions to heterodox movements connoted above all the *bāṭiniyya*, in the general sense of the term as well as in its specific application to the Ismaʿili *daʿwa*, it is quite likely that he regarded local religious–political disturbances as potential examples of the same paradigm. Religious figures, sometimes associated with revolts, appeared regularly in the region. Ibn Abī Zakariyyā, who appeared in 319/931, has already been mentioned. Al-Kaʿbī, Pseudo-Māwardī's contemporary and fellow citizen, composed a book in refutation of 'a pseudo-prophet in Khurasan'.[124] The Ḥanafī heresiographer Makḥūl al-Nasafī (d. 318/930) reported that a movement known as the Mutarabbiṣa ('those who wait in expectation'), followers of an individual from Nishapur, Ṭāhir b. Saʿīd b. ʿAbd al-Majīd al-Iskāf[ī?], proclaimed him the *mahdī*, the rightly guided figure whose rule, preceding the end-time, would restore religion and justice to the earth, and rose in revolt.[125] No later than 322/934, a pseudo-prophet (*mutanabbī*) and claimant to the status of *mahdī* appeared in Chaghaniyan, where he initiated an uprising that lasted at least until 339/950–1. Abū ʿAlī Aḥmad Chaghānī (d. 344/955), who in 327/939 followed his father Abū Bakr Muḥammad in the governorship of Khurasan, finally oversaw his capture and execution.[126] The eleventh-century Persian historian Gardīzī and the Arabic scholar and historian Ibn al-Athīr (555–630/1160–1233) describe this last individual's activities in accordance with some of the established stereotypes: the pseudo-prophet was not only effective, partly through his skills in trickery, in attracting large numbers of followers to his *da^cwa*, but was also belligerent towards those who disagreed with his claims to prophethood; he killed many of his opponents, and, according to Ibn al-Athīr, he claimed that after his death he would return to the world.[127] Contemporaneous depictions of al-Muqanna^c are likely to have shaped the authors' accounts of the Chaghani figure as well as their audiences' perceptions of the alleged pseudo-prophet. That the events in Chaghaniyan might have contributed to Pseudo-Māwardī's perception of the pressing danger of heterodoxy finds possible further support in the report of Niẓām al-Mulk that a certain Abū Manṣūr Chaghānī, the *^cāriż* (quartermaster general) of the army in Bukhara, converted to Isma^cilism towards the end of the reign of Naṣr.[128] Of these various revolts, that of the Isma^ciliyya aroused particular apprehension, since the high rank of its adherents meant that it combined the realms of the political and the religious in a potent challenge to the order envisaged and sought by, for example, the shaykhs who produced *al-Sawād al-a^cẓam*.

In this cogently argued exposition of the ills that he observed in the Samanid polity, Pseudo-Māwardī offered his royal readership a reasoned analysis of the kingdom's predicament. He described and accounted for the kingdom's ills, and proposed solutions that addressed not only the symptoms, but also the causative factors of each problem. He sought to persuade by means of rational argument, in which he proceeded from the general to the particular, from the universal and timeless to the current and immediate. His conception of his subject and his analytical method suggest his familiarity with the intellectual tools of Mu^ctazilite theology and Kindian philosophy. Pseudo-Māwardī depended not only on the techniques of logical exposition, but also on the persuasive power of an overwhelming variety of authoritative voices. By way of allusion and direct citation, he integrates a vast number and wide range of supporting texts, drawn from a diverse repertoire of sacred materials and human wisdom, into his work of counsel. To render his advice as effective as possible, Pseudo-Māwardī made use of his fluency in the full set of intellectual and literary resources available in Arabic. After his analysis of the kingdom's problems and his equally carefully plotted explanation of the remedies available to the king, Pseudo-Māwardī adduced the instructive examples of the prophets, caliphs and kings discussed in Chapter 1. His chronologically ordered depiction of exemplary rulers concludes, it will be remembered, with Aḥmad II, the murdered father of Naṣr II. By this arrangement Pseudo-Māwardī sought to exert the full force of the remembered past, and to evoke the compelling obligation on the present amir to equal or surpass the fine deeds of his predecessors.

In this chapter, as throughout *Naṣīḥat al-mulūk*, Pseudo-Māwardī presents advice intended to address the specific circumstances of his time and place against a universal backdrop. Since the beginnings of humankind, communities and kingdoms, in their composition and in their experience, have resembled one another, and the community and kingdom for whose benefit he offers his counsel follow the patterns set by their counterparts and predecessors. In parts of his text, Pseudo-Māwardī adopts a vocabulary applicable exclusively to the Muslim *milla*; at the same time, he urges the king to promote the well-being of the pluralistic society of *ahl al-milla wa-l-dhimma*, in the context of a mirror in which he juxtaposed Muslim and non-Muslim authorities in a deliberate and pointed manner.

In the preceding chapters I have drawn attention to three interrelated factors that, I propose, contributed to Pseudo-Māwardī's treatment of religious-political dissent. First, the circumstances of his time provided the context and occasion for his warning of the contemporary king(s) against groups whose rejection or subordination of external religious forms he regarded as the principal sign of a challenge to the social and political structure of the polity. Secondly, the textual legacies of late antiquity, with which he was deeply acquainted, provided him with a conceptual framework and an authoritative vocabulary by which to analyse and describe the processes involved in the formation of religious divisions. Thirdly, Pseudo-Māwardī's composition permitted him to assert his rejection of *ilḥād* and *zandaqa*, the charges that had been levelled against his fellow citizens Abū Zayd al-Balkhī and al-Kaᶜbī. Given his affinities with the philosopher and theologian, it is possible that Pseudo-Māwardī experienced the same accusations, and that, like other Muᶜtazilites, he wrote in part in defence of the application of rationality to religious knowledge.

8

The Religious Sensibility of *Naṣīḥat al-mulūk*

After the preceding discussion of Pseudo-Māwardī's religious–cultural context and his treatment of the religious–political problems that beset kingdoms, the present chapter seeks to locate him in the vibrant and varied religious life of the tenth-century Samanid domains. As the previous pages have demonstrated, *Naṣīḥat al-mulūk* displays a religious sensibility dominated by certain characteristics: a strong sense of ethical responsibility, expressed in part in observance of the divine law; conviction of the indispensable nature of rational speculation in the pursuit of religious understanding; and an austere way of living in the world, informed by an abiding consciousness of its transience and relativity. This chapter addresses these characteristics with reference to the predominant intellectual and religious configurations in early tenth-century eastern Iran and Transoxiana, namely, the Ḥanafiyya, the Muᶜtazila (and the forming theological school of the 'scholars of Samarqand') and the movement of renunciation that would eventually contribute to the formation of *taṣawwuf* or Sufism.

Pseudo-Māwardī's upholding of the Rāshidūn as exemplars of moral leadership and his subscription to the principle of *ijmāᶜ*, consensus, indicate his position among the *ahl al-sunna wa-l-jamāᶜa*.[1] As his reference to the Imamiyya demonstrates,[2] he was familiar with Shiᶜite doctrine and he also adduces several examples of ᶜAlī's conduct, especially in his discussion of military matters.[3] Pseudo-Māwardī's awareness of Imami doctrine is consistent with the widespread attachment to ᶜAlī in the eastern regions in this period.[4] As young men, the Amir Ismāᶜīl b. Aḥmad and the philosopher Abū Zayd al-Balkhī had both reportedly held Shiᶜite beliefs, which they later relinquished.[5] Al-Kaᶜbī, moreover, reported that almost all the Muᶜtazila regarded ᶜAlī as the most worthy of all persons (*kāna afḍala jamīᶜ al-khalq*) after the Messenger of God, but also held that at the time of their caliphates, Abū Bakr, ᶜUmar and ᶜUthmān were more suitable candidates for the office than ᶜAlī.[6] It is consistent with this outlook that Pseudo-Māwardī cites a ḥadīth that recognises the status of Abū Bakr and ᶜUmar, but presents ᶜAlī as superior to both of them.[7] He also refers to ᶜAlī as *al-imām al-fāḍil*.[8] As Wilferd Madelung has indicated, the Muᶜtazilite doctrine established only general conditions for the imamate; the decision regarding which caliph or claimant might be regarded as just and legitimate was a matter for the individual.[9] Pseudo-Māwardī's familiarity with Shiᶜite doctrine and the status he assigns to ᶜAlī, notwithstanding his affiliation with *ahl al-sunna wa-l-jamāᶜa*, find a context in the attachment to ᶜAlī prevalent in his environment.

Part I of this book presented evidence in support of the argument that Pseudo-Māwardī lived and wrote *Naṣīḥat al-mulūk* in Balkh; I argued further that some aspects of the text would support the hypothesis of its composition in Samarqand. Fuᵓād ᶜAbd al-Munᶜim Aḥmad's tentative suggestion, in 1988, of Abū Zayd's authorship, and Ḥasan Anṣārī's firm association of *Naṣīḥat al-mulūk* with the circle of Abū l-Qāsim al-Kaᶜbī,[10] both imply Pseudo-Māwardī's residence in or connection with Balkh, a point that, as Chapter 2 sought to demonstrate, finds support in several other aspects of the text as well. *Naṣīḥat al-mulūk*, I suggest, bears the clear imprint of the techniques and doctrines of both the Kindian tradition and the Baghdadi Muᶜtazila. These characteristics increase the likelihood of the book's production in Balkh, where Abū Zayd al-Balkhī continued the intellectual tradition associated with al-Kindī, and al-Kaᶜbī continued the theological–philosophical approach of the Muᶜtazila of Baghdad.

Although the evidence of *Naṣīḥat al-mulūk* suggests its composition in Balkh, it is quite likely that Pseudo-Māwardī encountered individuals linked with Samarqand and was to some extent familiar with intellectual trends in that city. Numerous scholars and merchants moved between Balkh and Samarqand, and their families intermarried. Both cities offered a milieu steeped in religious scholarship and the cultivation of ethical behaviour. Ulrich Rudolph has suggested that the metaphysics of al-Māturīdī, in Samarqand, reflect an acquaintance with the thought of Abū Zayd al-Balkhī, and perhaps an acquaintance with Ismaᶜili teachings.[11] Particularly indicative of the intellectual contacts between Samarqand and Balkh are al-Māturīdī's detailed representations, and criticisms, of the Muᶜtazilite doctrines of al-Kaᶜbī,[12] whose status in the region he acknowledges in his designation of him as *imām ahl al-arḍ*, 'leader of the earth's people'.[13] These examples suggest possible interconnections among intellectual figures whose dispositions were Kindian, Muᶜtazilite and Māturīdī–Samarqandī.

Even in Balkh, however, al-Kaᶜbī's teachings met with opposition.[14] The charges against Abū Zayd for *ilḥād* and al-Kaᶜbī for *zandaqa* perhaps contributed to Pseudo-Māwardī's formulation of a 'sum' of beliefs upon which members of the *milla* agreed, and for his setting as a boundary for the *milla* the acknowledgement of the exterior (*ẓāhir*) dimension of the sharīᶜa. His boundaries would have accommodated Abū Zayd, whose exegesis avoided *bāṭinī* speculation, and al-Kaᶜbī, whose theology held individuals responsible for their obedience or disobedience to the divine will. The notion of a minimalist 'sum' allowed for an internally diverse *milla* that included a spectrum of interpretations, limited by the acknowledgement of the exterior dimension of the law.

The Ḥanafiyya

As Aḥmad has demonstrated, Pseudo-Māwardī's treatment of several legal issues indicates his position among the Ḥanafiyya, the legal school generally prevalent in Khurasan and Transoxiana by the ninth century.[15] It was not only in legal matters, but also in his intellectual and doctrinal approach that Pseudo-Māwardī, a strong proponent of rational judgement, displayed an affinity with the Ḥanafiyya. Balkh had developed into a particularly strong centre for Ḥanafism as early as the lifetime of Abū Ḥanīfa (d. 150/767) himself. According to *Fażāᵓil-i Balkh*, some shaykhs and scholars of Kufa (presumably opponents of Abū Ḥanīfa) used to refer to Balkh as Murjiᵓābād, because Abū Ḥanīfa was considered a Murjiᵓite (that is, an affiliate of the political–religious movement associated with the doctrine of *irjāᵓ*, 'postponement' (of judgement on the status of the sinning Muslim) and later with the definition of faith in terms of belief and its profession rather than acts), and all the inhabitants of Balkh were followers of his school.[16] When the people of Khurasan travelled to Iraq in pursuit of knowledge, they visited some other scholars, 'except for the people of Balkh', who always studied with Abū Ḥanīfa.[17] Balkh emerged as the chief centre of Ḥanafī learning in the east, and after the death in 197/812–13 of the Ḥanafī judge Abū Muṭīᶜ al-Balkhī, who had held the judgeship for sixteen years, all the city's judges were Ḥanafīs. Numerous early scholars mentioned in Balkh's history were immediate students of Abū Ḥanīfa or one of his most famous companions, Abū Yūsuf (d. 182/798), al-Shaybānī (132–87 or 189/750–803 or 805) and Zufar b. al-Hudhayl (110–58/728–75). The renunciant Shaqīq al-Balkhī studied under Abū Ḥanīfa and retained an association with Abū Yūsuf.[18] *Fażāʾil-i Balkh*, perhaps conveying earlier materials, equates the categories of the Muslim, Sunni and Ḥanafī communities, when Shaykh al-Islām Vāᶜiẓ boasts, in enumerating the distinctive positive attributes of the city, that Balkh's population consists only of *ahl-i Islām*, only of the *madhhab-i sunnat va-jamāᶜat*, and that its only *millat* is the *millat-i Ḥanafī*. In his conception, the Ḥanafīs constituted a *millat*, comparable to the communities of non-Muslim (Jewish, Christian, Zoroastrian and (other) 'protected') confessional groups (*milal-i mukhtalifeh . . . az yahūdī wa-naṣrānī va-majūsī va-ahl-i dhimmat*).[19] Perhaps in an echo of the Ḥanafī-inflected discourse of his milieu, al-Kaᶜbī, a Ḥanafī jurist as well as a Muᶜtazilite theologian, composed a *Kitāb al-Sunna wa-l-jamāᶜa*.[20]

If in the early Islamic period the *madhhab* of Abū Ḥanīfa was especially rooted in Balkh, it became established elsewhere among the towns of eastern Khurasan and Transoxiana, and in the latter region it came to constitute the mainstream religious orientation of the population at large, *al-sawād al-aᶜẓam*.[21] It became so prevalent, in fact, that the text of that name, like *Fażāʾil-i Balkh*, equates the 'path' (*madhhab*) of Abū Ḥanīfa, on whom the author or translator bestows a set of exalted epithets, with that of the *ahl-i sunnat va-jamāᶜat*: as if the coincidence were self-evident, the author(s) link(s) the *madhhab-i sunnat va-jamāᶜat* with the *madhhab-i imām-i imāmān va-sayyid-i fuqahā va-kadkhudā-yi dīn va-ᶜilm va-shāhanshāh-i fiqh Abū Ḥanīfa Nuᶜmān b. Thābit*, 'the path of the Imam of Imams, the leader of the jurists, the lord of religion and knowledge, the King of Kings of jurisprudence, Abū Ḥanīfa Nuᶜmān b. Thābit'.[22]

Although the equation was by no means universal, Muᶜtazilite theological inclinations frequently accompanied Ḥanafī juristic affiliations in Khurasan and Transoxiana.[23] Pseudo-Māwardī provides an example of that conjunction. *Naṣīḥat al-mulūk* reflects a Ḥanafī proclivity with regard to its treatment of legal issues and an accompanying Muᶜtazilite orientation in theological matters.

In another important indication of Pseudo-Māwardī's affinity with the Ḥanafī tradition, he follows Abū Ḥanīfa's recognition of an affinity among religions. He too associates a set of common beliefs, principles and orientations with religions past and present, and envisages Islam not as different in kind from other religions, but rather as the finest realisation of a universal religious consciousness.

The Muᶜtazila and the *Mutakallimūn*

Pseudo-Māwardī displays a profound engagement with the discourse and activities of the *mutakallimūn* of his region. As Anṣārī has pointed out, *Naṣīḥat al-mulūk* displays a Muᶜtazilite approach and presupposes a number of Muᶜtazilite doctrines.[24] Among the examples mentioned in previous chapters are Pseudo-Māwardī's criticism of most of the Umayyad caliphs and his praise of the Muᶜtazilite-leaning Abbasid caliphs, particularly al-Maᵓmūn, al-Muᶜtaṣim and al-Wāthiq; his references to *tawḥīd* and *ahl al-tawḥīd*; his discussion of the status of rebels (*ahl al-baghy*) and his treatment of revolt (*khurūj*) against the unjust ruler; his assertion of the limits of the subjects' obedience; and his endorsement of 'minimalism'. Further examples of Muᶜtazilite concepts and doctrines, such as his inclusion amongst the required articles of belief of 'the promise and threat' (of divine reward and punishment) (*al-waᶜd wa-l-waᶜīd*), and 'commanding right and forbidding wrong' (*al-amr bi-l-maᶜrūf wa-l-nahy ᶜan al-munkar*), as well as his implied position on the theological status of the sinner, will be seen in Volume II.[25] Equally important is the Muᶜtazilite-associated intellectual approach that Pseudo-Māwardī demonstrates throughout his mirror.

To these points might be added further references that suggest not only Pseudo-Māwardī's Muᶜtazilite leanings, but also, more specifically, his affinity with the Baghdadi branch associated in the eastern regions with al-Kaᶜbī. Pseudo-Māwardī's adherence to the Baghdadi as opposed to the Basran branch emerges from a comparison of his assertions and implications with the evidence of, in particular, *al-Masāᵓil fī l-khilāf bayn al-Baṣriyyīn wa-l-Baghdādiyyīn* ('Theological Questions on the Disagreement Between the Basrans and Baghdadis') of Abū Rashīd al-Nīsābūrī, a theologian who began as a follower of al-Kaᶜbī and the Baghdadi school, but later joined ᶜAbd al-Jabbār and the Basran school, and devoted a treatise to the differences between the two branches of Muᶜtazilism.[26] Pseudo-Māwardī's support of the Baghdadi branch associates him, in all likelihood, with al-Kaᶜbī, who disseminated the teachings of the Baghdadi Muᶜtazila in Khurasan and Transoxiana. Among the features that point to an association with the Baghdadi Muᶜtazila is Pseudo-Māwardī's repeated reference to God's doing that which is optimal, *aṣlaḥ*, for all His servants: he writes that God, 'in His wisdom, mandated the commands and prohibitions, and their worship, in accordance with that which was most fitting (*aṣlaḥ*) for them', and He 'favours each one of them with that which He knows is best (*aṣlaḥ*) for him'.[27] In the earlier phase of Muᶜtazilism, the doctrine that God, as a corollary of His justice, must act in accordance with the best or most fitting is associated with several Muᶜtazilite theologians, including Abū l-Hudhayl al-ᶜAllāf (*c.* 135–227/752–841) and his student and nephew Abū Isḥāq al-Naẓẓām (*c.* 165–221/782–836); al-Kaᶜbī states that Bishr b. al-Muᶜtamir (d. *c.* 210–26/825–40) also affirmed the doctrine.[28] In the later period, however, the Baghdadi Muᶜtazila adopted and developed the doctrine into a form that elicited the rebuttals of Abū ᶜAlī al-Jubbāʾī (d. 303/915–16), ᶜAbd al-Jabbār and other later Muᶜtazilites of the Basran branch.[29] The evidence of *Naṣīḥat al-mulūk* suggests that Pseudo-Māwardī followed al-Kaᶜbī and the Muᶜtazila of Khurasan in this matter.

Pseudo-Māwardī's several invocations of the Balkh-born theologian ᶜAmr b. ᶜUbayd, later identified with the beginnings of the Muᶜtazila, are similarly compatible with a Muᶜtazilite perspective.[30] It is probably germane to note ᶜAmr's forceful encouragement of the performance of *al-amr bi-l-maᶜrūf*, 'commanding right', one of the 'five principles' of the Muᶜtazila, and a duty that Pseudo-Māwardī also affirms.[31] Pseudo-Māwardī's references to ᶜAmr stress his exemplary austerity and moral courage as an individual who did not shy away from offering sincere advice and admonition to a powerful caliph.[32] Pseudo-Māwardī also cites, on separate occasions, the Muᶜtazilite theologian and secretary Thumāma b. al-Ashras (d. *c.* 213/828) and al-Jāḥiẓ, both of whom appear in al-Kaᶜbī's *Maqālāt* ('Doctrines').[33] Al-Jāḥiẓ had been a student of al-Naẓẓām, and Pseudo-Māwardī, who was well acquainted with and cited his writings, follows the mention of al-Jāḥiẓ's name with a petition for God's mercy upon the earlier writer.[34]

As these indications already suggest, Muᶜtazilism, especially in the forms in which it flourished in Khurasan during his lifetime, greatly shaped Pseudo-Māwardī's mentality. In the light of his larger environment, it is worth noting that in their intellectual approach and in their general disposition towards certain topics, Pseudo-Māwardī and many Muᶜtazilite theologians were not altogether dissimilar from the scholars of Samarqand. Al-Māturīdī, who through his extensive refutation of al-Kaᶜbī's doctrines incidentally provides much of the extant information regarding his opponent's teachings, still shared significant common ground with him.[35] Certain Muᶜtazilite principles, indeed, found widespread acceptance, and ceased to indicate an exclusively Muᶜtazilite affiliation.[36]

If Ḥanafism frequently coincided with Muᶜtazilism in Khurasan and Transoxiana, it also contributed to the formation in Transoxiana of the distinctive theological disposition first described as the path of 'the scholars of Samarqand' and later associated with one of its leading exponents, al-Māturīdī.[37] Although al-Māturīdī and 'the scholars of Samarqand' were, as their designation indicates, closely associated with that city,[38] the developing network of scholars embraced a secondary connection with Balkh. Al-Māturīdī adhered to the doctrine of Abū Ḥanīfa as it had been transmitted and elaborated by the Ḥanafī scholars of Balkh and Transoxiana, and having originated in Samarqand, the emerging theological outlook became established in eastern Khurasan, especially in Marv and Balkh, a process that is likely to have begun during the lifetime of Pseudo-Māwardī.

Pseudo-Māwardī urged his royal audience to pursue and promote the science of *kalām*, which, as Volume II will indicate, he considered prior to jurisprudence.[39] He asserted the essential function of the *mutakallimūn*, rationally trained and skilled in the arts of debate, in the 'defence' of religion. He further urges his audience not to follow without question the opinions of others (*taqlīd*), but to employ rational speculation, *naẓar*, in the pursuit of religious truth. In these respects Pseudo-Māwardī's position is consistent with the perspectives and practices of both Muᶜtazilite and Samarqandī–Māturīdī theologians, who argued against members of other confessional groups and against representatives of opposing theological schools. Almost all Muᶜtazilites endorsed, as one of their foundational principles, the defence and dissemination of religious doctrine. The principle is also thoroughly demonstrated in the assertive literature of refutation produced among scholars of the emerging Māturīdī theological school.[40] Pseudo-Māwardī's repeated recommendation of the use of rational speculation, *naẓar*, in order to arrive at religious truth, and especially to adjudicate among differing religious claims and evaluate the strengths and weaknesses of religious arguments, is similarly in keeping with both a Muʿtazilite and a Ḥanafī–Māturīdī outlook.[41] In these aspects, Pseudo-Māwardī also followed the Kindian philosophical tradition, which likewise promoted the use of reason and rational speculation in the pursuit of religious truth, and rejected *taqlīd*.[42]

Renunciation

In keeping with certain strands of Muʿtazilite intellectualism and a strong current in the religious cultures of Balkh and Samarqand, Pseudo-Māwardī evinces a disposition towards the practices and mentality associated with *zuhd*. The term *zuhd* connotes an attitude of self-restraint manifested in the control of passion and appetite, associated with the lower self (*nafs*); on occasion Pseudo-Māwardī specifically associates the *nafs* with the 'animal appetites' (*al-shahawāt al-ḥayawāniyya*) and accentuates its distance from reason, *ʿaql*.[43] For some of Pseudo-Māwardī's contemporaries, the struggle against the lower self represented the true struggle; the mystic al-Ḥakīm al-Tirmidhī, for instance, devotes a lengthy excursus to 'exertion for the truth', *al-mujāhada ʿalā l-ḥaqīqa*.[44] Pseudo-Māwardī repeatedly urges the king to restrain rather than indulge his passions, to choose the path dictated by reason rather than succumb to the impulses of nature.[45] The worst kind of slavery, he asserts, is enslavement to passion; the king should practise renunciation of his desires (*tazhīd ʿan al-shahawāt*).[46] Pseudo-Māwardī's portrayal of the illusory promise of satisfied desire recalls Buddhist teachings: 'Let the person who dedicates himself to his appetites and devotes himself to his pleasures remember that he craves, desires, yearns and longs for nothing in this world but that when he attains it and triumphs over it, it wearies him and becomes tedious to him.'[47] Pseudo-Māwardī discerns in the divine description of worldliness as 'play and diversion' (*laʿb wa-lahw*, Q 6: 32) an expression of God's desire to rebuke the lower world (*dhamm al-dunyā*) and encourage men of intellect and virtue (*al-ʿuqalāʾ . . . wa-l-fuḍalāʾ*) to practise renunciation in it (*al-tazhīd fīhā*).[48] It was especially necessary that the king resist his desires when they induced him to transgress the religious law not only for the sake of his moral welfare, but also because his example would initiate a pattern of imitation amongst his *khāṣṣa* and eventually the generality of his subjects.

In a sequence adduced in his epilogue, in which he incorporated materials apart from the argument of his text, Pseudo-Māwardī describes three categories of persons with regard to their observance of the permitted and the forbidden, the *ḥalāl* and the *ḥarām*. The first category is that of the scrupulous ascetic (*al-nāsik al-wariᶜ*) who declines much of that which God has made lawful to him, and contents himself in the world with the food that his day brings him, out of distaste for the world and renunciation of it. He recognises and perceives the transience and instability of worldly things, the world's frequent treachery towards its denizens, its humbling of persons who exalt it and its rejection of those who seek to make it prosperous. By virtue of his far-reaching aspiration and pure soul, this individual rises towards a felicity that does not dissipate and an abode from which there is no transfer; in the world, he becomes a king by the goodness of his life and in the afterlife, a king by virtue of his attainment of divine rewards and blessings (*fa-ṣāra fī l-dunyā malikan bi-ṭīb al-ḥayāt wa-fī l-ākhira malikan bi-nayl al-mathwabāt wa-l-makramāt*). The second category is that of the person who abandons himself to the things that God has forbidden, does not consider consequences or reflect on his final end, pays no heed to hostile speech and a poor reputation in this world, and draws no lesson from (the threat of) painful and imminent punishments (*al-ᶜuqūbāt al-muʾlima al-muᶜjila*); the person who adopts this path should be shunned and avoided. The third category is that of the person who in this world desires the pleasure and sweetness of life, and in the afterlife hopes to attain divine reward and recompense. Accordingly, he pursues the permitted and avoids the forbidden, enjoys the world and upholds the duties of religion, and hopes that he will be among those to whom God brings good things in the world and in the afterlife; among those who mix good and bad works, in the hope that God will accept their repentance and forgive them if they repent and are remorseful.[49] The intelligent and virtuous king should know that if his lower or carnal self (*nafs*) will not submit to him in rejecting the world to the point that he reaches the station of the good and austere (*al-zuhhād al-akhyār*), he should at least rise above the station of the corrupt and debauched (*al-fussāq al-fujjār*).[50]

This passage appears in the epilogue to *Naṣīḥat al-mulūk.* Pseudo-Māwardī wished to leave his royal audience with the reflection that, as al-Ḥakīm al-Tirmidhī implied, it was mastery of the self that constituted the highest level of governance; the virtuoso in austerity was the true king.[51] At an earlier point in his mirror, Pseudo-Māwardī cited 'a renunciant' (*ba*ᶜ*ḍ al-zuhhād*), who pronounced, 'By patience (*ṣabr*) and godliness (*taqwā*), slaves become kings; by avidity (*ḥirṣ*) and desire (*shahwa*), kings become slaves'.[52]

As noted previously, Pseudo-Māwardī refers repeatedly, often as a pair, to austerity (*zuhd*) and worship or devotion (ᶜ*ibāda*). Sometimes he combines other qualities with this pairing; for example, he ascribes wisdom (*ḥikma*), austerity (*zuhd*), worship (ᶜ*ibāda*) and virtuous conduct (*sīra fāḍila*) to the Prophet's Companions.[53] His mirror contains not a single reference, however, to mystic speculation (*taṣawwuf*). The absence of the term *taṣawwuf* from *Naṣīḥat al-mulūk* is consistent with an early tenth-century date of composition. At least by this name, Sufism appears to have arrived late in Khurasan and Transoxiana. Bulliet has established that *zuhd* and ᶜ*ibāda* became established in Nishapur well before *taṣawwuf*, and the absence of the term in *Fażā*ʾ*il-i Balkh*, which records the biographies of certain figures identified as Sufis elsewhere, suggests its late arrival in that region as well.[54] By contrast, al-Maqdisī, who wrote in Sistan in the third quarter of the century, was aware of the *ṣūfiyya*, whom he held in low regard.[55] In connection with emerging practices that would become assimilated to *taṣawwuf*, Pseudo-Māwardī demonstrates strong disagreement with excessive dependence on the principle of *tawakkul*, 'trust in God' (often, to provide). Juxtaposing *tawakkul* with the virtues of resolve (*ḥazm*) and determination (ᶜ*azm*), Pseudo-Māwardī warns against 'beguilement by persons who call for trust in God (*tawakkul*) while finding a way to protect themselves and a proof that covers an opinion'.[56] The definition of *tawakkul*, and the development of an interpretation that rejected all forms of *kasb*, gain, is associated with the Balkhi renunciants Shaqīq al-Balkhī and his disciples Ḥātim al-Aṣamm and Aḥmad b. Khiḍrawayh.[57] It is possible that Pseudo-Māwardī endorsed the view that even in *zuhd*, individuals should avoid excess, and would have agreed with the proverb, recorded in the collection of al-Maydānī (d. 518/1124) of Nishapur, 'The utmost austerity is to limit hope and behave well' (*ghāyat al-zuhd qaṣr al-amal wa-ḥusn al-*ᶜ*amal*).[58]

Among the figures who appear in *Fażāʾil-i Balkh* and are presented as exemplars of *taṣawwuf* in later collections, such as the *Ṭabaqāt al-ṣūfiyya* ('Generations of the Sufis') of the hagiographer and Qurʾānic commentator al-Sulamī (325 or 330–412/937 or 942–1021), is Shaqīq al-Balkhī.[59] Paul has noted the presence by the tenth century of two styles of religious virtuosity, both grounded in *zuhd*, but one centred towards the contemplative way, the other activist and even militant.[60] He has shown the combination of these styles in the presentations of Shaqīq in *Kitāb al-Qand fī dhikr ʿulamāʾ Samarqand* and *Fażāʾil-i Balkh*.[61] According to the first of these sources, when Shaqīq arrived in Samarqand, he chose a life of solitude, in order to 'remain alone with God, and He with me' (*urīdu an abqā fardan maʿa Allāh wa-yabqā huwa maʿī*).[62]

Pseudo-Māwardī affirms the virtues of learning, quiet concentration and detachment from worldly ephemera. He also exhibits a characteristic that he shares with Shaqīq. When Shaqīq travelled to Turkistan in order to trade with the Kharlukhiyya (Karluks), he met an elderly man, the 'servant of the idols', who observed the discrepancy between Shaqīq's words and actions and thereby occasioned his repentance (*tawba*), and his subsequent turn to austerity (*zuhd*) and godliness (*taqwā*).[63] In a similarly explicit acknowledgement of a non-Muslim worthy of emulation, Pseudo-Māwardī concludes his epilogue with an extended narrative in which a king of China, being hard of hearing, devised a stratagem to ensure that no petitioner should fail to attract his attention. Addressing the Abbasid Caliph al-Manṣūr, the leading protagonist in the anecdote asks, 'If a polytheist (*mushrik bi-llāh*) behaves this way, how much more should you [al-Manṣūr] ensure that you enact justice?'[64] Shaqīq and Pseudo-Māwardī both assume the universality of wisdom; the use of images, while attesting to religious difference, was irrelevant to the general human potential to embody sincerity and moral virtue. Pseudo-Māwardī conceived of 'this community' as being constituted along lines that run parallel in other communities: the difference between Islam and other religions was not one of kind, but rather one of rank or precedence within a shared system. For Pseudo-Māwardī, as his copious quotations from and allusions to Ardashīr and Aristotle convey, the experiences of other peoples and the wisdom that they had attained and expressed provided an instructive context for the experiences, past and present, of the Muslim community, which, while constituting the perfected form of religiously founded humanity, was nevertheless situated in relationship to other communities. Pseudo-Māwardī's receptivity to, and integration of, diverse expressions of wisdom regardless of its provenance emerges clearly in the material we shall present in Volume II.

The Samanids

204/819	Aḥmad I b. Asad b. Sāmān Khudā
250/864	Naṣr I b. Aḥmad I
279/892	Ismāᶜīl b. Aḥmad I, Abū Ibrāhīm al-Amīr al-Māḍī
295/907	Aḥmad II b. Ismāᶜīl, Abū Naṣr al-Amīr al-Shahīd
301/914	Naṣr II b. Aḥmad II, al-Amīr al-Saᶜīd
331/943	Nūḥ I. b. Naṣr II, al-Amīr al-Ḥamīd
343/954	ᶜAbd al-Malik I b. Nūḥ I, Abū l-Fawāris al-Amīr al-Muᵓayyad or al-Muwaffaq
350/961	Manṣūr I b. Nūḥ I, Abū Ṣāliḥ al-Amīr al-Sadīd
365/976	Nūḥ II b. Manṣūr I, al-Amīr al-Raḍī
387/997	Manṣūr II b. Nūḥ II, Abū l-Ḥārith
389/999	ᶜAbd al-Malik II b. Nūḥ II, Abū l-Fawāris
390–5/1000–5	Ismāᶜīl II b. Nūḥ II, Abū Ibrāhīm al-Muntaṣir

Figure 1 The Samanids, 204–395/819–1005

Source: Clifford Edmund Bosworth, *The New Islamic Dynasties: A Chronological and Genealogical Manual* (New York, Columbia University Press, 1996), p. 170.

The Samanid Dynastic Family

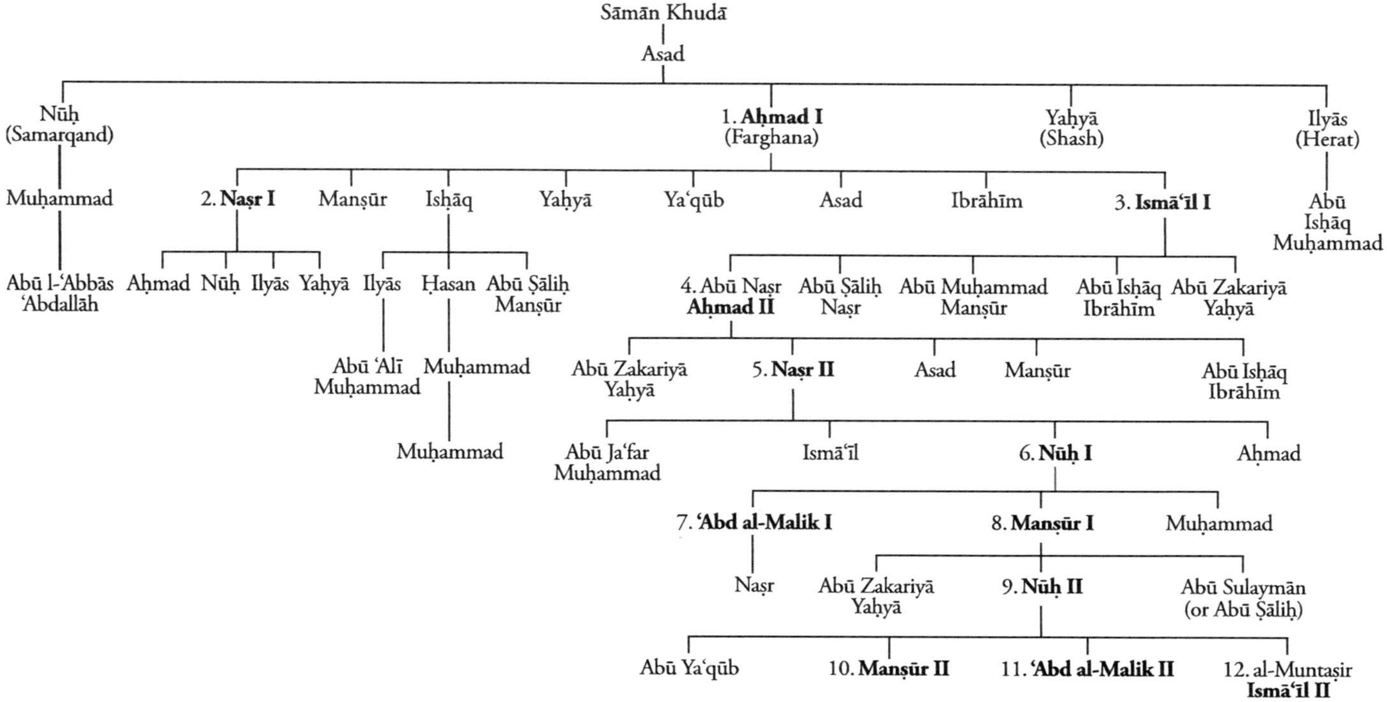

Figure 2 Genealogical Chart of the Samanid Dynastic Family

Adapted from E. de Zambaur, *Manuel de généalogie et de chronologie pour l'histoire de l'Islam*, Hannover, Lafaire, 1927. Unveränderter Neudruck, Bad Pyrmont, Orientbuchhandlung Heinz Lafaire, 1955, p. 203.

Notes

1. Introduction

1. Ibn Razīn, *Ādāb al-mulūk* ('The Customs of Kings'), p. 48.
2. Ibn Razīn's *Ādāb al-mulūk* represents an abbreviated version of the *Akhlāq al-mulūk* ('Dispositions of Kings') of al-Taghlibī, better known under the title *Kitāb al-Tāj* ('Book of the Crown', see below, p. 56). This section of al-Taghlibī's work appears only in the unpublished Berlin MS, and not in the manuscripts from which Ahmed Zeki Pacha prepared his published version of *Kitāb al-Tāj*; see Touati, 'Pour une histoire de la lecture', pp. 14–20.
3. The three editions are those of Khiḍr Muḥammad Khiḍr (hereafter NM-Kh), Muḥammad Jāsim al-Ḥadīthī (hereafter NM-Ḥ), and Fuʾād ᶜAbd al-Munᶜim Aḥmad (hereafter NM-A). Most references in the following chapters are to NM-A.
4. Sarıbıyık, *Siyaset Senati.*
5. Among these scholars are Khiḍr and al-Ḥadīthī, whose editions appeared in 1983 and 1986, respectively (NM-Kh, p. 20; NM-Ḥ, p. 17); Brockelmann, *GAL* I: 336, SI: 663; Zaydān, *Taʾrīkh ādāb al-lugha al-ᶜarabiyya* ('History of Arabic Literature'), III: 333–4; al-Ziriklī, *al-Aᶜlām* ('Distinguished Persons'), IV: 327; Sadan, '"Community" and "Extra-Community"', p. 113; Dankoff, *Wisdom of Royal Glory*, p. 270, n. 27; Bosworth, 'Mirrors for Princes', p. 528. The most substantial arguments in favour of al-Māwardī's authorship are those of Mikhail, *Politics and Revelation*, pp. 65–8, and Riḍwān al-Sayyid, who annotated the published version of Mikhail's work; see below, p. 12. Both scholars recognised the grounds for uncertainty with regard to the attribution, but decided, in significant measure because of the similarities in content and style of parts of *Naṣīḥat al-mulūk* with al-Māwardī's works, that the mirror belonged in the Māwardian corpus.

6. Aḥmad, *al-Tuḥfa al-mulūkiyya* ('The Royal Gift'), p. 32.
7. NM-A, pp. 5–33; Aḥmad, *al-Māwardī wa-kitāb Naṣīḥat al-mulūk* ('Al-Māwardī and the Book *Naṣīḥat al-mulūk*').
8. Leder, 'Aspekte arabischer und persischer Fürstenspiegel', p. 31; Crone, *God's Rule*, p. 439; Marlow, 'Samanid Work'; Anṣārī, 'Yek andīsheh-nāmeh' (accessed 3 October 2013).
9. MS Arabe, No. 2447 (= Ancien fonds arabe, No. 893). See de Slane, *Catalogue des manuscrits arabes*, Premier fascicule, B, XI, 428-9, MS 2447; Vajda, *Index général des manuscrits arabes musulmans*, p. 522.
10. Balayé, *La Bibliothèque nationale*, pp. 70, 72–3, 84–6, 88–9, 95–6.
11. Balayé, *La Bibliothèque nationale*, p. 87. (In a separate acquisition in the same year, the library acquired Persian manuscripts and a Qurʾān.)
12. Garel-Grislin, *Les manuscrits arabes et persans du cardinal Mazarin* (accessed 22 April 2013), p. 130, listed under the heading 'Recueil de textes de morale', in the Anciennes cotes: A. F. 893.
13. On these aspects of Arabic manuscripts, see especially the articles collected in Görke and Hirschler, *Manuscript Notes*, and the glossary and extensive bibliography assembled in Gacek, *Arabic Manuscript Tradition*.
14. See further Serikoff, 'Beobachtungen', pp. 165–71.
15. Gacek, *Arabic Manuscript Tradition*, p. 80.
16. MS Arabe 2447, f. 3a. The folios of the manuscript have been numbered more than once; the system followed in the present work follows the Arabic enumeration found in the upper left-hand corner of the left-hand folios, where divisions into portions (*ajzāʾ*) also appear. This system of numbering applies only to *Naṣīḥat al-mulūk*; the folios of *Muʿīd al-niʿam*, which appears first in the collection, are numbered separately.
17. The formulation 'In the name of God, the Merciful, the Compassionate'; this propitiary formula, often written alone, opens compositions (Gacek, *Arabic Manuscript Tradition*, pp. 12–13; Gacek, 'Copying and Correction', pp. 52–3).
18. MS Arabe 2447, f. 2b.
19. Cf. Gacek, *Arabic Manuscript Tradition*, pp. 14–15, 82.
20. MS Arabe 2447, f. 97b. In accordance with common practice, an honorific attribute accompanies the name of the month ('the good month of Safar'); cf. Gacek, 'Ownership Statements', p. 89 and n. 10.
21. MS Arabe 2447, f. 97b. In the context of a different manuscript germane to the Khalwatiyya in Egypt, Bannerth rendered a comparable phrase as 'serviteur [ms. des souliers] des pauvres (foqarāʾ), le parasite de leurs tables' (Bannerth,

'La Khalwatiyya en Égypte', p. 44). On the office of *khādim* in the Egyptian milieu, see also Gril, *La* Risāla *de Ṣafī al-Dīn*', p. 41.

22. Chih and Mayeur-Jaouen, 'Introduction', pp. 7–8; Bannerth, 'La Khalwatiyya en Egypte', p. 2.
23. Chih, 'Cheminements', pp. 181–201.
24. Rescher paraphrased the title as 'über die richtige Lebensart in praktischen und moralischen Dingen' (Rescher, *Das 'kitâb adab ed-dunjâ wa 'ddîn'*).
25. Al-Dhahabī, *Siyar aʿlām al-nubalāʾ* ('Biographies of the Eminent and Distinguished'), XVII: 14–15; cf. Melchert, 'Māwardī, Abū Yaʿlá, and the Sunni Revival', p. 43.
26. Ibn Khallikān, *Wafayāt al-aʿyān* ('Obituaries of the Notables'), I: 72–4; al-Dhahabī, *Siyar aʿlām al-nubalāʾ*, XVII: 193–7.
27. Sometimes al-Jabalī; see al-Subkī, *Ṭabaqāt al-shāfiʿiyya*, V: 272 and n. 6; al-Dhahabī, *Taʾrīkh al-Islām* ('History of Islam'), IX: 751; al-Dhahabī, *Siyar aʿlām al-nubalāʾ*, XVIII: 64; al-Samʿānī, *al-Ansāb* ('Genealogies'), III: 192 (v. al-Jabalī).
28. Al-Subkī, *Ṭabaqāt al-shāfiʿiyya*, III: 306.
29. Ibn Khallikān, *Wafayāt al-aʿyān*, III: 283. On *ṣuḥba* ('companionship', 'discipleship') and *riwāya* ('the capacity . . . to memorise and transmit'), see Berkey, *Transmission of Knowledge*, pp. 26, 30, 34–5; cf. Makdisi, *Rise of Colleges*, pp. 128–9, 141, 144.
30. MS Arabe 2447, ff. 97b–98a. This biography largely follows the information provided in al-Khaṭīb al-Baghdādī, *Taʾrīkh Baghdād* ('History of Baghdad'), XII: 102–3; Ibn Khallikān, *Wafayāt al-aʿyān*, III: 282–4, No. 428; Yāqūt, *Muʿjam al-udabāʾ* ('Collection of Littérateurs'): V: 1955–7, No. 822; al-Samʿānī, *al-Ansāb*, XII: 60 (v. al-Māwardī). The final report in the manuscript's biography does not appear in the earlier accounts.
31. MS Arabe 2447, f. 98a.
32. The *wālī* presided over the high council, *al-dīwān al-ʿālī*, which included the heads of the military regiments and treasury, the four jurisconsults (*muftī*s) and the chief military judge (*qāḍī ʿaskar*, Turkish *kadıasker*); this council met three times a week. A smaller council, known simply as the *dīwān* (Turkish *divan*), met daily; it was presided over by the lieutenant of the viceroy, and included the treasurer and a qāḍī of the *dīwān* (El-Nahal, *Judicial Administration*, pp. 91–2, n. 90). In the sixteenth century, the flexible term *tezkereci* described a variety of functions in different branches of the central and provincial administrations; in these different settings, a *tezkereci* might have been charged with

various secretarial, recording and administrative tasks, including the writing of documents or memoranda (sing. *tezkere*) (see Fleischer, *Bureaucrat and Intellectual*, p. 81 and n. 30, p. 214 and n. 2; Darling, *Revenue-Raising and Legitimacy*, pp. 49–80, esp. 53).

33. MS Arabe 2447, *Muᶜīd al-niᶜam*, f. 58a.
34. Al-Subkī, *Muᶜīd al-niᶜam*, p. 1. In its fullest version, the book treats 113 trades, professions and offices with a view to the proper conduct of their practitioners and the earning of divine favour.
35. Cf. Winter, 'Ottoman Egypt', pp. 11–13.
36. Martin, 'Short History', pp. 278–80.
37. Ohlander, '"Crude of Speech"', pp. 111–35.
38. MS Arabe 2447, f. 58a. On *istiktāb*, see Gacek, *Arabic Manuscript Tradition*, p. 123.
39. On the multiple positions held by members of the middle class, see Hanna, *In Praise of Books*, pp. 40–4.
40. On the offices of the *kâtib* and *nâzır*, see Shaw, *Financial and Administrative Organization*, pp. 43–5, 146–7, 155.
41. Hanna, *In Praise of Books*, pp. 79–103; see esp. pp. 83–4, 99.
42. See, for example, al-Sayyid, 'Tamhīd' ('Foreword'), *Tashīl al-naẓar*, pp. 93, 98; al-Sayyid, 'al-Māwardī: al-rajul wa-l-ᶜaṣr' ('Al-Māwardī, the Man and his Age'), pp. 102, 118. The single known manuscript of *Durar al-sulūk fī siyāsat al-mulūk* ('Pearls of Conduct in the Governance of Kings') was also almost certainly produced in Egypt in the early sixteenth century, since it was intended for the library of al-Malik al-Ashraf Abū l-Naṣr Qānṣūh al-Ghūrī (Ghawrī) (r. 906–22/1501–16) (Aḥmad, 'Muqadimmat al-dirāsa wa-l-taḥqīq' ('Introduction to the Study and Edition'), pp. 45–7).
43. Hanna, *In Praise of Books*, pp. 120–1, 137–8.
44. Geoffroy, *Le soufisme en Égypte*, pp. 59, 121, 160 and n. 108.
45. See Fleischer, *Bureaucrat and Intellectual*, esp. pp. 95–105; Howard, 'Genre and Myth'; Darling, *History of Social Justice*, pp. 127–54.
46. See, for example, Ḥājjī Khalīfa, *Kashf al-ẓunūn*, I: 35–8, 336–7; II: 1011–15, 1958. The period witnessed a strong interest in the varied oeuvre of al-Ghazālī; see Chih and Mayeur-Jaouen, 'Introduction', p. 11; Geoffroy, 'La soufisme au verdict de la fatwa', pp. 119, 123. On the Egyptian interest in the *Naṣīḥat al-mulūk* of al-Ghazālī in particular, see Wormser, 'La rencontre de l'Inde et de l'Égypte', pp. 215, 217.
47. Chih and Mayeur-Jaouen, 'Introduction', p. 9; Hathaway, *Arab Lands*,

pp. 7–9, 59–78; Howard, 'Ottoman Historiography'; Fleischer, *Bureaucrat and Intellectual*, pp. 8, 101–2.

48. It is perhaps notable that both authors express a certain disdain for entertaining stories. Al-Subkī warns copyists against the reproduction of such works (Irwin, 'al-Subkī'). On the reservations expressed in *Naṣīḥat al-mulūk*, see Volume II, pp. 39–40, 156–7.
49. Cf. Hathaway, *Arab Lands*, pp. 129–31, 214–17.
50. Yāqūt, *Muᶜjam al-udabāᵓ*, V: 1955–7, No. 822; Ibn Khallikān, *Wafayāt al-aᶜyān*, III: 282–4; Ibn Kathīr, *Ṭabaqāt al-shāfiᶜiyya*, I: 397–8 (No. 352); al-Dhahabī, *Taᵓrīkh al-Islām*, IX: 752–3; al-Dhahabī, *Siyar aᶜlām al-nubalāᵓ*, XVIII: 64–9, No. 29; al-Ṣafadī, *al-Wāfī bi-l-wafayāt* ('The Complete Guide to Obituaries'), XXI: 451–3, No. 310; al-Subkī, *Ṭabaqāt al-shāfiᶜiyya*, V: 267–85.
51. Serikoff, 'Beobachtungen', p. 170, n. 38. In the case of the littérateur al-Thaᶜālibī, a contemporary of al-Māwardī, biographers' records of the numbers and titles of his compositions exhibit a marked variation; see Orfali, 'Works of Abū Manṣūr al-Thaᶜālibī'.
52. *Taᵓrīkh Baghdād aw-Madīnat al-salām* ('History of Baghdad or the City of Peace'), XII: 102 (*lahu taṣānīf ᶜidda fī uṣūl al-fiqh wa-furūᶜihi wa-fī ghayr dhālika*). Al-Samᶜānī uses the same locution: *lahu taṣānīf ᶜiddatan fī uṣūl al-fiqh wa-furūᶜihi wa-fī ghayr dhālika* (*al-Ansāb*, XII: 60).
53. Fīrūzābādī, *Ṭabaqāt al-fuqahāᵓ* ('Generations of the Jurists'), p. 125. Cf. al-Subkī, *Ṭabaqāt al-shāfiᶜiyya*, V: 268; al-Dhahabī, *Taᵓrīkh al-Islām*, IX: 751–2.
54. Al-Subkī, *Ṭabaqāt al-shāfiᶜiyya*, V: 267. Cf. *GAL* GI 386, SI 668. On the question of whether *Qānūn al-wizāra wa-siyāsat al-mulk* refers to one or two books, see below, n. 56.
55. Ibn Kathīr, *Ṭabaqāt al-shāfiᶜiyya*, I: 397–8 (No. 352).
56. The uncertainty regarding the title of this work arises from the listing among the writings of al-Māwardī by some of his pre-modern biographers of *qawānīn al-wizāra wa-siyāsat al-mulk*. It is possible to read this entry, with Brockelmann and al-Sayyid, as a single title or, with Hanna Mikhail, Fuᵓād ᶜAbd al-Munᶜim Aḥmad and Muḥammad Sulaymān Dāᵓūd, as two titles, the second of which, *Siyāsat al-mulk*, Mikhail has identified with *Naṣīḥat al-mulūk* (*Politics and Revelation*, p. 67). See Ibn Khallikān, *Wafayāt al-aᶜyān*, III: 282; al-Dhahabī, *Siyar aᶜlām al-nubalāᵓ*, XVIII: 65–6 (in this case, the editor takes the entry *Qānūn al-wizāra wa-siyāsat al-mulk* to refer to a single book, p. 66, n. 1); al-Ṣafadī, *al-Wāfī bi-l-wafayāt*, XXI: 452; al-Subkī, *Ṭabaqāt al-shāfiᶜiyya*, V: 267; Ḥājjī Khalīfa, *Kashf al-ẓunūn* ('The Disclosure of Doubts'), II: 1011 (*Siyāsat*

al-mulk li-Abī l-Ḥasan ᶜAlī b. Muḥammad al-Māwardī al-Shāfiᶜī); al-Ziriklī, *al-Aᶜlām*, IV: 327. Some authors, such as Ibn al-Jawzī and Yāqūt, record only the first element (*Qawānīn al-wizāra*) of the title (Ibn al-Jawzī, *al-Muntaẓam* ('The Well-Ordered'), VIII: 199; Yāqūt, *Muᶜjam al-udabāʾ*, V: 1958).

57. See al-Sayyid, 'al-Māwardī: al-rajul wa-l-ᶜaṣr', pp. 10–11.
58. Al-Sayyid, 'al-Māwardī: al-rajul wa-l-ᶜaṣr', 8, cf. pp. 56–62. Al-Khaṭīb al-Baghdādī begins the long sequence of authors who report that al-Māwardī held many judgeships, but neither he nor his successors list them (noted in Melchert, 'Māwardī, Abū Yaᶜlá, and the Sunni Revival', p. 43).
59. Yāqūt, *Muᶜjam al-udabāʾ*, V: 1955; al-Ṣafadī, *al-Wāfī bi-l-wafayāt*, XXI: 453. On the objections of al-Ṣaymarī and the judge Abū l-Ṭayyib Ṭāhir b. ᶜAbdallāh al-Ṭabarī (348–450/959–1058), see Ibn al-Jawzī, *al-Muntaẓam*, VIII: 198.
60. Yāqūt, *Muᶜjam al-udabāʾ*, V: 1955.
61. *Politics and Revelation* represents Hanna Mikhail's doctoral dissertation, completed at Harvard University in 1968 and published posthumously. Riḍwān al-Sayyid added annotations in the published version. Donald Little ('New Look', p. 6) recognised the importance of Mikhail's dissertation two decades before its publication. Among other points in support of al-Māwardī's authorship, Mikhail and al-Sayyid note similarities in content and style between *Naṣīḥat al-mulūk* and al-Māwardī's writings, especially *Adab al-dunyā wa-l-dīn*.
62. Al-Māwardī, *Adab al-dunyā wa-l-dīn*, p. 212.
63. Mikhail, *Politics and Revelation*, pp. 67 and 83, n. 319.
64. Aḥmad, 'Muqaddimat al-dirāsa wa-l-taḥqīq', pp. 35–40.
65. Aḥmad, *al-Māwardī wa-kitāb Naṣīḥat al-mulūk*, pp. 19–23.
66. Aḥmad, *al-Tuḥfa al-mulūkiyya*, pp. 32–46; see further Dāʾūd and Aḥmad, *Min aᶜlām al-Islām* ('Of the Distinguished Persons of Islam'), p. 114.
67. Ḥājjī Khalīfa, *Kashf al-ẓunūn*, II: 1958.
68. See further NM-A, 'Muqaddimat al-taḥqīq wa-l-dirāsa', p. 7, and Aḥmad, *al-Māwardī wa-kitāb Naṣīḥat al-mulūk*, pp. 16–18. Mikhail also noted the 'puzzling' nature of Ḥājjī Khalīfa's reference (*Politics and Revelation*, p. 66).
69. Aḥmad, *al-Māwardī wa-kitāb Naṣīḥat al-mulūk*, pp. 16–18; see al-Ghazālī, *al-Tibr al-masbūk* ('Fashioned Gold'), p. 83.
70. NM-A, 'Muqaddimat al-taḥqīq wa-l-dirāsa', pp. 13–31; *al-Māwardī wa-kitāb Naṣīḥat al-mulūk*, pp. 29–68.
71. Aḥmad demonstrated the juristic differences between Pseudo-Māwardī and

al-Māwardī with reference to five issues: the share of 'those whose hearts are to be reconciled' (*al-mu*ʾ*allafa qulūbuhum*, Q. 9: 60) as a valid expenditure of the revenues from the obligatory charitable donation, *zakāt*; the allowance due to the collectors of *zakāt*; the matter of taking a fifth from the spoils (*fay*ʾ) acquired in military campaigns; the statutory punishment for drunkenness; and the minimum value of the stolen goods related to the statutory penalty for theft (Aḥmad, 'Muqaddimat al-taḥqīq wa-l-dirāsa', pp. 13–31; *Abū l-Ḥasan al-Māwardī*, pp. 55–68).

72. Aḥmad, 'Muqaddimat al-taḥqīq wa-l-dirāsa', NM-A, p. 33.
73. On the 'Kindian tradition', see Adamson, *Al-Kindī*, pp. 12–17.
74. Anṣārī, 'Yek andīsheh-nāmeh'. Aḥmad, too, noted the author's emphasis on rational theology and his invocation of individuals linked with the Muʿtazila ('Muqaddimat al-taḥqīq wa-l-dirāsa', p. 32).
75. On the development and branches of the Muʿtazila, see Gimaret, 'Muʿtazila'; van Ess, *Theologie und Gesellschaft*, III: 31–92, 199–508.
76. Yāqūt reports the account that al-Māwardī was a Shāfiʿī in *furū*ʿ (the branches of jurisprudence) and Muʿtazilite in *uṣūl* (the principles of jurisprudence), although he abstains from judgement as to the accuracy of the report (*Muʿjam al-udabā*ʾ, V: 1955). On the suspicions of al-Māwardī's Muʿtazilism, see the reports in al-Subkī, *Ṭabaqāt*, V: 270; al-Dhahabī, *Ta*ʾ*rīkh al-Islām*, IX: 752–3; al-Dhahabī, *Siyar a*ʿ*lām al-nubalā*ʾ, XVIII: 67. Melchert, 'Māwardī, Abū Yaʿlá, and the Sunni Revival', pp. 46–7 and Cook, *Commanding Right*, p. 344 also find evidence of al-Māwardī's Muʿtazilite views.
77. Anṣārī, 'Yek andīsheh-nāmeh', pp. 1–15, esp. pp. 8–9, 13.
78. On the relationship of *Naṣīḥat al-mulūk* to Abū Zayd al-Balkhī and the Kindian tradition, see Marlow, 'Abū Zayd al-Balkhī'.
79. Ibn al-Nadīm, *al-Fihrist* ('The Catalogue'), I: ii: 429; Yāqūt, *Muʿjam al-udabā*ʾ, I: 275–6, IV: 1491–2; al-Tawḥīdī, *al-Baṣā*ʾ*ir wa-l-dhakha*ʾ*ir* ('Insights and Treasures'), VIII: 66; Ibn Ḥajar, *Lisān al-mīzān* ('The Tongue of the Balance'), I: 283. On Aḥmad b. Sahl, see below, pp. 112–13.
80. To minimise confusion between Abū Zayd al-Balkhī and Abū l-Qāsim al-Balkhī, I shall refer to the latter as al-Kaʿbī in the remainder of this work. On the affinities with Muʿtazilite thought in al-Kindī's writings, see Adamson, 'Al-Kindī and the Muʿtazila'.
81. Ibn al-Nadīm, *al-Fihrist*, I: ii: 429.
82. Al-Tawḥīdī, *al-Baṣā*ʾ*ir wa-l-dhakhā*ʾ*ir*, VIII: 66. On al-Tawḥīdī's combination of philosophical and literary pursuits, see Rowson, 'Philosopher as Littérateur'.

83. Yāqūt, *Muᶜjam al-udabāᵓ*, IV: 1491–3, No. 634. For other reports of al-Kaᶜbī's eloquence, see El-Omari, 'Theology of Abū l-Qāsim al-Balḫī/al-Kaᶜbī', pp. 18, 31–2, 34–5.
84. Bonebakker, 'Early Arabic Literature and the Term *adab*'.
85. Sadan, '*Ādāb* – règles de conduite et *ādāb* – dictons, maximes', pp. 288–9.
86. Khalidi, *Arabic Historical Thought*, pp. 83–96.
87. Khalidi, *Arabic Historical Thought*, p. 83.
88. Ferster, *Fictions of Advice*, p. 4.
89. See further Ferster, *Fictions of Advice*, pp. 1–14; on the inherent constraints and contradictions of mirrors, see also Neguin Yavari's discussion of the role of vizier-advisers ('Mirrors for Princes or Hall of Mirrors?').
90. Gustav Richter, however, in his pioneering *Studien zur Geschichte der älteren arabischen Fürstenspiegel* of 1932, offered a perceptive treatment of the place of Arabic mirrors in the formation of *adab* (Richter, *Studien*, esp. pp. 5–6, 36–7, 75), and C. E. Bosworth has drawn attention to the extremely valuable historical information, sometimes unavailable in any other source, that mirrors sometimes provide ('Mirrors for Princes', p. 527).
91. The approach became established in the second half of the twentieth century with the publications of E. I. J. Rosenthal and, especially, A. K. S. Lambton, both of whom recognised the genre's debt to the literary culture of *adab*, but examined mirrors principally as contributions to political thought (Rosenthal, *Political Thought*, p. 77; Lambton, 'Islamic Mirrors for Princes', p. 419; cf. Lambton, *State and Government*, pp. xvi, xvii).
92. For examples, see Arjomand, 'Medieval Persianate Political Ethic'; Crone, *God's Rule*, pp. 148–64; Yavari, *Advice for the Sultan*.
93. Bosworth, 'An Early Arabic Mirror for Princes'; Bosworth, 'Mirrors for Princes'; Meisami, *Sea of Precious Virtues*; Bray, 'Local Mirror'; Marlow, 'Advice and Advice Literature'; Marlow, 'Teaching Wisdom'.
94. As subsequent chapters will demonstrate, Pseudo-Māwardī cites several texts from the literary corpus that transmitted this heritage, and refers to *mulūk Āl Sāsān* (the kings of the Sasanian dynastic family) as monarchs whose example remained valuable and instructive.
95. Mottahedeh, 'Shuᶜûbîyah Controversy', pp. 167–70; on Firdawsī's *Īrān-zamīn*, see p. 172.
96. On the terms 'Iran' and 'Iranian', as well as 'Persia' and 'Persian', see Savant, *New Muslims*, pp. 8–11, and the references cited in the notes thereto.
97. He also refers to *mulūk al-ᶜarab*, 'the Arab kings', and *mulūk al-hind*, 'the kings

of India' or 'Indian kings', from whom, by inference, he distinguished *mulūk al-ᶜajam*.

98. Savant, *New Muslims*, pp. 11–12, 233–4.
99. Indeed, the meaning of *Īrān-shahr* itself would cease to connote the full set of territories subsumed within the former empire and would become limited to its western part.
100. Bray, 'Local Mirror', p. 33.
101. For comparisons of *Naṣīḥat al-mulūk* with these and other examples of advisory literature, see Volume II, Chapter 1.

Chapter 1

1. Narshakhī, *Tārīkh-i Bukhārā* ('History of Bukhara'), pp. 104–5. Cf. Beckwith, *Tibetan Empire*, p. 158; de la Vaissière, *Samarcande et Samarra*, pp. 125–31.
2. Narshakhī, *Tārīkh-i Bukhārā*, p. 105.
3. Al-Iṣṭakhrī, *Masālik al-mamālik* ('Routes of the Kingdoms'), p. 292; Narshakhī, *Tārīkh-i Bukhārā*, p. 82; *Ḥudūd al-ᶜālam* ('Regions of the World'), p. 102; Gardīzī, *Zayn al-akhbār* ('Ornament of Historical Narratives'), p. 320; Treadwell, 'Account of the Samanid Dynasty', Text p. 136 = Translation p. 152; Ibn al-Athīr, *al-Kāmil* ('The Complete [History]'), VII: 279. Of special interest are the remarks of al-Bīrūnī, who averred that 'nobody contests who it was who was the first of their *dawla*', namely, Ismāᶜīl b. Aḥmad, whose lineage al-Bīrūnī traces to 'Bahrām Shūbīn, son of Bahrām J.sh.n.sh, the *marzubān* of Azerbaijan' (*al-Āthār al-bāqiya* ('Enduring Traces'), p. 39). (References to *al-Āthār al-bāqiya* indicate Sachau's edition unless otherwise indicated.) Cf. Bosworth, 'Heritage of Rulership', pp. 58–9.
4. On Bahrām's rebellion, see Pourshariati, *Decline and Fall*, pp. 122–30, 397–414. Pourshariati regards the rebellion as a major, and presaging, manifestation of the collapse of the 'Sasanian–Parthian confederacy' on which, she has argued, the stability of the empire had depended. See also Shahbazi, 'Bahrām', pp. 519–22.
5. See Pourshariati, 'Parthians and the Production of the Canonical Shāhnāmas', p. 353. Al-Iṣṭakhrī nevertheless considered the Samanids to be *furs*, and discussed their rule in his section on Fars (al-Iṣṭakhrī, *Masālik al-mamālik*, p. 293). Cf. above, pp. 18–19.
6. Al-Iṣṭakhrī, *Masālik al-mamālik*, p. 292; Ibn Ḥawqal, *Ṣūrat al-arḍ* ('The Form of the Earth'), II: 468–9. The two geographical works, whose authors met in person, are closely associated with one another. Al-Iṣṭakhrī developed further

the geographical and cartographical work of his predecessor, Abū Zayd al-Balkhī (d. 322/934); Ibn Ḥawqal embarked on his travels in 331/943, and his last datable appearance occurs in Sicily in 362/973. Ibn Ḥawqal depended heavily on al-Iṣṭakhrī's work, portions of which he reproduced verbatim; he also modified and added to his predecessor's text. See Miquel, *La géographie humaine*, I: 292–309; 'Ibn Ḥawḳal', 'al-Iṣṭakhrī'.

7. Al-Iṣṭakhrī ascribes the same pair of qualities to other non-Arab, and sometimes non-Muslim, military commanders of Ushrusana, Samarqand, Sogdia and Bukhara (*Masālik al-mamālik*, 292; cf. Ibn Ḥawqal, *Ṣūrat al-arḍ*, II: 468). As Julie Scott Meisami has observed, the historical accounts of Dīnavarī, Balʿamī and Gardīzī present favourable portraits of Bahrām, whereas the poet Firdawsī's portrayal is less positive (Meisami, *Persian Historiography*, pp. 34–5).
8. On the Samanids' origins in Balkh, see Narshakhī, *Tārīkh-i Bukhārā*, p. 81; Ḥamza al-Iṣfahānī, *Taʾrīkh*, p. 172; Gardīzī, *Zayn al-akhbār*, p. 319, n. 5. Bahrām-i Chūbīn's widely reported background in Rayy (Pourshariati, *Decline and Fall*, pp. 122–30, 463) probably assisted the Samanids' promotion of their claims to that city (Meisami, *Persian Historiography*, p. 34). Bahrām was also associated to some extent with Balkh, where he was killed (Howard-Johnston, 'The Sasanians' Strategic Dilemma', pp. 58–60). Vaziri has noted the Samanids' possible Buddhist past (*Buddhism in Iran*, pp. 159–60).
9. Treadwell, 'First Islamic Dynasty', pp. 5–6. Treadwell indicates that the medallion resembles Hephthalite rather than Sasanian models.
10. The term 'senior amir', employed by Treadwell ('Political History'), is adopted in the present study to indicate the leading dynastic figure; contemporaries employed no particular or exclusive title to denote this person. On the title *amīr*, see below, pp. 127–8.
11. Narshakhī, *Tārīkh-i Bukhārā*, pp. 105–6; Ibn al-Athīr, *al-Kāmil*, VII: 279–80. On the branches of the Samanid family, see Zambaur, *Manuel*, pp. 202–3, and Figure 2.
12. Narshakhī, *Tārīkh-i Bukhārā*, p. 109 (where, perhaps more accurately, it is the caliph's brother Abū Aḥmad al-Muwaffaq (d. 278/891) who effected the investiture; cf. Kennedy, 'al-Muwaffaḳ'). Narshakhī supplies the earlier date of 260, while al-Ṭabarī (*Taʾrīkh*, IX: 514), Ibn al-Athīr (*al-Kāmil*, VII: 280) and Ibn Ẓāfir (whose account is published and translated in Treadwell, 'Account of the Samanid Dynasty', p. 136 = p. 152) give the date of Naṣr's investiture as 261. On the term *al-mashriq*, see below, n. 166.
13. Narshakhī, *Tārīkh-i Bukhārā*, p. 109; Ibn al-Athīr, *al-Kāmil*, VII: 280 (the two

sources reflect the same discrepancy regarding the year of Ismāᶜīl's appointment and its acknowledgement in the *khuṭba*). On the evolution of the *khuṭba*, a formal public address, and its religious–political importance, see Qutbuddin, 'Khuṭba', esp. pp. 207–8.

14. Narshakhī provides an extensive account of Ismāᶜīl's gradual establishment of his authority in Bukhara, and the prelude to and course of his conflict with Naṣr (*Tārīkh-i Bukhārā*, pp. 106–18). For reasons that will be addressed shortly, Narshakhī's depiction of Ismāᶜīl favours him over his brothers. Despite Naṣr's displeasure, Ismāᶜīl, in Narshakhī's account, behaves with respectful courtesy, and at the conclusion of the conflict the victorious Ismāᶜīl offers apologies, begs forgiveness for his error and accepts responsibility for his aberration in a dramatic ritual of reconciliation with his brother (*Tārīkh-i Bukhārā*, p. 117). In the similar account of ᶜAlī b. Zayd Bayhaqī, known as Ibn Funduq, Naṣr asks if Ismāᶜīl's remorseful posture is meant in earnest (*jadd*) or in jest (*hazl*), and accepts his brother's assurance of seriousness (*Tārīkh-i Bayhaq* ('History of Bayhaq'), p. 68, where, incidentally, six sons of Aḥmad are named).
15. Ibn al-Athīr, *al-Kāmil*, VIII: 78. Cf. Treadwell, 'Political History', p. 144.
16. Bosworth, 'Afšīn'; 'Banīdjūrids'; 'Āl-e Moḥtāj'; 'Rulers of Chaghāniyān'.
17. On these developments, see Bosworth, 'Sāmānids', pp. 1026–7; Frye, 'Sāmānids', pp. 138–9.
18. Ibn al-Faqīh, *Kitāb al-Buldān* ('Book of Countries'), p. 313; Narshakhī, *Tārīkh-i Bukhārā*, pp. 106, 119–27; Ibn al-Athīr, *al-Kāmil*, VII: 490–516. For a detailed discussion of the sequence, see Bosworth, *History of the Saffarids*, pp. 223–35.
19. Ḥamza al-Iṣfahānī, *Taʾrīkh*, pp. 171–2; Narshakhī, *Tārīkh-i Bukhārā*, p. 127.
20. Cf. Paul, 'Nachrichten arabischer Geographen', p. 181; Fragner, 'Concept of Regionalism', pp. 345–7; Shaban, 'Khurāsān at the Time of Arab Conquest', pp. 479–90; Arjomand, 'Evolution of the Persianate Polity', pp. 116–20.
21. *Ḥudūd al-ᶜālam*, p. 102. The anonymous *Ḥudūd al-ᶜālam* reflects an association with the provincial location of Kāth and its ruling dynastic family, the Āl-i Afrīgh; or possibly with the family that supplanted them in 385/995, the Maʾmunids (Āl-i Maʾmūn) of Gurganj. Minorsky speculated that the author might have been a member of the Farighunid dynastic family. In the ninth century, the indigenous Afrighid dynasty of Khwarazmshahs probably became nominal vassals of the Samanids. See Bosworth, 'Chorasmia II', p. 517; 'Āl-e Afrīġ', pp. 743–5; 'Āl-e Maʾmūn', pp. 762–4; Spuler, 'Gurgandj', p. 1142.
22. The use of the term 'state' acknowledges the varying degrees of power vested

in pre-modern Iranian structures of statehood, all of which shared their power over persons with other institutions and agents. On the concept and definition of the 'state', see Paul, *Herrscher, Gemeinwesen, Vermittler*, p. 3. The term 'monarchical state' is Treadwell's (Treadwell, 'Political History', p. 104). The description of Ismāᶜīl as *avval-i salāṭīn-i Sāmān* ('first of the *sulṭān*s of the Samanids', *Tārīkh-i Bukhārā*, p. 106) confirms Treadwell's emphasis on the importance of Ismāᶜīl, although the use of the term *sulṭān* to designate a specific person is likely to reflect not Narshakhī's text, but a later recension of *Tārīkh-i Bukhārā* (on the history of the text, see below, n. 119).

23. Al-Iṣṭakhrī, *Masālik al-mamālik*, p. 315; Ibn Ḥawqal, *Ṣūrat al-arḍ*, p. 491. As a second criterion underlying Ismāᶜīl's choice of location for his capital, the geographers mention the tractability of the people of Bukhara (al-Iṣṭakhrī, *Masālik al-mamālik*, p. 315, Ibn Ḥawqal, *Ṣūrat al-arḍ*, p. 491). Previously, al-Iṣṭakhrī observes, the rulers of Transoxiana had settled either in Samarqand or Shash and Farghana 'facing the Turks' (*fī wujūh al-turk*); al-Iṣṭakhrī, *Masālik al-mamālik*, p. 315, cf. p. 318. Narshakhī, by contrast, attributes Ismāᶜīl's choice solely to his personal attachment to Bukhara, which he considered auspicious for the establishment of the dynastic capital (*dār al-mulk*) and court (*ḥażrat*) (*Tārīkh-i Bukhārā*, pp. 127–8).
24. Treadwell, 'First Islamic Dynasty', p. 7. See also Ibn Ḥawqal, *Ṣūrat al-arḍ*, p. 467.
25. Canfield, 'Introduction', pp. 1, 6–18.
26. Bonner, 'Waning of Empire', pp. 344, 358.
27. Chabbi notes the difficulty of producing an unequivocal definition of the term *ribāṭ*, the application of which evolved continuously and depended on widely varying contexts ('Ribāṭ', pp. 493–506, esp. 499–501).
28. Al-Iṣṭakhrī, *Masālik al-mamālik*, p. 291; Ibn Ḥawqal, *Ṣūrat al-arḍ*, 467 (chiefly with reference to Naṣr [I] b. Aḥmad); cf. Treadwell, 'Political History', p. 80.
29. Narshakhī, *Tārīkh-i Bukhārā*, pp. 118–19. It was at Ṭarāz that Abbasid forces, under the command of Ziyād b. Ṣāliḥ, had engaged Chinese forces in a major battle in 133/751 (cf. al-Maqdisī, *al-Badʾ wa-l-taʾrīkh* ('The Creation and History'), VI: 74–5; Daniel, *Khurasan*, p. 89). The tribal composition of the Karluk confederation changed between the ninth and the twelfth centuries; their centre in the ninth and tenth centuries was apparently at Balasaghun in the Chu valley (Golden, 'Karakhanids', pp. 348–58).
30. Peter Golden writes, 'The entire Oghuz–Karluk border with the Muslim world is described as being in a state of constant warfare, with the raids of the "Turks"

reaching deep into Khorasan' ('Karakhanids', p. 348). In 290/903–4, Ismāᶜīl faced a major Turkic invasion, possibly the Karluk response to the attack of Talas ('Karakhanids', p. 352); see al-Ṭabarī, *Taʾrīkh*, X: 116 (*sub anno* 291); Ibn al-Athīr, *al-Kāmil*, VII: 532–3 (*sub anno* 291).

31. Narshakhī, *Tārīkh-i Bukhārā*, pp. 118–19; al-Ṭabarī, *Taʾrīkh*, X: 34; Ibn al-Athīr, *al-Kāmil*, VII: 464–5 (*sub anno* 280); Golden, 'Karakhanids', p. 352; Bosworth, *Ghaznavids*, p. 31. See further below, pp. 179–80.
32. Al-Iṣṭakhrī, *Masālik al-mamālik*, pp. 288–9; Ibn Ḥawqal, *Ṣūrat al-arḍ*, p. 465. See further Golden, 'Karakhanids', pp. 346–7, and Bregel, 'Turko-Mongol influences', pp. 56–7.
33. Paul, 'Nachrichten arabischer Geographen', p. 189; see also Treadwell, 'Urban Militias', pp. 128–44, esp. 136–42. Al-Iṣṭakhrī mentions numerous *ribāṭāt* in Khurasan, Sijistan and Transoxiana, and comments specifically on their large numbers, approximately a thousand, near Karminiyya (*Masālik al-mamālik*, pp. 314; 273, 288, 290–1 and passim); cf. Ibn Ḥawqal, *Ṣūrat al-arḍ*, pp. 422–5, 466–7, 489, 504–5.
34. On the currencies of Bukhara and Samarqand, respectively, see al-Iṣṭakhrī, *Masālik al-mamālik*, pp. 314, 323; Ibn Ḥawqal, *Ṣūrat al-arḍ*, pp. 490, 500. On the production and distribution of Samanid coins, see Mitchiner, *Multiple Dirhems*.
35. Miles, 'Numismatics', p. 374; Heidemann, 'Numismatics', p. 662.
36. Al-Muqaddasī, *Aḥsan al-taqāsīm fī maᶜrifat al-aqālīm* ('The Best Divisions in the Knowledge of the Climes'), p. 4.
37. Al-Muqaddasī, *Aḥsan al-taqāsīm*, p. 10. Al-Muqaddasī also reports on the impressive holdings of the libraries of ᶜAḍud al-Dawla (r. 338–72/949–83) and the vizier al-Ṣāḥib b. ᶜAbbād (d. 386/996) in Baghdad.
38. *Risālat Ibn Faḍlān*. The opening sections of Ibn Faḍlān's account describe the party's dispatch by al-Muqtadir (pp. 97–8), the date of their departure (p. 103), and their arrival in Bukhara, where 'we went to al-Jayhānī, secretary of the Amir of Khurasan' (*ṣirnā ilā l-Jayhānī wa-huwa kātib amīr Khurāsān*); the embassy stayed in the capital for some days and were well looked after (pp. 107–8). The sources for the earlier Samanid period mention various individuals named 'al-Jayhānī' (see following note). The individual to whom Ibn Faḍlān refers was Abū ᶜAbdallāh Aḥmad b. Muḥammad, vizier to Naṣr until the amir replaced him with Abū l-Fażl Balᶜamī in about 310/922 or perhaps 313/925 (Pellat, 'al-Djayhānī', p. 265; Treadwell, 'Political History', p. 122; Crone and Treadwell, 'New Text', pp. 54–5, n. 85).

39. The plurality of similarly named individuals who carried the *nisba* al-Jayhānī has complicated efforts to identify the individual(s) involved in the composition of the apparently lost geographical work. Ducène identified the geographer as Abū ᶜAbdallāh Muḥammad b. Aḥmad al-Jayhānī, and placed the redaction of his work between 301/913–14 and his death between 310/922 and 322/934 ('Al-Ğayhānī', p. 261). Pellat, however, has proposed that the geographical work associated with 'al-Jayhānī' consisted of a collective family work, perhaps begun by Abū ᶜAbdallāh Muḥammad b. Aḥmad, but continued by his son Muḥammad b. Muḥammad, and completed by his grandson Aḥmad b. Muḥammad in the years immediately following 330/941–2 (Pellat, 'al-Dj̲ayhānī', pp. 265–6). On the three generations of viziers from the Jayhānī family, see Crone and Treadwell, 'New Text', pp. 54–5.
40. Al-Muqaddasī, *Aḥsan al-taqāsīm*, pp. 3–4. Of his own composition, al-Muqaddasī states that the knowledge he seeks to impart is not only indispensable to travellers and merchants, but also popular with kings and other powerful persons, while judges and jurists seek it out, and the common people and leaders of urban quarters take pleasure in it (*huwa ᶜilm targhabu fīhi al-mulūk wa-l-kubarāʾ wa-taṭlubuhu al-quḍāt wa-l-fuqahāʾ wa-tuḥibbuhu al-ᶜāmma wa-l-ruʾasāʾ*, p. 2). On the interpretation of *ruʾasāʾ* as 'leaders of urban quarters', see Cahen, 'Mouvements populaires', esp. II, 52–4 = *Mouvements populaires*, pp. 54–6; Paul, *Herrscher, Gemeinwesen, Vermittler*, pp. 7–8 and passim. On the recipient or anticipated audience for al-Muqaddasī's text, see Touati, 'La dédicace des livres', pp. 325–30.
41. Gardīzī, *Zayn al-akhbār*, pp. 612–13. Gardīzī praised the vizier's many compositions on every branch of the arts and sciences (*har fannī va-ᶜilmī*), including his letters to 'all the kingdoms of the world', and his soliciting of information from them regarding their governmental practices (*rasmhā-yi hameh dargāhhā va-dīvānhā bi-khwāst*) (*Zayn al-akhbār*, p. 330). On Gardīzī's history, which is almost exclusively concerned with Iranian, especially Khurasanian history, see Meisami, *Persian Historiography*, pp. 66–79.
42. Narshakhī, *Tārīkh-i Bukhārā*, pp. 128–9; Ibn Ẓāfir (Treadwell, 'Account of the Samanid Dynasty', pp. 138–9 = pp. 153–4); Gardīzī, *Zayn al-akhbār*, p. 326; Ibn al-Athīr, *al-Kāmil*, VIII: 7; Mīrkhwānd, *Rawżat al-ṣafāʾ* ('Garden of Purity'), IV: 37; Treadwell, 'Political History', pp. 89–91. Most of these accounts report that Aḥmad forestalled Isḥāq's efforts by arriving in Samarqand and arresting him; Narshakhī does not mention Isḥāq's challenge to Aḥmad.
43. Treadwell, 'Political History', pp. 94, 145.

44. On the *ʿaṣabiyya* (factionalism) and *fitna* (sedition) manifested in Samarqand, see Ibn Ḥawqal, *Ṣūrat al-arḍ*, p. 494; al-Yaʿqūbī, *Kitāb al-Buldān* ('Book of the Lands'), p. 293; al-Muqaddasī, *Aḥsan al-taqāsīm*, pp. 278, 336; Paul, 'Nachrichten arabischer Geographen', pp. 189–90. Al-Muqaddasī reported on the readiness of the Samarqandis to revolt against their leaders (*yashghabūna ʿalā l-umarāʾ*, p. 278), and Barthold commented on Isḥāq's reliance on 'the support of the population of that seditious town' (namely, Samarqand); *Turkestan*, p. 240. In an important observation, Paul has indicated that when the geographers refer to the *ahl* of a town, it is often difficult to ascertain whether the term denotes a garrison or the civil population (*Herrscher, Gemeinwesen, Vermittler*, pp. 96–7).
45. Ibn al-Athīr, *al-Kāmil*, VIII: 61 (*sub anno* 298).
46. Narshakhī, *Tārīkh-i Bukhārā*, pp. 128–9; Gardīzī, *Zayn al-akhbār*, p. 329; Ibn al-Athīr, *al-Kāmil*, VIII: 77–8; Treadwell, 'Murder of Aḥmad b. Ismāʿīl'; cf. Treadwell, 'Political History', p. 144. According to much later accounts, such as that of Qazvīnī (*Tārīkh-i guzīdeh*, p. 378), the assassination resulted from disaffection among Aḥmad's *mamlūk*s, but the later authors offer sparse and inconsistent explanations for this displeasure.
47. *Risālat Ibn Faḍlān*, p. 108. Ibn Ẓāfir's detailed account appears to be the sole source that gives Naṣr's age at his accession as not eight but twelve (Treadwell, 'Murder of Aḥmad b. Ismāʿīl', pp. 401, 411, 417).
48. According to al-Ṭabarī, Naṣr also possessed plentiful material resources (*al-amwāl wa-l-kurāʿ wa-l-silāḥ*); Isḥāq, meanwhile, had the support of the population of Samarqand and 'persons who had joined him among the inhabitants of nearby locations' (*wa-man kāna qad inḍamma ilayhi min ahl tilka l-nawāḥī*) (*Taʾrīkh*, X: 147-8 (*sub anno* 301)). See also Ibn al-Athīr, *al-Kāmil*, VIII: 78.
49. Treadwell, 'Murder of Aḥmad b. Ismāʿīl', esp. pp. 399, 406, 413; Treadwell, 'Political History', pp. 140–3. Depending on the context in which it is used, the term *ʿayyār* embraces several meanings and connotations, some positive, many negative; see Tor, 'ʿAyyār'. The Iranian background to the word, and perhaps the continuation of some of its meanings, have received considerable scholarly attention; Mohsen Zakeri has studied the Sasanian antecedents of numerous Arabic and Persian terms for categories, especially military or quasi-military cultural groupings, including *ʿayyārūn* (Persian *ayyārān*) and *fityān* (Zakeri, *Sāsānid Soldiers*); cf. Baldick, 'Iranian Origin of the *futuwwa*'. Pseudo-Māwardī does not refer to *muṭṭawwiʿa* or *ʿayyārūn*, but on one occasion he mentions *fityān* (see Volume II, pp. 145, 146, 163–4).

50. Ibn al-Athīr, *al-Kāmil*, VIII: 80. According to the twelfth-century writer al-Samʿānī, Isḥāq died in prison in Bukhara in Safar 301/913. Since this date falls some months before the widely attested date of Aḥmad's assassination in Jumada II 301, al-Samʿānī's dating of Isḥāq's death cannot be accurate (*al-Ansāb*, VII: 25).
51. Zambaur, *Münzprägungen*, p. 14; for Samarqand, p. 148 and n. 10; for Nishapur, p. 261 and n. 40. In both locations, the coins are dated 301; in Samarqand, coins minted in the name of Aḥmad II and Naṣr II were produced in the same year.
52. Narshakhī, *Tārīkh-i Bukhārā*, p. 130; Treadwell, 'Account of the Samanid Dynasty', pp. 140–2, 153–5, 162–3; Mīrkhwānd, *Rawżat al-ṣafāʾ*, IV: 39–40; Majd al-Dīn al-Ḥusaynī, *Zīnat al-majālis* ('Adornment of Assemblies'), p. 215.
53. Narshakhī, *Tārīkh-i Bukhārā*, p. 130.
54. NM-A, p. 100 (the full translation follows).
55. NM-A, p. 100. In this context, the word *awliyāʾ* apparently refers to human beings who, while not selected as prophets, enjoy a particular closeness to God. For another occurrence of the term in this sense, see below, p. 218.
56. See below, pp. 158–60.
57. As Khiḍr notes (NM-Kh, p. 79, n. 1), it was Sulaymān's father Dā'ūd for whom God softened iron (Q. 34: 10).
58. NM-A, pp. 100–1. The Qurʾānic references are to 21: 78–82; 27: 15–44; 34: 12 (Solomon); 38: 26 (David); 18: 83–98 (Dhū l-Qarnayn). Joshua does not appear by name in the Qurʾān, but certain passages allude to him (Heller [Rippin], 'Yūshaʿ b. Nūn', p. 351).
59. Doufikar-Aerts, *Alexander Magnus Arabicus*, esp. pp. 135–93; Mottahedeh, 'Eastern Travels of Solomon'; and see below, p. 275, n. 90, p. 281, n. 176.
60. For a near-contemporary example, see the *Bustān al-ʿārifīn* ('Garden of Those Who Know') of Abū l-Layth al-Samarqandī (d. 373/983), the Ḥanafī jurist, theologian and Qurʾān commentator (see further below, Chapters 2 and 6). In a treatment of prophets, Abū l-Layth notes the difference of opinion regarding Dhū l-Qarnayn and Luqmān; most scholars, he avers, consider Luqmān a sage rather than a prophet, and Dhū l-Qarnayn a righteous king rather than a prophet. Abū l-Layth cites ʿAlī's judgement that Dhū l-Qarnayn was a righteous man (*Bustān al-ʿārifīn*, pp. 66–8). On Alexander and Dhū l-Qarnayn, see also al-Thaʿālibī, *Histoire des rois des Perses*, p. 400; and on the disputed attribution of this work, known under various titles, most notably *Taʾrīkh*

ghurar al-siyar ('History of Illustrious Biographies'), see Orfali, 'Works of Abū Manṣūr al-Thaᶜālibī', pp. 297–8, No. 34 (Orfali places the entry in the section devoted to works that are 'Printed, Authenticity Doubtful'), and Rowson, 'al-Thaᶜālibī'.

61. NM-A, p. 101.
62. As the following passage, related to al-Walīd, will also suggest, *ᶜinād*, in Pseudo-Māwardī's Muᶜtazilī-inflected vocabulary, connotes stubborn resistance to the acceptance of religious truth (cf. van Ess, *Erkenntnislehre*, pp. 139, 177, 231).
63. Cursing of the dynasty's enemies, including ᶜAlī, became a periodic feature of the *khuṭba* in the Umayyad period; Qutbuddin, 'Khuṭba', p. 205, § 5, and p. 208. The precise nature of ᶜUmar's fiscal reforms, to which *bayᶜ al-khazāᵓin* (literally 'the sale of the treasuries') refers, remains uncertain (Hawting, *First Dynasty*, pp. 76–81).
64. NM-A, p. 101.
65. See Borrut, 'Entre tradition et histoire'. On Pseudo-Māwardī's use of the term *malik*, see below, Chapter 3.
66. Madelung, *Der Imam al-Qāsim*, p. 41.
67. van Ess, *Theologie und Gesellschaft*, II: 41–50.
68. Al-Kaᶜbī, *Faḍl al-iᶜtizāl* ('Excellence of Muᶜtazilism'), pp. 115–17; al-Masᶜūdī, *Murūj al-dhahab*, III: 221, 226.
69. As Steven Judd has pointed out, it was al-Walīd who became 'the caricature of Umayyad depravity, impiety, and licentiousness' (Judd, 'Reinterpreting al-Walīd b. Yazīd', p. 439).
70. On *wafāᵓ* and the obligations that it occasioned, see Chapter 3.
71. NM-A, pp. 102–3. Al-Ṭabarī, *Taᵓrīkh*, VII: 268–9 (*sub anno* 126) = *History of al-Ṭabarī*, XXVI: 193–5 (see n. 979 for additional occurrences of the text); Ibn al-Athīr, *al-Kāmil*, V: 292; al-Azdī, *Taᵓrīkh al-Mawṣil* ('History of Mosul'), pp. 57–8. Cf. Crone and Hinds, *God's Caliph*, p. 68; Hawting, *First Dynasty*, pp. 94–6.
72. van Ess, 'Les Qadarites'; Blankinship, *End of the Jihād State*, pp. 225–30; Judd, 'Reinterpreting al-Walīd b. Yazīd', pp. 455–6.
73. See further NM-A, pp. 156 (*ahl al-baghy*), 325–8 (*al-bāghūn*) ('rebels'). Cf. al-Ashᶜarī, *Maqālāt*, II: 348, § 197; Abou El Fadl, *Rebellion and Violence*, pp. 119 and n. 70, 134, 161.
74. NM-A, p. 103.
75. NM-A, p. 104. Pseudo-Māwardī cites three sets of verses in this account, the first attributed to 'his panaegyrist' (*mādiḥuhu*), the second and third to Abū

Nuwās. All three verses appear in Abū Nuwās's *Dīwān* (pp. 405, 401, 403), the last in a variant form. On Hārūn's custom of alternating *jihād* and *ḥajj*, cf. Tor, *Violent Order*, pp. 42–3.

76. Hinds, 'Miḥna'.
77. Cooperson, *Classical Arabic Biography*, pp. 32–4; Cooperson, *Al-Maʾmun*, pp. 115–21.
78. NM-A, p. 105. On the qualities associated with al-Maʾmūn in various sources, see Cooperson, *Classical Arabic Biography*, pp. 40–3. The attribute of *raʾy*, opinion, attributed to the caliph contrasts him with the most prominent opponent of *khalq al-Qurʾān*, Aḥmad b. Ḥanbal (d. 241/855) (*Classical Arabic Biography*, p. 36).
79. Al-Dīnawarī, *al-Akhbār al-ṭiwāl* ('Long Accounts'), pp. 585–6. With reference to al-Maʾmūn's ascribed attributes, Cooperson renders *ḥikma* as 'philosophical rationalism' (*Classical Arabic Biography*, p. 43).
80. Cf. Zaman, 'The Caliphs, the ᶜUlamāʾ, and the Law', pp. 29, 33–4; Cooperson, *Al-Maʾmun*, pp. 81–3.
81. Judd, 'Ghaylan al-Dimashqi'.
82. For an example, see Hamdani, 'Dialectic of Power'.
83. Cf. Hurvitz, *Formation of Hanbalism*, p. 120.
84. ᶜAbd al-Jabbār, *al-Mughnī*, VIII: 188; IX: 73; al-Ashᶜarī, *Maqālāt* ('Doctrines') I: 181–95. It is also consistent with points of view suggested in al-Kindī's writings, especially 'On Definitions'; see Adamson, 'Al-Kindī and the Muᶜtazila', pp. 67–76.
85. Al-Maqdisī, *al-Badʾ wa-l-taʾrīkh*, VI: 112. Al-Maqdisī composed his *Kitāb al-Badʾ wa-l-taʾrīkh* in Bust, Sistan in 355/966, perhaps, as Mahmoud Tahmi has suggested, for Khalaf b. Aḥmad (r. 352–93/963–1003) of the Saffarids (Tahmi, *L'Encyclopédisme musulman*, pp. 16–19). van Ess takes al-Maqdisī to have been a Muᶜtazilite (*Erkenntnislehre*, p. 177); see further Chapter 8, n. 41.
86. NM-A, p. 105.
87. On these terms, see Chapter 3.
88. NM-A, pp. 105–6.
89. On these events, see Kennedy, *Armies of the Caliphs*, pp. 133–4. Most accounts of al-Muᶜtaṣim's campaign against Amorium, in the course of which many Byzantine women were captured, do not mention the incident narrated in *Naṣīḥat al-mulūk*. The story does not appear in the lengthy account of al-Ṭabarī (*Taʾrīkh*, IX: 57–71 [*sub anno* 223] = *History of al-Ṭabarī*, XXXIII: 97–121), nor in that of al-Masᶜūdī (*Murūj al-dhahab*, III: 172–3); it does appear in the

much later, and brief, account of Ibn al-Athīr, who adds the detail that the woman was a Hāshimī (*imraʾa hāshimiyya*), that is, a member of the Prophet's family (*al-Kāmil*, VI: 480). Al-Ṭabarī's treatment of the incident, and its similarities to and differences from other accounts, are discussed at length in Bray, 'Al-Muᶜtaṣim's "Bridge of Toil"'. The campaign against Amorium provided the occasion for Abū Tammām's celebrated victory poem. Bray indicates that the reference to the captive Zibatran woman's call on al-Muᶜtaṣim for aid, or vengeance, appears in the commentaries on the poetry of Abū Tammām of Muḥammad b. Yaḥyā al-Ṣūlī (d. *c.* 335/946) and the fourteenth-century al-Khaṭīb al-Tibrīzī ('Al-Muᶜtaṣim's "Bridge of Toil"', p. 45). It is likely that Pseudo-Māwardī was familiar with his contemporary al-Ṣūlī's commentary. In al-Tibrīzī's later gloss, the caliph puts down a cup of wine in order to attend immediately to the Byzantine threat, and takes it up again on his victorious return (Stetkevych, *Abū Tammām*, p. 193, note to line 46, and p. 207; Bray, 'Al-Muᶜtaṣim's "Bridge of Toil"', p. 45); Pseudo-Māwardī's concise narrative omits this detail. On Abū Tammām's poem, see Bray, 'Al-Muᶜtaṣim's "Bridge of Toil"' (on the Zibatran woman, see p. 53 and n. 79); Stetkevych, *Abū Tammām*, pp. 187–211. Older studies include Badawi, 'Function of Rhetoric' (see p. 55), and Abdul Haq, 'Historical Poems' (see p. 25 and n. 5).

90. NM-A, p. 106.
91. Hinds, 'Miḥna', p. 4.
92. Madelung, *Der Imam al-Qāsim*, p. 41, and see below, pp. 214–15.
93. NM-A, pp. 106–7. In this passage the term *adab* appears twice, once in the singular and once in the plural; as observed in the Introduction, the term embraces many meanings, and I take it here to connote in broad terms the field of Arabic literary culture. The term *faḍl* is similarly complex, and defies adequate translation. In this instance, I take it to encompass moral excellence (cf. *faḍīla*, 'virtue'), intellectual and practical proficiency, and broadly humane learning of a sort that complemented more specifically religious learning (*ᶜilm*), with which, as in Pseudo-Māwardī's praise of al-Maʾmūn's exemplary qualities, it is often paired.
94. Among later historians, Gardīzī and Ibn al-Athīr both cited al-Sallāmī's *Taʾrīkh wulāt Khurāsān* ('History of the Rulers of Khurasan') extensively; Bosworth, 'al-Sallāmī', pp. 996–7. Al-Sallāmī was associated with the Chaghanids under Abū Bakr and Abū ᶜAlī. The designation *wulāt Khurāsān* is also common in the period's geographical literature; see, for example, Ibn Ḥawqal, *Ṣūrat al-arḍ*, p. 483.

95. NM-A, pp. 241–2, 351–2. See further Bosworth, 'Ṭāhirids and Arabic Culture', pp. 45–79.
96. Bayhaqī, *Tārīkh-i Bayhaq*, pp. 271, 296, 299, 115; al-Ṣafadī, *al-Wāfī bi-l-wafayāt*, p. 26.
97. NM-A, pp. 242, 351; in addition to these quotations of his sayings and poetry, Pseudo-Māwardī also cites an example of his conduct, NM-A, p. 278.
98. Ibn al-Nadīm, *al-Fihrist*, I: ii: 365 (*wa-qad naqala min rasāʾil Arisṭāṭālīs ilā l-Iskandar aw nuqila lahu wa-aṣlaḥa huwa*). Ibn al-Nadīm leaves unstated the language from which Sālim made his translations or corrections; van Bladel has argued persuasively that whereas scholars have long assumed that the original language was Greek, it is at least as likely to have been Middle Persian (van Bladel, 'Iranian Characteristics and Forged Greek Attributions').
99. Adamson, *Al-Kindī*, p. 26; Endreß, 'Circle of al-Kindī'.
100. Al-Bīrūnī, *al-Āthār al-bāqiya*, p. 99.
101. For the text of the Bāysunghurī Preface, see Riyāḥī, *Sar-chashmeh-hā-yi Firdawsī-shināsī*, pp. 364–418.
102. Riyāḥī, *Sar-chashmeh-hā-yi Firdawsī-shināsī*, pp. 368–9. See further Volume II, Chapter 2.
103. Bosworth, 'Ṭāhirids and Persian Literature', pp. 105–6.
104. On the concept of *dawla*, see Mottahedeh, *Loyalty and Leadership*, pp. 175–90, esp. 185–9. In the Iranian context, the notion of *farr(ah)*, in the royal applications that it acquired in the Sasanian period, found continued expression in the idea of *farr-i ilāhī* or *īzadī*, the divine nimbus of sovereignty (cf. de Fouchécour, *Moralia*, pp. 289–90, 397, 405; Gnoli, 'Farr(ah)', pp. 312–19), and perhaps contributed in part to the shaping of this concept of *dawla*.
105. Other strands relate the Tahirids' demise specifically to their failure to protect or their antipathy towards the ʿAlids, and locate predictions of their fall in dreams and horoscopes (for examples, see Mottahedeh, *Loyalty and Leadership*, pp. 69–71; Bernheimer, 'Rise of *sayyids* and *sādāt*', p. 43; Pingree and Madelung, 'Political Horoscopes', pp. 247–75).
106. Gardīzī, *Zayn al-akhbār*, pp. 303–4. See further Kaabi, *Les Tahirides*, pp. 299–312, 357–63; Tor, *Violent Order*, pp. 118–23, 147–53.
107. Meisami detects at least three hands in the composition of *Tārīkh-i Sīstān*. For full discussion of the historians' interests and proclivities, see Meisami, *Persian Historiography*, pp. 108–36. See also Bosworth, 'Sistan and its Local Histories', pp. 34–9.
108. *Tārīkh-i Sīstān*, p. 220. According to the account, the house had belonged

to Ṣāliḥ b. al-Naḍr, Ya^c^qūb's predecessor and rival in Bust. Cf. Bosworth, *History of the Saffarids*, p. 119; Meisami, *Persian Historiography*, pp. 117–18.

109. Of the originally thirty volumes, only six survive; these volumes detail the reign of the Ghaznavid Sultan Mas^c^ūd (r. 421–32/1030–41), and are sometimes known as *Tārīkh-i Mas^c^ūdī* ('The Mas^c^ūdian History'). This study refers to the work under the name *Tārīkh-i Bayhaqī* ('Bayhaqī's History').

110. After citing Q. 3: 26, 'Say, O God, possessor of sovereignty, you give sovereignty to whomever you choose and take it from whomever you choose', Bayhaqī describes God's removal of sovereignty from one group and His bestowal of it on another as a form of divine wisdom, its purpose the general welfare of humankind (*ḥikmat ast īzadī va-maṣlaḥat-i ^c^āmm mar khalq-i rū-yi zamīn*); *Tārīkh-i Bayhaqī*, pp. 97–8; cf. Mottahedeh, *Loyalty and Leadership*, pp. 186–7.

111. Pseudo-Māwardī's silence regarding the Saffarids indicates that he did not consider them to be exemplary. Like many later writers, he perhaps held a hostile view of the dynasty. If, as Chapter 2 seeks to demonstrate, the author lived in Balkh, such negative views would be consistent with Gardīzī's report that Ya^c^qūb devastated the city when he took it and Bamiyan in 256/870 (*Zayn al-akhbār*, pp. 306–7). It was also at Balkh that ^c^Amr b. al-Layth, having reportedly secured the acquiescence or allegiance of the local Banu Dawudid ruler, was defeated and captured by Ismā^c^īl.

112. Reading with Aḥmad *Sāmān* for *Sāsān* (NM-A, p. 107).

113. Treadwell has proposed the alternative translation 'the Efficacious Amir'; see 'Account of the Samanid Dynasty', p. 153, and n. 20.

114. NM-A, pp. 107–8.

115. I have discussed this passage, and the chief arguments for dating the text to the Samanid period, in 'Counsel and Commentary'.

116. Al-Ḥadīthī (NM-Ḥ, p. 140, n. 262) and Anṣārī ('Yek andīsheh-nāmeh', p. 10) take Pseudo-Māwardī's 'Naṣr b. Aḥmad' as a reference to Naṣr II. Anṣārī accordingly places the work's composition in approximately 332/943–4, late in the reign of Naṣr II, and proposes that its presentation was postponed until the reign of Naṣr's successor Nūḥ I b. Naṣr (r. 331–43/943–54) (pp. 10–13). In the view of the present author, the chronological sequencing and the description of Naṣr imply that Pseudo-Māwardī's reference is to Naṣr I rather than Naṣr II. Aḥmad also reads the text as referring to Naṣr I (NM-A, p. 107, n. 71).

117. Al-Nasafī, *al-Qand fī dhikr* ᶜ*ulamā*ᵓ *Samarqand* ('Book of Candy on the Record of the Scholars of Samarqand'), pp. 410–11, 630. On the title of 'amir', see below, pp. 127–8.
118. Numismatic evidence implies that the amirs began to adopt titles compounded with *malik* in the second half of the tenth century. Nūḥ b. Naṣr appears in the coinage as *al-malik al-mu*ᵓ*ayyad* (Bosworth, 'Titulature', p. 214; Treadwell, '*Shāhānshāh* and *al-Malik al-Mu*ᵓ*ayyad*', pp. 318–37).
119. Narshakhī, *Tārīkh-i Bukhārā*, pp. 3–4. Abū Naṣr Aḥmad b. Muḥammad Naṣr Qubāvī (d. 522/1128) expanded and translated the 'History' into Persian in 522 /1128 and continued it to the year 365/975–6. In 574/1178–9, Muḥammad b. Zufar abridged the Persian version, added to it, and presented the resulting product to the *ṣadr* of the Ḥanafīs in Bukhara, Burhān al-Dīn ᶜAbd al-ᶜAzīz II b. Muḥammad. An unknown author later added details concerning the Mongol conquest of Bukhara. Narshakhī's Arabic text is no longer extant, and it is not possible to gauge the impact of the several modifications to his composition in the available version.
120. Narshakhī, *Tārīkh-i Bukhārā*, pp. 106, 127.
121. Narshakhī, *Tārīkh-i Bukhārā*, p. 127. For further accounts of Ismāᶜīl, see al-Samᶜānī, *al-Ansāb*, VII: 24–5; Gardīzī, *Zayn al-akhbār*, pp. 323–5; al-Masᶜūdī, *Murūj al-dhahab*, IV: 156; Qazvīnī, *Tārīkh-i guzīdeh*, pp. 377–8; Treadwell, 'Account of the Samanid Dynasty', pp. 137–8, 153; Ibn al-Athīr, *al-Kāmil*, VIII: 5; Mīrkhwānd, *Rawżat al-ṣafā*ᵓ, IV: 32–6.
122. Bayhaqī, *Tārīkh-i Bayhaq*, p. 69, where Ismāᶜīl ascribes his efforts to the apprehension that an indigent stranger (*gharībī darvīsh*) might have a matter to bring to his attention, and might be moved, were the amir unavailable, to curse him in his prayers (literally, to offer unfavourable prayers) (*nabāyad keh marā du*ᶜ*ā-yi bad gūyad*). Cf. Niẓām al-Mulk, *Siyar al-mulūk*, pp. 28–9 = pp. 21–2; Mīrkhwānd, *Rawżat al-ṣafā*ᵓ, IV: 36; and on the subjects' duty to pray for the ruler, see below, p. 142, and Volume II, pp. 206–7.
123. Narshakhī, *Tārīkh-i Bukhārā*, p. 128.
124. Al-Samᶜānī, *al-Ansāb*, VII: 25; al-Nasafī, *al-Qand fī dhikr* ᶜ*ulamā*ᵓ *Samarqand*, p. 66, No. 60 (see below, p. 51).
125. *Tārīkh-i Sīstān*, pp. 253–4, 256. Cf. Tor, *Violent Order*, pp. 210, 215; Meisami, *Persian Historiography*, pp. 122–3.
126. Paul, 'Histories of Samarqand', pp. 86–7.
127. Paul, 'Nachrichten arabischer Geographen', pp. 188–9; 'Histories of Samarqand', p. 83; *Herrscher, Gemeinwesen, Vermittler*, pp. 103–17.

128. Abū l-Fażl Balᶜamī followed Abū l-Faḍl Yaᶜqūb al-Naysābūrī (al-Muqaddasī, *Aḥsan al-taqāsīm*, p. 337) as vizier to Naṣr in about 309/921 (Bosworth, 'Balᶜamī').
129. On Muḥammad b. Naṣr al-Marwazī, see al-Khaṭīb al-Baghdādī, *Taʾrīkh Baghdād*, III: 315–18, No. 1416; Sezgin, *GAS* I: 494.
130. Al-Nasafī, *al-Qand fī dhikr ᶜulamāʾ Samarqand*, p. 66, No. 60.
131. Al-Khaṭīb al-Baghdādī, *Taʾrīkh Baghdād*, III: 318. The accounts of Ibn al-Athīr (*al-Kāmil*, VII: 282) and al-Ṣafadī (*al-Wāfī*, V: 111) are virtually identical; see also Mīrkhwānd, *Rawżat al-ṣafāʾ*, IV: 32. Bonner ('Waning of Empire', p. 345 and n. 89) proposes, based on the date of al-Marwazī's death in 295/906, that the losing brother was Naṣr b. Aḥmad (d. 279/892) rather than Isḥāq, but the emendation seems unnecessary.
132. Al-Khaṭīb al-Baghdādī, *Taʾrīkh Baghdād*, III: 317.
133. Narshakhī, *Tārīkh-i Bukhārā*, p. 106. The term *salāṭīn* is likely to reflect not Narshakhī's original early tenth-century text, but one of the later redactions or versions of the *Tārīkh-i Bukhārā* (see above, nn. 22, 119).
134. Narshakhī, *Tārīkh-i Bukhārā*, p. 117. In Narshakhī's account, Isḥāq violated the expected ceremonial enactment of *khidma* (cf. the case of the Khwarazmshah Atsız, who in 543/1148 behaved similarly in rendering *khidma* to Sanjar; Paul, '*Khidma*', pp. 404, 410). See Chapter 3.
135. Gardīzī, *Zayn al-akhbār*, pp. 326, 330–1. In Gardīzī's narrative, at the time of Aḥmad (I)'s death, he left only two sons, Naṣr and Ismāᶜīl, who during the time of the Tahirids had held Samarqand and Bukhara, respectively, in a harmonious fashion; the conflict between them is attributed to the manipulations of evil talkers (*bad-gūyān*), its conclusion marked with elaborate emblems of reconciliation (*Zayn al-akhbār*, pp. 322–3).
136. NM-A, p. 107, and see above, p. 47.
137. I am grateful to Luke Treadwell for bringing this information to my attention. For an example of the numismatic appearance of this Qurʾānic language, see Mitchiner, *Multiple Dirhems*, p. 49.
138. *Tārīkh-i Sīstān*, p. 342; see further Bosworth, *History of the Saffarids*, pp. 301–2, 328–37; Meisami, *Persian Historiography*, pp. 128–9.
139. NM-A, p. 108. The wording resembles that employed for the Abbasids: *fa-ammā khulafāʾ banī l-ᶜAbbās fa-qalla man khalā minhum aw min afāḍilihim min khiṣāl ḥamīda* ('As for the Abbasid caliphs, few of them, or of the virtuous among them, were devoid of praiseworthy qualities') (NM-A, p. 103).
140. Cf. Khalidi, *Islamic Historiography*, pp. 74–8, 81–113.

141. It is difficult to assess the authorship and dating of many of these compositions, but the Arabic renderings are usually taken to reflect late Sasanian recensions (Safa, 'Andarz').
142. NM-A, pp. 108–9.
143. NM-A, p. 109.
144. NM-A, p. 108; *ᶜAhd Ardashīr*, p. 53. Cf. Shaked, 'Esoteric Trends', p. 214; and 'Notes', pp. 37–40.
145. NM-A, p. 108; *ᶜAhd Ardashīr*, p. 54. Cf. Shaked, 'Esoteric Trends', appendix D 'Secret Religion', pp. 214–19.
146. See Chapter 7.
147. In the published edition of *ᶜAhd Ardashīr*, a passage that appears between the two citations in *Naṣīḥat al-mulūk* (nn. 144, 145) draws attention to the potentially rebellious disposition of the lower classes: 'The first thing which I fear for you is that the lowly people (*al-sifla*) will get ahead of you in studying and reciting religion and becoming learned in it, and that your trust in the power of government will lead you to take this lightly; so that hidden leaderships will arise amongst those of the lowly people, the subjects and the ignorant commoners (*siflat al-nās wa-l-raᶜiyya wa-ḥashw al-ᶜāmma*) whom you have offended, treated harshly, deprived, intimidated and humiliated' (*ᶜAhd Ardashīr*, pp. 53–4; Steppat, 'From *ᶜAhd Ardashīr* to al-Maᵓmūn', pp. 451–2; Shaked, Esoteric Trends', appendix D 'Secret Religion', pp. 214–19). This passage does not appear in *Naṣīḥat al-mulūk*, despite the fact that Pseudo-Māwardī cites the passages that occur before and after it.
148. NM-A, p. 109. Cf. Grignaschi, 'La "Siyâsatu-l-ᶜâmmiyya"', p. 106; Maróth, *Correspondence*, p. 29; al-Mubashshir, *Mukhtār al-ḥikam wa-maḥāsin al-kalim* ('Choice Words of Wisdom and Fine Sayings'), p. 192; *Sirr al-asrār* ('Secret of Secrets'), in Badawī, *al-Uṣūl al-yūnāniyya*, p. 77.
149. NM-A, p. 109. Cf. Grignaschi, 'La "Siyâsatu-l-ᶜâmmiyya"', p. 110; Maróth, *Correspondence*, 32; al-Mubashshir, *Mukhtār al-ḥikam*, p. 193; Ibn Abī Uṣaybiᶜa, *Ṭabaqāt al-aṭibbāᵓ* ('Generations of the Physicians'), I: 99–100.
150. NM-A, p. 109. Grignaschi, 'La "Siyâsatu-l-ᶜâmmiyya"', p. 114; Maróth, *Correspondence*, p. 35.
151. NM-A, p. 109. Grignaschi, 'La "Siyâsatu-l-ᶜâmmiyya"', p. 118; Maróth, *Correspondence*, p. 37; al-Mubashshir, *Mukhtār al-ḥikam*, p. 193; Ibn Hindū, *al-Kalim al-rūḥāniyya min al-ḥikam al-yūnāniyya* ('Spiritual Sayings from the Greek Maxims'), p. 72; Ibn Abī Uṣaybiᶜa, *Ṭabaqāt al-aṭibbāᵓ*, I: 98; al-Shahrazūrī, *Nuzhat al-arwāḥ* ('The Amusement of Souls'), I: 202.

152. Cooperson, *Al-Maʾmun*, pp. 32–3, 83–106; Demichelis, 'Between Mu^{c}tazilism and Syncretism'; see also Yücesoy, 'Translation'.
153. Cf. al-Taghlibī, *Kitāb al-Tāj*, pp. 168–9.
154. Cf. al-Taghlibī, *Kitāb al-Tāj*, p. 169.
155. NM-A, pp. 277–8 = pp. 185–7. Niẓām al-Mulk cites ^{c}Abdallāh b. Ṭāhir in a somewhat similar context (*Siyar al-mulūk*, pp. 63–4 = *Book of Government*, pp. 47–8).
156. Formerly considered a work of the ninth-century littérateur al-Jāḥiẓ, *Akhlāq al-mulūk*, the work known under the title *Kitāb al-Tāj*, is the composition of an author named al-Taghlibī or al-Tha^{c}labī (Schoeler, 'Verfasser und Titel'; cf. Volume II, pp. 55–8). Of the two possible readings of the author's name, I have used the form al-Taghlibī throughout this book.
157. Cf. Volume II, pp. 56–8 and passim.
158. Narshakhī, *Tārīkh-i Bukhārā*, pp. 106, 127.
159. Bonner, 'Waning of Empire', p. 345.
160. Throughout this book, I have used the Persian form Chaghānī rather than the Arabic al-Ṣaghānī, except in quotations in which the Arabic form appears.
161. See Bosworth, 'Rulers of Chaghāniyān', pp. 5–9.
162. Kennedy, *The Prophet and the Age of the Caliphates*, pp. 210–47 and passim.
163. Daniel, 'The Islamic East', p. 499.
164. Daniel, 'Sāmānid "Translations"', pp. 290–2; see also Meisami, *Persian Historiography*, pp. 23–37, esp. 29–33.
165. Bonner, 'Waning of Empire', pp. 345–6; Frye, 'Sāmānids', pp. 143–5; Bosworth, 'Sāmānids', p. 1027.
166. On the terms 'the Islamic east' (*al-mashriq*) and 'regionalism', see Daniel, 'The Islamic East', pp. 448–9.
167. For Pseudo-Māwardī's discussion of this term, see below, pp. 119–20.
168. NM-A, p. 82.
169. Al-Tha^{c}ālibī, *Yatīmat al-dahr*, I: 124 (the entry on Ibn Khālawayh appears in the fourth section of al-Tha^{c}ālibī's first division, devoted to poets associated with Aleppo). Ibn Khallikān, on the authority of al-Tha^{c}ālibī, similarly ascribes the verse to Ibn Khālawayh (*Wafayāt al-a^{c}yān,* II: 178–9, No. 194); similarly Yāqūt (*Mu^{c}jam al-udabāʾ*, III: 1030–7, No. 367); Ibn Taghribirdī, *al-Nujūm al-zāhira* ('Shining Stars'), IV: 139 (citing al-Dhahabī). Cf. Spitaler, 'Ibn Khālawayh', pp. 824–5.
170. Mikhail, *Politics and Revelation*, pp. 66–7.
171. Rowson and Bonebakker, *A Computerized Listing*, pp. 7–25, esp. 8,

and 30, No. 20; Orfali, 'The Art of Anthology', ch. 5: 'An Anthologist at Work'.

172. Since in this first *qism* of his *Yatīma*, al-Thaʿālibī acknowledges as a guarantor Abū Bakr al-Khwārazmī (d. 383/993), who visited Syria, Bilal Orfali has suggested that some of the Syrian material that appears without an *isnād* may have been transmitted on his authority (Orfali, 'Sources of al-Thaʿālibī').

Chapter 2

1. Barthold, *Turkestan*, pp. 64–179. Definitions of the region varied; al-Iṣṭakhrī assimilates Khwarazm to Mā warāʾ l-nahr rather than to Khurasan, but treats Balkh and Tukharistan separately, as belonging to Khurasan; *Masālik al-mamālik*, pp. 253, 254.
2. de la Vaissière, *Marchands sogdiens*, pp. 263, 295.
3. On the possible origins of the name Bukhara, see Frye, 'Notes', pp. 106–19. In another suggestion of the city's Buddhist past, al-Iṣṭakhrī and Ibn Ḥawqal mention a nearby location, important for the supply of water, called al-Nawbahār (*Masālik al-mamālik*, pp. 308–9; Ibn Ḥawqal, *Ṣūrat al-arḍ*, II: 484); cf. Bulliet, 'Naw Bahār', p. 140. Maria Eva Subtelny suggests that the perception of Bukhara as a former centre for idolatry may have intensified its association with the Islamic religious sciences and its connections with Biblical and Islamic figures, such as Job, who was believed to have visited Bukhara ('Making', p. 81).
4. Subtelny, 'Making', p. 78. See also Bosworth, 'Bukhara', pp. 511–45, esp. 513–15.
5. de la Vaissière has indicated that Bukharans joined the Muslim élites rather more rapidly than Samarqandīs; *Marchands sogdiens*, p. 286.
6. Paul, 'Buchara die Edle', p. 64; Subtelny, 'Making', p. 82.
7. Paul, 'Buchara die Edle', p. 66. On the topography, urban landscape and markets of Bukhara, see al-Iṣṭakhrī, *Masālik al-mamālik*, pp. 305–16.
8. Al-Muqaddasī, *Aḥsan al-taqāsīm*, p. 270.
9. Al-Iṣṭakhrī, *Masālik al-mamālik*, p. 316; al-Muqaddasī, *Aḥsan al-taqāsīm*, p. 278.
10. Al-Iṣṭakhrī, *Masālik al-mamālik*, pp. 317–18; cf. *Ḥudūd al-ʿālam*, p. 113. Cf. Schaeder [Bosworth], 'Samarḳand'.
11. On the complex evolution of this work and its relationship to other works, in Arabic and in Persian, that include *qand* or *qandiyya* in their titles, see Weinberger, 'Authorship', pp. 369–82, and Paul, 'Histories of Samarqand', pp. 69–92. The published text is generally taken to represent al-Nasafī's

continuation (*dhayl*), recorded by Ḥājjī Khalīfa, to the earlier (lost) city chronicle of ᶜAbd al-Raḥmān b. Muḥammad al-Idrīsī al-Astarābādī, who died in Samarqand in 405/1015.

12. *Ḥudūd al-ᶜālam*, p. 102. *Mīr* is a common shortening for *amīr* in Persian sources.
13. Bosworth, 'Khurāsān', pp. 55–6. The designation 'Khurasan' derives from Middle Persian *xwarāsān*, meaning 'sunrise' or 'east', the name of a province to the eastern side of the Sasanian empire and one of the four quarters into which the empire was divided in the sixth century under Khusraw Anūshīrvān. The region described by this name in the Islamic period lacks clear and consistent boundaries, but is usually distinguished from Mā warāᵓ al-nahr, 'that which lies beyond the river', namely, Transoxiana (sometimes [Mā] warāᵓ nahr Balkh, as in al-Ṭabarī, *Taᵓrīkh*, X: 30).
14. Pourshariati also points out the limited means of communication between Inner and Outer Khurasan in the late antique period (*Decline and Fall*, pp. 417–19).
15. Bulliet, 'Medieval Nishapur', pp. 67–89; *Conversion*, esp. pp. 16–79, 33–74.
16. de Planhol, 'Bal<u>k</u>', pp. 587–8; Shaban, 'Khurāsān', pp. 479–90.
17. Spuler infers that Chaghaniyan, previously Hephthalite and Buddhist, took its culture from Balkh rather than from Bukhara or Samarqand ('Čaghāniyān', p. 1; with reference to al-Ṭabarī, *Taᵓrīkh*, VI: 424–5 [*sub anno* 86] = *History*, XXIII: 127–8; al-Dīnawarī, *al-Akhbār al-ṭiwāl*, p. 330; cf. Spuler, *Iran*, p. 29 and n. 6). Under Naṣr II, Abū Bakr Muḥammad of Chaghaniyan became governor of Balkh and Tukharistan, and in 321/933 of Khurasan.
18. The Farighunids were rulers of Guzgan from some time before the beginning of the tenth century until Guzgan was incorporated into the Ghaznavid Empire in the early eleventh century; see Bosworth, 'Āl-e Farīġūn', pp. 756–8. Kāykāᵓūs, author of the *Qābūsnāmeh*, relates an anecdote concerning Aḥmad b. Farīghūn, in which the latter received a defective 'gift' on the occasion of the Iranian New Year festival of Nawruz (*Qābūsnāmeh*, p. 127 = *Mirror for Princes*, pp. 115–16). On the Farighunids, whose patronage of scholarship and learning are often noted, see Manīnī, *al-Fatḥ al-wahbī*, II, pp. 101–5; Nāẓim, *Sulṭān Maḥmūd*, pp. 177–8; Spuler, *Iran*, p. 311; al-Bīrūnī, *al-Āthār al-bāqiya*, ed. Ażkāᵓī, pp. 491–2 ('Taᶜlīqāt-i kitāb' [notes]), n. 22; Narshakhī, *Tārīkh-i Bukhārā*, pp. 300–2; *Ḥudūd al-ᶜālam*, p. 178 (see also the 'improved translation' of the section on Guzganan in the Second Series of Addenda, p. xxi); Barthold, 'Preface', p. 5.

19. Narshakhī, *Tārīkh-i Bukhārā*, pp. 119, 122–6; cf. notes, pp. 300–2. See above, p. 28.
20. A parallel branch of the family may have ruled north of the Oxus in Khuttal well into the tenth century; see Barthold [Bosworth], 'Ṭukhāristān', pp. 599–602.
21. Treadwell, 'Political History', pp. 110–11.
22. On the plentiful deposits of silver at Andarab and Panjhir, see al-Iṣṭakhrī, *Masālik al-mamālik*, pp. 279, 280; cf. 281, 288. See further Marquart, *Ērānšahr*, pp. 301–2; Bosworth, 'Andarāb', p. 10. On the coins of the Abu Daʾudids minted principally at Andarab but also at Panjhir, Balkh, Khuttal and elsewhere, as well as the appearance of combinations of Abbasid, Samanid and Banijurid names in the region's coinage, see Vasmer, 'Beiträge, I', pp. 49–62; Zambaur, *Münzprägungen*, I: 54; Mitchiner, *Multiple Dirhems*, pp. 3–4 and passim.
23. Cf. Bosworth, 'Balḵ', p. 589.
24. Alliances among the empires of Tibet, China, the Caliphate, and the Western and Eastern Turks in their contests for domination over large parts of Eurasia were commonplace; see Beckwith, *Tibetan Empire*, pp. 117–18, 123 (with reference to al-Ḥārith).
25. Al-Ḥārith availed himself of this connection too, and latterly allied with the Khaqan of the Turgesh or Western Turks.
26. *Ḥudūd al-ʿālam*, pp. 62, 94–9; Commentary, 286–97; cf. Barthold, 'Preface', pp. 28, 35.
27. Sims-Williams, *Bactrian Documents*, II: 122–6 (documents eh, ja, jb).
28. In the full passage, al-Khwārazmī described *al-hayāṭila* as 'groups [*jīl/jiyal*] of people who possessed power (*shawka*) and possessed the lands of Tukharistan, the Turks of Khalaj and Kanjina; among what remains of them is the khāqān, the greatest king of the Turks, the khān, and he is the chief; *khāqān* means khān of khāns (*khāqān huwa khān khān*), that is, chief of chiefs (*raʾīs al-ruʾasāʾ*), as the Persians say *shāhānshāh*' (*Mafātīḥ al-ʿulūm* ('Keys of the Sciences'), pp. 119–20).
29. Geoffrey Khan surmises that the group of documents formed part of the royal archive of a petty prince of Siminjan and Rub in south-eastern Tukharistan. Most of the documents were composed in the Middle Iranian Bactrian language, written in a cursive script derived from the Greek alphabet, but some were written in Arabic. The latest document is dated 549 of the Bactrian era, probably to be equated with 781, and accordingly written in the early Abbasid period (Khan, 'Newly Discovered Arabic Documents').

30. Sims-Williams, *Bactrian Documents*, pp. 174–6 (documents za, zb; the former document, on cloth, features above and below the text two drawings, apparently representing a Buddha above and a wine-drinker wearing a turban and loincloth below; p. 33).
31. Jamsheed K. Choksy has noted the continuance of a Zoroastrian majority among the population of Balkh in the aftermath of the conquests; *Conflict and Cooperation*, pp. 27, 76.
32. Al-Yaᶜqūbī, *Kitāb al-Buldān*, p. 287 (*madīnat Balkh madīnat Khurāsān al-ᶜuẓmā . . . wa-hiya ᶜaẓīmat al-qadr*); al-Muqaddasī, *Aḥsan al-taqāsīm*, p. 302 and n. d.
33. Only the Persian text survives. Azad surmises that the Arabic author, identified in the surviving Persian version as Shaykh al-Islām al-Wāᶜiẓ (hereafter Vāᶜiẓ), was born no later than 565/1169–70; see Azad, 'The *Faḍāʾil-i Balkh*', pp. 80–1; *Sacred Landscape*, pp. 25–7. Although it dates from a much later period than Pseudo-Māwardī's lifetime, *Fażāʾil-i Balkh* draws on numerous earlier materials, including the *Manāqib* or *Faḍāʾil Balkh* of Abū Zayd al-Balkhī (Radtke, 'Theologen und Mystiker', p. 537).
34. Radtke, 'Theologen und Mystiker', pp. 538–49; Azad, 'The *Faḍāʾil-i Balkh*', pp. 88–98; al-Samᶜānī, *al-Ansāb*, II: 303–35 (v. 'al-Balkhī').
35. Al-Iṣṭakhrī, *Masālik al-mamālik*, p. 282.
36. NM-A, p. 214.
37. Cf. Versteegh, 'Linguistic Contacts', p. 492.
38. Cf. Cooperson, *Classical Arabic Biography*, pp. 2–6. Al-Wāqidī (d. 207/823) composed a book on the subject of *al-maghāzī*; the term had come to signify in particular the expeditions and raids of the Medinan period, but was extended to cover the general field of the Prophet's biography (Hinds, 'al-Maghāzī'; Raven, 'Sīra').
39. NM-A, pp. 215–16.
40. In the MS (f. 77a), the word appears to read *bāʾin*. Aḥmad and Khiḍr propose the reading *bustānī* (NM-A, p. 323, n. 1; NM-Kh, p. 251); al-Ḥadīthī, NM-Ḥ, p. 457, reads *bāghiyān*. I owe the further emendation to *bāghbān* to Jürgen Paul.
41. Al-Iṣṭakhrī, *Masālik al-mamālik*, p. 314 (*ammā lisān Bukhārā fa-innahā lisān al-Sughd illā annahu yuḥarrafu baᶜḍuhu wa-lahum lisān al-dariyya*); al-Muqaddasī, rather like al-Iṣṭakhrī, found Bukhara's language to be mixed, certainly not quite *darī* (*Aḥsan al-taqāsīm*, pp. 335–6). See further de la Vaissière, *Marchands sogdiens*, pp. 286–7; Treadwell, 'Political History', p. 56; and below, n. 43.

42. de la Vaissière, *Marchands sogdiens*, p. 287 ('il est possible que les connaissances sur le passé proprement sogdien de la ville soient alors en train de se perdre et qu'il faille en préserver la mémoire avant que les derniers témoins ne disparaissent').
43. Ibn al-Nadīm, *al-Fihrist*, I: i: 32. Citing Ibn al-Muqaffaᶜ as his source, Ibn al-Nadīm defines *dariyya* as the language of Madaᵓin ('the cities', the Arabic designation for the Sasanian capital of Ctesiphon), and the language in which persons at the royal court, after which it took its name, used to speak. In contemporary times, it was spoken by the people of Khurasan and the *mashriq*, and constituted the language of the people of Balkh. Cf. Marquart, *Ērānšahr*, p. 89; Pourshariati, 'The Parthians and the Production of the Canonical Shāhnāmas', p. 376; Meisami, 'Past in Service of the Present', pp. 262–3.
44. In the full narrative, the vizier declared the language of the Sijistani to be suitable for fighting (*qitāl*); that of the Nishapuri for legal argument (*taqāḍin*); that of the Marvazi for the vizierate (*wizāra*); that of the Balkhi for correspondence (*risāla*); and, in the culminating remark, that of the Herati for the privy (*kanīf*) (al-Muqaddasī, *Aḥsan al-taqāsīm*, pp. 334–5). Shaykh al-Islām Vāᶜiẓ, in enumerating the excellent qualities of Balkh, notes the sweetness of the inhabitants' speech and expression, and their use of Arabic idiom (*tarkīb-i ᶜarabī*) (Vāᶜiẓ, *Fażāᵓil-i Balkh*, pp. 45–6).
45. Vāᶜiẓ, *Fażāᵓil-i Balkh*, pp. 29–30. Cf. *GAL* II: 139; al-Ziriklī, *al-Aᶜlām*, VIII: 33 (al-Naḍr b. Shumayl).
46. Tor, 'Long Shadow', p. 155. Cf. Meisami, 'Past in Service of the Present'.
47. Cf. Volume II, Chapter 2.
48. He also cites an *āᵓīnnāmeh*; NM-A, pp. 162–3, 193, 281; see Volume II, pp. 53–5.
49. NM-A, p. 343. Cf. al-Taghlibī, *Kitāb al-Tāj*, pp. 173–4, where the titles appear in the forms *mūbadhān mūbadh*, *dabīrbadh* and *raᵓs al-asāwira* (p. 173). For *bazm-āvard*, see Nasrallah, *Annals*, pp. 149–50.
50. Compositions in the tradition of the *Shāhnāmeh* customarily group the kings of Iran into four successive dynasties: the Pishdadiyan, primordial kings, who in a mythological era oversaw the initial claiming of the world from demons and initiated human settlement; the Kayaniyan, a legendary dynasty; the Ashkaniyan or Arsacids, who pass virtually unmentioned; and, finally, the fully historical Sasanians. Integrated into this account is the Sistani cycle, tales of the exploits of the family of Sām, Zāl (Dastān), Rustam and Suhrāb, great heroes who perform the role of counsellors and protectors of the throne. As Dick

Davis has shown, Firdawsī's portrayal of kingship is rarely triumphalist, but rather highly subtle and complex (Davis, *Epic and Sedition*).

51. NM-A, p. 172. Aḥmad takes the Rustam in question to be the general (see n. 96), on whom see al-Ṭabarī, *Taʾrīkh*, II: 232. On the Tahirid connection with Rustam son of Dastān, see al-Masᶜūdī, *al-Tanbīh wa-l-ishrāf* ('Alerting and Oversight'), p. 347 (*Ṭāhir b. al-Ḥusayn b. Muṣᶜab b. Zurayf b. Ḥamza al-Rustamī min wuld Rustam b. Dastān al-shadīd*); cf. Bosworth, 'Heritage of Rulership', pp. 16–17; Tor, 'Long Shadow', pp. 152–3; Pourshariati, 'The Parthians and the Production of the Canonical Shāhnāmas', pp. 354–5.
52. NM-A, p. 348.
53. The reference is likely to be to the battle also known as Dhū Qār, one of the most celebrated battles (*ayyām*) of the Arabs, notable because it was fought against an army that included Persian forces. See al-Ṭabarī, *Taʾrīkh*, II: 193, 209–10, where the name of the Persian general rendered in Aḥmad's text as Hāmān is rendered as al-Hāmarz.
54. NM-A, pp. 348–9.
55. NM-A, p. 349. The reference is to Q. 27: 33, 'They said, We are possessed of strength and possessed of great courage' (*qālū naḥnu ūlū quwwatin wa-ūlū baʾsin shadīdin*). Pseudo-Māwardī's respectful and even admiring treatment of Rustam is in contrast to that in al-Ṭabarī, and resembles instead the accounts of Balᶜamī and Firdawsī (cf. Savant, '"Persians" in Early Islam', pp. 87–9).
56. NM-A, p. 349; Q. 61: 9 and 9: 33, 9: 40.
57. NM-A, pp. 76–7. Cf. Cook, *Commanding Right*, p. 475 and n. 37.
58. NM-A, pp. 114, 290–1.
59. 'Diversion and play' (*lahw wa-laᶜb*) constitutes a recurring theme in *Naṣīḥat al-mulūk*; see pp. 72, 196, 235. See also Ibn al-Muqaffaᶜ, *al-Ādāb al-kabīr*, in *Āthār Ibn al-Muqaffaᶜ*, p. 311.
60. NM-A, p. 380. Cf. Cook, *Commanding Right*, pp. 90–2 and passim.
61. On the identification of the Umayyads as 'Arabs', see Crone, *Nativist Prophets*, p. 20. An account in certain versions of the *Tārīkhnāmeh* ('History') of Balᶜamī records another example of 'the Arabs', this time sent by the Abbasids, in a Balkhi context (Crone and Jazi, 'Muqanna Narrative', I, Text p. 168 = Translation p. 175; II, p. 392). As Crone and Jazi note in this latter context, the designation indicates political loyalty, language and lifestyle, and not necessarily ethnicity (II: 392).
62. On this number and the reporting of numbers in general, see Crone, *Nativist Prophets*, pp. 7–8; Kennedy, *Armies of the Caliphs*, pp. 19–21.

63. After the *da*ᶜ*wa* had successfully overthrown the Umayyads, the second Abbasid Caliph al-Manṣūr ordered the execution of Abū Muslim, whose memory inspired several dissenting movements in the early Abbasid period; in many cases the adherents of these movements regarded him as a redemptive figure who would return. Cf. Yūsofī, 'Abū Moslem'; Crone, *Nativist Prophets*, passim.
64. I owe the reading of Abū Khālid al-Aᶜwar, as the name appears in the manuscript, as 'Abū [Dāʾūd] Khālid' to one of the anonymous readers for Edinburgh University Press.
65. On the composition of the Umayyad armies, see Kennedy, *Armies of the Caliphs*, esp. pp. 21–3, 42–51.
66. NM-A, p. 364.
67. MS Arabe 2447, f. 87b. On bridges near Balkh, see Ibn Ḥawqal, *Ṣūrat al-arḍ*, p. 475, where the bridge cited in *Naṣīḥat al-mulūk* is not mentioned.
68. Al-Ṭabarī, *Taʾrīkh*, VI: 454–64 (*sub anno* 91) = *History*, XXIII: 164–74. See further Barthold, *Turkestan*, p. 67.
69. Barthold, *Turkestan*, p. 65.
70. Esin, ' Tarkhan Nīzak or Tarkhan Tirek?', p. 329.
71. Al-Muqaddasī describes Siminjan as among the towns or urban districts of Balkh (*min muduniha*) (*Aḥsan al-taqāsīm*, p. 296), and notes the distances from Balkh to Khulm and from Khulm to Siminjan (p. 326). Cf. *Ḥudūd al-*ᶜ*ālam*, pp. 63, 108–9.
72. Le Strange, *Lands of the Eastern Caliphate*, p. 427; Barthold, *Turkestan*, p. 67; *Ḥudūd al-*ᶜ*ālam*, p. 338.
73. Al-Ṭabarī, *Taʾrīkh*, VII: 386–8; Vāᶜiẓ, *Fażāʾil-i Balkh*, p. 86. The account in *Fażāʾil-i Balkh* reads [l].S.r.ḥ.y.ā.n, probably Sarjanān, as in al-Ṭabarī, *Taʾrīkh*, VII: 387: 'They met at the River Sarjanan . . . and the generality of Ziyād's forces fell into the River Sarjanan . . . [Abū Dāʾūd] confiscated the possessions of the slain at Sarjanan and those who fled, Arabs and others alike' (*ijtama*ᶜ*ū* ᶜ*alā nahr al-Sarjanān . . . wa-waqa*ᶜ*a* ᶜ*āmmat aṣḥāb Ziyād fī nahr al-Sarjanān . . . wa-staṣfā amwāl man qutila bi-l-Sarjanān wa-man haraba min al-*ᶜ*arab wa-ghayrihim*). Ibn al-Athīr follows al-Ṭabarī almost verbatim (*al-Kāmil*, V: 383–5 (*sub anno* 130)). See also Daniel, *Khurasan*, pp. 86–7.
74. Al-Ṭabarī, *Taʾrīkh*, VII: 386–7 = *History*, XXVII: 105.
75. For the full account of these events, including the involvement of Judayᶜ al-Kirmānī, executed by Naṣr b. Sayyār, and his sons ᶜAlī and ᶜUthmān, both executed at the command of Abū Muslim, see al-Ṭabarī, *Taʾrīkh*, VII: 353–90

= *History*, XXVII: 61–109. See further Sharon, *Revolt*, pp. 173–4; Shaban, *ᶜAbbāsid Revolution*, pp. 159–63.

76. Vāᶜiẓ, *Fażāʾil-i Balkh*, pp. 86–9. The account appears in the author's treatment of Balkh's seventh shaykh, Mutawakkil b. Ḥamrān, one of the *tābiᶜūn*, Successors to the Prophet's Companions. Mutawakkil had assumed the judgeship of Chaghaniyan and later Balkh as well (85–6). Cf. Madelung, 'Early Murjiʾa', p. 38, n. 25.
77. Al-Iṣṭakhrī reports that Marv and Balkh had been the capital of Khurasan until the Tahirids joined them to Nishapur (*Masālik al-mamālik*, p. 258).
78. McChesney, 'Reconstructing Balkh', pp. 187–8; Azad, *Sacred Landscape*, pp. 2–4, 18–19.
79. Al-Iṣṭakhrī, *Masālik al-mamālik*, p. 278; Ibn Ḥawqal, *Ṣūrat al-arḍ*, II: 447–8. See also Schwarz, 'Bemerkungen', p. 439. According to Shaykh al-Islām Vāᶜiẓ, the urban population in his lifetime was exclusively Muslim, communities of Jews, Christians, Zoroastrians, *ahl-i dhimmat* 'and others', such as existed in other lands, being absent; he further mentions the absence of 'idol-worship' (*but-parast*) in the city (Vāᶜiẓ, *Fażāʾil-i Balkh*, p. 44). Further evidence of the Jewish community resident in the region of Balkh, Bamiyan and Ghazna has recently come to light in a cache of eleventh-century documents (Shaked, 'Early Persian Documents').
80. Al-Yaᶜqūbī, *Kitāb al-Buldān*, pp. 287–91.
81. It is of related interest that Balkh appears more than once in *Kalīla wa-Dimna*, the widely disseminated Arabic collection of animal fables derived in part from the Indian *Pañcatantra* (*Āthār Ibn al-Muqaffaᶜ*, pp. 164, 252); Pseudo-Māwardī knew this collection very well, and cited it and alluded to it in numerous instances; see Volume II, pp. 60–5 and passim. Balkh and Bami[yan] also appear in connection with contact with India (the sending of the game of chess to Nūshīrvān) in Firdawsī's *Shāhnāmeh* (*Le livre des rois*, VI: 307).
82. *Ḥudūd al-ᶜālam*, p. 108. See also van Bladel, 'Bactrian Background', p. 48.
83. On Kabul's role as an entrepôt for products from India, see Ibn Khurradādhbih, *al-Masālik wa-l-mamālik*, p. 38; al-Iṣṭakhrī, *Masālik al-mamālik*, p. 280; al-Muqaddasī, *Aḥsan al-taqāsīm*, p. 304.
84. On Ghazna, al-Iṣṭakhrī wrote, 'None of these towns in the environs of Balkh is greater in wealth and commerce than Ghazna, for it is the entrepôt of India (*furḍat al-hind*)' (*Masālik al-mamālik*, p. 280). Ibn Ḥawqal states that Ghazna's Indian trade did not suffer as a result of the incursions of Alptigin's army and the temporary severing of political links with India in 351/962 (*Ṣūrat al-arḍ*,

p. 450). The author of *Ḥudūd al-ᶜālam* wrote of Ghazna, 'It lies in Hindūstān and formerly belonged to it, but now is among the Muslim lands (*andar Islām-ast*). It lies on the frontier between the Muslims and the infidels' (p. 111); he also describes it as 'a resort of merchants'; cf. p. 346. Cf. al-Muqaddasī, *Aḥsan al-taqāsīm*, pp. 296–7, 303–4.

85. Nadwi, *Indo-Arab Relations*, p. 37; on the principal commodities involved in this trade from India, see pp. 39–41.
86. See Miquel, *La géographie humaine*, I: 153–89. Al-Muqaddasī described Ibn al-Faqīh's work in the introductory section to his *Aḥsan al-taqāsīm*, p. 4.
87. Of related interest, he also notes that the second clime, which stretched to Sind, near Kabul and Zabulistan, was a source of medicinal plants (*ᶜaqāqīr*), while the third clime, which began in Sogdia and Jurjan and ended in the lands of the Turks, from the borders of China to Egypt and up to Syria, Fars and Isfahan, was notable for the wisdom of some of its people, whom he describes as *nās ḥukamāʾ* ('wise people', p. 6).
88. *Mujmal al-tavārīkh*, p. 478.
89. Ibn al-Faqīh, *Kitāb al-Buldān*, p. 116.
90. Ibn al-Faqīh reports that Alexander (Dhū l-Qarnayn) built the city of Balkh (*Masālik al-mamālik*, p. 322). Yāqūt also states that it was Alexander who built Balkh, and that the city had been known as al-Iskandariyya in antiquity (*Muᶜjam al-buldān*, I: 479). The account appears in the various versions of Pseudo-Callisthenes; see Boyle, 'Alexander Romance', p. 19.
91. Ibn al-Faqīh records an account according to which when the daughter of the last Sasanian monarch Yazdagird was married to the Umayyad Caliph al-Walīd I b. ᶜAbd al-Malik (r. 86–96/705–15), she brought with her a basket that contained a book in Persian. The Umayyad governor of Iraq al-Ḥajjāj (b. Yūsuf, d. 95/714) called for the *dihqān* Zādān Farrukh b. Pīrī al-Kaskarī to translate it, and its contents included Qubād b. Fīrūz's assessment of his territories; seeking to build himself a city in which to settle, the monarch found thirteen places that seemed 'most pure' (*anzah*); among this number was Balkh (*Kitāb al-Buldān*, pp. 209, 236).
92. Among other accomplishments, Ṭahmūrath is reported to have built the citadel (*kuhandiz*) of Marv, the inner city (*shahristān*) of Babul, and Kardabad, greatest of the seven cities of Madaʾin (Ctesiphon) 'that are now in ruins' (*Mujmal al-tavārīkh*, p. 39). Notably, it was in the reign of Ṭahmūrath that, according to several reports, the figure of Būdhāṣaf appeared (Crone, 'Buddhism as Ancient Iranian Paganism', pp. 26–9); see below, pp. 82–3.

93. Rustam's exploits in Balkh include his battles with Afrāsiyāb (*Mujmal al-tavārīkh*, p. 49).
94. *Mujmal al-tavārīkh*, pp. 51–2. The author of this work identifies Zoroaster as the ninth son of Ibrāhīm (Abraham) (p. 92). Yāqūt cites a report according to which Luhrāsb, Gushtāsb's predecessor, had first constructed Balkh (*Mu*ᶜ*jam al-buldān*, I: 479).
95. *Mujmal al-tavārīkh*, pp. 54, 462.
96. van Bladel, 'Bactrian Background', p. 49.
97. Bulliet, 'Naw Bahār', pp. 140–5.
98. Bulliet, 'Naw Bahār'; Choksy, *Conflict and Cooperation*, pp. 4–5.
99. Beal, *Buddhist Records*, I: 39, 43.
100. Beal, *Buddhist Records*, I: 43–8. See also Frye, 'Sāmānids', p. 148.
101. Theravada or Hinayana Buddhism emphasises the individual nature of the Buddhist path that leads to nirvana; each individual possesses the potential to achieve nirvana, which cannot be gained other than by personal effort. The 'three jewels' (*triratna*) refer to the threefold Buddhist refuge: I take refuge in the Buddha, I take refuge in the teaching (*dharma*), I take refuge in the monastic order (*sangha*).
102. Fuchs, *Huei-ch*ᶜ*ao's Pilgerreise*, p. 26 [p. 449]. Paul Pelliot found the fragment that preserves Huei-chao's account at Dunhuang in 1908; the manuscript was subsequently deposited in the BnF ('Einleitung', pp. 3–4 (pp. 426–7)). I am grateful to John Moffett of the East Asian History of Science Library at the Needham Research Institute in Cambridge for assisting me in locating a copy of this publication.
103. Al-Yaᶜqūbī, *Kitāb al-Buldān*, pp. 289–90; al-Iṣṭakhrī, *Masālik al-mamālik*, pp. 275, 277, 283; *Ḥudūd al-*ᶜ*ālam*, p. 108; cf. p. 73.
104. Melikian-Chirvani, 'L'évocation littéraire', pp. 26, 30, 21; Crone, *Nativist Prophets*, pp. 121–8.
105. Beal, *Buddhist Records*, I: 49–53. The people, Xuanzang remarked, displayed 'a love of religion' 'from the highest form of worship to the three jewels', with 'earnestness and the utmost devotion of heart'.
106. Fuchs, *Huei-ch*ᶜ*ao's Pilgerreise*, pp. 25–6 [448–9]. See further Tarzi, 'History and Monuments', p. 658, and van Bladel, 'Bactrian Background', pp. 49–53.
107. Klimburg-Salter, 'Bāmiyān: Recent Research', p. 307.
108. van Bladel, 'Bactrian Background', p. 57. The same author observes that notwithstanding the presence of, or links with, Nestorian Christians and

Manichaeans, it was clearly Buddhism that predominated (van Bladel, 'Bactrian Background', pp. 53–5).

109. Al-Ya^c^qūbī, *Kitāb al-Buldān*, p. 289.
110. Kolesnikov, 'Information', p. 87.
111. Al-Iṣṭakhrī, *Masālik al-mamālik*, p. 280.
112. Ibn Ḥawqal, *Ṣūrat al-arḍ*, p. 450.
113. *Ḥudūd al-ʿālam*, p. 111; cf. pp. 346–7.
114. Al-Muqaddasī, *Aḥsan al-taqāsīm*, p. 304.
115. Khan, *Arabic Documents*, pp. 13–19; Khan, 'Newly Discovered Arabic Documents', pp. 201–15, esp. pp. 212–13.
116. Al-Nasafī, *al-Qand fī dhikr ʿulamāʾ Samarqand*, 238, No. 385; Vāʿiẓ, *Fażāʾil-i Balkh*, p. 132 (the Persian term for 'idol' is *but*). Paul cautions that whether or not the non-Muslim Turk represents a Buddhist monk, the story should not be taken to imply that the Karluks were all Buddhists at this time ('Islamizing Sufis', p. 312). On Shaqīq, see below, pp. 92, 141, 184, 231, 237–8.
117. Al-Yaʿqūbī, *Kitāb al-Buldān*, p. 289. In a reflection of the continuing status of the *dihqān*s, local landowners who played a significant role in the political and administrative life of the region, al-Yaʿqūbī describes the *shēr* as *rajul dihqān*; see further below, pp. 138–40.
118. For a discussion of the physical traces of Buddhism in Iran, see Vaziri, *Buddhism in Iran*, pp. 67–109.
119. Melikian-Chirvani, 'L'évocation littéraire', pp. 3, 33–4, 54 and passim.
120. Klimburg-Salter, 'Bāmiyān: An Obituary', pp. 5–6.
121. *Ḥudūd al-ʿālam*, p. 109.
122. Ibn al-Nadīm, *al-Fihrist*, II: i: 425 (following his account of Balkh). Ibn al-Nadīm records the names of Junbukt and Zunbukt for the two images.
123. Yāqūt, *Muʿjam al-buldān*, I: 330.
124. NM-A, pp. 196–7. Cf. Volume II, p. 131.
125. *Ḥudūd al-ʿālam*, pp. 108–9, 337–8, also p. 63. Minorsky interpreted the reference to the rock-dwellings as a reference to Dukhtar-i Nushirvan (p. 338).
126. Melikian-Chirvani, 'L'évocation littéraire', p. 23 and passim; cf. Azad, *Sacred Landscape*, pp. 77–86.
127. Albeit not in Buddhist contexts, the Barmakids appear singly and collectively in *Naṣīḥat al-mulūk* (NM-A, pp. 195, 224, 363–4).
128. Al-Yaʿqūbī, *Kitāb al-Buldān*, p. 288.
129. The name *barmak* perhaps derived from a Sanskrit word for 'chief' and applied to the head of a Buddhist monastery, as Bailey suggested ('Iranica', p. 2).

130. Narshakhī, *Tārīkh-i Bukhārā*, p. 67.
131. Al-Mas^{c}ūdī, *Murūj al-dhahab*, II: 228; cf. Marquart, *Ērānšahr*, p. 91.
132. See Schwarz, 'Bermerkungen', p. 443 and Vaziri, *Buddhism in Iran*, pp. 91–5. See further Vaziri, *Buddhism in Iran*, pp. 102–9.
133. Nadwi, *Indo-Arab Relations*, p. 68; van Bladel, 'Bactrian Background', pp. 64, 68. Yāqūt applies a similar term, *ustun*, to designate the 'dome' (*Mu^{c}jam al-buldān*, V: 307–8); cf. Melikian-Chirvani, 'L'évocation littéraire', pp. 2–3, 14–15; Azad, *Sacred Landscape*, p. 82. On the design of the Nawbahār, see further Beckwith, 'Plan of the City of Peace', p. 148, where, in a departure from the common interpretation of '*stupa*', the author proposes the emendation of *al-Ashbat* to *al-Athbat*, 'the most immovable', as a rendering of Acala, 'the Immovable'.
134. Ibn al-Faqīh, *Kitāb al-Buldān*, 322–3. See further Nadwi, *Indo-Arab Relations*, pp. 58–70; Melikian-Chirvani, 'L'évocation littéraire', pp. 11–19, 19–34.
135. As if it were self-evident, the Mu^{c}tazilite judge ^{c}Abd al-Jabbār (d. 415/1024–5) seems to imply that Buddhists deified the Buddha, as 'Copts', he held, had deified Pharaoh (*aqāwīl al-hind fī l-budd ma^{c}rūfa*, 'the doctrines of the Indians regarding the Buddha are well known') (*Tathbīt dalāʾil al-nubuwwa* ('Consolidation of the Proofs of Prophecy'), I: 106).
136. Crone, 'Buddhism as Ancient Iranian Paganism'.
137. For the sake of consistency, the spelling Būdhāṣaf will be adopted throughout, with the exception of transliterated passages.
138. Al-Mas^{c}ūdī, *Murūj al-dhahab*, II: 225–7; cf. I: 246.
139. Al-Bīrūnī, *al-Āthār al-bāqiya*, p. 204. See Crone, 'Buddhism as Ancient Iranian Paganism', p. 32; and below, p. 165.
140. See Tafażżolī, *Tārīkh-i adabīyāt-i Īrān*, pp. 301–2; Toral-Niehoff, 'Die Legende "Barlaam und Josaphat"'.
141. Crone, 'Buddhism as Ancient Iranian Paganism'. Crone suggests that the term *shamanān* also originated in this area. On the circulation of stories related to the life of the Buddha in Iran, see Vaziri, *Buddhism in Iran*, pp. 43–66, esp. pp. 43–54.
142. Al-Khwārazmī defines *al-budd* as 'the major idol of the Indians, to which they make pilgrimage; and every idol is called a *budd*' (*al-budd wa-huwa ṣanam al-hind al-akbar alladhī yaḥajjūnahu wa-yusammā kull ṣanam buddan*) (*Mafātīḥ al-^{c}ulūm*, p. 123). On usages of the terms *budd* and *but* (Persian), see Vaziri, *Buddhism in Iran*, pp. 36–7. On al-Khwārazmī's connections with Balkh, see Sabra, 'al-Khwārazmī'.

143. On al-Sāwī, see Kartanegara, 'Mukhtaṣar', I: 46–9.
144. ᶜUmar b. Sahlān al-Sāwī, *Mukhtasar Siwān al-hikma*, in Kartanegara, 'Mukhtasar', II, p. 142, No. 43.
145. Ibn al-Nadīm, *al-Fihrist*, II: i: 422.
146. Ibn al-Nadīm, *al-Fihrist*, II: i: 424–8.
147. Ibn al-Nadīm, *al-Fihrist*, II: i: 424–5. On the linking of *ᶜibāda* and *zuhd*, see below, pp. 181–6.
148. Ibn al-Nadīm, *al-Fihrist*, II: i: 428.
149. Al-Maqdisī, *al-Badʾ wa-l-taʾrīkh*, IV: 19. Crone, 'Buddhism as Ancient Iranian Paganism', p. 29, takes the *Kitāb al-Mamālik* to be that of al-Jayhānī. The assumption finds support in Gardīzī's explicit recognition of Abū ᶜAbdallāh Jayhānī as his source for information related to India (*Zayn al-akhbār*, pp. 612–13). It is possible that Ibn al-Nadīm's unidentified source was related to the work known under al-Jayhānī's name, or that a common source underlay Ibn al-Nadīm's source and al-Jayhānī's work.
150. Al-Bīrūnī, *Taḥqīq mā lil-hind*, pp. 57, 75. Al-Bīrūnī also reports *al-budd*'s assigning of the bodies of the dead to flowing water (p. 284). The limited nature of al-Bīrūnī's acquaintance with Buddhism, especially in comparison with his remarkable knowledge of other aspects of Indian culture, has surprised modern readers. Lawrence, 'Shahrastānī on Indian Idol Worship', p. 63 and n. 7, found al-Bīrūnī's failure to provide a comprehensive study of Buddhism 'baffling'. On the knowledge of Buddhism among writers in Arabic and Persian in the tenth and eleventh centuries, see further Lawrence, *Shahrastānī on the Indian Religions*, pp. 100–8, and Vaziri, *Buddhism in Iran*, pp. 135–66, passim.
151. On the term *zaᶜīm*, the legal scholar and secretary in the Mamluk chancery al-Qalqashandī (756–821/1355–1418) provides the definition *al-zaᶜīm al-kafīl . . . wa-yajūzu an yakūna bi-maᶜnā al-sayyid yuqālu li-sayyid al-qawm zaᶜīmuhum* ('the *zaᶜīm* is the person responsible . . . it is permissible to use the term in the sense of "leader", as it is said, the leader of a people is their *zaᶜīm*') (*Ṣubḥ al-aᶜshā*, VI: 51); cf. Picard, 'Zaᶜīm'. Closer in time to Pseudo-Māwardī, the theologian al-Baghdādī used the term to describe the leading figures of religious groups with whom he disagreed (see, for example, *Uṣūl al-dīn* ('Principles of Religion'), p. 335: 'Know that it is incumbent to consider every leader among the Muᶜtazila an infidel' (*iᶜlam anna takfīr kull zaᶜīm min zuᶜamāʾ al-muᶜtazila wājib*)). Al-Māwardī used the term repeatedly to denote the religious leader or founder of a religion (for example, 'It is incumbent

to establish a leader who will be the authority of the time and leader of the community' (*wajaba iqāmat imāmin yakūn sulṭān al-waqt zaᶜīm al-umma*), *Adab al-dunyā wa-l-dīn*, pp. 137–8); in some instances he too uses the term in a potentially pejorative sense ('In every religion, every one of its leaders has introduced an innovation', *fa-laysa dīna . . . illā . . . wa-kāna li-kull zaᶜīm fīhi bidᶜa, Adab al-dunyā wa-l-dīn*, pp. 137–8).

152. Al-ᶜĀmirī, *al-Iᶜlām*, p. 152; cf. Marlow, 'Kings and Sages', p. 54.
153. Azad, *Sacred Landscape*, pp. 68–100.
154. Al-Masᶜūdī, *Murūj al-dhahab*, II: 229. The use of *sulṭān*, apparently to suggest an individual, is perhaps anachronistic; cf. Chapter 3, p. 120.
155. See Thapar, *Aśoka*, pp. 250–66; cf. Shaked, 'Notes on the New Aśoka Inscription', pp. 118–22.
156. Bernard, 'Greek Colony', p. 124; Rapin and Hadot, 'Les textes littéraires grecs', pp. 259, 263. On the Hellenistic–Buddhist confluence in the region, see Haussig, *Die Geschichte Zentralasiens*, pp. 188, 198–9.
157. Al-Iṣṭakhrī, *Masālik al-mamālik*, p. 282, see above, p. 67 (cf. al-Iṣṭakhrī's glowing account of Transoxiana, p. 287); Vāᶜiẓ, *Fażā'il-i Balkh*, p. 29.
158. Yāqūt, *Muᶜjam al-udabā'*, I: 274. Most sources agree that al-Balkhī died in this year, although in two instances Ḥājjī Khalīfa reports the date of 340 (*Kashf al-ẓunūn*, I: 227, 602; cf. Bağdatlı, *Īḍāḥ al-maknūn*, II: 196; in one instance, he reports the date of 322 (*Kashf al-ẓunūn*, II: 1440; cf. *Keşf el-zunun zeyli*, I: 112).
159. The date of al-Kindī's death is uncertain; see Adamson, *Al-Kindī*, p. 4.
160. Adamson, *Al-Kindī*, p. 4.
161. NM-A, pp. 105–6, and see above, pp. 40–3.
162. Rosenthal, 'Abū Zayd al-Balkhī on Politics', p. 287.
163. Yāqūt, *Muᶜjam al-udabā'*, I: 277.
164. Biesterfeldt, 'Abū Zaid al-Balḫī', p. 159.
165. Yāqūt, *Muᶜjam al-udabā'*, I: 277.
166. Ibn al-Nadīm, *al-Fihrist*, I: ii: 430; Yāqūt, *Muᶜjam al-udabā'*, I: 275.
167. Barthold, finding no reports to indicate that al-Balkhī had returned to Balkh prior to the accession of Naṣr II b. Aḥmad in 301/914, when, if Yāqūt's dating is correct, he would have been approximately sixty-six years old, suggested that his travels may have lasted a good deal longer than eight years and that his return to his native town occurred only in his old age (Barthold, 'Preface', pp. 15–16).
168. Biesterfeldt, 'Die Zweige des Wissens: Theorie und Klassifikation der

Wissenschaften in der Darstellung des Ibn Farīġūn', Habilitationsschrift, Universität Bochum, 1985, I: 166, cited in Adamson, *Al-Kindī*, p. 12.

169. On the life and doctrines of al-Ka[c]bī, see El-Omari, 'Theology of Abū l-Qāsim al-Balḫī/al-Ka[c]bī'. El-Omari has demonstrated that the various, albeit antagonistic, perspectives of the theologians who recorded and refuted al-Ka[c]bī's doctrines permit a multifaceted reconstruction of his positions, and also facilitate the understanding of his situation in relation to other theological persuasions (pp. 5–6).
170. See El-Omari, 'Accommodation and Resistance'; on the *miḥna*, see above, pp. 40–4.
171. Significantly, Muḥammad's brother, predecessor and founder of the polity, al-Ḥasan b. Zayd, had supported both Shi[c]ite law and Mu[c]tazilite theology.
172. Yāqūt, *Mu[c]jam al-udabā[ɔ]*, IV: 1493. Cf. Madelung, *Der Imam al-Qāsim*, p. 77; van Ess, 'Abu'l-Qāsem Ka[c]bī', pp. 359–62; Anṣārī, 'Yek andīsheh-nāmeh', p. 13.
173. Al-Tawḥīdī, *al-Baṣā[ɔ]ir wa-l-dhakhā[ɔ]ir* ('Insights and Treasures'), VIII: 66.
174. van Bladel, 'Bactrian Background', p. 49.
175. Al-Iṣṭakhrī, *Masālik al-mamālik*, p. 316; Ibn Ḥawqal, *Ṣūrat al-arḍ*, pp. 492–3; al-Muqaddasī, *Aḥsan al-taqāsīm*, p. 278; Yāqūt, *Mu[c]jam al-buldān*, III: 246–50. See also Bosworth, 'Samarḳand', p. 1033.
176. According to al-Iṣṭakhrī, Tubba[c] of Yemen built Samarqand and Dhū l-Qarnayn completed part of it (*Masālik al-mamālik*, p. 318); Ibn al-Faqīh reverses the order, with Tubba[c] restoring Alexander's city to its former grandeur (*Kitāb al-Buldān*, pp. 325–6). Cf. Ibn Ḥawqal, *Ṣūrat al-arḍ*, p. 494; Yāqūt, *Mu[c]jam al-buldān*, III: 246, 247.
177. Ibn al-Faqīh and al-Iṣṭakhrī mention the existence of an inscription taken by the inhabitants to be in the Ḥimyarite language and linked to the founding role of Tubba[c] in the city. Al-Iṣṭakhrī reports having seen the inscription, located on the Bāb Kishsh, in person (*Masālik al-mamālik*, p. 318); Ibn al-Faqīh reports, on the authority of al-Aṣma[c]ī (d. *c.* 216/831), the existence of an inscription in Ḥimyariyya (*Kitāb al-Buldān*, pp. 325–6). Although no examples have survived, Samarqand probably possessed wall paintings as well (Karev, 'Qarakhanid Wall Paintings', pp. 47–8).
178. Al-Iṣṭakhrī, *Masālik al-mamālik*, p. 288; Ibn Ḥawqal, *Ṣūrat al-arḍ*, p. 465; al-Tha[c]ālibī, *Laṭā[ɔ]if al-ma[c]ārif*, pp. 161, 218 = Bosworth, *Book of Curious and Entertaining Information*, p. 140. Al-Tha[c]ālibī, incidentally, quotes *al-Masālik*

wa-l-mamālik for the information. Sharaf al-Zamān Marvazī, after noting 'In ancient times, all the districts of Transoxiana had belonged to the kingdom of China, with the district of Samarqand as its centre (*qaṣaba*)', remarks on the production of high quality paper remaining as a vestige of the earlier Chinese presence (Minorsky, *Marvazī on China, the Turks and India*, p. 18, § 18; see also Commentary, 67–8).

179. Al-Nasafī, *al-Qand fī dhikr ᶜulamāᵓ Samarqand*, p. 93, No. 112; p. 100, No. 132; p. 126, No. 190; p. 187, No. 288; p. 240, No. 388; p. 241, No. 389; p. 356, No. 586; p. 393, No. 664; p. 412, No. 703; p. 495, No. 862; p. 634, No. 1116; p. 654, No. 1144.
180. Al-Nasafī, *al-Qand fī dhikr ᶜulamāᵓ Samarqand*, p. 147, No. 227 (*khān al-khawāghidhīn*).
181. In his account of Samarqand, Xuanzang does not mention Buddhism, but comments on the city's prosperous and populous character (Beal, *Buddhist Records*, I: 32–3); Fuchs, *Huei-chᶜao's Pilgerreise*, 29 [452].
182. Al-Iṣṭakhrī, *Masālik al-mamālik*, p. 321.
183. Ibn Ḥawqal, *Ṣūrat al-arḍ*, p. 498; Bosworth, 'Samarḳand', p. 1032.
184. Colless, 'Nestorian Province', p. 52.
185. Ibn Ḥawqal, *Ṣūrat al-arḍ*, p. 493. See Paul, *Herrscher, Gemeinwesen, Vermittler*, p. 56 and n. 96 (with other references). Irrigation, as Paul has demonstrated, was among the primary areas that necessitated cooperation between the structures of power and society; *Herrscher, Gemeinwesen, Vermittler*, pp. 31–66.
186. *Ḥudūd al-ᶜālam*, p. 113; Commentary, p. 352. See also Monnot, *Penseurs musulmans*, pp. 97–8. The same author refers to Manichaean communities at locations in Tibet, Khaju and Saju (pp. 84–5).
187. Al-Muqaddasī, *Aḥsan al-taqāsīm*, p. 278.
188. NM-A, p. 325.
189. Crone and Jazi, 'Muqanna Narrative', II, esp. pp. 381–2, 396–401; and below, Chapter 6.
190. NM-A, 'Muqaddimat al-taḥqīq wa-l-dirāsa', pp. 13–31; see above, pp. 13–14 and n. 71.
191. Madelung, 'Spread of Māturīdism'.
192. van Ess, 'Abu'l-Layṯ Samarqandī', pp. 332–3. See also Pakatchi, 'Abū al-Layth al-Samarqandī', pp. 219–28.
193. Al-Samarqandī, *Tanbīh al-ghāfilīn*, p. 18 (Dhū l-Nūn); pp. 19, 20, 27 (Shaqīq); p. 26 (Sufyān al-Thawrī); pp. 15, 19 (*ḥakīm min al-ḥukamāᵓ*); the Persian text, followed by an Arabic translation, appears on pp. 25–6.

194. van Ess, 'Abu'l-Layt̲ Samarqandī', p. 333. Cf. Shaked, 'Andarz'; Safa, 'Andarz'; Marlow, 'Advice and Advice Literature'.

Chapter 3

1. See, for example, Crone, *God's Rule*, pp. 148–64; Arjomand, 'Medieval Persianate Political Ethic'; Arjomand, 'Salience of Political Ethic'.
2. See Gutas, 'Ethische Schriften'; Gutas, 'Classical Arabic Wisdom Literature'; Marlow, 'Advice and Advice Literature'; Leder, 'Aspekte arabischer und persischer Fürstenspiegel'.
3. On the advisory writings of these authors, see Marlow, 'Advice and Advice Literature'.
4. Pseudo-Māwardī, in accordance with common practice, employs formulaic expressions of glorification and benediction after mentioning God and His Prophet (see Gacek, 'Copying and Correction', p. 54).
5. This verse follows the verse that reads, 'It is God Who has subordinated the sea for you, so that the ships may course upon it by His command, and that you might seek His favour (*faḍl*), perchance you may be thankful (*tashkurūn*)' (45: 12). Pseudo-Māwardī's audience is likely to have associated the verse cited in the text with its predecessor. The terms *faḍl* and *tashkurūn* provide context for Pseudo-Māwardī's exploration of the concepts of favour and gratitude, which figure prominently in the subject matter of the present chapter.
6. NM-A, p. 61.
7. See above, n. 5.
8. Al-Ḥakīm al-Tirmidhī, *al-Riyāḍa wa-adab al-nafs*, p. 34.
9. In this passage, Pseudo-Māwardī alludes to the several Qurʾānic references to God's appointment or sending of 'armies', *junūd*, commonly interpreted as angels sent to provide invisible assistance to the Prophet and the first Muslims. See, for example, Q. 9: 26 (*thumma anzala llāhu sakīnatahu ʿalā rasūlihi wa-ʿalā l-muʾminīna wa-anzala junūdan lam tarawhā* ('Then God sent His peace of reassurance upon His Prophet and upon the believers, and He sent armies that you could not see')); 9: 40 (*wa-ayyadahu bi-junūdin lam tarawhā* ('And He supported him with armies you could not see')); 33: 9 (*fa-arsalnā ʿalayhim rīḥan wa-junūdan lam tarawhā* ('And We sent against them a wind and armies you could not see')) (al-Bayḍāwī, *Anwār al-tanzīl* ('Lights of Revelation'), pp. 382, 387, 123); cf. 48: 4, 7 (*wa-lillāhi junūdu l-samawāti wa-l-arḍ* ('God's are the armies of the heavens and the earth')). See also Nawas, 'Badr', pp. 196–7 (with reference to Q. 8: 9, 12).

10. On the meanings of *daʿwa*, see Canard, 'Daʿwa'.
11. NM-A, pp. 203–5. The ellipses mark a sequence of Qurʾānic quotations (6: 124; 22: 75; 4: 172; 82: 12, 13; 21: 20; 80: 15, 16; 81: 19–21; 4: 125; 20: 13; 28: 26; 12: 55; 19: 30–2; 68: 4; 4: 41).
12. See Adamson, *Al-Kindī*, esp. pp. 21–73, and Volume II, p. 102.
13. These doctrines and other Muʿtazilite features of Pseudo-Māwardī's mirror receive treatment in Part III of the present volume and in Volume II.
14. Al-Baghdādī, *Uṣūl al-dīn*, p. 295; al-Āmidī, *Abkār al-afkār*, IV: 225.
15. Ibn al-Nadīm, *al-Fihrist*, I: ii: 430; Yāqūt, *Muʿjam al-udabāʾ*, I: 275.
16. Cf. Mānkdīm (d. 425/1034), *Sharḥ al-uṣūl al-khamsa* ('Commentary on the Five Principles'), p. 780. (This work, properly titled *Taʿlīq Sharḥ al-Uṣūl al-khamsa* ('Notes to the Commentary on the Five Principles'), has been published and is cited here under the title *Sharḥ al-Uṣūl al-khamsa*. By the Zaydī ʿAlid Mānkdīm, it provides a compendium of Muʿtazilite doctrine; it is based on ʿAbd al-Jabbār's *Sharḥ al-Uṣūl al-khamsa*, which has not survived independently and from which Mānkdīm quotes extensively.) See also ʿAbd al-Jabbār, *al-Mughnī*, XV: 300–3, and for other contemporary discussions of *ʿiṣma*, see al-Ḥakīm al-Tirmidhī, *Thalātha muṣannafāt*, I: 105–6, 146, 182, 186, 188; al-Māturīdī, *Kitāb al-Tawḥīd*, pp. 14–15; Madelung, 'ʿIṣma', pp. 182–4.
17. On these doctrines and their appearance in *Naṣīḥat al-mulūk*, see Volume II, p. 83 and passim.
18. See, for example, NM-A, p. 92.
19. Mottahedeh, *Loyalty and Leadership*, pp. 178–9. Mottahedeh explains that the only category in which the king participated at all was the army, which, like the king, was overwhelmingly detached from special interests and not identified with the categories present in the population.
20. Marlow, *Hierarchy and Egalitarianism*, esp. pp. 66–90.
21. See Sadan, 'A "closed-circuit" saying', pp. 325–41; Pourshariati, *Decline and Fall*, pp. 342–4.
22. NM-A, p. 243. See also *ʿAhd Ardashīr*, p. 98, No. 16; al-Ābī, *Nathr al-durr*, IV: 233.
23. Cf. Darling, *History of Social Justice*, passim.
24. The major treatments of the idea and institution of *khidma* are Jurado Aceituno, *La 'ḫidma' selyuqí* (the present author has not seen this study), and now Paul, '*Khidma*'.
25. Paul, '*Khidma*'. I am most grateful to the author for providing me with a copy of this article before its publication.

26. Paul, '*Khidma*', pp. 397–408. See also below, p. 124.
27. Niẓām al-Mulk, *Siyar al-mulūk*, esp. pp. 138–60. This work is attributed to the vizier Niẓām al-Mulk, who was born in about 408/1018 or 410/1019–20 in Tus. His father, a native of Bayhaq, was employed as a tax collector under the Ghaznavids, who continued many features of Samanid political culture. The authorship of *Siyar al-mulūk* has occasioned long-standing doubts. A majority of scholars have accepted Niẓām al-Mulk's authorship, despite persisting questions surrounding his relationship to the surviving text, which, like the work entitled *Naṣīḥat al-mulūk* attributed to al-Ghazālī, is composed of two somewhat different parts; see Simidchieva, '*Siyāsat-nāme* Revisited'. The problem has recently received thorough study in the articles of A. Khismatulin, who has concluded that the author of *Siyar al-mulūk* foisted his work on the vizier in a case of 'forgery' ('To Forge a Book' and 'Art of Medieval Counterfeiting'). At the time of writing, Khismatulin's stimulating discussion has alerted scholars more fully to the problematic nature of the text, but has yet to find broad scholarly adoption. For purposes of the present project, whether or not Niẓām al-Mulk wrote *Siyar al-mulūk* is less important than its similarities with its Arabic predecessor.
28. Al-Iṣṭakhrī, *Masālik al-mamālik*, p. 291; Ibn Ḥawqal, *Ṣūrat al-arḍ*, p. 468.
29. Paul, 'Nachrichten arabischer Geographen', p. 190.
30. On the sense of *khādim* as 'eunuch', see Ayalon, 'On the Eunuchs in Islam', esp. pp. 74–89. On Ibn Khaldūn's view, see al-Sayyid, 'al-Māwardī', p. 87.
31. These *khadam* were responsible for the king's foods, beverages, clothing and mounts (Wakelnig, *Philosophy Reader*, pp. 344–7). The anonymous 'Philosophy Reader', probably the work of a member of the circle of Miskawayh, includes a lengthy section apparently by al-ᶜĀmirī (Wakelnig, *Philosophy Reader*, Introduction, pp. 4–7, 16, 21–2; see Commentary, 125–33; Text and Translation, pp. 313– 54, §§ 213–22). I am most grateful to the author for providing me with proofs of the *Philosophy Reader* prior to publication.
32. Lapidus, *History of Islamic Societies*, p. 63.
33. Crone, 'Maᶜūna'; Zakeri, *Sāsānid Soldiers*, pp. 173–5.
34. *Āthār Ibn al-Muqaffaᶜ*, pp. 346, 352, 356 = Pellat, *Conseilleur*, pp. 20–1, 38–9, 50–1. On this important example of advisory writing, see the studies of Goitein, 'Turning Point'; Latham, 'Ibn al-Muqaffaᶜ', pp. 64–72; Zaman, *Religion and Politics*, pp. 81–5; Zaman, 'The Caliphs, the ᶜUlamāᵓ and the Law', pp. 4–7; Lowry, 'First Islamic Legal Theory'; Kristó-Nagy, *La pensée d'Ibn al-Muqaffaᶜ*, pp. 213–66; and the edition and translation of Pellat, *Ibn al-Muqaffaᶜ . . . 'Conseilleur' du calife*. Cf. Volume II, pp. 9–10.

35. Cf. Montgomery, *In Praise of Books*, p. 140. On the *aᶜwān*, see below, pp. 131, 135 and passim.
36. Bayhaqī, *Tārīkh-i Bayhaqī*, p. 98 and passim.
37. Grignaschi, in his study of *Āʾīn li-Ardashīr* ('Ardashīr's Regulations'), takes the term *khadam* to represent a translation of the Middle Persian *parastār*, in general usage 'serviteur', but more specifically indicating service to the king at the court (Grignaschi, 'Quelques spécimens', Text pp. 91–2 = Translation p. 111). Grignaschi refers to the research of Geo Widengren, who, with particular reference to *Kārnāmak i Artaxšēr i Pāpakān* ('Book of Deeds of Ardashīr Son of Bābak', a short work that narrates the life of Ardashīr I [r. *c.* 224–240 or 242] in Middle Persian prose), indicated in the context of late antique Iran the requirement of a formal contract (*mihr* or *mihrān*) in the establishment of the status of vassal, and located parallels in the *Shāhnāmeh* (under the designations *manshūr*, *ᶜahd* and *nāmeh*) ('Recherches', pp. 84–5).
38. Étienne de la Vaissière has also noted parallels between the *ghulām* and the *chākar* (*Samarcande et Samarra*, pp. 59–88, esp. pp. 68–77; de la Vaissière, 'Čākar'). On the links between the Sogdian *chākar* and the *shākiriyya* of the Abbasid forces, see also Crone, *Slaves on Horses*, pp. 49 and 237, n. 354 (finding a near identity between *walāʾ khidma* and *shākirī*); Kennedy, *Armies of the Caliphs*, pp. 200–3.
39. Qazvīnī, 'Muqaddimeh-yi qadīm', p. 34. Following the terminology of Qazvīnī, who edited and published the text, and Minorsky, who translated it into English ('Older Preface'), this text is frequently referred to as the 'Older Preface' to the *Shāhnāmeh*.
40. Narshakhī, *Tārīkh-i Bukhārā*, p. 117.
41. Cf. Zakeri, *Sāsānid Soldiers*, pp. 79–91; Zakeri, '*ᶜAyyārān* and *Futuwwa*', pp. 748–9. For example, de la Vaissière emphasises that in Sasanian Iran, the lord's 'adoption' of his élite military personnel as foster-children was unknown; instead, it was the fiction of servitude that provided the symbolic affirmation of loyalty (*Samarcande et Samarra*, pp. 82–6, 82).
42. Cf. Daniel, 'Arabs, Persians, and the Advent of the Abbasids', pp. 546–7.
43. Al-Taghlibī, *Kitāb al-Tāj*, pp. 104–5.
44. NM-A, p. 390. Similarly cited on the authority of al-Wāqidī, the account appears in al-Ṭurṭūshī, *Sirāj al-mulūk*, II: 727–8, where the source states that the episode took place during the caliphate of Hishām (r. 105–25/724–43). See also Ibn al-Farrāʾ, *Rusul al-mulūk*, p. 34, where, on the authority of al-Wāqidī, the incident is said to have occurred during the time of Muᶜāwiya.

45. NM-A, p. 390.
46. On the concept of *ḥaqq* (pl. *ḥuqūq*), see Crone, *God's Rule*, pp. 281–2.
47. Paul's major study in this regard is his *Herrscher, Gemeinwesen, Vermittler*, to which, with other examples of Paul's research, I refer frequently in the following pages.
48. Khan, *Arabic Documents from Early Islamic Khurasan*, pp. 13–19; cf. Pourshariati, *Decline and Fall*, esp. pp. 33–59.
49. Bosworth dates this 'second' line of Saffarids to 297–393/911–1003; Bosworth, *History of the Saffarids*, pp. 267–339.
50. Treadwell, 'Political History', p. 194, n. 39; Barthold, *Turkestan*, p. 229.
51. See further Paul, *Herrscher, Gemeinwesen, Vermittler*, pp. 172–3; Mottahedeh, *Loyalty and Leadership*, pp. 48, 56 and passim.
52. Ibn al-Athīr, *al-Kāmil*, VIII: 87, 119.
53. Treadwell, 'Political History', pp. 107–8. As noted in Chapter 1, Isḥāq also minted coins in Samarqand and Nishapur in 301/914, the year of his attempted seizure of the senior amirate from Naṣr.
54. Gardīzī, *Zayn al-akhbār*, p. 324. On Aḥmad b. Sahl, see below, pp. 112–13.
55. *Tārīkh-i Sīstān*, pp. 290–4; Ibn al-Athīr, *al-Kāmil*, VIII: 60–1.
56. *Tārīkh-i Sīstān*, pp. 296–7.
57. The Kharijites, a diverse set of sectarians who resisted caliphal control and also diverged from the Shiᶜa, were active in Sistan in the ninth and tenth centuries (Bosworth, *History of the Saffarids*, pp. 67–9 and passim).
58. Abū ᶜImrān Sīmjūr had held the office of ceremonial ink-stand bearer (*dawātī*) to Ismāᶜīl b. Aḥmad; see *Tārīkh-i Sīstān*, pp. 293–4; Ibn al-Athīr, *al-Kāmil*, VIII: 60. On the meanings of *mawlā*, see Crone, 'Mawlā'.
59. See further Treadwell, 'Political History', pp. 148–9; Frye, 'Sāmānids', p. 141; Barthold, *Turkestan*, p. 241.
60. On these individuals and other figures involved in revolts against Naṣr, see Volume II, pp. 236–7.
61. Ibn al-Athīr, *al-Kāmil*, VIII: 80 (*sub anno* 301), 132–4 (*sub anno* 310); Gardīzī, *Zayn al-akhbār*, pp. 330–1; Treadwell, 'Political History', pp. 146–8. Naṣr II faced several further challenges; see Ibn al-Athīr, *al-Kāmil*, VIII: 78–9; and Volume II, pp. 236–7. Challenges from within the dynastic family included one mounted by Naṣr's brothers, whom he had imprisoned in Bukhara during an absence from the capital. In 317/929, one of the brothers, Yaḥyā, who had held the governorship of Samarqand in 306/918–19, was proclaimed amir, and attracted the support of another of Naṣr's former commanders, Muḥammad

b. Ilyās; Narshakhī, *Tārīkh-i Bukhārā*, pp. 130–1; Ibn al-Athīr, *al-Kāmil*, VIII: 208–12 (*sub anno* 317); Bosworth, 'Banū Ilyās', pp. 110–11; Treadwell, 'Political History', pp. 153–7.

62. Ibn al-Athīr, *al-Kāmil*, VIII: 134; Treadwell, 'Political History', pp. 146–8.
63. Abū l-Fażl Bal^camī secured the release from prison and restoration to favour of Muḥammad b. Ilyās of Kirman, described by Ibn al-Athīr as a companion (*ṣāḥib*) of Naṣr (*al-Kāmil*, VIII: 278; Bosworth, 'Banū Ilyās', p. 100); Abū ^cAbdallāh al-Jayhānī secured the release and return to Naṣr's service of the general Ḥusayn b. ^cAlī (Ibn al-Athīr, *al-Kāmil*, VIII: 88; see further below, n. 73). On another occasion, Bal^camī reportedly interceded for Ḥusayn's release (Bosworth, 'Bal^camī, Abu'l-Fażl Moḥammad', p. 573).
64. Ibn al-Athīr describes Sīmjūr al-Dawātī (see above, n. 58) as the 'father of the family of Sīmjūr, governors of Khurasan for the Samanids' (*wa-huwa wālid Āl Sīmjūr wulāt Khurāsān lil-Sāmāniyya*) (*al-Kāmil*, VIII: 60). See also al-Sam^cānī, *al-Ansāb*, VII: 351–5, 'al-Sīmjūrī', where Sīmjūr is described as *ghulām lil-Sāmāniyya wa-awlāduhu umarā^ɔ fuḍalā^ɔ*, 'military slave to the Samanids, and his sons were virtuous commanders' (p. 351); Bosworth, Sīmdjūrids', p. 612.
65. Qazvīnī Mustawfī, *Tārīkh-i guzīdeh*, pp. 379–81; Treadwell, 'Political History', pp. 168–70, 293, 298–9.
66. Narshakhī, *Tārīkh-i Bukhārā*, p. 39; Paul, *State and the Military*, p. 29.
67. Gardīzī, *Zayn al-akhbār*, p. 331.
68. Ibn al-Athīr, *al-Kāmil*, VIII: 87, cf. VIII: 119.
69. On these events, see *Tārīkh-i Sīstān*, pp. 294–305; Gardīzī, *Zayn al-akhbār*, pp. 326, 331; Ibn al-Athīr, *al-Kāmil*, VIII: 69–70 (*sub anno* 300), 87–9 (*sub anno* 302); Mīrkhwānd, *Rawżat al-ṣafā^ɔ*, IV: 40; Treadwell, 'Political History', p. 110 and n. 33, pp. 148–9, 151. According to *Tārīkh-i Sīstān*, on his release from the citadel Manṣūr left for Khurasan, and remarked that he had escaped from hell and reached paradise, and had no need of Sistan (p. 301).
70. See Stern, 'Early Ismā^cīlī Missionaries', pp. 77–9. On Ḥusayn b. ^cAlī, see Treadwell, 'Political History', pp. 110, 137, 326–8.
71. Ibn al-Athīr, *al-Kāmil*, VIII: 118. On Aḥmad b. Sahl, see Paul, 'Aḥmad b. Sahl'; Treadwell, 'Political History', p. 111 and n. 40, pp. 313–14; Bosworth, 'Aḥmad b. Sahl b. Hāšem'; and below, pp. 140–1.
72. Vasmer, 'Beiträge', pp. 58–9 (the article also discusses coins minted with the single name Aḥmad, some of which are likely to refer to Aḥmad b. Sahl); Zambaur, *Münzprägungen*, I: 54 (Andarab), 76 and n. 6 (Balkh), dated 303 in both locations.

73. Ibn al-Athīr, *al-Kāmil*, VIII: 88 (*sub anno* 302). Al-Thaᶜālibī refers to Ḥusayn b. ᶜAlī's poems on the subject of his conflict with Aḥmad b. Sahl, as well as his poems composed for other occasions, including his release from prison in Herat with the assistance of Abū l-Faḍl al-Bilghamī [= al-Balᶜamī] (*Yatīmat al-dahr*, IV: 96–7; for a translation of this poem, see Treadwell, 'Political History', p. 190, n. 24). Both viziers are named in this regard and it is not obvious whether the sources refer to the same occasion or whether the two viziers interceded for Ḥusayn on different occasions.
74. Ibn al-Athīr, *al-Kāmil*, VIII: 117–20 (*sub anno* 307); Barthold, *Turkestan*, p. 241; Treadwell, 'Political History', pp. 150–1. In a slightly later but analogous situation, Abū ᶜAlī Chaghānī, commander of the armies of Khurasan (*ṣāḥib jaysh Khurāsān*) would eventually revolt against Nūḥ b. Naṣr. In this case, Ibn Ḥawqal describes Abū ᶜAlī's virtues, but considers his revolt to have exceeded the due limits: 'In Khurasan, there was no one like him among the cavalry in the military virtues of excellence, nobility, probity and lineage (*fa-lam yura . . . min al-uswāriyya ka-huwa faḍlan wa-nubulan wa-ᶜiffatan wa-aṣlan*) in his time, with leadership and governance; everybody witnessed this [excellence] from him. But he was not impervious to wickedness (*ghayr annahu khutima lahu bi-sharr*); for he manifested disobedience to his lord (*ṣāḥib*) and went to excessive lengths in extirpating his benefits' (*bālagha fī istiʾṣāl niᶜamihi*) (*Ṣūrat al-arḍ*, II: 477).
75. Paul, 'Nachrichten arabischer Geographen', p. 180.
76. NM-A, p. 61; see above, pp. 97–8.
77. NM-A, pp. 62–3.
78. NM-A, p. 63.
79. Ibn Ḥawqal, *Ṣūrat al-arḍ*, I: 3.
80. Cf. Badawī, *Platon*, pp. 152, 164 and passim.
81. On the term *siyāsa*, see Arjomand, 'Perso-Indian Statecraft', p. 462.
82. Al-Muqaddasī, *Aḥsan al-taqāsīm*, p. 307.
83. For the writings on *siyāsa* of al-Kindī and his students, see Volume II, pp. 7–8.
84. Wakelnig, *Philosophy Reader*, p. 338 = p. 9.
85. NM-A, pp. 63–4. Al-Thaᶜālibī would also mention the use of the term *arbāb* 'in the time of the (pre-Islamic) Khusrows' (al-Thaᶜālibī, *Ādāb al-mulūk*, p. 38).
86. ᶜAdī b. Zayd, *Dīwān*, pp. 84–92 (No. 16), p. 89, line 27; NM-A, p. 64, and n. 20.
87. Mānkdīm, *Sharḥ al-uṣūl al-khamsa*, pp. 48, 232–61; van Ess, *Erkenntnislehre*, pp. 79, 166–7; al-Māturīdī, *Kitāb al-Tawḥīd*, pp. 120–34, esp. 127–9,

Rudolph, *Al-Māturīdī*, p. 326; Horten, *Die Philosophie des abu Raschíd*, p. 27; al-Ashʿarī, *Maqālāt*, I: 171–3 (*al-ruʾya*).

88. Al-Māturīdī, *Kitāb al-Tawḥīd*, p. 127; Rudolph, *Al-Māturīdī*, p. 326. On al-Māturīdī, see above, p. 91.
89. Mānkdīm, *Sharḥ al-uṣūl al-khamsa*, pp. 233, 262–5.
90. On the Muʿtazilite inflexions of these terms, see van Ess, *Erkenntnislehre*, pp. 91, 188. On reason (*ʿaql*) and the senses, see the Muʿtazilite ʿAbd al-Jabbār, *al-Mughnī*, XII: 58.
91. An Abbasid general, renowned for his generosity; he played an important role in securing al-Maʾmūn's caliphate against the challenge of his uncle Ibrāhīm b. al-Mahdī (162–224/779–839) (see Cooperson, *Al-Maʾmun*, pp. 67, 71).
92. Cf. above, p. 91; in this case, the term denotes Caliph al-Maʾmūn (Cooperson, *Classical Arabic Biography*, pp. 27, 34–5, 67–8).
93. NM-A, pp. 64–5.
94. Crone, *Pre-industrial Societies*, pp. 99–100; Al-Azmeh, *Muslim Kingship*, pp. 115–31.
95. As a rule, the term seems to have implied status rather than official investiture (Paul, 'Histories of Isfahan', pp. 129–32; Paul, *Herrscher, Gemeinwesen, Vermittler*, pp. 77–87, 213–15 and passim).
96. The ḥadīth appears in al-Kulaynī, *al-Uṣūl min al-Kāfī*, *al-Kutub al-arbaʿa*, I: 40, § 178, *Bāb anna l-arḍa lā takhlū min ḥujja*, Nos 447, 451, 452, 453 (in the last and closest parallel, ʿAlī states, 'The earth is never devoid of a proof, and by God, I am that proof' (*inna l-arḍa lā takhlū min ḥujjatin wa-anā wa-llāhi dhālika l-ḥujja*)). The ḥadīth is also recorded in a *waṣiyya* of ʿAlī: *lā takhlū al-arḍ min qāʾim lillāh bi-ḥujjatihi liʾallā tabṭula ḥujaj Allāh wa-bayyinātuhu* (Abū Nuʿaym, *Ḥilyat al-awliyāʾ wa-ṭabaqāt al-aṣfiyāʾ* ('The Adornment of the Friends and the Generations of the Pure'), I: 80).
97. NM-A, pp. 65–6.
98. Its use to denote a single person in his environment is attested later in the century in al-Muqaddasī's *Aḥsan al-taqāsīm*, where Balkh is able to raise each year more than the amount needed by the *sulṭān*'s treasury (*khizānat al-sulṭān*) (p. 302), and the Samanids convened debates in the presence of the *sulṭān* in Ramadan (p. 339). Al-Muqaddasī also uses the term in a general sense ('We have only mentioned in our book a celebrated person, a reputed scholar or an illustrious ruler (*lam nadhkur fī kitābinā illā ṣadran mashhūran aw-ʿāliman madhkūran aw-sulṭānan jalīlan*) when absolutely necessary', p. 8). Al-Muqaddasī also refers to his service to the kings (*khidmatī lil-mulūk*) of his

time (p. 2), and the items he has found in the libraries of kings (*fī khazāʾin al-mulūk*, p. 3).

99. The couplet reads: *ḥujjat-i yektā khudāy va-sāyeh-yi ūst / ṭāᶜat-i ū kardeh vājib āyat-i furqān* ('He is the proof of the One God and His shadow / The verse of the Furqān made obedience to him obligatory') (*Tārīkh-i Sīstān*, p. 319). See further Ross, 'A Qasida by Rudaki', p. 220; Bosworth, *History of the Saffarids*, pp. 287–9.
100. Niẓām al-Mulk, *Siyar al-mulūk*, pp. 261, 263 = *Book of Government*, pp. 193, 194.
101. Anon., *Ḥudūd al-ᶜālam*, pp. 102, 112, 118, 121. Al-Bīrūnī (*al-Āthār al-bāqiya*, p. 39) similarly referred to the Samanids as *mulūk Khurāsān*, as well as to the *mulūk* of several other regions, such as the Jibal. Ibn al-Faqīh refers to *mulūk al-atrāk* ('kings of the Turks') (*Kitāb al-Buldān*, p. 329). Paul has established that the term *malik* implied a relatively high level of independence, and that, as Ibn al-Faqīh's usage indicates, it applied across ethnic and linguistic groupings ('Nachrichten arabischer Geographen', p. 182).
102. Paul, 'Nachrichten arabischer Geographen', p. 182.
103. Narshakhī, *Tārīkh-i Bukhārā*, p. 127.
104. NM-A, p. 88.
105. On the Muᶜtazilite perspective that perhaps underlies this passage, see van Ess, *Une lecture*, p. 54 (with reference to al-Naẓẓām); van Ess, *Erkenntnislehre*, pp. 129, 169. Pseudo-Māwardī returns to the theme of the king's common humanity with his subjects more than once; see also Volume II, pp. 203–4.
106. NM-A, pp. 66–9. On the interpretation of 34: 16, see Khoury, 'al-ᶜArim'. The reference evokes the domesticated landscape endowed with two luxurious gardens and irrigation systems, and the flood that caused the rupture of the dam of al-ᶜArim in *c.* 542 in the Yemeni city of Mārib; Gonzalez, 'Sheba', p. 586.
107. *ᶜAhd Ardashīr*, p. 56; Ibn Qutayba, *ᶜUyūn al-akhbār*, I: 8. Ibn Qutayba introduces the passage with the formula, 'I read in the "Book of *Āʾīn*" that one of the kings of the *ᶜAjam* said in an oration' (*khuṭba*). (On the 'Book of *Āʾīn*', see Volume II, pp. 53–5.) Ibn Qutayba cites this example directly after a quotation ascribed to Aristotle's correspondence with Alexander (*qaraʾtu kitāban min Arisṭāṭālīs ilā l-Iskandar*, 'I have read in something that Aristotle wrote to Alexander'), and follows it with a similar formulation associated with the Iranian heritage (*wa-naḥwahu qawl al-ᶜajam, wa-qālū*, 'This is like the saying of the Persians'). See also Muḥammadī, *al-Tarjama wa-l-naql*, p. 359.

108. Crone, 'Ethiopian Slave'; Abou El Fadl, *Rebellion and Violence*, pp. 120–2 and n. 72. See above, p. 122.
109. Mottahedeh, *Loyalty and Leadership*, pp. 66–96, esp. pp. 72–82.
110. Schacht, 'ᶜAhd'; Hallaq, 'Contracts and Alliances'; Böwering, 'Covenants'; see further Mottahedeh, *Loyalty and Leadership*, pp. 45, 47, 53, 61, 66–72, 193.
111. Niẓām al-Mulk, *Siyar al-mulūk*, pp. 138, 158.
112. In the later Seljuk period, the figure of Atsız supplies a compelling example of the retraction of the ties of *khidma*; see Paul, 'Sanjar and Atsız', pp. 81–129, esp. 89–93. On the contraction, retraction and re-establishment of relationships of *khidma*, see further Paul, '*Khidma*'.
113. NM-A, p. 316.
114. NM-A, p. 100: '. . . the saying of a king, a caliph or an amir' (*bi-qawli malikin min al-mulūk aw khalīfatin min al-khulafāʾ aw amīrin min al-umarāʾ*).
115. NM-A, p. 154.
116. NM-A, p. 150.
117. NM-A, p. 106. Niẓām al-Mulk referred regularly to the Samanid senior amir as *amīr-i Khurāsān* (*Siyar al-mulūk*, pp. 144, 150, 287 and passim).
118. NM-A, p. 107. See Chapter 1, p. 47.
119. NM-A, p. 159. The payment of *zakāt*, one of the five pillars of Islam, is a religious obligation; the payment of additional charitable donations in the form of *ṣadaqa* is sometimes considered voluntary, but sometimes obligatory (see Zysow, 'Zakāt'; Weir [Zysow], 'Ṣadaḳa'). Cf. Volume II, p. 188–9.
120. Paul notes several indications that individuals described as *umarāʾ* paid no land tax (*kharāj*) to the Samanid senior amirs, and rendered only 'gifts'; 'Nachrichten arabischer Geographen', p. 183.

Chapter 4

1. I borrow this felicitous phrasing from Julia Bray ('Ibn al-Muᶜtazz and Politics', p. 143).
2. Paul, *Herrscher, Gemeinwesen, Vermittler*, pp. 147–233.
3. It is possible that, in a parallel to the *khazāʾin* and *buyūt* of the following clause, Pseudo-Māwardī's *manzila* and *manāzil* refer to physical places of residence, possibly as large as urban neighbourhoods, rather than social stations; Pseudo-Māwardī perhaps intends the social and the residential connotations of the term.
4. Christopher Melchert advises that the phrase is likely to signify 'political advisers', since *raʾy* retained its positive connotations in political contexts long after

it had lost them in juristic and theological matters; I am grateful for this communication. See further Melchert, 'Traditionist-Jurisprudents', pp. 386–7.

5. NM-A, pp. 253–4. On *umma* and *milla* see below, pp. 143–4.
6. Paul, *Herrscher, Gemeinwesen, Vermittler*, pp. 2–7, 237–51. The evidence of *Tārīkh-i Bayhaq* speaks especially eloquently of the prominence of ᶜAlid families; see Ibn Funduq, *Tārīkh-i Bayhaq*, pp. 54–65, 168, 169, 170, 179, 180, 186, 190, 221, 231, 232, 246, 250, 253–5, 284–6 and passim; see further *Herrscher*, p. 123, and Bernheimer, 'Rise of *Sayyids* and *Sādāt*', p. 46.
7. Cf. Paul, *Herrscher, Gemeinwesen, Vermittler*, pp. 6–7.
8. Cf. Mottahedeh, *Loyalty and Leadership*, pp. 82–93. Many historians have observed a general increase of *mamālīk*, and of their respective proportions in the ruler's armed forces, but, as Bregel observes, it is difficult to estimate their numbers (Bregel, 'Turko-Mongol Influences', pp. 57–8). The shift, whatever its degree, perhaps corresponds to the larger trend of decreasing direct contact between the ruler and the ruled from the earlier to the later Samanid period (Paul, *Herrscher, Gemeinwesen, Vermittler*, pp. 251–60).
9. Tor, in a re-examination of the matter, has stressed the limited extent to which *mamlūk*s replaced other groups within the amirs' armed forces ('Mamluks in the Military', pp. 213–24).
10. Niẓām al-Mulk, *Siyar al-mulūk*, p. 158.
11. Paul, *State and the Military*, esp. pp. 20–30.
12. See above, pp. 110–11.
13. In 381/991, Abū ᶜAlī Sīmjūri appropriated all the state revenues in Khurasan and assumed for himself the titles of *amīr al-umarāʾ* and *al-muʾayyad min al-samāʾ* (Bosworth, 'Titulature', p. 215).
14. Al-Iṣṭakhrī, *Masālik al-mamālik*, p. 292; Ibn Ḥawqal, *Ṣūrat al-arḍ*, p. 471. The language is that of Ibn Ḥawqal, who adds to his predecessor's text the *dahāqīn* and the reference to acquisition through purchase; al-Iṣṭakhrī wrote merely *fa-inna juyūshahum al-atrāk al-mamlūkūn wa-min al-aḥrār man yuᶜrafu dāruhu wa-makānuhu*.
15. For the passage in question, see Volume II, pp. 145, 163–5.
16. See above, p. 99.
17. See Zakeri, *Sāsānid Soldiers*, pp. 173–5. For the term *aᶜwān* in Abbasid contexst, see above, p. 104.
18. *ᶜAhd Ardashīr*, p. 52. Cf. Zakeri, *Sāsānid Soldiers*, pp. 176–7.
19. Grignaschi, 'Quelques spécimens', pp. 91–2 = p. 111 (*al-ahl wa-khawāṣṣ al-ḥidāth wa-l-aᶜwān wa-l-khadam*, 'family, close retainers, assistants and pledged

servants'). Grignaschi concluded that the *a*ᶜ*wān* were 'certainement les *ayyārān*' of Middle Persian texts.

20. Ibn Abī Dharr reports two instances of the term *a*ᶜ*wān* in ᶜ*Ahd Sābūr*. The first, cited through the *Khudaynāmeh*, links the categories of ᶜ*ummāl*, *a*ᶜ*wān* and *ahl mamlakatihi* (*Kitāb al-Sa*ᶜ*āda wa-l-is*ᶜ*ād*, pp. 296–7); the second links the *wuzarā*ᵓ and the *a*ᶜ*wān* (p. 443).
21. NM-A, p. 392. The passage appears in *al-Adab al-ṣaghīr*, in *Āthār Ibn al-Muqaffa*ᶜ, p. 325. Passages of a similar kind appear in the 'Epistolary Cycle' of Aristotle and Alexander (Maróth, *Correspondence*, p. 17 (*bi-ṣalāḥ al-a*ᶜ*wān wa-l-wuzarā*ᵓ *iṣlāḥ al-malik*, in *Waṣiyyat Arisṭāṭālīs*), p. 68 (*fa-hum wuzarā*ᵓ*ukum wa-a*ᶜ*wānukum* ᶜ*alā* ᶜ*adūwwikum*, in *al-Siyāsa al-āmmiyya*); Maróth reads *wuzarā*ᵓ and *a*ᶜ*wān* as parallel terms with the same meaning (Maróth, *Correspondence*, p. 89). On *al-Adab al-ṣaghīr*, see Zakeri, 'ᶜAlī b. ᶜUbaida al-Raihānī'; Volume II, p. 256, n. 35.
22. For example, Abū l-Fażl Balᶜamī played an important role in military as well as diplomatic activities during Naṣr's reign (Ibn al-Athīr, *al-Kāmil*, VIII: 125, 132, 263; Kirmānī, *Nasā*ᵓ*im al-asḥār*, p. 35).
23. NM-A, p. 350: '[The report] has reached me concerning a recent commander of the armies in this our time (*aḥad aṣḥāb al-juyūsh al-muḥdathīn fī* ᶜ*aṣrinā hādhā*), that the enemy clashed with him and faced him in many times his numbers. His military encampment faced the rising sun in the east, while the encampment of his enemy faced in the opposite direction. He therefore ordered his leading officer (*ṣāḥib*) to surprise the enemy by mobilising the armies and transferring them to a place where the sun would rise opposite them. He did so, and the enemy was forced to withdraw from his location and confront the sun in their eyes. Then he mounted and lay in wait for the enemy's men (*qawm*) until the sun rose in their faces; then he attacked them, and fought them, and that was one of the causes of his victory over them.'
24. See above, pp. 29–30, 33.
25. NM-A, pp. 323–34. The last category is related to the verse Q 29: 29 ('do not cut off the road [for travellers]'); on its meanings, see Abou El Fadl, *Rebellion and Violence*, pp. 51, 133. On the category of *mushrik*, see below, p. 154.
26. NM-A, p. 290; see Volume II, p. 241. On the avoidance of capital punishment, particularly with regard to the statutory penalties, see Rabb, *Doubt in Islamic Law*, pp. 114–23; cf. pp. 123–32.
27. Abou El Fadl, *Rebellion and Violence*, pp. 34–7, 40–6, 64–7 and passim.
28. Abou El Fadl, *Rebellion and Violence*, pp. 124–5, 127–30 and passim.

29. NM-A, p. 333; cf. p. 325, where he urges *wafā*ʾ, fulfilling the rights of and loyalty towards *ahl al-*ᶜ*ahd wa-l-dhimma*. See further Volume II, p. 203.
30. Paul, 'Nachrichten arabischer Geographen', pp. 187–8. Samanid Transoxiana was not, of course, the only period and region in which, as Paul has put it, 'the state had no monopoly in terms of power, even in the relatively narrow military understanding' (p. 191).
31. This reading follows Aḥmad, NM-A, p. 253.
32. Al-Iṣṭakhrī, *Masālik al-mamālik*, p. 290; Ibn Ḥawqal, *Ṣūrat al-arḍ*, p. 466.
33. Narshakhī, *Tārīkh-i Bukhārā*, p. 120.
34. Treadwell, 'Account of the Samanid Dynasty', p. 141 = p. 155, p. 139 = p. 154.
35. Ibn Funduq, *Tārīkh-i Bayhaq*, p. 285. On this history, see Meisami, *Persian Historiography*, pp. 209–29, and Pourshariati, 'Local Historiography', pp. 133–64; on its sources, pp. 133–4.
36. Al-Thaᶜālibī, *Ādāb al-mulūk*, pp. 152–3. On the Mīkālīs, see Bulliet, *Patricians*, p. 67.
37. Pourshariati provides the useful definition of the *dihqān* as a 'military landlord', presumably in the period following the reforms of Khusraw I (*Decline and Fall*, p. 500); see also Daryaee, *Sasanian Persia*, pp. 29, 54–5. The description of al-Samᶜānī, *al-Ansāb*, V: 423–4, for the epithet *al-dihqān* indicates the understanding of the term in his time: 'This term applies to persons who were prominent in a region and possessed estates and cultivated lands; a group in Khurasan and Iraq became well-known by [this epithet]' (*hādhihi l-lafẓa li-man kāna muqaddam nāḥiyatin min al-qurā wa-man yakūn ṣāḥib al-ḍay*ᶜ*a wa-l-kurūm wa-shtahara bihi jamā*ᶜ*a bi-Khurāsān wa-l-*ᶜ*Irāq*). On the *dihqān*s at the time of and in the aftermath of the conquests, see Zakeri, *Sāsānid Soldiers*, pp. 101–12 and passim.
38. de la Vaissière, *Marchands sogdiens*, p. 279.
39. de la Vaissière, *Marchands sogdiens*, pp. 280–1. With reference to *Kitāb al-Buldān* of al-Yaᶜqūbī, who, in his description of Samarra, consistently links but distinguishes between *al-jund*, the army and *al-shākiriyya* (pp. 259 (*quwwād Khurāsān wa-aṣḥāb[u]h[u]m min al-jund wa-l-shākiriyya*), 262 (*qaṭā*ʾ*i*ᶜ *al-jund wa-l-shākiriyya*), 268 (*dīwān al-jund wa-l-shākiriyya*) see further above, pp. 105, 135).
40. Al-Iṣṭakhrī, *Masālik al-mamālik*, p. 292; de la Vaissière, *Marchands sogdiens*, p. 283; *Samarcande et Samarra*, pp. 143–66.
41. Al-Iṣṭakhrī, *Masālik al-mamālik*, p. 323; Ibn Ḥawqal, *Ṣūrat al-arḍ*, pp.

499–500. Variants on the name include Kīs.fā, as in Ibn Ḥawqal (see al-Iṣṭakhrī, *Masālik al-mamālik*, p. 292 and n. b).

42. Bulliet, *Patricians*, p. 22.
43. Bosworth, *Ghaznavids*, p. 32.
44. *Tārīkh-i Sīstān*, p. 319; cf. Tafażżolī, 'Dehqān'. Ross, 'Qasida by Rudaki', p. 219, line 27.
45. Al-Nasafī, *al-Qand fī dhikr ᶜulamāᵓ Samarqand*, pp. 56, 57, 76, 140, 169, 201, Nos 31, 38, 81, 213, 260, 321.
46. Al-Nasafī, *al-Qand fī dhikr ᶜulamāᵓ Samarqand*, pp. 105–6, No. 148.
47. Al-Thaᶜālibī, *Ādāb al-mulūk*, pp. 153, 216. The listing of *dahqana* among the four primary functions probably implies the growing equation, in the course of the later tenth and eleventh centuries, of *dihqān*s with agricultural labour (cf. Paul, 'Where Did the *Dihqān*s Go?', pp. 20–2). Al-Sayyid has shown convincingly that the fourfold model of rulership, craftsmanship, commerce and agriculture is likely to have originated in Ḥanafī circles partly in response to interpretations of *tawakkul*, and partly in an effort to demonstrate the legitimacy of government and government service (al-Sayyid, 'Tamhīd', pp. 49–52; al-Sayyid, *Mafāhīm al-jamāᶜāt*, pp. 83, 89).
48. Paul, 'Nachrichten arabischer Geographen', pp. 184–5; cf. Paul, 'Histories of Samarqand', pp. 90–1 and n. 50. See also *Ḥudūd al-ᶜālam*, pp. 98, 99, 109 (where the term is rendered 'prince'); p. 116 ('The kings of Farghāna belonged formerly to (the class of) margraves and were called *dihqān*'), p. 117 ('Formerly the dihqāns in this province [Īlāq] were counted among the margraves' (*dihqān-i īn nāḥiyat-rā az mulūk-i aṭrāf būdandī*)). On *mulūk al-aṭrāf*, see further above, pp.121–2; see also al-Yaᶜqūbī's account of Bamiyan, p. 79 and n. 117.
49. Bulliet, *Patricians*, pp. 89, 201.
50. Al-Iṣṭakhrī, *Masālik al-mamālik*, pp. 291–2; Ibn Ḥawqal, *Ṣūrat al-arḍ*, p. 468 (*wa-dahāqīn mā warāᵓ al-nahr quwwāduhum wa-ḥāshiyatuhum wa-khawāṣṣ khadamihim li-luṭfihim fī l-khidma wa-ḥusn al-ṭāᶜa wa-l-hayᵓa fī l-malbas wa-l-zayy al-sulṭānī*).
51. Treadwell, 'Urban Militias', pp. 143–4.
52. See Volume II, Chapter 2.
53. Gardīzī, *Zayn al-akhbār*, p. 334. See also Ibn al-Athīr, *al-Kāmil*, VIII: 118; Mīrkhwānd, *Rawżat al-ṣafāᵓ*, IV: 40; Treadwell, 'Political History', pp. 124–5 and n. 101.
54. Pourshariati, 'Parthians and the Production of the Canonical Shāhnāmas', pp. 371–2. The name Āzādsarv is evocative of the pre-Islamic Iranian past: it

appears in Firdawsī's *Shāhnāmeh* at the beginning of the story of Rustam and Shaghād (see the discussion in Davidson, *Poet and Hero*, pp. 48, 71), and in an account of Buzurgmihr's sole ability to interpret Nūshīrvān's dream (Firdawsī, *Le livre des rois*, VI: 192).

55. They were *dabīrān*, secretaries, and *munajjimān*, astrologers, specialists in *ᶜilm al-nujūm* (astrology, a particular interest of Gardīzī's, as Meisami has indicated; *Persian Historiography*, p. 69). Their knowledge of astrology enabled them to predict, correctly, that they would all three be killed in a single day on account of the 'factionalism of the Arabs' (*taᶜaṣṣub-i ᶜarab*) (*Zayn al-akhbār*, p. 332). Ibn al-Athīr likewise reports that three of Aḥmad's brothers had been killed in Marv in 'the communal conflict (*ᶜaṣabiyya*) of the Arabs and the *ᶜajam*' (*al-Kāmil*, VIII: 118). Both authors also describe Aḥmad's imprisonment in Sistan at the hands of ᶜAmr b. al-Layth, whose deputy in Marv he had been. Ibn al-Athīr, *al-Kāmil*, VIII: 118, states that Aḥmad, in prison, had a vision of the Prophet Joseph, suggesting that, like Joseph, he was innocent and wrongfully imprisoned; Gardīzī narrates an elaborate story in which Aḥmad's sister Ḥafṣeh assisted him in devising a stratagem to escape from prison incognito (Gardīzī, *Zayn al-akhbār*, pp. 332–3).
56. As attested by the coinage issued in his name; see above, p. 113 and n. 72.
57. On Abū Zayd's relations with Aḥmad b. Sahl, see Yāqūt, *Muᶜjam al-udabāʾ*, I: 144–5, 147, 149 (for this episode, see p. 149); al-Ṣafadī, *al-Wāfī bi-l-wafayāt*, VI: 410–13 (pp. 411–12). On manners of address, including the avoidance of the ruler's patronymic, see Al-Azmeh, *Muslim Kingship*, p. 141; Cook, 'The Namesake Taboo'.
58. NM-A, p. 234.
59. Ibn al-Athīr, *al-Kāmil*, VIII: 119; see also Paul, *State and the Military*, pp. 27, 29.
60. Gardīzī, *Zayn al-akhbār*, p. 334.
61. Frye, 'Sāmānids', pp. 112–13; Frye, *Medieval Achievement*, pp. 32, 35, 43, 90–1, 156.
62. Bosworth, 'Sāmānids', p. 1029.
63. Paul, 'Where Did the *Dihqān*s Go?' (I am grateful to the author for providing me with a copy of this article prior to its publication).
64. Al-Nasafī, *al-Qand fī dhikr ᶜulamāʾ Samarqand*, p. 238; Vāᶜiẓ, *Fażāʾil-i Balkh*, pp. 130, 131. Cf. p. 79, above.
65. The term *zāhid* denotes an ascetic, a renunciant or a person committed to a life of austerity and moral integrity; the term is largely synonymous with *nāsik*, which, however, perhaps had a wider application, particularly with regard to

non-Muslim ascetics (see further below). In translated passages I have generally used 'renunciant' for *zāhid* and 'ascetic' for *nāsik*.

66. Radtke, 'Theologen und Mystiker', esp. p. 539, No. 9 (Ibrāhīm), p. 540, No. 12 (Shaqīq), p. 542, No. 19 (Ḥātim).
67. Paul, 'Histories of Samarqand', pp. 82–7; Paul, *State and the Military*, esp. pp. 20–30; Tor, 'Privatized Jihad'.
68. Although military activities at the frontier evolved into more professional and organised forms of warfare, even in later times, the initiative for campaigns did not always lie with the rulers, and *ghāzī* fighters had their own leaders (Paul, 'Histories of Samarqand', p. 87). On Ibrāhīm, see further pp. 179, 184.
69. See below, pp. 186–7.
70. It is conceivable that the author's choice of term is related to Persian *sarvar*; this term appears in ᶜAlī b. Zayd Bayhaqī's discussion of the *nuqabā-yi sādāt* in the formulation *sādāt Banī Hāshim va-sarvarān-i Baṭḥā* (*Tārīkh-i Bayhaq*, p. 253). See further below, p. 143.
71. Treadwell, 'Urban Militias'; cf. Paul, *Herrscher, Gemeinwesen, Vermittler*, pp. 123–7, and more generally pp. 98–102.
72. Treadwell, 'Urban Militias'.
73. In the political sense, Ibn Funduq describes the *bayt-i ḥukkām-i Mazīnān*, 'house of the rulers of Mazinan', of whom he writes that the Ghaznavid Sultan Maḥmūd b. Sebüktigin (r. 388–421/998–1030) gave the *riyāsat* (the office of *raʾīs*, urban leader) of Mazinan to Abū ᶜAlī al-Ḥasan b. ᶜAbbās, who had settled there; his sons became the *ḥukkām* of that district (*rabᶜ*; on this designation, see *Tārīkh-i Bayhaq*, pp. 34–5, and Pourshariati, 'Local Historiography', p. 149). They were 'men of fine qualities and manly virtue' (*mardumānī hunarmand va-bā-muruvvat*) (*Tārīkh-i Bayhaq*, p. 169). Ibn Funduq also frequently employs the term *ḥākim* when he refers to a jurist (*Tārīkh-i Bayhaq*, pp. 196–7, 206, 212, 214); on his ancestral house, see pp. 101–7. Cf. Pourshariati, 'Local Historiography', p. 142.
74. *Herrscher, Gemeinwesen, Vermittler*, pp. 91–2 and nn. 77, 78.
75. Bulliet, *Patricians*, p. 234.
76. Bernheimer, 'Rise of Sayyids and Sādāt'. On the *nuqabāʾ*, representative leaders, of the ᶜAlids in Bayhaq, see *Tārīkh-i Bayhaq*, pp. 253–5 (the Āl Zubāra feature prominently in this section and throughout the text).
77. See, for example, Q. 21: 92, 16: 120. As is well known, the *umma* of the Constitution of Medina includes the Jewish communities (Denny, 'Umma').
78. For the first version, see Abū Ḥanīfa (attrib.), *al-ᶜĀlim wa-l-mutaᶜallim* (Cairo),

p. 11 (*wa-lam yabᶜathhu li-yufarriqa l-kalima wa-yuḥarrisha al-muslimīna baᶜḍahum ᶜalā baᶜḍin*); the passage follows the mention of the Shiᶜa, Kharijites and the Murjiʾa. For the second version, in which the text 'instil discord' refers not to *al-muslimīn* but to, more inclusively, 'the people' (*al-nās*), see Riḍwān al-Sayyid, *Mafāhīm al-jamāᶜāt*, pp. 120–7, 120–1.

79. Abū Ḥanīfa (attrib.), *al-ᶜĀlim wa-l-mutaᶜallim* (Cairo), p. 11 = *al-ᶜĀlim wa-l-mutaᶜallim* (Aleppo), pp. 45–7 (additions between square brackets are from the Aleppo edition). This last passage is also cited by al-Sayyid (*Mafāhīm al-jamāᶜāt*, p. 121).
80. *ᶜAhd Ardashīr*, pp. 57, 63, and other utterances of Ardashīr (p. 95); al-Taghlibī, *Kitāb al-Tāj*, pp. 95–9. In *Kalīla wa-Dimna*, the term *zāhid* also appears occasionally. In Arabic tradition, Aristotle, like other Greek philosophers, was reputed to have pursued an ascetic way of life; the citation is from the anonymous author of *Nihāyat al-arab fī akhbār al-furs wa-l-ᶜarab* ('The Extremity of Desire on the Historical Accounts of the Persians and the Arabs'), p. 110, and see pp. 110–13. Given the prevalence of the term *zāhid* in the tenth-century *mashriq*, as well as these attestations of an association of *nussāk* with pre-Islamic antiquity, Pseudo-Māwardī's choice of term seems significant. Notably, his contemporary and probable fellow citizen Abū Zayd al-Balkhī wrote a book concerning *al-ᶜUttāk wa-l-nussāk*, 'Persons Pure and Ascetic' (Ibn al-Nadīm, *al-Fihrist*, I: ii: 430, following the emendation of *al-Futtāk wa-l-nussāk* in Biesterfeldt, 'Abū Zaid al-Balḫī', p. 161).
81. Following NM-A, p. 265; the editor rightly observes that the text of the MS is unclear (NM-A, p. 265, n. 54; MS f. 61b).
82. NM-A, pp. 264–5.
83. On the lands of the Āl Muḥtāj (also known as the Chaghānīs, see above, pp. 28, 57, 111), see Ibn Ḥawqal, *Ṣūrat al-arḍ*, p. 477. Bosworth has described the Chaghānīs' and the Sīmjūrīs' estates as 'virtually hereditary franchises' (Bosworth, 'Secretary's Art', pp. 116–17 and notes). Pseudo-Māwardī similarly supplies no indication that he wrote at a time when the granting of *iqṭāᶜāt*, grants of land, rather than salaries, had become a regular practice; see Volume II, pp. 166–8.
84. See Volume II, pp. 13, 16 and passim.

Chapter 5

1. NM-A, p. 45.
2. Golden, 'Karakhanids', p. 344.

3. See above, p. 66.
4. Golden, 'Karakhanids', p. 344; Canfield, 'Theological "Extremism" and Social Movements', p. 132; Daniel, *Khurasan*, p. 139.
5. See, for example, Crone, *Nativist Prophets*; Halm, *Kosmologie und Heilslehre*, pp. 142–3, 150.
6. Bulliet, *Conversion*, pp. 43–63; Bulliet, 'Conversion'.
7. See Chapter 2. Cf. Pourshariati, *Decline and Fall*, pp. 321–95, 417–20; Daniel, *Khurasan*, pp. 125–56; Bulliet, *Patricians*, pp. 14–19; Treadwell, 'Political History', pp. 48–63.
8. Paul has found little evidence to support the conjecture that Sufis were instrumental in Islamising the Turks of Central Asia ('Islamizing Sufis', p. 298).
9. *Ḥudūd al-ᶜālam*, p. 111, Commentary, pp. 346–8; al-Iṣṭakhrī, *Masālik al-mamālik*, p. 280; Ibn Ḥawqal, *Ṣūrat al-arḍ*, p. 450; Kolesnikov, 'Information', p. 87.
10. Al-Iṣṭakhrī describes Ghur as *dār kufr*, 'the Abode of Unbelief', and explains that he mentions it only because of the presence there of some Muslims (*wa-ammā al-Ghūr fa-innahā dār kufr wa-innamā dhakarnāhu fī l-Islām li-anna bihi muslimīn*), as well as in surrounding areas (*Masālik al-mamālik*, p. 272). At a later point, he describes the location as surrounded by *dār al-Islām*, 'the Abode of Islam', even though its people, with the exception of a few Muslims, are *kuffār* (*Masālik al-mamālik*, p. 281).
11. Al-Iṣṭakhrī, *Masālik al-mamālik*, p. 245 (*wa-hādhihi l-nawāḥī baᶜḍ hāʾulāʾi qad aslamū wa-baᶜḍuhum musālimūn*, '[In] these regions some of the inhabitants have adopted Islam and some of them live peaceably [with the Muslims]'); Ibn Ḥawqal, *Ṣūrat al-arḍ*, p. 419 (*wa-fī baᶜḍ hādhihi l-nawāḥī man qad aslama wa-hum musālimūn*). See further Kolesnikov, 'Information', p. 84.
12. Al-Muqaddasī, *Aḥsan al-taqāsīm*, pp. 336–7. Cf. Kolesnikov, 'Information', p. 86.
13. Contrary to this impression, *Fażāʾil-i Balkh* describes that city as devoid of the numerous non-Muslim communities that characterised other locations, although the period to which this description applied remains unspecified (Vāᶜiẓ, *Fażāʾil-i Balkh*, pp. 44–5).
14. See above, p. 144.
15. Ibn al-Nadīm, *al-Fihrist*, I: ii: 429.
16. The point recurs in the *Tafsīr al-Qurʾān al-karīm* of Abū l-Layth al-Samarqandī; see, for one example, the views of al-Ḍaḥḥāk and others on *yā ayyuhā alladhīna āmanū āminū bi-llāhi wa-rasūlihi* ('O You who believe: Believe in God and His Prophet', 4: 136) (II: 441–3).

17. For example, al-Masʿūdī, *Murūj al-dhahab*; al-Maqdisī, *al-Badʾ wa-l-taʾrīkh*; Ibn al-Nadīm, *al-Fihrist*. Cf. Khalidi, *Islamic Historiography*, esp. pp. 81–113; Tahmi, *L'Encyclopédisme musulman*, pp. 1–11; Marlow, 'Difference and Encyclopaedism'.
18. Cf. Monnot, *Penseurs musulmans*, pp. 110–18.
19. Ibn al-Nadīm, *al-Fihrist*, II: i: 378–403.
20. Cf. Tamer, 'Politisches Denken', p. 318.
21. Marlow, 'Difference and Encyclopaedism'.
22. See, for example, al-Maqdisī, *al-Badʾ wa-l-taʾrīkh*, II: 240–1 and passim. See further Tahmi, *L'Encyclopédisme musulman*, pp. 21–7.
23. Al-ʿĀmirī, *al-Iʿlām*, p. 167; cf. Monnot, *Islam et religions*, pp. 136–7 and n. 6.
24. See below, p. 156.
25. NM-A, pp. 333, 256.
26. Monnot, *Islam et religions*, pp. 83–96.
27. Ibn al-Nadīm, *al-Fihrist*, I: ii: 414, 512, 566, 574, 585, 597, 600, 608, 612, 645; I: ii: 512, 566, 586, 595, 600; I: ii: 512, 566, 574, 595, 600, 608, 619.
28. On al-Kindī's writings against the Manichaeans and others, see Adamson, *Al-Kindī*, p. 8; Akasoy, *Die erste Philosophie*, p. 26. This deployment of philosophy against other religious groups and perspectives did not deter the Muʿtazilite theologian and judge ʿAbd al-Jabbār from including al-Kindī in a list of persons 'in the Islamic dispensation' (*fī dawlat al-Islām*) who had composed works in rejection of prophecy; ʿAbd al-Jabbār also assimilated al-Kindī, with other individuals named in the previous context, to *al-bāṭiniyya* and *ṭabaqāt al-qarāmiṭa*, and associated him in a general fashion with 'these riffraff among the *zindīq*s of our time' (*hāʾulāʾi l-sufla min zanādiqat zamāninā*) (*Tathbīt dalāʾil al-nubuwwa*, II: 374, 508). See below, p. 156.
29. Ibn al-Nadīm, *al-Fihrist*, I: ii: 430. Cf. Biesterfeldt, 'Abū Zaid al-Balḫī'.
30. Al-Masʿūdī, *Murūj al-dhahab*, I: 94 (citing al-Kaʿbī's *ʿUyūn al-masāʾil wa-l-jawābāt*).
31. For the Muʿtazilite literature of refutation, see Ibn al-Nadīm, *al-Fihrist*, I: ii: 555–629. This industry was in part a response to the numerous refutations of which the Muʿtazila were the object. See also Schmidtke, 'Neuere Forschungen', pp. 382–3.
32. Ibn al-Nadīm, *al-Fihrist*, I: ii: 429; Yāqūt, *Muʿjam al-udabāʾ*, IV: 1491–2.
33. Ibn al-Nadīm, *al-Fihrist*, I: ii: 615. It is of related interest that Abū Zayd al-Balkhī and Abū l-Qāsim al-Kaʿbī, who appear to have enjoyed a lifelong friendship, also engaged in written debate with one another (Abū Zayd composed

a *Kitāb Ajwibat Abī l-Qāsim al-Ka*ᶜ*bī*, 'Book of Responses to Abū l-Qāsim al-Kaᶜbī') (*al-Fihrist*, I: ii: 430). The theologian al-Ashᶜarī (d. 324/935–6), ᶜAbd al-Jabbār, al-Baghdādī, the twelfth-century religious and philosophical historian al-Shahrastānī and the scholar and philologist Nashwān al-Ḥimyarī (d. perhaps 573/1178) made use of al-Kaᶜbī's *Maqālāt*, which provides an important indication of the context that produced *Naṣīḥat al-mulūk*. On al-Kaᶜbī's *Maqālāt*, see Ibn al-Nadīm, *al-Fihrist*, I: ii: 615; *GAS* I: 622–3; van Ess, 'Abu'l-Qāsem Kaᶜbī', p. 360; Madelung and Walker, *Ismaili Heresiography*, pp. 10–11. For the work itself, see the published extract in Fuʾād Sayyid (ed.), *Faḍl al-i*ᶜ*tizāl wa-ṭabaqāt al-mu*ᶜ*tazila* ('The Excellence of Muᶜtazilism and the Generations of the Muᶜtazila'), pp. 63–119.

34. ᶜAbd al-Jabbār, *Tathbīt dalāʾil al-nubuwwa*, II: 624–5. Al-Kaᶜbī also participated in a debate with a Jewish interlocutor (Ibn al-Nadīm, *al-Fihrist*, I: ii: 614; Yāqūt, *Mu*ᶜ*jam al-udabāʾ*, IV: 1492).
35. ᶜAbd al-Jabbār, *Tathbīt dalā*ᶜ*il al-nubuwwa*, I: 5. Cf. Monnot, *Penseurs musulmans*, pp. 43–51.
36. Monnot, *Islam et religions*, p. 137 and n. 2. See al-Māturīdī, *Kitāb al-Tawḥīd*, pp. 175–83, 216–68 and passim; cf. Madelung, 'al-Māturīdī', pp. 846–7; Vajda, 'Le témoignage d'al-Māturīdī'; Stroumsa and Stroumsa, 'Anti-Manichaean Polemics', p. 57.
37. Al-Māturīdī, *Kitāb al-Tawḥīd*, pp. 216–68; he argues, against the *sūfisṭāʾiyya*, that the true nature of things is fixed, and knowledge of them verifiable (*ḥaqāʾiq al-ashyāʾ thābita wa-l-*ᶜ*ilm bihā mutaḥaqqiq*, Abū l-Muᶜīn al-Nasafī, *al-Tamhīd*, p. 118).
38. Al-Māturīdī refutes al-Kaᶜbī specifically in his *Kitāb al-Tawḥīd* ('Book of the Doctrine of the Divine Unity'), pp. 78–82, 424–7, 469–79, 489–99, 504–8, 551–79. The writings to which he refers are al-Kaᶜbī's *Kitāb Awāʾil al-adilla* ('Book of the Primary Proofs'), *Kitāb Tahdhīb al-jadal* ('Book of the Discipline of Disputation') and *Kitāb fī wa*ᶜ*īd al-fussāq* ('Book on the Threat to Sinners').
39. Abū l-Muᶜīn al-Nasafī, *Tabṣirat al-adilla*, I: 22–4.
40. Abū l-Muᶜīn al-Nasafī, *Tabṣirat al-adilla*, I: 93–108 and passim.
41. For *ahl al-ahwāʾ* and *mulḥidūn*, I have provided both general translations and the more precise translations proposed in Bray, 'Local Mirror', p. 41 and nn. 22 and 23. Bray's translations draw on the definitions provided by al-Shahrastānī, who wrote in 521/1127–8. Although in several cases the stronger and more precise renderings would seem appropriate in Pseudo-Māwardī's much earlier text as well, it is difficult to assess his exact meaning, since he refrains from definitions

or identifications; for this reason I have sometimes provided, as in this instance, both a looser and a more precise term in rendering his vocabulary into English.

42. Al-Maqdisī, *al-Badʾ wa-l-taʾrīkh*, I: 1–8; Tahmi, *L'Encyclopédisme*, p. 26; Peacock, *Tārīkhnāma*, p. 42.
43. On the Ḥanafī usage of this title even before the lifetime of al-Māturīdī, see van Ess, *Erkenntnislehre*, p. 48.
44. Madelung, *Religious Trends*, p. 30.
45. Samarqandī, *al-Sawād al-aʿẓam*, p. 17; cf. Peacock, *Tārīkhnāma*, p. 46. References to the text are to the Persian translation.
46. Samarqandī, *al-Sawād al-aʿẓam*, pp. 17–19.
47. Samarqandī, *al-Sawād al-aʿẓam*, p. 19.
48. Samarqandī, *al-Sawād al-aʿẓam*, p. 19; cf. p. 22.
49. *Naṣīḥat al-mulūk* attests to the unfamiliarity of the religious culture to the *ghilmān* at the Samanid court in its advising of a consistent if rudimentary programme of instruction (see Volume II, pp. 163–5).
50. Samarqandī, *al-Sawād al-aʿẓam*, p. 166.
51. Samarqandī, *al-Sawād al-aʿẓam*, pp. 38, 46, 53.
52. Samarqandī, *al-Sawād al-aʿẓam*, p. 186. Andrew Peacock has argued that the Karrāmiyya perhaps provided the principal impetus for the tract's composition (Peacock, *Tārīkhnāma*, p. 47).
53. Bosworth, 'Karāmiyah'; cf. Melchert, 'Sufis and Competing Movements', and Malamud, 'Politics of Heresy', on the class-based marginalisation of the Karrāmiyya in Nishapur. For the Sasanian antecedents, see *ʿAhd Ardashīr*, pp. 60–1; cf. Shaked, 'Esoteric Trends', appendix D 'Secret Religion', p. 215.
54. Peacock, *Tārīkhnāma*, pp. 47–8.
55. Anṣārī, 'Yek andīsheh-nāmeh'.
56. NM-A, p. 157. See Volume II, p. 95.
57. Cf. Latham, 'Ibn al-Muqaffaʿ', pp. 49–50. On *zandaqa* as a social and religious phenomenon, see further van Ess, *Theologie und Gesellschaft*, I: 423–6.
58. Stroumsa and Stroumsa, 'Anti-Manichaean Polemics', p. 37.
59. Ibn al-Nadīm, *al-Fihrist*, II: i: 401–2, 406. In Ibn al-Nadīm's account, the 'king' conveys his personal adherence to Manichaeanism when he refers to the Manichaeans as 'the people of my religion' (*ahl dīnī*). Whatever the event that underlay Ibn al-Nadīm's account, the episode, as Monnot observes, cannot have involved the Samanids; the Kirgiz had destroyed the Uighur kingdom in 840, and Manichaeism was persecuted in China from 843 onwards (Monnot, *Islam et religions*, p. 130 and n. 2).

60. Anon., *Ḥudūd al-ᶜālam*, p. 113.
61. Al-Bīrūnī, *al-Āthār al-bāqiya*, p. 209 = p. 191. Outside the lands of Islam, al-Bīrūnī reports that most of the eastern Turks, the people of China and Tibet and some Indians followed Mānī's *dīn* and *madhhab*. For al-Masᶜūdī, it was Būdhāṣaf who was the first of the Sabians (*Murūj al-dhahab*, II: 226). Cf. Crone, 'Buddhism as Ancient Iranian Paganism'; Monnot, *Islam et religions*, p. 130 and nn. 2–3.
62. Abū l-Maᶜālī, *Bayān al-adyān* ('Clarification of the Religions'), p. 18.
63. Differently, Abū l-Maᶜālī regards the term as an Arabised form of Zandak, the name of a man from Fars (*Bayān al-adyān*, p. 22).
64. Al-Masᶜūdī, *Murūj al-dhahab*, I: 252–3, 275.
65. Al-Masᶜūdī, *Murūj al-dhahab*, I: 275. Monnot cites and translates the passage (*Penseurs musulmans*, pp. 309–10). Cf. de Blois, 'Zindīḳ', p. 510.
66. ᶜAbd al-Jabbār, *Tathbīt dalāʾil al-nubuwwa*, I: 170. Monnot, *Penseurs musulmans*, p. 278, reproduces the passage in translation.
67. Al-Samᶜānī, *al-Ansāb* ('Genealogies'), VI: 336–8.
68. Al-Khwārazmī, *Mafātīḥ al-ᶜulūm*, pp. 37–8.
69. Niẓām al-Mulk, *Siyar al-mulūk*, p. 259 = p. 191. Cf. Crone, *Nativist Prophets*, p. 249.
70. Mazdak, according to al-Bīrūnī, had claimed to be the author of the *tafsīr* and the *taᶜwīl* of the *Avesta* (Fück, 'Sechs Ergänzungen', p. 79). Cf. de Blois, 'Zindīḳ'; Monnot, *Penseurs musulmans*, pp. 98–101.
71. The Persian historian Abū ᶜAlī Balᶜamī, son of the vizier Abū l-Fażl Balᶜamī and also known as Amīrak Balᶜamī, became vizier towards the end of the reign of ᶜAbd al-Malik b. Nūḥ (r. 343–50/954–61) and retained office under Manṣūr b. Nūḥ (r. 350–65/961–76); he died between 382/992 and 387/997 (Khaleghi-Motlagh, 'Amīrak Balᶜamī').
72. Daniel, 'Sāmānid "Translations"', pp. 292–4; Meisami, *Persian Historiography*, pp. 23–37.
73. Crone, *Nativist Prophets*, pp. 176, 181, 208.
74. Abū l-Maᶜālī, *Bayān al-adyān*, p. 22. On *ibāḥa*, see Crone, *Nativist Prophets*, pp. 391–438.
75. Meisami, *Persian Historiography*, pp. 158–62; see also Yavari, *Advice for the Sultan*, pp. 32–7.
76. Ibn al-Balkhī, *Fārsnāmeh*, pp. 73, 76–7; Meisami, *Persian Historiography*, pp. 181–3.
77. Anṣārī also reached this conclusion ('Yek andīsheh-nāmeh').

78. Crone, *Nativist Prophets*, pp. 106–42.
79. Cf. Vaziri, *Buddhism in Iran*, pp. 29–39, esp. pp. 36–8.
80. Narshakhī, *Tārīkh-i Bukhārā*, p. 102; cf. Crone and Jazi, 'Muqanna Narrative', II: 394. See also Abū l-Maʿālī, who even a century after Pseudo-Māwardī cites the report of an individual whose female ancestor was the sole survivor of the conflagration (*Bayān al-adyān*, p. 60). For other accounts of his death, see Daniel, *Khurasan*, p. 143. Crone notes the possible Buddhist background reflected in the manner of al-Muqannaʿ's death (*Nativist Prophets*, pp. 133–4).
81. Daniel, *Khurasan*, p. 130; cf. Meisami, *Persian Historiography*, pp. 74, 160, 172, 183–5.
82. Crone, Nativist Prophets, pp. 144–51.
83. Al-Bīrūnī, *al-Āthār al-bāqiya*, pp. 204–14; Crone, 'Buddhism as Ancient Iranian Paganism', p. 32. On Ibn Abī Zakariyyāʾ, see Ażkāʾī, 'Taʿlīqāt', pp. 646–7.
84. The majority of sources report that al-Muqannaʿ's origins lay in Marv (Narshakhī, *Tārīkh-i Bukhārā*, p. 90; al-Maqdisī, *al-Badʾ wa-l-taʾrīkh*, VI: 97), and the tenth-century Ismaʿili heresiographer Abū Tammām refers to Hishām b. Ḥakīm with the *nisba* al-Marwazī (Madelung and Walker, *Ismaili Heresiography*, p. 76 = p. 75).
85. On al-Muqannaʿ's given name, see also Madelung and Walker, *Ismaili Heresiography*, p. 76 = p. 75; cf. Crone, 'Abū Tammām', pp. 168–9. For a full account of al-Muqannaʿ's early life and background, see Crone, *Nativist Prophets*, pp. 106–11. It is of some interest that the sudden death of Abū Dāʾūd Khālid in 140/757 occasioned some controversy, including the charge that it was the work of a certain grouping among the 'Wearers of White'. Gardīzī ascribes the murder to certain followers of Saʿīd-i Jūlāh, who was the *raʾīs* of the Sipīdjāmagān ('Wearers of White'); Gardīzī adds that this individual and his followers were captured and killed (*Zayn al-akhbār*, p. 273; cf. Crone, *Nativist Prophets*, p. 105).
86. See above, pp. 72–4.
87. According to *Fażāʾil-i Balkh*, the twenty-fifth shaykh of the city, Shihāb Ibn Muʿammar (203–96/818/19–908/9), a scholar and specialist in the transmission of ḥadīth, died in prison 'for religious reasons' (*bi-sabab-i dīnī*). His body was brought for burial to 'a place called Farrākhī-yi M.w.m.k (= Maydān-i M.w.m.k), which is Masjid-i Muqannaʿ'. The location acquired this latter name after a certain Muqannaʿ found a tablet of hard stone there amongst the old foundations and pillars, which he wished to remove. On hearing the voice of a great shaykh, who addressed him by his *kunya*, Abū ʿAbdallāh, and

warned him against disturbing and ruining the resting place (*marqad*) and tomb (*mashhad*) of Muᶜammarī, Muqannaᶜ replaced the tablets and built a wall there (Vāᶜiẓ, *Fażāʾil-i Balkh*, pp. 206–8, 207; cf. Daniel, *Khurasan*, p. 139 and n. 10; Azad, *Sacred Landscape*, p. 89). Conveyed on the authority of Muḥammad b. Abū [sic] Muṭīᶜ, the account does not specify the date of Muqannaᶜ's action, but it suggests that the site of the tomb of Shihāb Ibn Muᶜammar, who died in 296/908–9, had already fallen into disrepair.

88. Crone and Jazi, 'Muqanna Narrative', I: 164 = 172; II: 386, 404; Crone, 'Abū Tammām', p. 174; Crone, *Nativist Prophets*, pp. 112–13, 140.
89. de la Vaissière, *Samarcande et Samarra*, pp. 116–17, stresses this point and observes at the same time that al-Muqannaᶜ was not Sogdian.
90. On the taking of Samarqand, see certain versions of *Tārīkhnāmeh* (Crone and Jazi, 'Muqanna Narrative', I: 163 = 170; II: 381–2, 396–404). On the undated copper coinage, including the location of its production, see Kochnev, 'Les monnaies de Muqannaᶜ'; the enigmatic inscription on the coin (a *fels*) reads 'Hāshim walī Abā [sic] Muslim', 'Hāshim the friend of Abū Muslim' (pp. 143, 149); or perhaps more probably, *waṣī*, 'heir' or 'executor [of another person's will]' (Naymark and Treadwell, 'An Arab-Sogdian Coin', pp. 361–2, derive the inscription's sense as 'by the order of Hāshim, the executor of the will of Abī Muslim' (p. 361)). See further Crone and Jazi, 'Muqanna Narrative', II: 400; Crone, 'Abū Tammām', p. 170.
91. Crone and Jazi, 'Muqanna Narrative', II: 382, 406; 391–2.
92. Narshakhī, *Tārīkh-i Bukhārā*, pp. 92–101.
93. Crone and Jazi, 'Muqanna Narrative', I: 163 = 170; 164 = 171; 165 = 173; II: 384, 386, 395–6. See also Meisami, *Persian Historiography*, pp. 32–3; Meisami, 'Why Write History?', pp. 336–7. Similarly emphasising the political dimensions of al-Muqannaᶜ's movement, al-Khwārazmī attributes the name al-Mubayyiḍa, the 'Wearers of White', to the followers of Hāshim b. Ḥakam al-Marwazī due to their adoption of the colour white for their clothing, in opposition to al-Musawwida, the 'Wearers of Black', among the followers of the Abbasids (*aṣḥāb al-dawla al-ᶜAbbāsiyya*) (*Mafātīḥ al-ᶜulūm*, p. 28).
94. Crone and Jazi, 'Muqanna Narrative', I, p. 163, 1.5 and 2.1 = p. 170, 1.5 and 2.1.
95. Crone, 'Abū Tammām', pp. 168, 173–4.
96. On the life and writings of Abū Tammām, see Madelung and Walker, *Ismaili Heresiography*, pp. 1–12. For his detailed account of al-Muqannaᶜ and the revolt of the Sipīdjāmagān (*Tārīkh-i Bukhārā*, pp. 89–104), Qubāvī, a later

Persian adaptor of the text, supplements Narshakhī's report with materials drawn from various sources, including the *Tārīkhnāmeh* of Bal^{c}amī and the apparently otherwise lost *Akhbār-i Muqanna^{c}* of 'Ibrāhīm' (pp. 89–90), as well as the work of Abū Tammām. For a full analysis of the various accounts, see Crone and Jazi, 'Muqanna Narrative', II: 408–13.

97. Madelung and Walker, *Ismaili Heresiography*, pp. 10–14, 77, n. 177. Crone has demonstrated that al-Ka^{c}bī appears not to have included the Mubayyiḍa in his *Maqālāt* ('Abū Tammām', pp. 167–8).

98. Abū Tammām continues to relate that in every location (*balad*) the Mubayyiḍa had a leader (*ra$^{\circ}$īs*) drawn from the men of religion. They called this individual 'commander' (*farmānsālār*), and they met and conferred with him in secret (Madelung and Walker, *Ismaili Heresiography*, pp. 77–9 = pp. 76–7).

99. Narshakhī, *Tārīkh-i Bukhārā*, p. 103. Qubāvī writes as if he were drawing on his personal observation, but to a large extent his description displays a familiarity with Abū Tammām's account, presented in abbreviated form.

100. Al-Muqaddasī, *Aḥsan al-taqāsīm*, p. 323; al-Tha^{c}ālibī, *Ādāb al-mulūk*, p. 38. Cf. Kolesnikov, 'Information', p. 82; Crone, 'Abū Tammām', pp. 174–5.

101. Crone, *Nativist Prophets*, provides an exceptionally rich study of the beliefs and manifestations of the Khurramiyya; for a brief description, see pp. 22–7, 253. The term *dīn al-Khurramiyya* is first attested in Khurasan in 118/736. Akin to and probably related historically to Mazdakism, but attested over several centuries of the Islamic era and across a vast geographical area, Khurramism connoted the elimination of desire through the provision of equal access to women and property, with abstention from harm to any living being. Abū Muslim and other exponents of the Abbasid *da^{c}wa* recruited among Khurramis in Iran, and the connection continued in the emergence of individual religious figures and movements after Abū Muslim's execution (pp. 42–5 and passim).

102. Ibn al-Nadīm, *al-Fihrist*, II: i: 422. See further Crone, 'Abū Tammām', p. 174.

103. Niẓām al-Mulk, *Siyar al-mulūk*, p. 300 (*bāṭinīyān-i ḥażrat bi-sipīdjāmagān-i Farghāna va-Khujand va-Kāsān nāmeh nebishtand*) = p. 222. Cf. Crone and Treadwell, 'New Text'.

104. Al-Iṣṭakhrī, *Masālik al-mamālik*, p. 149.

105. See, for example, ^{c}Abd al-Jabbār, *Tathbīt dalā$^{\circ}$il al-nubuwwa*, I: 80; see further below.

106. Cf. Crone, *Slaves on Horses*, p. 64.

107. Halm, *Kosmologie*, pp. 9, 16.

108. The report derives from Niẓām al-Mulk (*Siyar al-mulūk*, p. 286 = p. 211);

cf. Daftary, 'History and Doctrines', pp. 112, 152; Stern, 'Early Ismāʿīlī Missionaries', pp. 62–3 = p. 198.

109. See Ḥamza al-Iṣfahānī, *Taʾrīkh*, pp. 182–3; al-Masʿūdī, *Murūj al-dhahab*, IV: 278–89. On Asfār b. Shīrūya's attraction to Ismaʿilism, see also al-Baghdādī, *al-Farq bayn al-firaq* ('The Difference among the Sects'), p. 267. On Mardāvīj's designs, see also al-Suyūṭī, *Taʾrīkh al-khulafāʾ* ('History of the Caliphs'), p. 390. Mardāvīj reportedly persecuted Ismaʿilis, probably in 321/933–4 during a campaign against the Samanids in Gurgan (see Treadwell, 'Political History', pp. 161–3, 189, 208–9; Stern, 'Early Ismāʿīlī Missionaries', pp. 63–7, 70–1 = pp. 198–204, 208–9).

110. Stern, 'Early Ismāʿīlī Missionaries', p. 82 = p. 223; Walker, *Abū Yaʿqūb al-Sijistānī*, p. 17.

111. Niẓām al-Mulk, *Siyar al-mulūk*, pp. 297–9 = pp. 220–1; cf. Treadwell, 'Political History', pp. 187, 329–30. Ismaʿilis promoted further unrest at Herat in the course of the tenth century. In one instance, 'the Qarāmiṭa' killed the *muḥaddith* (traditionist, specialist in the reports (*aḥādīth*, sing. *ḥadīth*) of the Prophet's *sunna*, normative practice) Abū Isḥāq Ibrāhīm b. Muḥammad al-Qarrāb in Herat (*al-Qand fī dhikr ʿulamāʾ Samarqand*, p. 45, No. 2); Faṣīḥ Khvāfī provides the date of 364/974–5, and states that he was killed in the street (*Mujmal-i Faṣīḥī* ('Faṣīḥī's Compendium'), II: 531); cf. Ibn Ḥajar al-ʿAsqalānī, *Tabṣīr al-muntabih* ('Alerting of the Attentive'), III: 1068.

112. Crone and Treadwell, 'New Text', pp. 61–7; Daftary, *History and Doctrines*, pp. 137–237.

113. Stern, 'Ismāʿīlī Propaganda and Fāṭimid Rule in Sind', esp. pp. 179–80, 183; Halm, *Das Reich des Mahdi*, pp. 341–7.

114. ʿAbd al-Jabbār, *Tathbīt dalāʾil al-nubuwwa*, I: 80; Monnot, *Penseurs musulmans*, pp. 279–80.

115. Stern suggested in a tentative fashion that whereas in Iraq, al-Bahrayn, Yemen and North Africa, the Ismaʿili missionaries sought broad support among the population and only then initiated revolts against the authorities, in north-western and especially north-eastern Iran, they concentrated their efforts on the conversion of members of the ruling élite (Stern, 'Early Ismāʿīlī Missionaries', p. 81 = pp. 222–3). See further Treadwell, 'Political History', pp. 186 ff; Crone and Treadwell, 'New Text'; Daftary, *History and Doctrines*, pp. 121–3. It has been suggested that the spate of conversions among the Samanid élites, including the conversion of the amir, perhaps represented a deliberate estrangement from the Abbasid caliphate; Meisami sees in Naṣr's conversion, as well as in

his patronage of Persian culture, a desire to distance himself from the Abbasids (*Persian Historiography*, p. 19).

116. Al-Nasafī, *al-Qand fī dhikr ʿulamāʾ Samarqand*, p. 203, No. 323. The passage appears in the entry on Abū ʿUthmān Saʿīd b. Ibrāhīm b. Maʿqil b. al-Ḥajjāj b. Khidāsh b. Naw Shabīr al-Raʾīs al-Nasafī, who 'consumed his life' (or whose life was consumed) (*afnā ʿumrahu*/*ufniya ʿumruhu*) in *taʿaṣṣub al-qarāmiṭa* ('the factionalism of the Qarāmiṭa [Ismaʿilis]') and who was 'afflicted with many tribulations' (*miḥan*) on that account 'until God made his religion triumphant', presumably a reference to the eventual suppression of the Ismaʿilis; cf. Paul, 'Histories of Samarqand', p. 90 and n. 49. If the final phrase refers to a specific incident, the account does not specify its date or location.
117. Treadwell, 'Political History', p. 110.
118. Gardīzī, *Zayn al-akhbar*, p. 331. Ḥusayn's release from prison was secured by Abū l-Fażl Balʿamī, according to al-Thaʿālibī, *Yatīmat al-dahr*, IV: 97, or by Abū ʿAbdallāh Jayhānī, according to Ibn al-Athīr (*al-Kāmil*, VIII: 88); see above, pp. 113. 289 n. 73. Cf. Treadwell, 'Political History', pp. 189–90; Stern, 'Early Ismāʿīlī Missionaries', p. 78 = p. 218.
119. On Ḥusayn's conversion and elevation to leadership of the *daʿwa*, see Niẓām al-Mulk, *Siyar al-mulūk*, pp. 285, 287–8 = pp. 210, 212; al-Baghdādī, *al-Farq bayn al-firaq*, p. 267. Cf. Treadwell, 'Political History', pp. 189–90; Stern, 'Early Ismāʿīlī Missionaries', pp. 77–8 = pp. 217–28; cf. pp. 60–1 = p. 195.
120. Treadwell, 'Political History', pp. 111, 190.
121. Niẓām al-Mulk, *Siyar al-mulūk*, p. 285 = p. 210; Stern, p. 78 = p. 217; Treadwell, p. 189, n. 19.
122. Niẓām al-Mulk, *Siyar al-mulūk*, p. 287 = p. 212. Niẓām al-Mulk also emphasises the activities of heterodox missionaries among the élites in his discussion of Mazdak, *Siyar al-mulūk*, pp. 257–8 = p. 190; on his approach to and conversion of Qubād, see *Siyar al-mulūk*, pp. 259–60 = 192.
123. Niẓām al-Mulk, *Siyar al-mulūk*, p. 288–9 = p. 213. Cf. Crone and Treadwell, 'New Text', pp. 52–8.
124. Niẓām al-Mulk, *Siyar al-mulūk*, p. 288 = p. 213.
125. Ibn al-Nadīm, *al-Fihrist*, I: ii: 429; and see below, p. 319, n. 34. At II: i: 405, Ibn al-Nadīm lists Muḥammad b. Aḥmad al-Jayhānī among the *zanādiqa*. On the dates of his vizierate, see Crone and Treadwell, 'New Text', pp. 54–5, n. 85.

126. Al-Thaᶜālibī, *Ādāb al-mulūk*, p. 169; Niẓām al-Mulk, *Siyar al-mulūk*, p. 299 = p. 222. See further Crone and Treadwell, 'New Text', esp. pp. 54–5.
127. On the various Muṣᶜabīs and their treatment in different sources, see Paul, 'Histories of Samarqand', p. 90, n. 49. Ibn Sawāda (Pesar-i Savādeh) is also mentioned in Niẓām al-Mulk, *Siyar al-mulūk*, pp. 288, 295 = pp. 212, 218. The relevant section of *Ādāb al-mulūk* has been translated and analysed in Crone and Treadwell, 'New Text', pp. 37–67; Julia Bray has provided an emended translation of parts of this text in 'Local Mirror', pp. 41–2. On the relevant material in Niẓām al-Mulk's *Siyar al-mulūk*, see Meisami, *Persian Historiography*, pp. 145–62.
128. On Abū Yaᶜqūb, see Stern, 'Early Ismāᶜīlī Missionaries', pp. 80–1 = pp. 220–2, and Walker, *Early Philosophical Shiism*.
129. Al-Thaᶜālibī, *Ādāb al-mulūk*, p. 171, § 460 (on the responsiveness to Ismaᶜili teachings of 'Abū Jaᶜfar Ibn Bānū, the father of Khalaf', namely, Abū Jaᶜfar Aḥmad b. Muḥammad); cf. Crone and Treadwell, 'New Text', pp. 57–8. On Abū Jaᶜfar's engagement with philosophy, see Dunlop, 'Philosophical Discussions in Sijistan'. On Khalaf's departure from his father's philosophical interests, see Bosworth, *History of the Saffarids*, pp. 292–4, 301–2, 328–37; Rowson, 'Philosopher as Littérateur', p. 85.
130. Ibn al-Nadīm, *al-Fihrist*, I: ii: 669.
131. Ibn al-Nadīm, *al-Fihrist*, I: ii: 668–9.
132. Al-Thaᶜālibī, *Ādāb al-mulūk*, pp. 168–71, passim; Niẓām al-Mulk, *Siyar al-mulūk*, pp. 282–311 = pp. 208–31, passim. See also Crone and Treadwell, 'New Text', pp. 38, 58–61; Bray, 'Local Mirror', pp. 41–2.
133. Aigle, 'La conception du pouvoir', p. 17.
134. Neguin Yavari has described this feature of mirrors as 'a combined denunciation of heresy with a subtle attack on fanaticism and dogmatism' (*Advice for the Sultan*, p. 7).

Chapter 6

1. Golden, 'Karakhanids', pp. 354–61.
2. See pp. 158–60.
3. Anṣārī, 'Yek andīsheh-nāmeh', pp. 12–13; cf. above, p. 48 and n. 116.
4. Paul, 'Histories of Samarqand', p. 88.
5. Zaman, 'Death, Funeral Processions, and the Articulation of Religious Authority', p. 36.
6. Al-Nasafī, *al-Qand fī dhikr ᶜulamāʾ Samarqand*, p. 216, No. 347.

7. Al-Nasafī, *al-Qand fī dhikr ᶜulamāᵓ Samarqand*, p. 211, No. 336. For further examples, see Paul, 'Histories of Samarqand', pp. 88–9; Paul, *State and the Military*, pp. 20–1.
8. Al-Nasafī, *al-Qand fī dhikr ᶜulamāᵓ Samarqand*, p. 298, No. 472.
9. Al-Nasafī, *al-Qand fī dhikr ᶜulamāᵓ Samarqand*, p. 187, No. 288.
10. Al-Nasafī, *al-Qand fī dhikr ᶜulamāᵓ Samarqand*, p. 209, No. 332.
11. Al-Nasafī, *al-Qand fī dhikr ᶜulamāᵓ Samarqand*, p. 276, No. 441.
12. Vāᶜiẓ, *Fażā'il-i Balkh*, pp. 246–8, 246; Radtke, 'Theologen und Mystiker', p. 545, No. 33. On Dāwūd, see also al-Nasafī, *al-Qand fī dhikr ᶜulamāᵓ Samarqand*, p. 148, No. 228.
13. Paul, 'Histories of Samarqand', pp. 84, 88; al-Nasafī, *al-Qand fī dhikr ᶜulamāᵓ Samarqand*, p. 183, No. 284.
14. Al-Nasafī, *al-Qand fī dhikr ᶜulamāᵓ Samarqand*, pp. 296–7, No. 471.
15. Al-Nasafī, *al-Qand fī dhikr ᶜulamāᵓ Samarqand*, p. 296; cf. Paul, 'Histories of Samarqand', p. 88.
16. Al-Nasafī, *al-Qand fī dhikr ᶜulamāᵓ Samarqand*, p. 671, No. 1182; p. 47, No. 5. This individual was known as M.ḥ.
17. See, for example, al-Dhahabī, *Siyar aᶜlām al-nubalāᵓ*, X: 684–5 (ᶜAbdallāh b. Ṭāhir).
18. Narshakhī, *Tārīkh-i Bukhārā*, p. 105; Ibn al-Athīr, *al-Kāmil*, VII: 456.
19. Al-Samᶜānī, *al-Ansāb*, VII: 25 (v. al-Sāmānī); al-Nasafī, *al-Qand fī dhikr ᶜulamāᵓ Samarqand*, 65, No. 60 (where the author mentions the four brothers in this order, and states that all of them related ḥadīth (*kulluhum yuḥaddithūna*)); *al-Qand fī dhikr ᶜulamāᵓ Samarqand*, pp. 587–8, No. 1035.
20. Mottahedeh, *Loyalty and Leadership*, p. 142; cf. Peacock, *Tārīkhnāma*, p. 23.
21. Al-Samᶜānī, *al-Ansāb*, VII: 24–5; Treadwell, 'Political History', p. 99, n. 129.
22. Al-Nasafī, *al-Qand fī dhikr ᶜulamāᵓ Samarqand*, pp. 469–70, No. 808; Paul, 'Histories of Samarqand', p. 88.
23. Al-Kaᶜbī, *Qubūl al-akhbār* ('The Acceptance of Transmitted Reports'), I: 229–44, passim.
24. NM-A, p. 375.
25. Al-Nasafī, *al-Qand fī dhikr ᶜulamāᵓ Samarqand*, pp. 587–8, No. 1035.
26. Al-Nasafī, *al-Qand fī dhikr ᶜulamāᵓ Samarqand*, p. 65, No. 60. The designation *kātib* in this period connotes a position closer to that of the vizier; cf. the description of Naṣr's vizier al-Jayhānī as *kātib amīr Khurāsān* in the *Risālat Ibn Faḍlān* (see above, p. 254, n. 38).
27. Al-Nasafī, *al-Qand fī dhikr ᶜulamāᵓ Samarqand*, p. 81, No. 92.

28. Al-Nasafī, *al-Qand fī dhikr ᶜulamāᵓ Samarqand*, p. 411, No. 700 (al-Amīr Abū Yaᶜqūb Isḥāq b. Aḥmad b. Asad b. Sāmān, on the authority of the judge al-Haytham b. Abī l-Haytham).
29. Al-Nasafī, *al-Qand fī dhikr ᶜulamāᵓ Samarqand*, p. 630, No. 1109.
30. Al-Dhahabī, *Siyar aᶜlām al-nubalāᵓ*, X: 684–5. Cf. Bosworth, 'Tahirids and Arabic Culture', esp. pp. 54, 58.
31. NM-A, p. 107.
32. Ibn al-Nadīm, *al-Fihrist*, I: i: 237, 216, 271; the work in question is a collection of ḥadīth that seldom occur. Abū ᶜUbayd was a grammarian, Qurᵓānic scholar and jurist; born in Herat, he was engaged as a tutor to two families in Khurasan, enjoyed the patronage of ᶜAbdallāh b. Ṭāhir in Baghdad, and died in Mecca.
33. Al-Nasafī, *al-Qand fī dhikr ᶜulamāᵓ Samarqand*, p. 65, No. 60.
34. Lamoreaux, *Early Muslim Tradition of Dream Interpretation*, p. 83; Kinberg, 'Qurᵓān and Ḥadīth', pp. 26–7 and passim.
35. Al-Nasafī, *al-Qand fī dhikr ᶜulamāᵓ Samarqand*, pp. 141–2, No. 215. Khiḍr, described as 'one of Our servants, unto whom We had given mercy from Us, and whom We had taught knowledge from Our presence' (*ᶜabdan min ᶜibādinā ātaynāhu raḥmatan min ᶜindinā wa-ᶜallamnāhu min ladunnā ᶜilman*), appears in Q 18: 60–82.
36. Al-Nasafī, *al-Qand fī dhikr ᶜulamāᵓ Samarqand*, p. 66, No. 60.
37. For the 'scholar-ascetics' involved in fighting on the Byzantine border, see Bonner, *Aristocratic Violence*, esp. pp. 107–34; Bonner, 'Some Observations Concerning the Early Development of Jihad', esp. pp. 402–15. Certain reports suggest that some individuals considered fighting at the Byzantine frontier to be more meritorious than engaging in warfare at the frontier against the steppe; see Bonner, *Aristocratic Violence*, pp. 108–9; Tor, 'Islamization of Central Asia', pp. 284–5.
38. Touati, *Islam et voyage*, pp. 249–58; Bonner, *Aristocratic Violence*, pp. 125–30; Tor, *Violent Order*, pp. 46–8; Paul, 'Histories of Samarqand', p. 82 and n. 36.
39. Paul, *State and the Military*, p. 13; Paul, 'Histories of Samarqand', p. 82; Touati, *Islam et voyage*, pp. 242–58; Tor, *Violent Order*, pp. 44–68; Tor, 'Privatized Jihad', esp. pp. 559–60, 567. See further above, p. 50.
40. Cf. Tor, 'Privatized Jihad'; Tor, *Violent Order*, esp. pp. 81–4, 85–116. In her studies of the *mutaṭawwiᶜa*, Tor observes that these individuals, who sometimes supported state-sponsored initiatives of *ghazw*, were nevertheless distinct from the *ghuzāt*. She notes the common ideology, in particular a devotion to

Prophetic tradition (ḥadīth), which bound the *mutaṭawwiʿa* to one another, and their distance from, and even antipathy towards caliphal authority, a feature that illuminates the rise of the Saffarids.

41. NM-A, p. 107.
42. Narshakhī, *Tārīkh-i Buhkārā*, pp. 118–19; and see above, p. 30.
43. NM-A, p. 107. Cf. Bonner, *Aristocratic Violence*, pp. 99–106.
44. Al-Nasafī, *al-Qand fī dhikr ʿulamāʾ Samarqand*, pp. 65–6, No. 60 (*kāna min afāḍil al-umarāʾ mimman yaʿdilu fī aḥkāmihi mushfiqan ʿalā raʿiyyatihi bihi yuḍrabu al-mathal fī ḥusn al-khulq wa-l-ʿishra wa-l-raghba fī l-jihād wa-qitāl al-kafara wa-kāna kathīr al-jund*, p. 65). Cf. Paul, 'Histories of Samarqand', p. 84. On Ismāʿīl's commitment to religiously associated warfare, see al-Ṭabarī, *Taʾrīkh*, X: 34; *Tārīkh-i Sīstān*, pp. 254, 256; al-Masʿūdī, *Murūj al-dhahab*, IV: 156; Ibn al-Athīr, *al-Kāmil*, VII: 533, 547; Tor, 'Islamization of Central Asia', pp. 282–4.
45. Narshakhī, *Tārīkh-i Bukhārā*, p. 118.
46. NM-A, pp. 52, and Volume II, p. 22.
47. Samarqandī, *al-Sawād al-aʿẓam*, pp. 17–18.
48. NM-A, p. 107; and see above, p. 47.
49. Al-Muqaddasī, *Aḥsan al-taqāsīm*, pp. 338–9. On this practice, see Al-Azmeh, *Muslim Kingship*, pp. 140–1.
50. Al-Khaṭīb al-Baghdādī, *Taʾrīkh Baghdād*, III: 317; cf. al-Subkī, *Ṭabaqāt al-Shāfiʿiyya*, II: 248.
51. Josef van Ess has discerned in this example an indication of the relative openness of the religious culture of Samarqand, despite the dominance of the Ḥanafīs (van Ess, *Theologie und Gesellschaft*, II: 566). Balʿamī enjoyed a close association with Muḥammad b. Naṣr, a possible indication, as the Syrian historian and theologian al-Dhahabī (d. 748/1348) would state explicitly, of the vizier's adherence (and perhaps that of the Balʿamī family) to the Shāfiʿī *madhhab* and a reflection of a less than uniformly Ḥanafī orientation among the political élites of the Samanid polity (al-Dhahabī, *Siyar aʿlām al-nubalāʾ*, XV: 292, No. 133 (*al-wazīr al-kāmil al-imām al-faqīh Abū l-Faḍl Muḥammad . . . al-Balʿamī . . . samiʿa Abā l-Muwajjah Muḥammad b. ʿAmr wa-l-faqīh Muḥammad b. Naṣr fa-akthara ʿanhu wa-lāzamahu muddatan wa-kāna ʿalā madhhabihi*)). Cf. Daniel, 'Sāmānid "Translations"', p. 284.
52. Al-Nasafī, *al-Qand fī dhikr ʿulamāʾ Samarqand*, pp. 65–6, No. 60.
53. Al-Nasafī, *al-Qand fī dhikr ʿulamāʾ Samarqand*, p. 66, No. 60.
54. Cf. Paul, 'Histories of Samarqand', p. 88.

55. Paul, 'Histories of Samarqand', pp. 89–90; Paul, *State and the Military*, pp. 20–3.
56. Al-Nasafī, *al-Qand fī dhikr ᶜulamāᵓ Samarqand*, p. 614, No. 1078.
57. Al-Muqaddasī, *Aḥsan al-taqāsīm*, p. 339.
58. Kinberg, 'What is Meant by *Zuhd*'.
59. Ibn al-Nadīm, *al-Fihrist*, I: ii: 662. On *taqwā*, see Volume II, pp. 76–88.
60. Ibn al-Nadīm, *al-Fihrist*, I: ii: 658–9.
61. Al-Jāḥiẓ, *al-Bayān wa-l-tabyīn*, III: 125–202, with sections on the *nussāk* and *zuhhād* of Basra and Kufa (pp. 193–202); Ibn Qutayba, *ᶜUyūn al-akhbār*, II: 261–376.
62. Cf. Hamori, 'Ascetic Poetry'.
63. NM-A, pp. 58, 75, 232; Hamori, 'Ascetic Poetry', pp. 268–9.
64. Ibn al-Nadīm, *al-Fihrist*, I: ii: 657–8. On Bishr, see Cooperson, *Classical Arabic Biography*, pp. 154–87.
65. Radtke, 'Ḥakim al-Termeḏi'. In the previous century, the warrior ascetic ᶜAbdallāh b. Mubārak of Marv (118–81/736–97) had composed a *Kitāb al-Zuhd wa-l-raqāᵓiq* ('Book of Austerity and Exhortations') (Ibn al-Nadīm, *al-Fihrist*, II: i: 97; cf. van Ess, *Theologie und Gesellschaft*, II: 551–5, 553); Muḥammad b. ᶜImrān al-Marzubānī (297–384/910–94) of Khurasan also wrote a treatise on the subject (*al-Fihrist*, I: ii: 413).
66. Muslim, *Kitāb al-Zuhd wa-l-raqāᵓiq*, 1231–51 (the latter term (sing. *raqīqa*) connoted stirring exhortation); Ibn Māja, *Sunan*, IV: 462–586 (*Kitāb al-Zuhd*); al-Tirmidhī, *al-Jāmiᶜ al-ṣaḥīḥ* ('The Comprehensive and Sound Collection [of Prophetic ḥadīth]'), III: 284–339 (*Kitāb al-Zuhd*); al-Dārimī, *Sunan*, *Kitāb al-Riqāq*, II: 179–230.
67. On the religious culture of Balkh, see van Ess, *Theologie und Gesellschaft*, II (1992): 508–47; on that of Samarqand, II: 560–7.
68. See pp. above, pp. 130, 141–2, 144–5.
69. In addition to the examples mentioned in the text above, al-Nasafī documents the cases of Abū ᶜAyyāsh ᶜAbd b. ᶜAyyāsh al-Samarqandī al-ᶜĀbid (p. 339, No. 774); Abū Saᶜd Saᶜīd b. ᶜUthmān b. al-Minhāl al-Zāhid al-Shāshī, who entered Samarqand in 313 (pp. 193–4, No. 302); Abū ᶜAbd al-Raḥmān ᶜAbd b. Sahl b. Muḥammad al-Zāhid al-Ḥaddād al-Samarqandī (pp. 448–9, No. 772); Saᶜd b. Ṣāliḥ al-Zāhid al-Samarqandī (*al-Qand fī dhikr ᶜulamāᵓ Samarqand*, p. 210, No. 335); Abū Isḥāq Ibrāhīm b. Aḥmad b. Muḥammad al-Sarakhsī al-Zāhid, who died in 417 (*al-Qand fī dhikr ᶜulamāᵓ Samarqand*, p. 45, No. 21); and further examples (*al-Qand fī dhikr ᶜulamāᵓ Samarqand*,

Nos 302, 318, 335, 336, 373, 385, 772). Ibn al-Nadīm records a *Kitāb al-Zuhd* of Abū Naṣr Muḥammad b. Masᶜūd al-ᶜAyyāshī of Samarqand (d. 320 /932) (*al-Fihrist*, I: ii: 685). Cf. *Tārīkh-i Bayhaq*, pp. 158, 159, 185, 199, 246.

70. Ibn al-Nadīm, *al-Fihrist*, I: ii: 655–65 and passim. The epithets *al-mutaṣawwif* or *al-ṣūfī* do not appear in *al-Qand fī dhikr ᶜulamāᵓ Samarqand* or *Fażāᵓil-i Balkh*.
71. Narshakhī, *Tārīkh-i Bukhārā*, p. 127; and see above, pp. 49–50.
72. Al-Nasafī, *al-Qand fī dhikr ᶜulamāᵓ Samarqand*, p. 211, No. 336.
73. Al-Nasafī, *al-Qand fī dhikr ᶜulamāᵓ Samarqand*, p. 145, No. 223.
74. Samarqandī, *al-Sawād al-aᶜẓam*, p. 19.
75. Cf. Madelung, 'Abuᵓl-Qāsem Esḥāq Samarqandī', p. 358; Ibn Funduq, *Tārīkh-i Bayhaq*, pp. 241, 242; and the utterances of Fuḍayl b. ᶜIyāḍ (Abū Nuᶜaym, *Ḥilyat al-awliyāᵓ*, VIII: 92).
76. Radtke, 'Theologen und Mystiker', p. 537, no. 8; Azad, 'The *Faḍāᵓil-i Balkh*', p. 95. This ᶜAbbād b. Kathīr was perhaps al-Thaqafī al-Baṣrī (d. after 140/757) or al-Ramlī al-Filasṭīnī (d. after 170/786); Azad, *Sacred Landscape*, p. 55.
77. Radtke, 'Theologen und Mystiker', p. 551.
78. Al-Nasafī, *al-Qand fī dhikr ᶜulamāᵓ Samarqand*, pp. 237–9, No. 385; van Ess, *Theologie und Gesellschaft*, II: 545 (Shaqīq).
79. Al-Nasafī, *al-Qand fī dhikr ᶜulamāᵓ Samarqand*, p. 238; Vāᶜiẓ, *Fażāᵓil-i Balkh*, pp. 130, 131.
80. Radtke, 'Theologen und Mystiker', esp. p. 539, No. 9 (Ibrāhīm), p. 540, No. 12 (Shaqīq), p. 542, No. 19 (Ḥātim).
81. Azad, 'Female Mystics', p. 57; *Sacred Landscape*, p. 144.
82. See Chapter 4, pp. 130, 141–2, 144–5.
83. He was the teacher of the eminent scholar Abū Jaᶜfar Muḥammad b. ᶜAbdallāh al-Hinduwānī (d. Bukhara, reportedly poisoned, 362/972–3) (Vāᶜiẓ, *Fażāᵓil-i Balkh*, pp. 299–310; Radtke, 'Theologen und Mystiker', p. 547, No. 49). Shaykh al-Islām Vāᶜiẓ presents the seventy shaykhs, pre-eminent religious figures and scholars, in chronological order; see Azad, *Sacred Landscape*, pp. 170–3.
84. Vāᶜiẓ, *Fażāᵓil-i Balkh*, pp. 291–4 (Abū Bakr Muḥammad b. Saᶜīd Balkhī, the forty-fifth shaykh), pp. 293–4; Radtke, 'Theologen und Mystiker', p. 547, No. 45, and p. 550. Radtke takes Ḥasan to be the son of the vizier; Paul states that it is impossible to ascertain whether or not Ḥasan is the son of the vizier (Paul, 'Histories of Samarqand', p. 90, n. 49). Abū l-Qāsim Ṣaffār Balkhī was the forty-fourth shaykh (*Fażāᵓil-i Balkh*, pp. 288–91).
85. See above, pp. 163, 171. The comment may refer to his fate in the afterlife.

86. Ibn al-Nadīm, *al-Fihrist*, I: ii: 669. In Ibn al-Nadīm's account, Naṣr regrets his acquiescence to al-Nasafī's suasion. His son Nūḥ then assembles the *fuqahāʾ* and summons al-Nasafī, whom the *fuqahāʾ* debated, exposed (*hatakū*) and disgraced (*faḍaḥū*), and whom Nūḥ had executed.
87. Al-Thaʿālibī, *Ādāb al-mulūk*, p. 169; = Crone and Treadwell, 'New Text', p. 38; cf. p. 43.
88. NM-A, p. 103 (Yazīd); Volume II, pp. 93, 94 and passim (rebels).
89. Cf. Treadwell, 'Political History', pp. 185, 188–200.
90. Among the dead in an occurrence 'in the days of Saʿīd b. Maʿqil' in Isfijab was Abū ʿUthmān Saʿīd b. al-Khiḍr al-Kasbawī (al-Nasafī, *al-Qand fī dhikr ʿulamāʾ Samarqand*, p. 204, No. 324). See further Paul, 'Histories of Samarqand', p. 89.
91. Niẓām al-Mulk, *Siyar al-mulūk*, p. 289 (*turkān va-sarān-i lashkar-rā khush nayāmad keh pādshāh qarmaṭī shod*) = p. 214 ('Now the Turks and officers of the army were displeased that the king had become a Qarmaṭī').
92. Al-Nasafī, *al-Qand fī dhikr ʿulamāʾ Samarqand*, pp. 437–9, 438–9, No. 756 (Abū Yaʿlā ʿAbd al-Muʾmin b. Khalaf al-ʿAmmī); pp. 202–4, 203, No. 323 (Abū ʿUthmān Saʿīd b. Ibrāhīm al-Raʾīs al-Nasafī). Elsewhere ʿAbd al-Muʾmin appears with the *nisba* al-Tamīmī; see El-Omari, 'Theology of Abū l-Qāsim al-Balḫī/al-Kabʿī', p. 29, n. 71.
93. Crone and Treadwell, 'New Text', pp. 41–8.
94. Crone and Treadwell, 'New Text', pp. 45–6.
95. Al-Nasafī, *al-Qand fī dhikr ʿulamāʾ Samarqand*, pp. 412–13, No. 704.
96. Al-Nasafī, *al-Qand fī dhikr ʿulamāʾ Samarqand*, pp. 202–3, No. 323. Compare al-Baghdādī, *al-Farq bayn al-firaq*, p. 267.
97. Narshakhī, *Tārīkh-i Bukhārā*, p. 132; Crone and Treadwell, 'New Text', pp. 43–8; Peacock, *Tārīkhnāma*, p. 26.
98. Niẓām al-Mulk, *Siyar al-mulūk*, pp. 299–305 = pp. 221–6; Crone and Treadwell, 'New Text', pp. 48–52. Niẓām al-Mulk mentions Farghana, Khujand and Kasan. See above, p. 167 and p. 307, n. 103.
99. Narshakhī, *Tārīkh-i Bukhārā*, pp. 131–2.
100. The term *dahriyya* lacks a clear definition, but evokes a range of materialist opinions, loosely linked with Q 45: 24, 'They say: There is nothing but our life of the world; we die and we live, and nothing destroys us but time (*dahr*).'
101. Ibn al-Zubayr, *Kitāb al-Dhakhāʾir* ('Book of Treasures', perhaps composed *c.* 463/1070–1), pp. 139–40; Bosworth, 'Alleged Embassy', pp. 18–19 (for the little information that may be surmised concerning the author, apparently a Shiʿite who wrote in Fatimid Egypt, see Bosworth, 'Alleged Embassy', p. 17).

It is unclear from the account whether Naṣr I or Naṣr II is intended: the stated genealogy of Naṣr b. Aḥmad b. Nūḥ b. Asad belongs to Naṣr I, but the dating of 327/939 for the episode falls during the reign of Naṣr II. In any event, the amir is portrayed as the great defender of the Muslim realms.

102. Ibn al-Zubayr, *Kitāb al-Dhakhāʾir*, pp. 145–6. On these terms, see above, pp. 32–3, 137–8, 142; the translations here follow Bosworth, 'Alleged Embassy', pp. 19, 21.
103. Meisami, 'Why Write History in Persian?' pp. 356–7; Daniel, 'Manuscripts and Editions', p. 286; Arjomand, 'Salience of Political Ethic', pp. 9–11; Meisami, *Persian Historiography*, pp. 27–37, esp. p. 29.
104. Kraemer, *Philosophy*, pp. 8–24; Bosworth, *History of the Saffarids*, pp. 282–301; Dunlop, 'Philosophical Discussions'; and see above, p. 171.
105. *Tārīkh-i Sīstān*, p. 342. Cf. Meisami, *Persian Historiography*, pp. 128–9 (my translation follows that of Meisami); Bosworth, *History of the Saffarids*, pp. 301–2, 328–37.
106. Al-Manīnī, *al-Fatḥ al-wahbī*, I: 375. Cf. Tahmi, *L'Encyclopédisme musulman*, pp. 18–19; Rowson, 'Philosopher as Littérateur', p. 85 and n. 127.
107. Stern, 'Early Ismāʿīlī Missionaries', pp. 80–1; Bosworth, *History of the Saffarids*, p. 331.

Chapter 7

1. This ḥadīth is found in Muslim, *Ṣaḥīḥ*, p. 1116 = *Kitāb al-ʿIlm* ('Book of Knowledge'), Bāb 3, No. 2669; Ibn Māja, *Sunan*, IV: 393 = *Kitāb al-Fitan* ('Book of Trials'), Bāb 17: *Iftirāq al-umam*, No. 3994; Aḥmad b. Ḥanbal, *Musnad*, XIV: 81 (No. 8340); XV: 508 (No. 9819); XVI: 375, 483 (Nos 10641, 10827); XVIII: 322 (No. 11800), 357 (No. 11843), 393–4 (No. 11897).
2. Reading, with the MS, *sharāʾiṭ* and *furūḍ*; the readings *sharāʾiʿ* and *furūʿ*, 'laws' and 'legal rulings', are also possible.
3. NM-A, pp. 85–6.
4. *ʿAhd Ardashīr*, p. 53.
5. NM-A, p. 108; see above, p. 53.
6. For a somewhat similar interpretation in the case of Niẓām al-Mulk, see Yavari, *Advice for the Sultan*, p. 37.
7. See Adamson, *Al-Kindī*, pp. 22–5; Zimmermann, 'Al-Kindī', pp. 364–9.
8. See Chapter 4, p. 143.
9. Al-ʿĀmirī, *al-Iʿlām*, p. 195.
10. See Volume II, Chapter 3.

11. The phrase represents a variant on the term *abnāʾ al-dunyā*, 'sons of the (mundane) world', which recurs in *Naṣīḥat al-mulūk*; the verb *tadāwala* evokes the concept of *dawla*, the 'turn in power'.
12. NM-A, p. 86. Cf. al-Ṭurṭūshī, *Sirāj al-mulūk*, II: 504–5.
13. See al-Fārābī, *La religion*, pp. 66–71 ('le fondateur de la Loi'), and *Iḥṣāʾ al-^{c}ulūm* ('Enumeration of the Sciences'), p. 107; cf. Heck, *Construction of Knowledge*, p. 209.
14. NM-A, p. 45; Volume II, p. 12.
15. See above, pp. 186, 187. The factionalism of the schools of law in Nishapur and other cities of the eastern regions largely postdates *Naṣīḥat al-mulūk*.
16. NM-A, p. 86.
17. Pseudo-Māwardī's references to the 'root' and 'branches' of the kingdom evoke a parallel with the 'roots' or principles of jurisprudence (*uṣūl al-fiqh*) and the 'branches' (*furū^{c}*, sing. *far^{c}*) of jurisprudence, that is, the body of positive rules derived from the principles. Ghazālī likened faith to a tree, with ten roots and ten branches (*Naṣīḥat al-mulūk*, pp. 2–3).
18. Cf. al-Mubashshir b. Fātik, *Mukhtār al-ḥikam*, p. 254 (in the variant *man tāha fī wilāyatihi dhulla fī ^{c}azlili* (instead of *fī ^{c}izzihi*), attributed to Baṭlamiyūs, Ptolemaeus or Ptolemy).
19. NM-A, pp. 86–7.
20. *Bilawhar wa-Būḏāsf*, p. 10 = *Le livre de Bilawhar et Būḏāsf*, p. 65.
21. Ibn al-Muqaffa^{c}, *al-Ādāb al-kabīr*, in *Āthār Ibn al-Muqaffa^{c}*, p. 300. Cf. Arjomand, '^{c}Abd Allah Ibn al-Muqaffa^{c}', p. 19.
22. *^{c}Ahd Ardashīr*, p. 49. Cf. Shaked, 'Notes', p. 57, and below, p. 197.
23. *^{c}Ahd Ardashīr*, p. 50.
24. NM-A, pp. 120–1; *^{c}Ahd Ardashīr*, pp. 49–50 (with minor variants). Cf. Shaked, 'Notes', p. 57, and n. 29 (Shaked notes the echo of the Zoroastrian triad of thought, speech and action).
25. Al-Tha^{c}ālibī, *Ādāb al-mulūk*, p. 51 and n. 61. See also a reminiscent section in Ibn al-Jawzī, *al-Miṣbāḥ al-muḍīʾ fī khilāfat al-Mustaḍī^{c}* ('The Illuminating Lamp on the Caliphate of al-Mustaḍī^{c}', composed for Caliph al-Mustaḍī^{c} (r. 566–75/1170–80)), pp. 157–63; although much later, Ibn al-Jawzī's writings perhaps continue some features of *Naṣīḥat al-mulūk*.
26. Cf. Volume II, pp. 19–20, 21, where kings are *maḥjūbūn*, 'concealed' or 'secluded'.
27. NM-A, pp. 87–8.
28. Niẓām al-Mulk, *Siyar al-mulūk*, pp. 31–40 = pp. 23–31. See further Yavari,

'Mirrors for Princes or a Hall of Mirrors?'; Yavari, *Advice for the Sultan*, pp. 122–3. A briefer version of the narrative appears in Ghazālī, *Naṣīḥat al-mulūk*, 154–5 = pp. 93–4.

29. See above, pp. 167–8.
30. Bayhaqī, *Tārīkh-i Bayhaqī*, p. 106.
31. Bayhaqī, *Tārīkh-i Bayhaqī*, pp. 107–8; Bosworth–Ashtiany, *History of Beyhaqi*, I: 190–1; cf. I: 64 and III: 94–5.
32. NM-A, p. 88.
33. Treadwell, 'Account of the Murder', pp. 401, 410–11.
34. Ibn al-Nadīm, *al-Fihrist*, I: ii: 429; Yāqūt, *Muᶜjam al-udabāʾ*, I: 274; al-Ṣafadī, *al-Wāfī bi-l-wafāyāt*, VI: 409. The implication is that al-Jayhānī was a Zoroastrian or a Manichaean.
35. Treadwell, 'Account of the Samanid Dynasty', pp. 143, 156–7; Treadwell, 'Political History', pp. 318–19; Crone and Treadwell, 'New Text', pp. 54–5.
36. On al-Muṣᶜabī, see al-Thaᶜālibī, *Ādāb al-mulūk*, p. 169; Niẓām al-Mulk, *Siyar al-mulūk*, p. 299 = p. 222. Cf. Crone and Treadwell, 'New Text', esp. pp. 54–5. See further above, pp. 163, 171.
37. Gardīzī, *Zayn al-akhbār*, p. 330, and see above, p. 255, n. 41; Bayhaqī, *Tārīkh-i Bayhaqī*, pp. 107–8.
38. See above, p. 187.
39. El-Omari, 'Theology of Abū l-Qāsim al-Balḫī/al-Kabᶜī', pp. 29, 46, 252; see above, pp. 155, 230.
40. Al-Thaᶜālibī, *Ādāb al-mulūk*, p. 169; Niẓām al-Mulk, *Siyar al-mulūk*, p. 299 = p. 222. Cf. Crone and Treadwell, 'New Text', esp. pp. 54–5.
41. Al-ᶜĀmirī, *al-Iᶜlām*, p. 193.
42. Al-ᶜĀmirī, *al-Iᶜlām*, p. 195. Rowson translates 'political bias' (*taᶜaṣṣub malakī*) and 'ethnic bias' (*taᶜaṣṣub nasabī*); see the following note.
43. Al-ᶜĀmirī, *al-Iᶜlām*, p. 195; cited and partially translated in Rowson, *Muslim Philosopher*, pp. 186–7.
44. For a recent discussion of this ubiquitous and foundational theme in mirrors for princes, see Yavari, *Advice for the Sultan*, esp. pp. 7–44.
45. Cf. al-Māwardī, *Aᶜlām al-nubuwwa*, pp. 127–56.
46. NM-A, pp. 88–9.
47. See above, pp. 161–3.
48. Niẓām al-Mulk, *Siyar al-mulūk*, p. 259 = p. 191.
49. Galli, 'Some Aspects', esp. pp. 14–16.
50. Galli, 'Some Aspects'; Götz, 'Māturīdī'.

51. In the derivation of legal principles, the term *ta'wīl* was employed broadly; Abou El Fadl, *Rebellion and Violence*, pp. 126–30, 149–52 and passim.
52. Al-Baghdādī, *al-Farq bayn al-firaq*, pp. 270 (*inna al-bāṭiniyya . . . ta'awwalat uṣūl al-dīn ᶜalā l-shirk ... murād[u]hum bi-ta'wīl al-sharīᶜa* [*rafᶜ al-sharīᶜa*], 'the *bāṭiniyya* . . . have applied a metaphorical interpretation to the principles of religion in a manner tantamount to association (the assigning of partners to the divine) . . . their objective in interpreting the religious law [is the abolition of the religious law]'); 280 (*ta'awwalū li-kull rukn min arkān al-sharīᶜa ta'wīlan yūrithu taḍlīlan*, 'for every pillar of the law they have produced a metaphorical interpretation that has bequeathed error'); 293. Cf. Ibn al-Balkhī, for whom the *mulḥidān*, under the category of *ta'vīl*, engaged in 'contradiction' (*naqż*) of the Qur'ān as part of their deception (see above, p. 164).
53. ᶜAbd al-Jabbār, *Tathbīt dalā'il al-nubuwwa*, I: 118; see also I: 135, 170. Cf. Monnot, *Penseurs musulmans*, p. 278.
54. Al-Kaᶜbī and al-Māturīdī addressed the idea of the 'natures' (*ṭabā'iᶜ*) of things; van Ess, 'Abu'l-Qāsem Kaᶜbī', p. 361; van Ess, *Erkenntnislehre*, pp. 133, 136–7; Rudolph, *Al-Māturīdī*, pp. 281–8, 290–1.
55. Al-Kindī, *al-Ibāna ᶜan sujūdi l-jirm al-aqṣā*, pp. 244–61. See also Abū Rīda's introduction to the treatise, pp. 238–44; Walzer, *Greek into Arabic*, pp. 180–6, 196–9.
56. Al-Kindī, *al-Ibāna ᶜan sujūd al-jirm al-aqṣā*, esp. pp. 245–6.
57. Al-Kindī, *Risālat al-Kindī fī kammiyyat kutub Arisṭūṭālīs*, pp. 363–84 (Abū Rīda, 'Muqaddima', pp. 359–62), pp. 372–3, 372–6 (with reference to 36: 79–82); cf. Adamson, *Al-Kindī*, pp. 43–4.
58. Rudolph, *Al-Māturīdī*, pp. 149–50, 152.
59. Al-Samarqandī, *Bustān al-ᶜārifīn*, pp. 51–1.
60. Yāqūt, *Mu'jam al-udabā'*, I: 278.
61. Yāqūt, *Mu'jam al-udabā'*, I: 259, 278 (citing al-Tawḥīdī's lost *Taqrīẓ al-Jāḥiẓ*); cf. *al-Imtāᶜ wa-l-mu'ānasa* ('Delight and Entertainment'), II: 38–9; Rowson, *Muslim Philosopher*, p. 19; Rowson, 'Philosopher as Littérateur', p. 66.
62. Al-ᶜĀmirī, *al-Iᶜlām*, pp. 77–8, 87; cf. Rowson, *Muslim Philosopher*, pp. 20, 184, 220.
63. Reading with the MS (f. 15b) *ᶜawāmm*.
64. On *lahw wa-laᶜb*, 'diversion and play', see Q 6: 70, 23: 115, and above, Chapter 2, n. 59.
65. The passage refers to the disputed status of music, especially instrumental music. The term *malāhī*, in the previous phrase, connotes musical instruments

as well as, in a general sense, 'distractions' (see previous note). Negative associations of musical instruments (*ma^cāzif*), and their association with licentiousness, unclean animals and forbidden activities, are evident in Ibn Abī l-Dunyā's collection of ḥadīth and *akhbār*, *Kitāb Dhamm al-malāhī* ('Book in Censure of Musical Instruments'), pp. 67–87. Cf. Cook, *Commanding Right*, pp. 90–1 and passim.

66. NM-A, p. 89. Pseudo-Māwardī makes a similar point in his second chapter, where, again employing the plural forms, he writes that virtues can only be attained by exertion of one's nature (*ṭab*[c]), urging one's body and soul to root out destructive desires (*shahawāt*) and fancies (*ahwā*ʾ) ruinous to reputations (*a*[c]*rāḍ*) or religions (*adyān*) (NM-A, p. 74).
67. NM-A, pp. 157–8; cf. pp. 222–5.
68. Al-[c]Āmirī, *Kitāb al-Amad*, in Rowson, *Muslim Philosopher*, p. 76 = p. 77.
69. Al-Tha[c]ālibī, *Ādāb al-mulūk*, p. 169; cf. Crone and Treadwell, 'New Text', pp. 38, 58–61; Bray, 'Local Mirror', pp. 41–2.
70. NM-A, pp. 93–6, 257. Al-Tha[c]ālibī places considerable emphasis on the same point (Bray, 'Local Mirror', p. 41).
71. [c]*Ahd Ardashīr*, p. 76; cf. Shaked, 'Esoteric Trends', appendix D 'Secret Religion', p. 217.
72. Pseudo-Māwardī discusses 'hypocrites' at a later point in his mirror as well; see Volume II, p. 240.
73. Khalidi, *Islamic Historiography*, p. 53; al-Mas[c]ūdī, *Murūj al-dhahab*, I: 154–5, 316; II: 107–8, 226–7.
74. NM-A, p. 90 (*lā ya*[c]*rifūna fīhi manqabatan lā yablughūnahā bi-l-taqdīr fī anfusihim*).
75. This proverb appears in al-Maydānī, *al-Amthāl*, II: 636, No. 4044, and is listed as a proverbial saying in *Lisān al-*[c]*arab* (under [c]*-z–z*, *man* [c]*azza bazza* = *man ghalaba salaba*), IV: 2972. See also al-Ābī, *Nathr al-durr*, IV: 223.
76. NM-A, pp. 89–90.
77. Niẓām al-Mulk, *Siyar al-mulūk*, p. 285 = p. 210; Stern, 'Early Ismā[c]īlī Missionaries', p. 78 = p. 217.
78. See above, pp. 112–13.
79. Samarqandī, *al-Sawād al-a*[c]*ẓam*, pp. 40–2; cf. Madelung, 'Abu'l-Qāsem Esḥāq Samarqandī', p. 358. See further Paul, 'Histories of Samarqand', p. 88; Tor, *Violent Order*, pp. 160–4.
80. Al-Ash[c]arī, *Maqālāt*, II: 348, § 197; cf. Abou El Fadl, *Rebellion and Violence*, p. 119 and n. 70, p. 143.

81. Al-Ashᶜarī, *Maqālāt*, II: 348–9, §§ 197, 198.
82. Al-Kaᶜbī, *Faḍl al-iᶜtizāl*, pp. 115–19; Cook, *Commanding Right*, p. 204 and n. 48.
83. NM-A, pp. 101–3. See above, pp. 37–9.
84. NM-A, p. 103; cf. NM-A, p. 76. Ibn al-Muqaffaᶜ had also addressed the question of obedience in *al-Risāla fī l-ṣaḥāba* (*Āthār Ibn al-Muqaffaᶜ*, pp. 348–50 = Pellat, *Conseilleur*, pp. 24–9; cf. Lowry, 'First Islamic Legal Theory', p. 30).
85. Al-Kaᶜbī, *Faḍl al-iᶜtizāl*, p. 117. Cf. van Ess, *Une lecture*, p. 123.
86. In religious and edificatory discourse, Pharaoh is synonymous with oppressive rule, religious obstinacy and overweening pride; cf. Firestone, 'Pharaoh'.
87. For the hadīth cited in this section, see Ibn Māja, *Sunan*, IV: 468 (= *Kitāb al-Zuhd*, No. 4110); al-Tirmidhī, *al-Jāmiᶜ al-ṣaḥīḥ*, III: 293 (= *Kitāb al-Zuhd*, 13: *Bāb mā jāʾa fī hawān al-dunyā ᶜalā Allāh ᶜazza wa-jalla*, No. 2321); al-Dārimī, *Sunan*, II: 190 (= *Kitāb al-Riqāq*, 26: *Bāb fī hawān al-dunyā ᶜalā Allāh*, No. 2737).
88. Cf. al-Ṭabarī, *Taʾrīkh*, IV: 204.
89. NM-A, pp. 90–2. The last phrase alludes to ᶜUmar b. ᶜAbd al-ᶜAzīz, and possibly Yazīd III, who reportedly took ᶜUmar b. ᶜAbd al-ᶜAzīz as a model; unlike most reports, certain Muᶜtazilite accounts portray Yazīd as equal in legitimacy to ᶜUmar (Hawting, *First Dynasty*, p. 94).
90. See above, pp. 100–1; cf. al-Ashᶜarī, *Maqālāt*, I: 209; Mānkdīm, *Sharḥ al-uṣūl al-khamsa*, p. 780.
91. NM-A, p. 92.
92. NM-A, pp. 92–3; cf. p. 85. His final cross-reference is to his fourth chapter.
93. NM-A, pp. 93–4.
94. van Ess renders *naẓar* as 'Spekulation' or 'Denken'; see *Erkenntnislehre*, pp. 237–363. The Shāfiᶜī theologian al-Āmidī (551–631/1156–1233) glossed the term, in its specialised use among theologians, as *tafakkur* or *iᶜtibār*, the two words possessing the same meaning (*Abkār al-afkār*, I: 125).
95. See Abū Rashīd al-Nīsābūrī, *Masāʾil*, pp. 345–6; Horten, *Die Philosophie des abu Raschíd*, pp. 203–4.
96. On the Muᶜtazilite involvement in inter-confessional debates at the caliphal courts, see van Ess, *Erkenntnislehre*, pp. 18–19. On the role of the *mutakallimūn* as religious specialists or instructors, see Pines, 'Early Meaning of the Term *Mutakallim*', p. 232; cf. Crone, 'Post-Colonialism', p. 24; Crone, *Slaves on Horses*, p. 64, cf. p. 246, nn. 452, 453. In the case of the Ismaᶜili *dāᶜī* Muḥammad Nakhshabī (= Muḥammad b. Aḥmad Nasafī), Niẓām al-Mulk

notes that he was a *mutakallim*, as well as one of the *falāsifeh-yi Khurāsān* (p. 287 = p. 212, p. 295 = p. 218).

97. NM-A, p. 93. Cf. al-ᶜĀmirī, *al-Iᶜlām bi-manāqib al-Islām*, pp. 129–83.
98. NM-A, p. 94. The concluding aphorism is variously attributed in other sources; see, for example, Ibn Qutayba, *ᶜUyūn al-akhbār*, I: 2; al-Ṭurṭūshī, *Sirāj al-mulūk*, I: 121 (in both cases attributed to Abū Ḥāzim (Salama b. Dīnār) and addressed to the Umayyad Caliph Sulaymān b. ᶜAbd al-Malik (r. 96–9/715–17)). The first half of the aphorism appears without attribution in al-Maydānī, *Majmaᶜ al-amthāl* ('Collection of Proverbs'), I: 128. See also Volume II, p. 134.
99. Al-Tirmidhī, *al-Jāmiᶜ al-ṣaḥīḥ*, III: 108 (= *Kitāb al-Birr wa-l-ṣila*, 58: *Bāb mā jāʾa fī l-mirāʾ*, No. 1993); Ibn Māja, *Sunan*, I: 53 (*Muqaddima, Bāb* 7: *Ijtināb al-bidaᶜ wa-l-jadal*, No. 51).
100. Al-Nasāʾī, *Sunan*, II: 89–90 (*Kitāb al-Imāma, Kayfa yuqawwimu l-imām al-ṣufūf*).
101. On the numerous traditions concerning Salmān and their interpretations, see Savant, *New Muslims*, pp. 61–89.
102. NM-A, pp. 95–6. Ellipses mark Pseudo-Māwardī's citation of 3: 103 and 3: 105.
103. NM-A, pp. 96–7.
104. NM-A, pp. 96–7. On *ahl al-jumal* or *aṣḥāb al-jumal*, see ᶜAbd al-Jabbār (*al-Mughnī*, XII: 533; cf. XII: 525–33, and van Ess, *Erkenntnislehre*, p. 50, with van Ess's emendation of *aṣḥāb al-jumal* for *aṣḥāb al-ḥaml*).
105. Cf. van Ess, *Erkenntnislehre*, pp. 50, 314–15 (on the limitation of the imposition of *naẓar*). Al-Tawḥīdī reports an exchange between al-Kaᶜbī and Abū l-Hudhayl, in which the latter also argues that for the common people (*al-ᶜāmma*) it is required only that they assent to the doctrines that are agreed upon, and not to doctrines, such as the createdness of the Qurʾān, that are subject to disagreement (*al-Baṣāʾir wa-l-dhakhāʾir*, IV: 215–15).
106. See van Ess, 'Abu'l-Qāsem Kaᶜbī', p. 362; van Ess, *Erkenntnislehre*, pp. 46, 73; Horten, *Philosophie des abu Raschid*, pp. 178, 193; El-Omari, 'Theology of Abū l-Qāsim al-Balḫī/al-Kabᶜī', pp. 184–5, 187–8.
107. ᶜAbd al-Jabbār, *al-Mughnī*, XII: 123, 125, 526; van Ess, *Erkenntnislehre*, p. 46.
108. Al-Maqdisī, *al-Badʾ wa-l-taʾrīkh*, I: 1–2.
109. Rudolph, *Al-Māturīdī*, pp. 215, 151–2 and 152, n. 95. Rudolph surmises that Abū Salama was a student of Abū Aḥmad al-ᶜIyāḍī, rather than a direct student of al-Māturīdī (pp. 151–3).

110. *ᶜAhd Ardashīr*, p. 54; cf. Shaked, 'Esoteric Trends', appendix D 'Secret Religion', p. 215.
111. *ᶜAhd Ardashīr*, pp. 60–1; cf. Shaked, 'Esoteric Trends', appendix D 'Secret Religion', p. 215.
112. See NM-A, pp. 232–3, and Volume II, p. 174.
113. Zaman, 'The Caliphs, the ᶜUlamāᵓ, and the Law', p. 6.
114. Cf. NM-A, p. 202.
115. NM-A, p. 97.
116. NM-A, pp. 97–8. The Pseudo-Aristotelian passages correspond to Grignaschi, 'La "Siyâsatu-l-ᶜâmmiyya"', p. 108, Maróth, *Correspondence*, p. 31; cf. al-Mubashshir, *Mukhtār al-ḥikam*, p. 193; al-Shahrazūrī, *Nuzhat al-arwāḥ*, I: 201. Al-Ṭurṭūshī attributes the saying to al-Khalīl b. Aḥmad (*Sirāj al-mulūk*, II: 472).
117. NM-A, p. 98.
118. NM-A, pp. 98–9.
119. NM-A, p. 99. The ḥadīth appears in al-Tirmidhī, *al-Jāmiᶜ al-ṣaḥīḥ*, III: 114 (= *Kitāb al-Birr wa-l-ṣila*, 63: *Bāb mā jāᵓa fī l-iḥsān wa-l-ᶜafw*, No. 2007).
120. NM-A, p. 99. The saying appears in Abū Nuᶜaym, *Ḥilyat al-awliyāᵓ*, II: 157 (the opening lines in an address of al-Ḥasan al-Baṣrī); al-Jāḥiẓ, *al-Bayān wa-l-tabyīn*, III: 132 (also citing al-Ḥasan al-Baṣrī).
121. NM-A, p. 99. In variant forms, the final saying appears in, among many other sources, Ibn Qutayba's *ᶜUyūn al-akhbār*, where Ziyād is said to have heard 'a man' utter a similar saying (Ibn Qutayba, *ᶜUyūn al-akhbār*, I: 5), and al-Ghazālī, *al-Tibr al-masbūk*, where the Umayyad Caliph Muᶜāwiya asks al-Aḥnaf b. Qays about the age (*al-zamān*), and receives this statement in response (*al-Tibr al-masbūk*, p. 207).
122. NM-A, p. 149; see also pp. 135, 156.
123. Cf. NM-A, pp. 135, 139, 149, 156, and Volume II, pp. 87, 93.
124. On Ibn Abī Zakariyyāᵓ see above, p. 165. According to Ibn al-Nadīm, al-Kaᶜbī entitled his refutation *Fuṣūl al-khiṭāb fī l-naqḍ ᶜalā rajul tanabbaᵓa bi-Khurāsān* (Ibn al-Nadīm, *al-Fihrist*, I: ii: 615); Yāqūt and al-Dhahabī knew of the text as a refutation of a pseudo-prophet in Khurasan (*kitāb fī l-radd ᶜalā mutanabbiᵓ bi-Khurāsān*) (*Muᶜjam al-udabāᵓ*, IV: 1493; *Siyar aᶜlām al-nubalāᵓ*, XIV: 313).
125. Bernand, 'Le *Kitāb al-Radd*', p. 86.
126. Bosworth, 'Rulers of Chaghāniyān', pp. 5, 8; Gardīzī, *Zayn al-akhbār*, p. 347; Ibn al-Athīr, *al-Kāmil*, VIII: 289–90; Abū l-Maᶜālī, *Bayān al-adyān*, p. 70.
127. Gardīzī, *Zayn al-akhbār*, p. 347; Ibn al-Athīr, *al-Kāmil*, VIII: 289–90.

128. Niẓām al-Mulk, *Siyar al-mulūk*, pp. 288, 295 = pp. 213, 218; Bosworth, 'Rulers of Chaghāniyān', p. 5; Barthold, *Turkestan*, p. 243. It is conceivable that this individual was the brother of Abū Alī, who perhaps oversaw his execution as well; indeed, Crone and Treadwell have suggested that Isma[c]ilism might have constituted a factor in the downfall of the Chaghānī family (Crone and Treadwell, 'New Text', pp. 53–4, 56–7). It is perhaps significant that Nūḥ b. Naṣr engaged in a contest for authority with Abū [c]Alī, whom he removed from office as Amir of Nishapur and replaced with Ibrāhīm Sīmjūr; Abū [c]Alī, however, did not acquiesce in this reversal (Narshakhī, *Tārīkh-i Bukhārā*, pp. 132–3); see above, pp. 57, 110–11, 133.

Chapter 8

1. NM-A, p. 85, and see Volume II, p. 107.
2. NM-A, pp. 65–6; and see above, pp. 119–20. Compare al-Ka[c]bī's comments on the Imami conception of the imam (Mānkdīm, *Sharḥ al-uṣūl al-khamsa*, pp. 758–9).
3. See, for example, NM-A, pp. 156–7. Pseudo-Māwardī's invocations of [c]Alī as the leading exemplar for military conduct link him to the juristic discourse concerning the status and treatment of Muslim rebels (Abou El Fadl, *Rebellion and Violence*, pp. 34–7, 125 and n. 91, and passim). Cf. Anṣārī, 'Yek andīsheh-nāmeh', p. 7.
4. Al-Muqaddasī, *Aḥsan al-taqāsīm*, p. 323; cf. Treadwell, 'Political History', pp. 191–2.
5. Al-Nasafī, *al-Qand fī dhikr [c]ulamā[ɔ] Samarqand*, p. 66, No. 60; Yāqūt, *Mu[c]jam al-udabā[ɔ]*, I: 277.
6. Madelung, *Der Imam al-Qāsim*, pp. 35, 77–8, 157, 159. See also Abū Tammām, in Madelung and Walker, *Ismaili Heresiography*, p. 13 = p. 30. *Al-Sawād al-a[c]ẓam*, by contrast, makes a point of emphasising the sequential excellence of the four Rāshidūn, for example, pp. 85–90.
7. NM-A, p. 235; see Volume II, pp. 176, 177.
8. NM-A, p. 152.
9. Madelung, *Der Imam al-Qāsim*, p. 74.
10. See above, 'Introduction'.
11. Rudolph, *Al-Māturīdī*, pp. 174, 192, 307–8; cf. pp. 335, 352.
12. Rudolph, *Al-Māturīdī*, pp. 251, 253. On al-Ka[c]bī's activity at Nasaf, near Samerkand, see Gilliot, 'La théologie musulmane en Asie centrale', p. 146.
13. Al-Māturīdī, *Kitāb al-Tawḥīd*, p. 78.

14. Yāqūt reports the extremely high reputation that al-Kaᶜbī's writings enjoyed in Baghdad, but also that the worthy people of Balkh (*ṣulaḥāᵓ ahl Balkh*) cast aspersions on his religion and his religious belief on account of his Muᶜtazilism, and that they accused him of *zandaqa* in Balkh (*Muᶜjam al-udabāᵓ*, IV: 1491–2).
15. Barthold, *Turkestan*, p. 232; Madelung, 'Spread of Māturīdism', p. 115.
16. Gilliot, 'La théologie musulmane en Asie centrale', p. 147. As it did elsewhere, the association of Abū Ḥanīfa with *raᵓy* (opinion, rational judgement) remained prevalent in the eastern regions. Al-Khwārazmī knew the followers of Abū Ḥanīfa as *aṣḥāb al-raᵓy*, and he grouped them among the six *firaq* or 'sects' of the Murjiᵓa; *Mafātīḥ al-ᶜulūm*, p. 28.
17. Vāᶜiẓ, *Fażāᵓil-i Balkh*, pp. 28–9; Madelung, 'Early Murjiᵓa', p. 36.
18. Vāᶜiẓ, *Fażāᵓil-i Balkh*, p. 131; Radtke, 'Theologen und Mystiker', p. 540; Madelung, 'Early Murjiᵓa', pp. 36–8.
19. Vāᶜiẓ, *Fażāᵓil-i Balkh*, pp. 44–5. The observations occur in the context of Shaykh al-Islām Vāᶜiẓ's account of the blessings particular to the city of Balkh. He distinguishes between blessings of religion and blessings of this world (*niᶜmat-i dīn va-niᶜmat-i dunyā*). In enumerating the city's blessings of the former category, he notes its construction in the era of Islam, since it had fallen into ruin previously and had been made prosperous in the Islamic period (pp. 43–4); the confessional composition of its population, which consisted only of Muslims (p. 44); and the exclusive presence in the city of the Ḥanafī *madhhab*, other than which no other *millat* existed (p. 44).
20. Ibn al-Nadīm, *al-Fihrist*, I: ii: 615; Yāqūt, *Muᶜjam al-udabāᵓ*, IV: 1493; van Ess, 'Abu'l-Qāsem Kaᶜbī', p. 360; Madelung, 'Spread of Māturīdism', p. 117.
21. Madelung, *Religious Trends*, pp. 18–20, 30.
22. Samarqandī, *al-Sawād al-aᶜẓam*, p. 22.
23. Madelung, 'Spread of Māturīdism', pp. 114–15. Bulliet found that in Nishapur, as elsewhere, the Ḥanafīs antedated the Shāfiᶜīs, and many Ḥanafīs were Muᶜtazilite (Bulliet, *Patricians*, pp. 36–7).
24. Anṣārī, 'Yek andīsheh-nāmeh'.
25. NM-A, pp. 147–8. Moreover, Pseudo-Māwardī's reference to the impact of the *kabīra*, major sin, on the status and destiny of the Muslim is consistent with Muᶜtazilite teachings regarding 'the promise and the threat'; see Volume II, pp. 78–9, 83.
26. Born no later than 360/970, Abū Rashīd Saᶜīd b. Muḥammad al-Nīsābūrī followed the doctrine of al-Kaᶜbī prevalent in Khurasan and Transoxiana.

Later he studied in Rayy with ᶜAbd al-Jabbār, to whose doctrine he transferred his adherence. His *Masāʾil*, in which he refutes the doctrines of al-Kaᶜbī and supports those of ᶜAbd al-Jabbār, reflects his fluency in the teachings of both branches of the Muᶜtazila (Madelung, 'Abū Rašīd Nīsābūrī', pp. 367–8).

27. NM-A, pp. 203, 286. On the doctrine of *al-aṣlaḥ*, see al-Ashᶜarī, *Maqālāt*, II: 414–16; ᶜAbd al-Jabbār, *al-Mughnī*, XIV: 7–180.
28. Al-Kaᶜbī, *Faḍl al-iᶜtizāl*, p. 72.
29. In an expression of his disagreement over the doctrine with al-Jubbāʾī, al-Kaᶜbī composed a *Kitāb al-Nihāya fi l-aṣlaḥ ᶜalā Abī ᶜAlī* (Ibn al-Nadīm, *al-Fihrist*, I: ii: 615; Yāqūt, *Muᶜjam al-udabāʾ*, IV: 1493). ᶜAbd al-Jabbār cited al-Kaᶜbī's pronouncements regarding the topic in *al-Mughnī*, XIV: 55, 61. Cf. Mānkdīm, *Sharḥ al-uṣūl al-khamsa*, p. 134, where the doctrine is attributed to the Baghdadi Muᶜtazila without specific reference to al-Kaᶜbī. Cf. van Ess, 'Abu'l-Qāsem Kaᶜbī', pp. 360, 362; Ormsby, *Theodicy*, p. 233.
30. According to al-Kaᶜbī, ᶜAmr b. ᶜUbayd hailed from Kabul, which he located at the borders of Balkh (*Faḍl al-iᶜtizāl*, p. 68); cf. van Ess, *Une lecture*, p. 118.
31. Cook, *Commanding Right*, pp. 53, 197 and n. 7.
32. NM-A, pp. 51, 71, 79, 103, 129, 211, 309. For a discussion of the context and nature of the reports concerning ᶜAmr, see van Ess, *Une lecture*, pp. 118–20; on his austerity, see esp. pp. 117–18.
33. NM-A, pp. 199 (ᶜAmr b. Baḥr = al-Jāḥiẓ), 71 (Thumāma). Cf. *Faḍl al-iᶜtizāl*, p. 73; Abū Tammām, in Madelung and Walker, *Ismaili Heresiography*, p. 19 = p. 34, and n. 56 (see also 'Introduction', p. 11); van Ess, *Erkenntnislehre*, p. 17. Cf. al-Āmidī, *Abkār al-afkār*, V: 48–50. Thumāma and al-Jāḥiẓ were both associated with the Muᶜtazilite grouping known as *aṣḥāb al-maᶜārif*. Cf. van Ess, *Erkenntnislehre*, pp. 132, 159, 329.
34. See Volume II, p. 133.
35. Rudolph, *Al-Māturīdī*, pp. 173–5, 251, 290–1, 351.
36. See, for example, Abou El Fadl's discussion of al-Jāḥiẓ's presentation of the Muᶜtazilite position regarding rebels (*Rebellion and Violence*, p. 161; on al-Jāḥiẓ's views, see also p. 119, n. 70).
37. Madelung, 'Spread of Māturīdism', pp. 114–15.
38. Madelung, 'Spread of Māturīdism', p. 111.
39. See Volume II, pp. 99, 101.
40. The Muᶜtazilī and Māturīdī position was at variance with that of many Ḥanbalīs in the ninth and early tenth centuries (Melchert, 'Traditionist-Jurisprudents', p. 396). The tendency receded in the course of the tenth century, however.

41. Pessagno, 'Intellect and Religious Assent', pp. 18–27. Tahmi indicated the same affinity in the case of al-Maqdisī, whose writings are evocative of Mu^{c}tazilite doctrines and patterns of thought, but who, in Tahmi's view, may have been more inclined to a Māturīdī disposition (Tahmi, *L'encyclopédisme musulman*, pp. 132–3). Van Ess, however, considers al-Maqdisī a Mu^{c}tazilite (*Erkenntnislehre*, p. 118). The supposition finds support in al-Maqdisī's favourable reference to al-Ka^{c}bī, I: 135.
42. See Zimmermann, 'Al-Kindī', p. 367; Adamson, *Al-Kindī*, pp. 46–73 and passim; al-^{c}Āmirī, *Kitāb al-Amad*, in Rowson, *Muslim Philosopher*, p. 94 = p. 95, p. 98 = p. 99. Al-^{c}Āmirī acknowledges al-Kindī in this work (p. 76 = p. 77).
43. NM-A, pp. 70, 87, 131.
44. Al-Tirmidhī, *Adab al-nafs*, pp. 147–51, 152–6, and passim.
45. See, for instance, NM-A, pp. 69–70, 70 (and n. 43), 97, 119–24, 130–3, 164, 182.
46. NM-A, p. 131.
47. NM-A, p. 133.
48. NM-A, p. 164 (cf. Q 6: 32). Pseudo-Māwardī employs the verb *arāda* to refer to this divine desire. On the divine attribute of *irāda*, cf. al-Ash^{c}arī, *Maqālāt*, I: 152–3; on Mu^{c}tazilite views, including those of al-Ka^{c}bī, see Mānkdīm, *Sharḥ al-uṣūl al-khamsa*, p. 440; Madelung, *Der Imam al-Qāsim*, pp. 164–6; al-Baghdādī, *al-Farq bayn al-firaq*, pp. 166–7; van Ess, 'Abuʾl-Qāsem Ka^{c}bī', p. 361. Racha El-Omari, in a thorough study of al-Ka^{c}bī's doctrine, has argued that in his doctrine of the divine will al-Ka^{c}bī 'betrayed his commitment to an archaic form of Mu^{c}tazilism that may have played a crucial role in hindering the survival of his school' ('Theology of Abū l-Qāsim al-Balḫī/al-Ka^{c}bī', p. ii; see further pp. 135–61).
49. NM-A, pp. 373–4.
50. NM-A, p. 374.
51. An anonymous tenth-century manual for Sufis employs the same conceit in its title, *Adab al-mulūk*, so-called because 'the Sufis have renounced all the appurtenances of the world, and have accordingly become kings' (*li-anna al-ṣūfiyya zahadū ^{c}an jamī^{c} asbāb al-dunyā fa-ṣārū mulūkan*) (*Adab al-mulūk*, pp. 6–7).
52. NM-A, p. 132. The citation appears in Pseudo-Māwardī's fourth chapter, which includes several other articulations of the sentiment that desire transforms even the most powerful individuals into prisoners under bondage.

53. NM-A, p. 202.
54. Bulliet, *Patricians*, pp. 40–42; see also Melchert, 'Asceticism to Mysticism'.
55. Al-Maqdisī, *al-Bad*ʾ *wa-l-ta*ʾ*rīkh*, V: 138.
56. NM-A, p. 189; see also Volume II, pp. 123–6. On the reservations of ninth-century traditionalists regarding *tawakkul*, see Melchert, 'Piety of the Hadith Folk', p. 430.
57. Melchert, 'Sufis and Competing Movements', p. 237.
58. Al-Maydānī, *Majma*ᶜ *al-amthāl*, II: 75, no. 2695.
59. Al-Sulamī, *Ṭabaqāt al-ṣūfiyya*, pp. 63–7, No. 7.
60. Paul, 'Islamizing Sufis', pp. 310–14; cf. van Ess, *Theologie und Gesellschaft*, II: 545–7.
61. Al-Nasafī, *al-Qand fī dhikr* ᶜ*ulamā*ʾ *Samarqand*, pp. 237–9, No. 385; Vāᶜiẓ, *Fażā*ʾ*il-i Balkh*, pp. 129–42 (shaykh 12).
62. Al-Nasafī, *al-Qand fī dhikr* ᶜ*ulamā*ʾ *Samarqand*, p. 237.
63. Al-Nasafī, *al-Qand fī dhikr* ᶜ*ulamā*ʾ *Samarqand*, p. 238, No. 385. On Shaqīq's wealth, see above, p. 141.
64. NM-A, p. 399. The anecdote appears in several sources, including al-Ghazālī, *al-Tibr al-masbūk*, p. 108.

Index